Strategies for College Writing

Strategies for College Writing

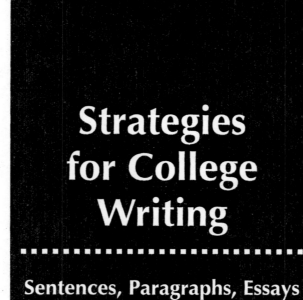

Sentences, Paragraphs, Essays

SECOND EDITION

Jeanette Harris
Texas Christian University

Ann Moseley
Texas A&M University—Commerce

PEARSON
Longman

New York San Francisco Boston
London Toronto Sydney Tokyo Singapore Madrid
Mexico City Munich Paris Cape Town Hong Kong Montreal

Editor-in-Chief: Joseph Terry
Senior Acquisitions Editor: Steven Rigolosi
Associate Editor: Barbara Santoro
Senior Supplements Editor: Donna Campion
Media Supplements Editor: Nancy Garcia
Senior Marketing Manager: Melanie Craig
Production Manager: Eric Jorgensen
Project Coordination, Text Design, and Electronic Page Makeup: Electronic Publishing Services Inc., NYC
Cover Design Manager: John Callahan
Cover Designer: Maria Ilardi
Cover Photo: © William Whitehurst/CORBIS
Manufacturing Manager: Roy Pickering

For permission to use copyrighted material, grateful acknowledgment is made to the copyright holders on pp. 519–523, which are hereby made part of this copyright page.

Library of Congress Cataloging-in-Publication Data
Harris, Jeanette, 1936–
    Strategies for college writing:sentences, paragraphs, essays/Jeanette Harris, Ann
Moseley—2nd ed.
        p. cm.
    Includes bibliographical references and index.
    ISBN 0-321-10436-6
    1. English language—Rhetoric. 2. English language—Sentences. 3. English
    language—Paragraphs. 4. English language—Grammar. 5. Report writing. I. Moseley,
    Ann. II. Title.

PE1408.H3457 2003
808'.042—dc21   2003043395

Please visit our Web site at **http://www.ablongman.com/harris**

ISBN 0-321-10436-6

For our children and grandchildren

—*JH*

—*AM*

CONTENTS

PART TWO
■ ■ ■ ■ ■ ■ ■ ■ ■ ■ ■
Methods of Development   113

PART THREE
▪ ▪ ▪ ▪ ▪ ▪ ▪ ▪ ▪ ▪ ▪ ▪
Writing and Editing Sentences   235

PREFACE

This second edition of *Strategies for College Writing*, like the first, is designed to prepare students for the academic writing assignments required of them in college. Our goal in writing this book was to bridge the gap many students face between the writing skills they currently possess and the writing skills they need to be successful in college-level courses. Like most developmental writing textbooks, *Strategies for College Writing* provides complete coverage of basic writing skills and clear, thoughtful instruction in writing correct, well-structured, and adequately developed sentences, paragraphs, and essays. But it also challenges students and helps them advance beyond fundamental writing skills—to construct paragraphs and essays based on varied patterns of organization, and to learn effective strategies for revising and editing. *Strategies for College Writing* also offers students abundant examples of student writing, collaborative learning activities, and a variety of exercises.

Because we are convinced that reading as well as writing instruction helps students acquire the academic skills they need to become successful college students, we integrate reading and writing instruction throughout this book. Therefore, *Strategies for College Writing* includes not only thematically arranged high-interest readings, which serve as effective prompts for writing assignments, but also instruction in critical reading and basic reading/writing skills such as outlining, summarizing, and taking essay exams.

Last but not least, we believe instructors will find *Strategies for College Writing* a comprehensive yet flexible textbook. Instructors can follow the organization of the book as it is written or can adapt the book to correspond to their class needs by choosing from the wealth of material provided. In addition, the book is supplemented by strong instructional support—a Web site as well as a manual that includes suggestions for teaching, additional resources, and a test bank.

ORGANIZATION AND SCOPE

Part One, "Writing Paragraphs and Essays," provides students with basic instruction on the writing process, invention strategies, topic sentences and theses, structure of paragraphs and essays, processes of gathering information through observations and interviews, achieving coherence, and revising.

Part Two, "Methods of Development," provides extensive instruction in using traditional patterns of development: description, narration, process, example, comparison/contrast, classification, cause and effect, definition, and persuasion. Each chapter focuses on both paragraphs and essays and presents student as well as professional writing.

Part Three, "Writing and Editing Sentences," provides instruction on basic sentence patterns and sentence-level editing concerns. Instruction focuses on sentence structure and style, major sentence errors, punctuation, capitalization, and spelling. Each chapter presents appropriate exercises to reinforce instruction.

Part Four, "Critical Reading and Writing Strategies," focuses on skills such as outlining and summarizing, reviewing books and movies, and taking essay exams.

Part Five, "A Mini-Reader on American Culture," includes fourteen selections that are divided into four thematic units: Identity, College Life, Lifestyles, and Diversity. Each reading selection is preceded by a preview, journal assignment, and reading strategy. Following each reading students are also asked to summarize, respond to, discuss, and write about each selection. The thematic arrangement and the cumulative assignments at the end of each unit encourage students to make critical connections among related readings.

FEATURES NEW TO THIS EDITION

As a result of the experiences we and other instructors have had in teaching with the first edition of *Strategies for College Writing*, we have added the following features to this edition:

- **Additional visuals to support alternative learning styles.** The increased use of visuals in this edition not only makes the book more interesting but also benefits those students who learn most effectively via visual representations of concepts.

- **New chapter on writing film and book reviews.** This chapter provides students with basic instruction on writing reviews—an assignment they frequently encounter in a variety of courses.

- **Additional instruction for students of English as a second language (ESL) that focuses on articles, prepositions, and order of adjectives.** Students whose native language is not English often need special assistance with these aspects of English usage.

- **Ten new reading selections in Part Five.** The new reading selections plus the more popular selections from the previous edition now constitute a mini-reader on American lifestyles and issues—topics that interest not only American students but also those from other countries.

- **New chapter on gathering information that focuses on interviews and observations.** This chapter introduces students to two basic types of field research and to the concept of using and documenting sources.
- **Appendix that focuses on using and documenting sources.** The new appendix can be included in class instruction or can simply be available for students to use on their own.

ENDURING FEATURES

Features that have continued from the previous edition include the following:

- **Extensive instruction on the writing process,** including separate chapters on invention and revision.
- **Numerous exercises,** including cloze and sentence-combining types, that focus on the discrete skill being taught and then present the skill in the context of a paragraph or essay.
- **Group activities,** designated as "Participating in the Academic Community," at the end of each chapter to help promote active learning through collaboration.
- **Emphasis on academic writing skills** as well as basic writing instruction.
- **Many examples of student writing,** to provide both realistic models and increased motivation for students.
- **Flexible organization** that accommodates a variety of course structures and teaching styles.
- **Instruction on modes of discourse** as patterns for organizing both paragraphs and essays.
- **Section on critical reading and writing skills** that also includes instruction on outlining and summarizing, writing reviews, and taking essay exams.
- **Thematically grouped reading selections** that address topics of interest to students.

CONCLUSION

Strategies for College Writing is the product of our many years of teaching writing—both in the classroom and in writing centers. We hope that the instructors who use this book will benefit from our experience and that students will find in it a way of becoming more effective readers and writers.

BOOK-SPECIFIC ANCILLARIES

The **Instructor's Manual and Test Bank**, prepared by the authors, offers teaching suggestions, supplemental activities and exercises as well as chapter tests and reading quizzes. To order a copy of this ancillary, please contact your Longman book representative. 0-321-10438-2.

For additional writing assignments, Internet-based activities, and gradable quizzes, be sure to visit *Strategies for College Writing's* Companion Web site at **http://www.ablongman.com/harris.** This companion Web site was prepared by Charlsye Smith.

THE TEACHING AND LEARNING PACKAGE

In addition to the book-specific supplements discussed above, many other skills-based supplements are available for both instructors and students. All of these supplements are available either free or at greatly reduced prices.

For Additional Reading and Reference

The Dictionary Deal. Two dictionaries can be shrinkwrapped with this text for a nominal fee. *The New American Webster Handy College Dictionary* is a paperback reference text with more than 100,000 entries. *Merriam Webster's Collegiate Dictionary*, 10th edition, is a hardback reference with a citation file of more than 14.5 million examples of English words drawn from actual use. For more information on how to shrinkwrap a dictionary with your text, please contact your Longman sales representative.

Penguin Quality Paperback Titles. A series of Penguin paperbacks is available at a significant discount when shrinkwrapped with this text. Some titles available are Toni Morrison's *Beloved*, Julia Alvarez's *How the Garcia Girls Lost Their Accents*, Mark Twain's *Huckleberry Finn, Narrative of the Life of Frederick Douglass*, Harriet Beecher Stowe's *Uncle Tom's Cabin*, Dr. Martin Luther King, Jr.'s *Why We Can't Wait*, and plays by Shakespeare, Miller, and Albee. For a complete list of titles or more information, please contact your Longman sales consultant.

Penguin Academics: *Twenty-Five Great Essays, Fifty Great Essays,* and *One Hundred Great Essays*, edited by Robert DiYanni. These alphabetically organized essay collections are published as part of the Penguin Academics series of low-cost, high-quality offerings intended for use in introductory college courses. All essays were selected for their teachability, both as models for writing and for their usefulness as springboards for student writing. For more information on how to shrinkwrap one of these anthologies with your text, please contact your Longman sales consultant.

100 Things to Write About. This 100-page book contains 100 assignments for writing on a variety of topics and in a wide range of formats, from expressive to analytical. Ask your Longman sales representative for a sample copy. 0-673-98239-4.

Newsweek **Alliance.** Instructors may choose to shrinkwrap a twelve-week subscription to *Newsweek* with any Longman text. The price of the subscription is 59 cents per issue (a total of $7.08 for the subscription). Available with the subscription is "Interactive Guide to *Newsweek*"—a free workbook for students who are using the text. In addition, Newsweek provides a wide variety of instructor supplements free to teachers, including maps, Skills Builders, and weekly quizzes. For more information on the *Newsweek* program, please contact your Longman sales representative.

Electronic and Online Offerings

The Longman Writer's Warehouse. This innovative and exciting online supplement is the perfect accompaniment to any developmental writing course. Designed by English instructors specially for developing writers, the Writer's Warehouse covers every part of the writing process. Also included are journaling capabilities, multimedia activities, diagnostic tests, an interactive handbook, and a complete instructor's manual. The Writer's Warehouse requires no space on your school's server; rather, students complete and store their work on the Longman server and are able to access it, revise it, and continue working at any time. For more details about how to shrinkwrap a free subscription to the Writer's Warehouse with this text, please consult your Longman sales representative. For a free guided tour of the site, visit **http://longmanwriterswarehouse.com**.

The Writer's ToolKit Plus. This CD-ROM offers a wealth of tutorial, exercise, and reference material for writers. It is compatible with both the PC and Macintosh platforms, and is flexible enough to be used either occasionally for practice or regularly in class lab sessions. For information on how to bundle this CD-ROM free with your text, please contact your Longman sales representative.

iSearch Guide for English, **2nd Edition by H. Eric Branscomb and Doug Gotthoffer.** A guide to online research. Featuring the Longman Internet Guide and access to the Research Navigator Database, the iSearch guide gives students and instructors instant access to thousands of academic journals and periodicals any time from any computer with an Internet connection. With helpful tips on the writing process, online research, and finding and citing valid sources, starting the research process has never been easier! Free when packaged with this textbook. 0-321-20277-5.

For Instructors

Electronic Test Bank for Writing. This electronic test bank features more than 5,000 questions in all areas of writing, from grammar to paragraphing, essay writing, research, and documentation. With this easy-to-use CD-ROM, instructors simply choose questions from the electronic test bank, then print out the completed test for distribution. CD-ROM: 0-321-08117-X Print version: 0-321-08486-1.

Competency Profile Test Bank, **2nd Edition.** This series of sixty objective tests covers ten general areas of English competency, including fragments, comma splices and run-ons, pronouns, commas, and capitalization. Each test is available in remedial, standard, and advanced versions. Available as reproducible sheets or in computerized versions. Free to instructors. Paper version: 0-321-02224-6 Computerized IBM: 0-321-02633-0 Computerized Mac: 0-321-02632-2.

Diagnostic and Editing Tests and Exercises, **5th Edition.** This collection of diagnostic tests helps instructors assess students' competence in standard written English for purpose of placement or to gauge progress. Available as reproducible sheets or in computerized versions, and free to instructors. Paper: 0-321-11730-1 CD-ROM: 0-321-11731-X.

ESL Worksheets, **3rd Edition.** These reproducible worksheets provide ESL students with extra practice in areas they find the most troublesome. A diagnostic test and posttest are provided, along with answer keys and suggested topics for writing. Free to adopters. 0-321-07765-2.

Longman Editing Exercises. Fifty-four pages of paragraph editing exercises give students extra practice using grammar skills in the context of longer passages. Free when packaged with any Longman title. 0-205-31792-8 Answer key: 0-205-31797-9.

80 Practices. A collection of reproducible, ten-item exercises that provide additional practices for specific grammatical usage problems such as comma splices, capitalization, and pronouns. Includes an answer key, and free to adopters. 0-673-53422-7.

CLAST Test Package, **4th Edition.** These two forty-item objective tests evaluate students' readiness for the CLAST exams. Strategies for teaching CLAST preparedness are included. Free with any Longman English title. Reproducible sheets: 0-321-01950-4 Computerized IBM version: 0-321-01982-2 Computerized Mac version: 0-321-01983-0.

TASP Test Package, **3rd Edition.** These 12 practice pretests and posttests assess the same reading and writing skills covered in the TASP examination. Free with any Longman English title. Reproducible sheets: 0-321-01959-8.

Teaching Online: Internet Research, Conversation, and Composition, **2nd Edition.** Ideal for instructors who have never surfed the Net, this easy-to-follow guide offers basic definitions, numerous examples, and step-by-step information about finding and using Internet sources. Free to adopters. 0-321-01957-1.

Using Portfolios. This supplement offers teachers a brief introduction to teaching with portfolios in composition courses. This essential guide addresses the pedagogical and evaluative use of portfolios and offers practical suggestions for implementing a portfolio evaluation system in a writing class. 0-321-08412-8.

The Longman Instructor's Planner. This all-in-one resource for instructors includes monthly and weekly planning sheets, to-do lists, student contact forms, attendance rosters, a gradebook, an address/phone book, and a mini almanac. Ask your Longman sales representative for a free copy. 0-321-09247-3.

The Longman Electronic Newsletter. Twice a month during the spring and fall, instructors who have subscribed receive a free copy of the Longman Developmental English Newsletter in their e-mailbox. Written by experienced classroom instructors, the newsletter offers teaching tips, classroom activities, book reviews, and more. To subscribe, send e-mail to **BasicSkills@ablongman.com.**

For Students

Researching Online, **5th Edition.** A perfect companion for a new age, this indispensable new supplement helps students navigate the Internet. Adapted from *Teaching Online,* the instructor's Internet guide, *Researching Online* speaks directly to students, giving them detailed, step-by-step instructions for performing electronic searches. Available free when shrinkwrapped with this text. 0-321-09277-5.

Learning Together: An Introduction to Collaborative Theory. This brief guide to the fundamentals of collaborative learning teaches students how to work effectively in groups, how to revise with peer response, and how to coauthor a paper or report. Shrinkwrapped free with this text. 0-673-46848-8.

A Guide for Peer Response, **2nd Edition.** This guide offers students forms for peer critiques, including general guidelines and specific forms for different stages in the writing process. Also appropriate for a freshman-level course. Free to adopters. 0-321-01948-2.

Ten Practices of Highly Successful Students. This popular supplement helps students learn crucial study skills, offering concise tips for a successful career in college. Topics include time management, test taking, reading critically, stress, and motivation. 0-205-30769-8.

The Longman Student Planner. This daily planner for students includes daily, weekly, and monthly calendars as well as class schedules and a mini-almanac of useful information. It is the perfect accompaniment to a Longman reading or study skills textbook and is available free to students when shrinkwrapped with this text. 0-321-04573-4.

The Longman Writer's Journal. This journal for writers, free with any Longman English text, offers students a place to think, write, and react. For an examination copy, contact your Longman sales consultant. 0-321-08639-2.

The Longman Researcher's Journal. This journal for writers and researchers, free with this text, helps students plan, schedule, write, and revise their research project. An all-in-one resource for first-time researchers, the journal guides students gently through the research process. 0-321-09530-8.

The Longman Writer's Portfolio. This unique supplement provides students with a space to plan, think about, and present their work. The portfolio includes an assessing/organizing area (including a grammar diagnostic test, a spelling quiz, and project planning worksheets), a before and during writing area (including peer review sheets, editing checklists, writing self-evaluations, and a personal editing profile), and an after-writing area (including a progress chart, a final table of contents, and a final assessment). Ask your Longman sales representative for 0-321-10765-9.

State-Specific Supplements

[FOR FLORIDA ADOPTIONS] *Thinking Through the Test,* by D.J. Henry. This special workbook, prepared specially for students in Florida, offers ample skill and practice exercises to help student prepare for the Florida State Exit Exam. To shrinkwrap this workbook free with your textbook, please contact your Longman sales representative. Available in two versions: with answers and without answers. Also available: two laminated grids (one for reading, one for writing) that can serve as handy references for students preparing for the Florida State Exit Exam.

[FOR NEW YORK ADOPTIONS] Preparing for the CUNY-ACT Reading and Writing Test, edited by Patricia Licklider. This booklet, prepared by reading and writing faculty from across the CUNY system, is designed to help students prepare for the CUNY-ACT exit test. It includes test-taking tips, reading passages, typical exam questions, and sample writing prompts to help students become familiar with each portion of the test. 0-321-19608-2.

[FOR TEXAS ADOPTIONS] *The Longman TASP Study Guide,* by Jeanette Harris. Created specifically for students in Texas, this study guide includes straightforward explanations and numerous practice exercises to help students prepare for the reading and writing sections of the Texas Academic Skills Program Test. To shrinkwrap this workbook free with your textbook, please contact your Longman sales representative. 0-321-20271-6.

THE LONGMAN SERIES OF MONOGRAPHS FOR DEVELOPMENTAL EDUCATORS

Ask your Longman sales consultant for a free copy of these monographs, written by experts in their fields.

#1: *The Longman Guide to Classroom Management.* Written by Joannis Flatley of St. Philip's College, the first in Longman's new series of monographs for developmental English instructors focuses on issues of classroom etiquette, providing guidance on dealing with unruly, unengaged, disruptive, or uncooperative students. Ask your Longman sales representative for a free copy. 0-321-09246-5.

#2: *The Longman Guide to Community Service-Learning in the English Classroom and Beyond.* Written by Elizabeth Rodriguez Kessler of California State University in Northridge, this is the second monograph in Longman's series for developmental educators. It provides a definition and history of service-learning as well as an overview of how service-learning can be integrated effectively into the college classroom. 0-321-12749-8.

ACKNOWLEDGMENTS

We are indebted not only to the students who contributed samples of their writing to this book but also to those who provided us with valuable insights into the teaching of writing.

We would also like to thank the following individuals, who reviewed this book during various stages of development: Debra Anderson, Indian River Community College; Deborah Andres, University of Delaware; Deborah Bradford, University of Massachusetts, Dartmouth; Thomas Burns, Butler County College; Rick Casper, Prestonsburg Community College; Ann Higgins, Gulf Coast Community College; Michael Hricik, Westmoreland County Community College; Ann Lambert, Guilford Technical Community College; Alfred Guy Litton, Texas Woman's University; Janeen Myers, Oklahoma State University at Oklahoma City; and Jeff Thompson, Tennessee State University.

JEANETTE HARRIS
ANN MOSELEY

Writing Paragraphs and Essays

This textbook provides effective strategies for the writing you will be expected to do as a college student. The writing instruction includes not only explanations, exercises, and assignments but also patterns that provide you with simple visual representations of the basic forms of most academic writing. Once you have mastered these basic concepts, you will be able to apply them in all your writing assignments.

Part One, Writing Paragraphs and Essays, gives you the foundation you will need to become a better writer. The nine chapters included in Part One provide you with basic instruction in writing—the importance of a controlling idea, the structure of paragraphs and essays, the ways in which ideas are arranged and connected, and the process of gathering information. Most important, Part One includes patterns and strategies to help you construct effective paragraphs and essays.

Understanding the Writing Process

As a first-year college student, you will be writing and reading for every class you take. Your academic assignments during a typical week might include writing an essay for your English composition class, reading an article and writing a summary for your sociology class, and writing an essay examination in your history class. Because writing is an important part of nearly all college classes, you will probably be writing more than you ever have before.

In your previous writing experiences, you probably thought more about *what* to write than *how* to write. Although the content of your writing is very important, we begin this book by discussing the **process** of writing. By understanding this process, you will be able to make better decisions as you write and become a more successful academic writer.

Asked to describe what happens when she writes, one of our students responded:

> My writing is a process of thinking, writing, thinking, scratching out, thinking, writing again, and sometimes starting the whole process over. Writing is a struggle with the pen to sort out a complex bundle of words.

This description of the writing process is both accurate and perceptive. For most of us, writing is a struggle that involves rewriting as well as writing. And each time we write, the process varies a little because it is not an exact process such as turning on a computer or solving a math problem. Using a word processor will make this process easier for you, but writing will remain a difficult and demanding—yet also rewarding—task.

The writing process also varies from one person to the next. No two people go through exactly the same process when they write, even if they are writing to the same audience for the same purpose. You should understand that the writing process is not a precise formula but rather a general pattern. However, understanding this general process—even though it is sometimes messy and inexact—will help you become a better writer and a better student.

In general, effective writers go through the following three stages:

1. Prewriting
2. Writing
3. Rewriting

Although most writers move through these stages in this order, each stage actually merges with the others. That is, one stage does not have to end completely before another stage begins. When you are writing, you move back and forth among these stages, starting one stage before you complete another or returning to an earlier stage before moving forward again. Or you may work on two stages at the same time, as when you discover new ideas while rewriting or discard an idea even before you actually begin to write. In addition, you usually go through each stage repeatedly. All writers write, read their work, and rewrite, trying to understand their own ideas, to anticipate their readers' needs, and to communicate their ideas clearly and effectively to those readers. Many rereadings and rewritings may be necessary before this process is complete.

The following diagram emphasizes that the various stages of the writing process do not always follow each other in a neat, sequential order:

Even though these stages vary each time you write, you will be a better writer if you understand how these stages relate to one another.

PREWRITING

Some of the most important writing you do never reaches the page or is written and then thrown away. When you are given a topic or a writing assignment, ideally you should think about it before you begin to write. If your assignment is a final course project in a psychology or political science class, you will have weeks or even months for the idea to "incubate" or "cook," to use metaphors other writers have used. If the assignment is a freshman English essay due in a couple of weeks, you will have only a couple of days to think about the topic before you start working on it. In writing an essay examination for your history class, you will have only a few minutes to consider the topic before you respond to it—although you should, of course, have prepared by studying the material.

The thinking period that occurs in the earliest stage of prewriting is important, but beware of letting this stage turn into procrastination. Early in this first stage, you should begin to explore your topic in writing; indeed, if your assignment is a general one that allows you to determine your own specific topic, this early prewriting exploration can help you *find* your topic. Therefore, **prewriting** involves not only *thinking* about your topic but also *writing* about it. For example, when his English teacher asked him to write a paragraph about the course requirements at his university, a student named Jerry made the following list:

history

English composition

math—basic math and algebra

computer science—not required (I wonder why?)

speech

science

government

This list eventually led Jerry to argue in the paragraph he wrote that computer science should also be a required course. (Specific prewriting strategies will be discussed in detail in Chapter 3, Setting Goals and Generating Ideas.)

Considering Subject, Purpose, and Audience

An important part of preparing to write is considering not only the **subject** you are writing about but also your **purpose** and your **audience**, those who will read your work. Indeed, the process of writing is, in large part, a struggle to discover the answers to the important questions of *What? Why?* and *Who?* As shown in the following figure, writers and speakers produce a text (anything that is written or spoken) by considering subject (*What?*), purpose (*Why?*), and audience (*Who?*):

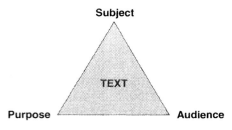

Because these three elements—subject, purpose, and audience—are all basic to the writing process, a writer should consider each of them before and during writing. For example, as he thought about his writing assignment, Jerry made the following decisions:

Subject: I will write about a computer science class as a basic skills requirement.

Purpose: I will recommend that a computer science class be added to the list of basic skills requirements.

Audience: I will write to college administrators who decide what basic skills courses should be required.

As Jerry discovered, the elements of subject, purpose, and audience are so dependent on one another that one choice affects, or determines, another. For example, in order to achieve his purpose of trying to get a computer science class added to the list of basic skills courses, Jerry must write to convince a particular audience: college administrators who would make such a decision.

WRITING

Although **writing** requires preparation, it is also an act of discovery. You may begin with a mental plan—or even an outline (see Chapter 3). Or you may find—as Jerry did in the following draft of his paragraph—that your writing process works better if you just begin writing, discovering the structure of your paragraph or essay as you write and revise:

> The ability to use a computer is necessary for college and work. The first day of class this semester, all of my instructors gave assignments that would require me to use a computer. Three out of the four classes that I am taking gave sights on the Internet to access for homework assignments. Since I graduated from high school ten years ago. I have not had one job that has not required me to use a computer. These examples shows that computers play a major role in this world. Therefore, I urge the administrators of our college to add a basic computer science course to the list of basic skills requirements.

Whatever process you use to create your draft, however, you should not hesitate to make changes as new ideas or discoveries come to you.

Remember that a good writer is flexible. Do not limit yourself to the ideas you had before you began to write. In both this drafting stage and your final revision stage, you may have new ideas and insights that will strengthen your writing, making it more vivid, more interesting, and more readable.

The number of drafts you write will depend on how many discoveries you make as you write. The writer who requires several drafts is often a better writer than the one who thinks he or she has gotten it right the first time. Just as an artist shapes and reshapes, colors and recolors, so a writer writes and rewrites until the finished product achieves its purpose.

REWRITING

The **rewriting** stage is not limited to the final part of the process but may occur at any point. As you work back and forth through the writing process, you may see your subject, purpose, or even audience in a different light. This act of *revising* (or "reseeing") your writing then prompts you to rewrite your draft, to make changes in everything from a single word to the focus of your entire composition.

In rewriting, you assume the difficult role of being a reader of your own writing. To rewrite effectively, you must learn to look at your own writing objectively—to *resee* it as your reader will see it.

As illustrated in the following figure, the process of rewriting is both a part of the larger writing process and a process in itself:

As shown here, rewriting includes three functions: revising, editing, and proofreading. To *revise* means to make important changes in the content, focus, or organization of a draft; to *edit* means to make changes or corrections in sentence structure, usage, and word choice; and to *proofread* means to make minor corrections in the final copy.

For example, as Jerry reread his paragraph, he decided that he had not given enough examples to convince college administrators to consider his recommendation seriously. Therefore, he rewrote it, adding the examples that appear in bold type:

The ability to use a computer is necessary for college and

work. The first day of class this semester, all of my instructors

gave assignments that would require me to use a computer.

For example, **my political science, history, and business instructors all** gave sights on the Internet to access for homework assignments. Furthermore, **my English instructor explained that I would be required to write and revise my papers on a computer**. Since I graduated from high school ten years ago. I have not had one job that has not required me to use a computer. **The two workplaces where I have used computers the most were a farm supplies store and a law enforcement agency. At the farm supplies store, I used computers for making sales, ordering merchandise, and keeping inventory records. At the law enforcement agency where I am currently working, I use computers for keeping records of offense reports, accident reports, and traffic violations as well as for checking a person's criminal history and driver's license record**. These examples shows that computers play a major role in this world. Therefore, I urge the administrators of our college to add a basic computer science course to the list of basic skills requirements.

In addition to adding specific examples, Jerry also inserted the transitions *for example* and *furthermore*, which are highlighted.

After Jerry revised his paragraph by adding examples and transitions, he edited and proofread it, making the following changes:

[1]The ability to use a computer is necessary for college and work. [2]The first day of class this semester, all of my instructors gave assignments that would require me to use a computer. [3]For example, my political science, history, and business instructors

sites   all gave ~~sights~~ on the Internet to access for homework assignments. [4]In addition, my English instructor explained that I would be required to write and revise my papers on a computer. [5]Since I graduated from high school ten years ago., I have not had one job that has not required me to use a computer. [6]The two workplaces where I have used computers the most were a farm supplies store and a law enforcement agency. [7]At the farm supplies store. I used computers for making sales, ordering merchandise, and keeping inventory records. [8]At the law enforcement agency where I am currently working, I use computers for keeping records of offense reports, accident reports, and citations for traffic violations as well as for checking a person's criminal history and driver's license record. [9]These

show   examples ~~shows~~ that computers play a major role in this world. [10]Therefore, I urge the administrators of our college to add a basic computer science course to the list of basic skills requirements.

As shown, Jerry found that in sentence 3 he needed the word *sites*, meaning "location," as in "websites," rather than *sights*, meaning "views" or "visions." He also found and corrected a fragment in sentence 5 and a subject-verb agreement error in sentence 9. Like Jerry, you should wait until your ideas are down on paper and developed fully before you worry about spelling errors and punctuation. If you become too concerned with correctness (editing and proofreading) during your early drafts, you may inhibit your writing process. Knowing that you can attend to matters of style and correctness on later drafts frees you to think more clearly and creatively on early drafts. Save editing and proofreading, as Jerry did, primarily for the final stages. (For more information about rewriting, see Chapter 9.)

Your writing process is uniquely your own, but it is also an evolving process. That is, you probably write best at a particular time—maybe early in the morning or late at night—and in a particular place—perhaps at a computer in the library or propped on a pillow in your room. Yet as your writing process develops throughout your study of this textbook, you will learn new strategies that will make you a better writer. If you take the time to let your writing process work *for* you, you will also become a much more successful college student.

CHAPTER REVIEW

- The writing process involves the three stages of prewriting, writing, and rewriting.
- These three stages of the writing process overlap and recur.
- The writing process is shaped by the elements of subject, purpose, and audience.
- The rewriting stage includes the substages of revising, editing, and proofreading.

■ WRITING ASSIGNMENT

Write a description of your own writing process. How is it similar to or different from the process described in this chapter?

■ PARTICIPATING IN THE ACADEMIC COMMUNITY

Discuss your writing process with a small group of your classmates. Compare your writing processes and discuss how they are similar to or different from the general process described in this chapter.

CHAPTER

2

Selecting and Limiting a Topic

Your first reaction to a writing assignment may be that you do not know what to write about. Knowing how to select a topic and limit its scope is an important first step to becoming a confident academic writer. Occasionally, your instructor will give you a topic and a detailed assignment. More often, however, your instructor will expect you to come up with a topic on your own. In still other cases, an instructor will give you a general topic and expect you to modify it. In this chapter, you will learn how to get started on a writing assignment by doing the following:

- Selecting a topic on your own
- Modifying an assigned topic
- Limiting, or narrowing, a topic

SELECTING YOUR OWN TOPIC

Sometimes an instructor, especially in a composition course, will give you a writing assignment but not a topic. The instructor will say something like this: "Write a three- to five-page essay on any topic that interests you" or "Write a one-page definition of something." If you receive this type of open-ended assignment in a writing course, you are indeed free to choose any topic you like. However, you should be aware that certain topics will be valued more than others. If you write about a clichéd topic—such as what you did on your summer vacation or why you do not like living in the dorm—you may satisfy the requirements of the assignment but will probably not produce an essay that earns a very good grade.

Even more constraints are involved when the instructor in a history or sociology course tells you to write a five- to ten-page paper on any topic that interests you. In this situation, there are definite constraints. The instructor assumes that you will write about something associated with the course. You are not free to write about what you did on your summer vacation or even how you feel about the pollution problems created by increasing traffic in your city. Your history instructor will expect you to write on a topic related to history, and your sociology instructor will assume you will write about some sociological issue. So you need to realize that in almost every situation, your choices are somewhat limited. But these limitations can actually be helpful because they focus your thinking and provide you with insight into your instructor's intentions yet allow you to personalize the topic.

Guidelines for Selecting a Topic

The following guidelines will help you select a topic for a writing assignment:

1. *Focus on your own experiences, interests, and attitudes.* In selecting your specific subject, do not concentrate on the instructor's likes or dislikes. For example, if your freshman composition instructor tells you to write an essay about anything that interests you, do not try to think of a topic that will impress her. Sure, she is interested in politics and classical music, but you may know very little about these subjects and have practically no personal experience with either. Instead, select a topic that you know something about and are interested in—something, if possible, with which you have had extensive, firsthand experience. For example, you may know a great deal about cars, small children, or jazz. If you write on one of these topics, your instructor may learn something by reading your paper. Each writing assignment is an opportunity to demonstrate what you know. If you choose a topic that you know nothing about, have had no experience with, and have little interest in exploring, you cannot hope to write intelligently about it. Your primary concern in selecting a topic for a writing assignment, therefore, should be to choose something you know well and in which you are interested. For example, you might write about what you learned about responsibility while working at a job, how tennis shoes have changed, or why you think grades should be abolished. These topics are not earth-shattering but can be the subjects of thoughtful, academically appropriate essays.

2. *Tailor your topic to the class for which the assignment is required.* The kinds of topics you explore and the types of sources you use will vary in different classes. For instance, your English composition instructor may encourage you to rely primarily on your personal experiences. Your history and political science classes will probably require you to write about topics primarily based on background reading. Your sociology and psychology classes, however, will probably allow you to select writing topics—such as family problems or ways to achieve self-esteem—that will allow you to combine your personal experience and your reading. In selecting topics for any of these classes, however, remember that you can write most intelligently and convincingly about subjects that you know well and in which you are interested.

As you will discover in Chapter 3, Setting Goals and Generating Ideas, the tasks of choosing and focusing a topic go hand in hand with invention strategies such as freewriting and brainstorming, which help you not only discover topics for writing but also generate ideas for developing these topics.

EXERCISE

2.1   Brainstorm for a few minutes on a list of topics that are of interest to you (see pages 20–21). Be as complete as possible. Do not be concerned with whether these topics are appropriate or safe or interesting to anyone else. The list should reflect *your* interests and experiences—not what you think anyone else might be interested in.

MODIFYING AN ASSIGNED TOPIC

If your writing assignment specifies a certain topic, you must focus on that subject. For example, if a history instructor tells you to write about John F. Kennedy, you cannot write about Abraham Lincoln instead (even if you know more about Lincoln). However, you can focus on Kennedy and still use what you know about Lincoln by comparing Kennedy to Lincoln in some way. Even when the assignment is fairly explicit, you can usually modify the topic to take into account your own interests and knowledge.

In fact, instructors usually expect and encourage you to personalize the topics they assign. While you should not radically change the assigned topic or completely ignore it, you can certainly shape it to conform to your own interests. If you are in doubt about modifying an assigned topic, speak with your instructor. Of course, drastic changes in an assignment always need to be approved.

EXERCISE

2.2   The following five writing assignments provide topics. Modify and focus each assignment by changing the topic to one that reflects your own interests and knowledge.

1. Argue for or against an environmental issue.

   Your topic: _____

2. Evaluate some product with which you are familiar.

   Your topic: _____

3. Compare two movies that have the same theme.

   Your topic: _____

4. Analyze a problem that exists in your community or school.

   Your topic: _____

5. Explain how some aspect of popular American culture has changed in your lifetime.

   Your topic: _____

LIMITING A TOPIC

Whether your topic has been assigned or chosen by you, it likely needs to be limited, or narrowed. For example, suppose you are free to choose a topic on your own and decide to write about your experiences on a certain job you held. You still need to narrow this topic so it focuses on one particular aspect of your experience—say, what you learned, how the working conditions created problems, or why the job was stressful. Following are several examples of the process of limiting a topic. Notice that as you move down each list, the topics become increasingly more specific:

1. *Transportation*
   vehicle
   trucks
   domestic versus foreign pickups
   Chevrolet versus Mazda pickups

2. *Music*
   popular music
   jazz
   Nat King Cole's influence on jazz
   Cole's influence on modern jazz

3. *Education*
   college
   first-year students
   problems first-year students face

Although you may fear that you will not have enough to say if you limit your topic, you will discover that you actually have much more information to draw on if you write on a narrowed topic that you know something about and then focus on providing your reader with lots of specific details. Narrower topics almost always result in stronger compositions.

If an instructor gives you a general topic, it is especially important for you to narrow it. For example, if you are asked to write about nutrition, you might narrow this topic to nutrition for a particular age group, perhaps your own. Then you can further tailor the topic to fit your knowledge and experiences by narrowing it to an even more specific topic, such as how good nutrition can benefit college students or the difference between the diets of male and female students.

EXERCISE

2.3

Limit each of the following topics so it is appropriate for a three- to five-page writing assignment.

1. Using the Internet

   _____

2. How to be a good consumer

   _____

3. Current trends in lifestyles

   _____

4. How education has failed

   _____

5. Causes of stress

   _____

EXERCISE

2.4

The following topics are typical of freshman composition assignments. Narrow each to a limited subject on which you could write an essay.

1. An autobiography about your reading and writing experiences

   _____

2. Profile of a family member

   _____

3. Campus crimes

   _____

4. Problems caused by television

_____

5. Modern heroes

_____

EXERCISE

2.5   Choose one of the topics you included in your brainstorming list in Exercise 2.1 and brainstorm again on this topic. Create a list of your new ideas; then again choose one. Repeat this process of brainstorming and then selecting a topic from your new list until you have a limited topic that would be appropriate for an essay.

CHAPTER REVIEW

- When selecting a topic of your own, write on a subject (1) that interests you, (2) that you know well, and (3) that reflects your own experience.
- When possible, modify assigned topics to reflect your own interests, expertise, and experience.
- Narrow _all_ topics.

WRITING ASSIGNMENT

Select one of the topics you provided in Exercise 2.3, 2.4, or 2.5 and write a discovery draft, in which you tell what you know about this subject. Do not worry about organization or structure at this point. The purposes of a discovery draft are to get your ideas on paper and to generate as much information on the subject as possible.

PARTICIPATING IN THE ACADEMIC COMMUNITY

Meet with others members of your class who have chosen to write about the same general topic for the preceding writing assignment. Compare your limited topics, and share the information you have generated.

CHAPTER

3

Setting Goals
and Generating Ideas

Once you have selected and limited your topic, you need to explore that topic to decide what you want to say about it and how you want to say it. Although you will need to research some topics (see Chapter 7), you can use your own knowledge, your reading, and your experience to generate ideas for many of your writing assignments. As this chapter will show, you can also use specific strategies during the prewriting stage to find and focus (or refocus) your topic, discover your ideas for writing, and plan possible ways of organizing these ideas. These strategies can be helpful not only in your composition class but also in other classes.

USING INVENTION STRATEGIES

The task of generating ideas is often called **invention**. Of course, you do not "invent" ideas that have never existed before. What you actually do is use strategies for tapping into knowledge and experiences you already have, rediscovering them, so to speak, by making connections between these ideas and your topic and by seeing these ideas as possible subjects for writing. Some of the most helpful invention strategies are freewriting, journal writing, brainstorming, clustering, mapping, questioning, and discussing.

Freewriting

As a beginning writer, you may be intimidated by the task of getting started. You might be interested to know that even famous writers often share this fear. The writer Truman Capote, for example, once admitted that he hated "facing that blank piece of paper every day and having to reach up somewhere into the clouds and bring something down out of them" (Jon Winokur, *Writers on Writing*, Philadelphia: Running Press,

1986, p. 101). One of the most helpful techniques for getting ideas down on paper is **freewriting**.

To freewrite, simply write rapidly for five or ten minutes without stopping and without worrying about form or correctness. If you do not have a particular topic in mind, or if you are writing to discover a general topic, write whatever comes to mind, repeating words or phrases if you cannot think of something else to write. The key is to keep writing without stopping for several minutes, letting the ideas flow freely, as Shana did in the following example:

> Well, here is the first day of freshman English and what a suprise! The teacher asks me to write. But write what? Freewrite, she says, so OK. Write, write, write. It seems as if that is what I've done all my life, and I've never liked it. What should I write about? School is writting, and I guess college is writting too. I guess if I have to write about something I can write about writting—why I don't like it. Maybe it goes back to my third grade teacher Mrs. Jaggart who never liked my stuff. Worst teacher I ever had. Put red marks all over my papers. Never said anything nice about it. Wonder what this teacher will say when I—

When you finish freewriting, reread to see if certain words and ideas are especially interesting to you or related to one another; then underline those ideas. For example, as shown in the following underlined phrases, when Shana reread her freewriting, she discovered that she had actually found a possible idea for an essay:

> Well, here is the first day of freshman English and what a suprise! The teacher asks me to write. But write what? Freewrite, she says, so OK. Write, write, write. It seems as if that is what I've done all my life, and I've <u>never liked it</u>. What should I write about? School is writting, and I guess college is writting too. I guess if I have to write about something I can write about <u>writting—why I don't like it</u>. Maybe it goes back to my third grade teacher Mrs. Jaggart who <u>never liked my stuff</u>. Worst teacher I ever had. Put <u>red marks all over my papers</u>. <u>Never said anything nice about it</u>. Wonder what this teacher will say when I—

As shown by the words she underlined, Shana has started to focus on her own attitude toward writing and reasons for that attitude.

Helpful variations of freewriting are **looping** and **focused freewriting**. In looping, you take an idea that surfaced in one freewriting and do a focused freewriting, writing whatever comes to mind about that particular topic. For example, Shana could develop her ideas further with a focused freewriting on her attitude toward writing. You can open up almost any topic through focused freewriting. (*Note:* Focused freewriting can be part of the looping process or a separate activity.)

EXERCISE

3.1   Do a five- to ten-minute freewriting about your most memorable teacher—perhaps your best or worst one. Remember not to worry about form or correctness and not to stop writing until time is up. When you are finished, reread your freewriting and underline phrases that particularly interest you or that form a connected pattern. Write these phrases here.

_____

_____

_____

_____

If you wish, you may do a more focused freewriting on one of the ideas about your teacher that emerged in your first freewriting.

Journal Writing

Although a **journal** entry has more structure and order than freewriting, it is similar to freewriting in that one of its purposes is to generate ideas. Because your primary audience for your journal is yourself, this format allows you to discover—to question and explore, to think critically, and to write freely about your thoughts, observations, questions, and feelings. In the following journal entry, Housein explores the idea of a special teacher:

> A special teacher, or mentor, becomes a leader for the students and is not seen as a boss who is always right. Looking back in my past high school years, I had a few teachers that taught me by using this leadership approach. These were the only classes in which I got A's and A⁺'s, primarily because I liked going to class.
>
> I remember being in my geometry class just waiting for time to go, as I looked forward to my anatomy class. This class was considered the hardest course at Emporia High School and even had a harder grading scale than regular classes. I was asked by my geometry teacher why I was failing her class when I had an A in my anatomy class. I

didn't have the answer for her then. I knew only that I liked going to the anatomy class because it was interesting, and because the class was fun, I did the best I could without even questioning the amount of work I was putting into the class.

Unlike my geometry class, where I just sat there bored out of my mind and getting in trouble for talking and getting out of my seat. I thought my lack of interest in geometry was just because I couldn't do math, and I dropped her class. My theory for having failed the class changed, as the next year (my Junior year) I got a different teacher and a B⁺ in geometry. In my new geometry class. I had a teacher who was also my track and field coach. I thought he was the craziest teacher, he was very funny and expected us to do the best we could, because we could.

These two teachers made me feel part of their classes and if I missed or did poorly in class it would affect the whole group. As mentor teachers, they focused on a student centered education.

Housein's journal entry is thoughtful and well developed, but you may have noticed that it has some errors in sentence structure. Although most instructors react to journal entries with written comments, they usually do not evaluate them in the same way they evaluate other written assignments. Thus, you should not be overly concerned with correctness in a journal. Instead, you should feel free to experiment not only with new ideas but also with new words, forms, and styles of writing.

You may write about anything you wish in your journal—your feelings about a relationship, your doubts about college, what you did over the weekend, your baby's first steps. Journal entries focused on topics assigned by an instructor, however, can also provide excellent ideas for academic writing. Rereading one of your academic entries a few days later can remind you of ideas you had about the assignment that you might otherwise have forgotten; rereading one of your personal entries a few years later can remind you of special events and feelings in your life. Here are just a few topics that you might explore in your journal:

1. Tell about a time that you did something right.
2. Write about a day when everything seemed to go wrong.
3. What person do you admire most in the world? Why?
4. What is your favorite book or movie? Why?
5. If you could change identities with another person, whom would you choose? Why?

6. Where do you see yourself in ten years?

7. If you could relive any part of your life, what would it be and why?

8. How would you change your life if you could?

9. If you had only a year to live, what would you do?

10. If you could live in another time, past or future, when would it be?

Writing in a journal can become an enjoyable routine if you have a particular time and place to write. Many people like to write in their journals just before they go to bed. You may buy a special notebook or create a computer file for your journal. You may write in your journal as often as you wish, but you will find the task easier and more enjoyable if you write in it for ten or fifteen minutes each day. As you get used to writing in your journal, you will probably spend more time with it, and your journal entries may grow to be as long as Housein's.

EXERCISE

3.2

Write a journal entry on one of the ten topics just listed. Feel free not only to tell about your experience, real or imaginary, but also to describe your feelings and to comment on the importance of the experience.

Brainstorming

Like freewriting, **brainstorming** is a quick and easy method for getting ideas down on paper. To brainstorm, you simply jot down rapidly in list form whatever words, phrases, names, details, or ideas come to mind. Although you can do an unfocused brainstorming to generate—or invent—ideas about a topic, you will get more helpful ideas for writing if you do a focused brainstorming on a particular topic you have already chosen. In the following brainstorming, for example, Amy focused on problems in public schools:

drugs	violence
failure	shootings in Colorado
fights in classroom	drug testing
kids don't pay attention	discipline problems
teachers don't care	math classes too hard
kids don't care	not enough money
bomb threat at Emory HS graduation	need more books

As you can see, brainstorming is an effective technique for gathering ideas for writing. You can even use a form of brainstorming when you are taking an in-class essay examination, jotting down main points or examples in the margins of your examination sheet. By writing down ideas for a paper or an exam as soon as you think of them, you can avoid the memory block that sometimes occurs because of writing anxiety.

EXERCISE

3.3   Brainstorm for about five minutes on the goals that you have for your life. What would you like to accomplish right away? What would you like to achieve in the future? In the following spaces, write a list of ideas that come to mind about this topic.

_____

_____

_____

_____

Clustering

When you brainstorm, one idea leads to another so that many of the items you list are connected in some way. If you draw circles and lines to show connections among these related ideas, you will have a **cluster** of ideas to use in a paragraph or an essay. In the following example, notice how Amy created a cluster from her earlier brainstorming:

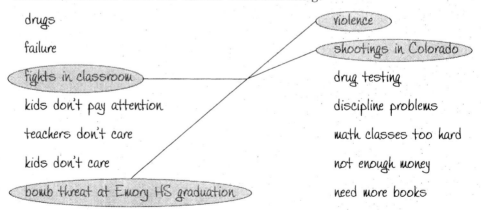

As you can see, Amy noticed she had listed in her brainstorming several items about violence in the public schools. She identified these items and grouped them together. Later, she can add ideas and examples to this original cluster to make a plan for writing about this topic.

EXERCISE

3.4   Review the brainstorming about your goals that you created in Exercise 3.3. Then draw circles and lines to cluster related ideas.

Mapping

If you are a visual learner, you may find the technique of **mapping** particularly helpful. Just as a road map helps you to find your destination and gives you information about the stops on the way when you are on a trip, a visual idea map helps you know where you want to go in your writing and how you can get there. Just as one road leads to another, one thought will lead to another and take you to interesting ideas for writing that you might never have thought of without this exercise. To map an idea, write your general topic in the middle of a piece of paper and then branch out from the topic with related ideas, examples, and details, as shown in Jerry's mapping on the subject of educational methods:

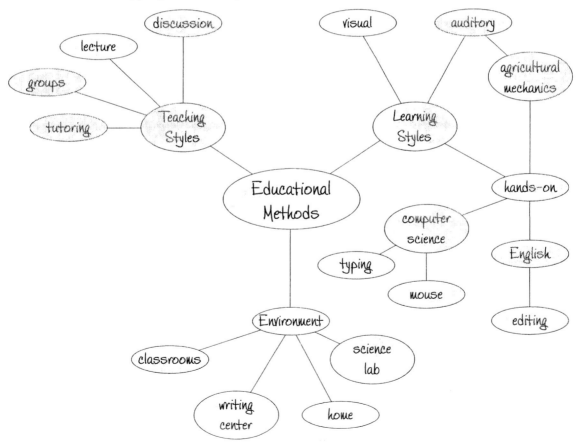

In Jerry's map, you can immediately see a visual diagram of how ideas are related. From such a map, you can often determine which ideas have the potential for development and which do not, thus helping you identify your best choices for writing. In Jerry's map, for example, hands-on learning style emerges as a good topic.

EXERCISE

3.5   Add subtopics and examples as necessary to complete the following map on the benefits of a college education. (Use a separate sheet of paper.)

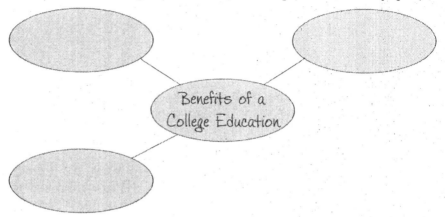

Questioning

To generate ideas for writing, you can also use the technique of **questioning**. When newspaper reporters cover an event or do an interview, they often use questions to be sure they get all the information they need. You can also use these reporters' questions to help you select a topic and gather information to develop that topic. You can remember them as the 5-*W* questions—*Who? What? When? Where? Why?*—and *How?*

Notice how Tomas adapted these questions to explore the topic of an influential teacher:

Who influenced you?   Mrs. Roberts, my English teacher when I was a junior in high school.

What did she do?   She showed an interest in me as a person. She also showed an interest in my culture when she assigned our class Rudolfo Anaya's <u>Bless Me, Ultima</u> to read. As we talked about this book she helped other students to understand about Mexican American culture.

When did she do this?	She talked about <u>Bless Me, Ultima</u> and Mexican American culture when I was sixteen years old and a high school junior.
Where did she do this?	She discussed this book in my English class. It was in a small town somewhere in southern California, but my family was moving around so much that year that I don't remember the name of the town.
Why did she do this?	At first I wondered why Mrs. Roberts, an Anglo, would teach a Mexican American book in an American literature class. I thought books like this should be taught, but at other schools teachers just talked about Poe and Twain and stuff like that. I think Mrs. Roberts tried to find a book that the Mexican Americans in the class could relate to. But she also seemed to really like the book herself. I think she thought it was just as good as I did.
How did she influence you?	Reading that book got me a lot more interested in school. I saw that I could explain about some of the customs in the book that others didn't know about, and I felt smart. Before we moved, Mrs. Roberts even talked to me about going to college. If it hadn't been for her, I don't think I would be in this class.

EXERCISE

3.6   Use the questioning technique to explore the college major or career that you plan to pursue.

What is your intended career or major?

_____

_____

Who influenced you to make this decision?

_____

_____

When did you decide on this career or major?

_____

_____

Where do you hope to work?

_____

_____

Why did you choose this career
or major?

_____

_____

How do you plan to achieve
your goal?

_____

_____

Discussing

Discussing your writing with your classmates, a tutor, or your instructor can also help you think of new ideas for your writing. Moreover, testing your own ideas against the ideas of others—comparing and evaluating these ideas—is important for developing the critical thinking skills necessary for all of your academic writing and reading assignments.

Consider the following transcription of a class discussion on the value of great books such as Homer's *The Odyssey* and Nathaniel Hawthorne's *The Scarlet Letter*:

Clay: I disagree with the great books approach. People need to be able to think for themselves. How is all of this classical reading going to prepare students for the real world? The answer is, it isn't.

Maggie: But isn't college about a well-rounded education? Reading the classics is a good way to learn about literature, science, art, and mathematics. And it certainly isn't boring!

Cherie: Well, Charles Dickens's *A Tale of Two Cities* is supposed to be a classic, isn't it? I had an English teacher in high school who made us read it, and I didn't even read the whole book. I bought the CliffsNotes™ and read enough to pass my tests. What did I get from that? It's not that I was bad at reading, but the book could not keep my interest long enough for me to gain anything from it.

Maggie: I had a different experience in a summer college class in science fiction. We read books like *Brave New World, Flatland*, and *War of the Worlds*. In class we talked about scientific advances in each book and how far technology has come today to catch up with the fiction. I learned more about physics in this class than in my high school physics class.

Housein: Also, the classics help us learn about life, not just learn for a piece of paper that says we have sat through so many classes to qualify us for a specific job. I like the idea of the classics, but the problem is that it's hard to define a classic or a "great book." Is a book great just because it's on somebody's list? And why aren't there more books by Hispanics and African Americans on the list of classics?

Cherie: Yeah, that's a problem, too. Just who says a book is great? But mostly I agree with Clay that these books just don't apply to my life today. And I don't appreciate being forced to read a long, boring book I have no interest in. I didn't like it in high school, and I don't like it now, especially when I have to pay for it.

Housein: Maybe books don't have to be long and hard to be great. I even think Dr. Seuss's books are great because they teach kids to read and to love language, and they are fun. I think that's really great!

After participating in this discussion, these students may be better prepared to write a paper on some of the advantages and disadvantages of requiring students to read the classics. A discussion such as this enables you to clarify and sharpen your ideas and exposes you to the ideas of others.

EXERCISE

3.7   With a small group of your classmates, discuss the freewriting that you did on your best or worst teachers in Exercise 3.1. What conclusions can you draw about effective teaching from these examples? Write two or three of these conclusions in the following space:

1. _____
2. _____
3. _____

USING INFORMAL PLANNING OUTLINES

Outlining is a method of organizing ideas by indicating their relationship to one another. Like a diagram, an outline is a blueprint or plan of a completed work. It is a skeleton that allows you to see the essential framework of a piece of writing.

Because an outline visually represents general and specific relationships, you must understand how to distinguish between general and specific concepts in order to outline. For example, elementary, secondary and postsecondary are three general categories of education. Thus, on an outline, you would arrange them as three equal headings:

▶ **Example**

elementary education

secondary education

postsecondary education

Then, if you wanted to include specific examples of each of these three general categories, you could place them under the appropriate headings:

▶ **Example**

Postsecondary education

  technical school

  community college

  four-year college

  university

You could also add letters or numbers to your outline to make the relationships clearer:

▶ **Example**

1. Postsecondary education

   a. technical school

   b. community college

   c. four-year college

   d. university

Or you could use a different system of representation as long as you continued to indicate that *postsecondary education* is the most general term and that the other terms are specific examples or types of postsecondary education:

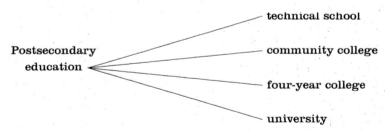

Outlines can appear in various forms as long as they communicate accurately the relationships that exist among the items of information included. The outline form that is probably most familiar to you is the **formal outline**. Writers use formal outlines to give their readers information about the material being outlined. Formal outlines are most appropriately used as tables of contents. They are frequently included with long reports, research papers, and proposals as a guide to the contents. Because formal outlines must communicate clearly to a reader, the writer uses a traditional form that is familiar to everyone. A formal outline is illustrated here:

Main idea: Literature has traditionally been divided into three categories.

   I. Fiction
     A. Novel
     B. Short story

  II. Drama
     A. Tragedy
     B. Comedy
       1. Low comedy
       2. High comedy

 III. Poetry

This outline could serve as an effective introduction to a chapter or essay on the types of literature. As a reader, you can determine from this formal outline that the three main types of literature are fiction, drama, and poetry. You can also see that fiction can be divided into the subcategories of novel and short story and that drama can be divided into tragedy and comedy. Further, you can see that comedy can be divided into low comedy and high comedy. Not only do the numbers and letters assigned to the entries on the outline and the system of indentation indicate the relative importance of the entries and their relationships to one another but also the use of numbering and capitalization is consistent. (For information on using outlines for studying, see Chapter 32.)

When you are planning a paragraph or an essay, however, you may find a formal outline too limiting. Whereas a formal outline usually requires at least two items in each category, you may find that in some categories you have only one point to make. In addition, the fact that a formal outline is so neat and balanced may discourage you from making changes in your plan as you work. For these reasons, writers usually find that some type of **informal outline** is more helpful for establishing goals before they begin to write.

Because you are the only person who will be using your planning outline, you should select the format that is most helpful for you. Indeed, your planning outline may simply be scratches on a piece of paper—what is called a *scratch outline*—if these scratches communicate to you. However, you may find it helpful to learn several possible formats for planning outlines. Following are four formats for exploring the topic of hands-on learning:

► **Example A: Informal Topic Outline**

1. English class (editing)
2. agricultural mechanics class
   —plumbing (copper pipe and PVC pipe)
   —wiring
   —carpentry
3. computer science class (typing and mouse skills)

► **Example B: Flow Diagram**

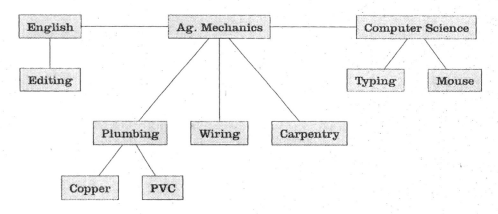

► **Example C: Mapping**

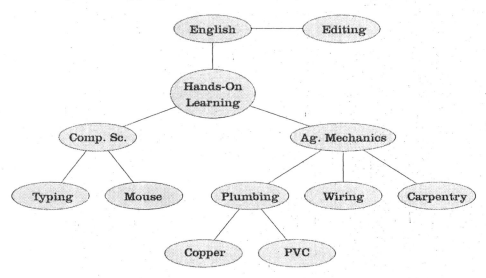

▶ Example D: Informal Sentence Outline

1. In my English class we practice hands-on editing.

2. In my agricultural mechanics class we get hands-on practice.
   —We plumb with both copper and PVC pipe.
   —We install electrical wiring.
   —We practice carpentry skills.

3. In my computer science class we use both keyboard and mouse skills.

Any one of these planning outlines can help you write a paragraph or brief essay on learning with a hands-on approach. Or, you may want to experiment with two or three planning formats to determine which ones work best for you.

EXERCISE

3.8   Write an informal outline based on the brainstorming you did about your goals in life in Exercise 3.3 or on one of the other prewriting exercises you have completed. Use whichever planning format you prefer.

CHAPTER REVIEW

■ Invention strategies help you discover what you have to say about an idea or topic.

1. **Freewriting** is writing your thoughts rapidly for a few minutes without worrying about form or correctness.

2. **Journal writing** allows you to explore your thoughts and feelings in depth.

3. **Brainstorming** is a rapid listing of ideas.

4. **Clustering** identifies and shows connections among ideas generated by brainstorming.

5. **Mapping** creates a visual diagram of your ideas.

6. **Questioning** gathers information from the queries *who, what, when, where, why*, and *how*.

7. **Discussing** allows you to compare your ideas with others.

■ Informal planning outlines, which can occur in various forms, can be helpful working plans for writing.

▦ WRITING ASSIGNMENT

Write a paragraph, journal entry, or brief essay using the planning outline you created for Exercise 3.8.

▦ PARTICIPATING IN THE ACADEMIC COMMUNITY

Compare the planning outline you created in Exericise 3.8 with the outlines of a small group of your classmates. Discuss why you each chose the type of format you used.

Constructing Paragraphs: Topic Sentences

As a college student, you will be assigned a variety of writing tasks. Instructors will ask you to write essays, memos, reports, research papers, critiques, reviews, and response papers. Most instructors will assume that you know what is involved in writing these types of assignments. One of the purposes of this book is to provide you with the strategies you need to produce a variety of writing assignments. Rather than focusing on each type of assignment individually, this book emphasizes the basic patterns and concepts that make up most academic writing assignments. If you master these concepts, you will know the general shape of all academic discourse and be able to adapt the basic patterns to any assignment. One of the most important of these concepts is the paragraph.

BASIC STRUCTURE OF A PARAGRAPH

A **paragraph** consists of a series of sentences related to a single idea that is identified in the **topic sentence.** In simple terms, the topic sentence tells the reader what the paragraph will be about. It is usually stated at the very beginning of the paragraph, as in the example that follows:

The terrorists who destroyed the World Trade Center and killed almost 3,000 people in New York City on September 11, 2001, changed the way Americans view the world. In a few minutes, America became a different place to live—a place that is less safe and secure, more vulnerable. For the first time in the memory of anyone now alive, the mainland of America was successfully attacked, and Americans knew what it is like to be afraid. But the attack changed more than our own sense of security; it also changed the way we view the rest of the world and our relationships with other nations. In the future, we can no longer assume that what happens even in remote, poverty-stricken nations will not affect us. The terrorists not only changed our perception of ourselves but also made us world citizens in ways we had never been before.

Notice that this paragraph begins with a general statement, which serves as the topic sentence for the paragraph, establishing the idea that the 2001 terrorist attacks changed the way we view the world. This sentence serves as the introduction and establishes the controlling idea for the paragraph. The next four sentences in the paragraph support the topic sentence by providing specific details about how our view of the world has changed. These specific details further explain and reinforce the topic sentence. Then the final sentence in the paragraph functions as a conclusion.

Model of a Basic Paragraph

The following diagram shows the form and proportions of a model paragraph. Notice that the first word in the paragraph is indented several spaces (usually five to ten) from the margin. Notice, too, that the body of the paragraph is much longer than either the introduction or the conclusion.

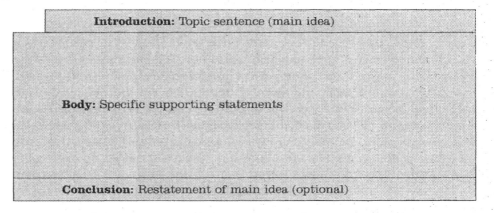

Introduction: Topic sentence (main idea)

Body: Specific supporting statements

Conclusion: Restatement of main idea (optional)

This paragraph model is just that—a model, or pattern, to help you visualize the shape and proportions of a well-developed paragraph. Other patterns exist, but in general they are variations of this basic model. If you observe paragraphs in books, magazines, and newspapers, you will notice that professional writers often write paragraphs that do not follow this pattern. Experienced writers may omit topic sentences or place their main ideas in the middle or at the end of the paragraph if that arrangement suits their subject and purpose. However, in learning to write and read academic discourse, you will find this pattern useful.

EXERCISE

4.1

The following paragraphs use the pattern of the model paragraph, except that the topic sentence has been omitted. For each paragraph, you are given three sentences, each of which could function as a topic sentence. However, only one of the sentences is really appropriate. Read each paragraph carefully, examining the supporting details and the conclusion. Then select the topic sentence that best expresses the main idea. Write the sentence in the space provided.

PARAGRAPH A

1. Movies are more emotional than recorded music or books.
2. Audiences prefer movies to other forms of entertainment.
3. Movies have a hold on people, at least while they are watching one, that is more intense than any other medium.

Topic sentence _____

_____

It is not unusual for a movie reviewer to recommend taking a handkerchief, but never will you hear such advice from a record reviewer and seldom from a book reviewer. Why do movies have such powerful effects? It is not movies themselves. With rare exception, these evocative efforts occur only when movies are shown in a theater. The viewer sits in a darkened auditorium in front of a giant screen with nothing to interrupt the experience. The rest of the world is excluded. Movies, of course, can be shown outdoors at drive-in theaters and on television, but the experience is strongest in the darkened cocoon of a movie house.

—John Vivian, *The Media of Mass Communication*, 4th ed.

PARAGRAPH B

1. College students often face a challenge when trying to eat healthy foods.
2. Most college students do not make the effort to eat a healthy diet.
3. College cafeterias do not provide the variety of foods required by a healthy diet.

Topic sentence: _____

_____

Some students live in dorms and do not have their own cooking or refrigeration facilities. Others live in crowded apartments where everyone forages in the refrigerator for everyone else's food. Still others eat at university food services where food choices are limited. Most students have time constraints that make buying, preparing, and eating healthy food a difficult task. In addition, many lack the financial resources needed to buy many foods that their parents purchased while they lived at home. What's a student to do? . . .

—Rebecca J. Donatelle and Lorraine G. Davis, *Health: The Basics*, 2nd ed.

EXERCISE

4.2   After reading the three specific statements for each of the following paragraphs, supply an appropriate topic sentence.

1. *Topic sentence:* _____

_____

Specific statement: Smoking can cause permanent stains on teeth.

Specific statement: It also contributes to heart disease.

Specific statement: The most significant health risk for most smokers is lung cancer.

2. *Topic sentence:* _____

_____

Specific statement: In the past, a college education prepared people for professional degrees or for a position in a family business.

Specific statement: In more recent years, college degrees have increasingly been perceived as the best way to prepare for a career.

Specific statement: Most recently, people have begun to view college degrees as preparation for life.

WRITING EFFECTIVE TOPIC SENTENCES

Academic writing nearly always begins with a single, well-defined idea that is expressed in a clear, forceful sentence. You have already learned in this chapter that this statement of the main idea is referred to as a *topic sentence* if you are writing a paragraph. You have also learned that the topic sentence expresses a general concept, which is then supported by more specific ideas—other sentences that elaborate, explain, or expand on it. Now you are ready to learn how to write effective topic sentences.

An effective topic sentence consists of a **topic** (what you are writing about) and an **assertion** (the point you are making about the topic). In other words, the assertion makes a statement about the topic. It may express an attitude or opinion (*Recycling should be enforced by law*), or it may simply indicate what is to follow (*We should recycle for three reasons*). Together, the topic and assertion let your reader know the point you are making or the idea you are developing in your paragraph.

Please keep these points in mind:

- Statements of fact do not usually serve as topic sentences because such statements need no further development or support.
- Titles cannot take the place of topic sentences because they tell what the paragraph is about (*Recycling*) but not what you are going to say (assert) about your topic (*Recycling can be an important step toward an environmentally sound conservation policy*).

Narrowing Topic Sentences

Although a topic sentence is a general statement in relation to the other sentences in the paragraph, it should not be so broad that you cannot develop the idea it expresses in a page or less. Often, a statement that is too general to serve as an effective topic sentence can be narrowed by the addition of more specific information. Consider the following sentence:

1. Conservation is important.

This statement is so broad that it cannot possibly be developed adequately in a single paragraph. If you narrow the statement by specifying a particular type of conservation, you will have a more workable topic sentence:

2. Recycling is an important form of conservation.

If you narrow further, you will have an even more effective topic sentence:

3. Local efforts to recycle paper help us conserve our natural forests.

Notice that as you narrow your topic sentence by adding more specific details, it becomes not only a longer sentence but also a stronger topic sentence—one that could be developed in a paragraph. Notice also that both the topic and the assertion are more specific in sentence 3.

Topic	Assertion
1. Conservation	is important.
2. Recycling	is an important form of conservation.
3. Local efforts to recycle paper	help us conserve our forests.

EXERCISE

4.3   Working individually or with your classmates, read the following topic sentences and underline the topic once and the assertion twice. Then write several specific statements that could be used to support the topic sentence.

1. Most older Americans have a strong work ethic.

   Topic: _____

   Assertion: _____

   Specific supporting statements:

   (1) _____

   (2) _____

   (3) _____

   Conclusion: _____

   _____

   _____

2. Telephones intrude into the privacy of our daily lives.

   Topic: _____

   Assertion: _____

   Specific supporting statements:

   (1) _____

   (2) _____

   (3) _____

   Conclusion: _____

   _____

   _____

3. Many gun-related accidents involve children.

   Topic: _____

   Assertion: _____

   Specific supporting statements:

   (1) _____

   (2) _____

   (3) _____

Conclusion: _____

_____

_____

EXERCISE

4.4

This exercise provides you with practice in narrowing topic sentences. As you revise these sentences, keep in mind the following guidelines:

- A topic sentence should always be a complete sentence.
- A topic sentence should not merely state a single fact.
- A topic sentence should be a general statement but should not be so broad or vague that it cannot be developed adequately in a paragraph of five to ten sentences.

Rewrite each of the following statements, narrowing both topic and assertion. (*Note*: You will need to change words and add new words.)

1. Education is important.

   _____

2. Exercise improves a person's health.

   _____

3. Technology has changed the way we live.

   _____

4. Personal relations are often difficult.

   _____

5. Young people ignore rules.

   _____

PLACEMENT OF TOPIC SENTENCES/ MAIN IDEAS IN PARAGRAPHS

Much academic reading depends on your ability to identify main ideas and to distinguish them from supporting details in order to summarize what the writer is saying. Understanding the various patterns in which topic sentences occur in paragraphs will help you identify main ideas when you read.

Topic Sentence as First Sentence

Often, the main idea appears only once in a paragraph. Most frequently, the topic sentence, or main idea statement, occurs at or near the beginning of the paragraph, usually as the first sentence. Remaining sentences, then, give explanations, examples, and details. This pattern (general to specific) is illustrated in the figure and the sample paragraph that follow. (The topic sentence in the paragraph is set in bold type.)

Topic sentence
Specific detail
Specific detail
Specific detail

The American breakfast changed dramatically in the past century. In the first fifty or sixty years of the twentieth century, a typical breakfast consisted of bacon and eggs or cereal. Although some people occasionally liked a gooey donut or a sweet roll for breakfast, most Americans preferred the standard fare—day after day. Beginning in the 1960s, however, breakfasts because increasingly exotic. Traditional breakfast fare gave way to Belgian waffles, French omelettes, or huevos rancheros (eggs topped by a spicy Mexican salsa). Breakfasts also became healthier. Yogurt, granola, bagels, and fruit were considered better for people than bacon and eggs accompanied by buttery hot biscuits smothered in gravy.

Topic Sentence as Last Sentence

The topic sentence can occur as the last sentence of a paragraph. In this case, the paragraph starts with details or examples and concludes with the main idea. This paragraph pattern (specific to general) is illustrated in the figure and the sample paragraph that follow:

Specific detail
Specific detail
Specific detail
Topic sentence

In the past, student writers occasionally resorted to using the words or ideas of others simply because they didn't know any better or were just desperate or lazy. More recently, people, even famous people, seem to "borrow" from other people's work almost casually, and plagiarism, especially among college students, has become all too common. The Internet has contributed to the problem by making not only articles and essays but also entire books and even music readily available on-line. In addition, the Internet has blurred the concept of what constitutes intellectual property. **Thus, plagiarism has become not only an increasingly prevalent but also a more complex problem**.

Topic Sentence as First and Last Sentences

Some writers state the topic sentence at both the beginning and the end of a paragraph. In this case, the final statement of the main idea is not merely a restatement of the topic sentence. The last sentence reinforces the main idea but also reflects the conclusions that the writer has reached. This pattern (general to specific to general) is illustrated in the figure and the sample paragraph that follow:

| **Topic sentence** |
| Specific detail |
| Specific detail |
| Specific detail |
| **Concluding topic sentence** |

The weather in West Texas is completely unpredictable. Winter often brings warm, sunny days while summer and spring may surprise residents with periods of cool, cloudy weather. The wind may blow fiercely one day and be completely calm the next. Drought may plague the region at times, only to be followed by heavy rainfall and even flooding. At one time or another, and in no particular order, West Texans experience blinding dust storms, record-breaking heat waves, tornadoes, hail, thunderstorms, and "blue northers"—those sudden cold spells that sweep across the Panhandle and into the state from the north. **The climate throughout West Texas is often dramatic, sometimes disagreeable, but seldom dull**.

Topic Sentence as Second/Middle Sentence

The topic sentence may also be stated in the second (or even the third or fourth) sentence of a paragraph. In this pattern, the first sentence or sentences serve as an introduction to the main idea. Or the first sentence(s) may function as a transition, linking the paragraph to the preceding one.

This paragraph pattern (introduction/transition to general to specific) is illustrated in the figure and the sample paragraph that follow:

Introduction/transition
Topic sentence
Specific detail
Specific detail
Specific detail

In the past few years, millions of Americans have begun to exercise. **Unfortunately, many of these energetic but amateur athletes have sustained serious injuries**. Tennis players have ruined their elbows, joggers their knees, and aerobic dancers their ankles. More serious injuries are often sustained by those who play competitive sports such as basketball or football. Even lifting weights involves certain risks to muscle tissue and bones.

Implied Main Idea

In some paragraphs, the topic sentence is not stated. Rather, it is suggested or *implied* throughout the paragraph. In the following sample paragraph, the main idea is implied rather than stated. Read the paragraph carefully; then state the main idea in your own words. Key words that provide you with clues to the main idea of the paragraph appear in bold type.

On his **inauguration day, Andrew Jackson** mounted his horse and rode to the White House, followed by a **crowd** of 10,000 visitors. The people **pushed** into the White House, **climbing on delicate furniture** to see the new president. **Excited supporters trod on valuable rugs** with muddy boots, **turned over pieces of furniture**, and **broke expensive glassware**. They **pushed and shoved** to get next to the new president, who, after being backed helplessly against a wall, climbed out a back window.

Main idea: _____

_____

_____

Although this paragraph does not have a stated main idea (topic sentence), each sentence provides an important detail that suggests or implies the main idea. One way to state the main idea would be *On Andrew Jackson's inauguration day, his excited supporters destroyed valuable White House property and even endangered the president.*

In your reading, you will sometimes find paragraphs in which the main idea is implied rather than stated. When you read a paragraph with an implied main idea, you must use the supporting details to help you determine—or infer—the main idea. The main idea you formulate from these details is an *inference.* The process of inferring a main idea from the details within a paragraph is similar to the process of inferring the meaning of an unfamiliar word from its context. In both situations, you use the information given to help you infer what the writer implies.

As a writer, you may occasionally write a paragraph with an implied main idea. If you choose not to include a topic sentence, however, you should keep your main idea clearly in mind, being sure that each detail develops the main idea so clearly that your reader will have no difficulty understanding it.

EXERCISE
4.5

In the three paragraphs that follow, the main idea is implied rather than stated. Read each paragraph carefully; then state in your own words its main idea.

PARAGRAPH A

Li Jian was the only international student in the history class. Because most of the discussions focused on American history and culture, he had little to contribute. He was also very shy, especially when he was called on to answer a question. To make matters even worse, he had to work on a group project with three girls, a situation that only increased his normal shyness.

Main idea: _____

_____

PARAGRAPH B

In the distant past, writers labored with quill pens and ink, carefully forming each letter by hand. The fountain pen, when it appeared on the writing scene, was viewed as a marvelous convenience. Then the typewriter provided writers with a much more efficient method of writing, a method that for many years was viewed as the ultimate in writing convenience. When the correcting typewriter came along, writers thought they had died and gone to heaven. Today, however, writers who write with computers and word-processing programs scorn "old-fashioned" typewriters.

Main idea: _____

_____

PARAGRAPH C

Chemical plants dump their waste in our rivers and streams. The smokestacks of refineries belch poisonous black clouds into our air. Car manufacturers produce monstrous utility vehicles that guzzle gas and emit noxious fumes along the highways that crisscross our nation. Lumber companies level our forests, utility companies contaminate our drinking water, and oil freighters spill oil on our beaches. Meanwhile, our politicians worry about big problems like whether to cut taxes and how to please the voters.

Main idea: _____

_____

CHAPTER REVIEW

- A paragraph consists of a series of sentences that develop a single idea, which is usually stated in a topic sentence.
- A topic sentence usually occurs at the beginning of a paragraph.
- An effective topic sentence includes both a topic and an assertion that makes a statement about the topic.
- A topic sentence should be narrowed so that it can be developed adequately in a single paragraph.
- Knowing the placement options for topic sentences helps readers identify main ideas in paragraphs.
- A main idea can be implied rather than stated but should always be clear.

WRITING ASSIGNMENT

Limit the following topic sentence by making the idea more specific; then write five specific sentences that support it.

Topic sentence: Dating is (or is not) the best way to find a mate.

Limited topic sentence: _____

_____

Specific supporting sentences:

1. _____
_____

2. _____
_____

3. _____
_____

4. _____
_____

5. _____
_____

PARTICIPATING IN THE ACADEMIC COMMUNITY

Meet with a group of your classmates to discuss the topic sentences you have written. Evaluate each topic sentence to determine if it is sufficiently limited and includes both a topic and an assertion.

Constructing Paragraphs: Supporting Details

You learned in Chapter 4 that a topic sentence expresses the general idea of a paragraph. But it is the specific details in a paragraph that develop the general idea, providing the information readers need to understand what the writer means. Good writers not only state the main ideas of their paragraphs clearly but also support them with specific facts and details. Read the following paragraph carefully, noticing the details used to support the main idea:

> It was a land tortured by weather. There were wet springs when days of pouring rain put creeks out of banks and washed away cotton and corn. At times, before the water could drain off, dust storms blew down from the western plains, clouding the sky and making mouths gritty. Summers were long, hot, dry—worst in the dog days of August, when creeks ran low and scummy and the earth cracked in the sun. The people learned to be grateful for the first cool days of fall, and to bundle up in hard winters when blue northers swept down across Kansas and Oklahoma. They shivered in their shacks and said there was "nothing between them and the North Pole but a bobbed-wire fence."
>
> —William A. Owens, *This Stubborn Soil*

Identify three specific details from this paragraph that support the main idea that the land was "tortured by weather."

1. _____

2. _____

3. _____

These specific details about the weather make the main idea vivid and meaningful. The details tell *how* the land was tortured by weather— that it was not floods, hurricanes, or earthquakes the people feared but rather heat, dust storms, rain, and "blue northers." The general statement that introduces William Owens's paragraph tells very little about the land or the weather. The details that support the main idea, however, offer a vivid image of the effects the weather had on the people and the land.

USING SPECIFIC DETAILS TO SUPPORT TOPIC SENTENCES

Inexperienced writers often write paragraphs that have too many general statements and too few specific details. A paragraph that consists of a series of general statements is difficult for a reader to understand, but a paragraph that consists of a general statement supported by specific details is much easier to comprehend.

Thus, a well-structured paragraph usually consists of one general statement, which functions as the topic sentence, and a series of specific statements, which support the topic sentence. This pattern—general idea plus supporting details—is an important one to remember.

The following paragraph illustrates this pattern:

The Olympic Games have increasingly become a form of entertainment as well as a sporting event. [general statement] The opening ceremonies feature not only the athletes but also famous entertainers and other well-known personalities. Every part of this ceremony is carefully choreographed and staged with elaborate costumes, music, and even firework displays. To a lesser extent, the awards ceremonies at the end of each event also involve music and spectacle. And it is no longer just the figure skaters who are viewed as stars but all of the athletes. Primarily as a result of their being televised, the Olympic Games are now viewed as one big show.

EXERCISE
5.1

Write three or more sentences that include specific supporting details for each of the following topic sentences.

▶ **Example:** The house at the end of the road looked deserted. (1) The grass was waist high and brown. (2) Several windows in the house were missing. (3) And the brick chimney that had once topped the steeply pitched roof was now just a few crumbling bricks.

1. College teachers usually expect students to be independent and self-motivated.

_____

_____

_____

_____

_____

2. A college education has become very expensive.

_____

_____

_____

_____

_____

3. College students are increasingly diverse.

_____

_____

_____

_____

_____

Factual and Sensory Details

Supporting details may be factual or sensory. **Factual details** help readers by giving them exact information. They usually answer questions such as *Who? What? When? Where? Why? How?* and *How many?* Often these details provide names, dates, places, numbers, measurements, or statistics. In contrast, sensory details appeal to the senses of sight, hearing, smell, taste, or touch. These details help readers not only to visualize the writer's words but also to hear, feel, smell, and taste what the writer is expressing. The following sentence includes both factual and sensory details:

> The runner had completed the race in less than three minutes but was so exhausted that her legs were trembling and her breath came in short, painful gasps.

Write the factual detail.

_____

Write the two sensory details.

_____

_____

In supporting your topic sentences, use both types of specific details. Factual details help your readers understand your meaning, while sensory details help them experience that meaning. Together, these two types of details enable you to communicate more precisely and effectively.

EXERCISE

5.2   For each of the following general statements, write two supporting sentences—one that includes factual details and one that includes sensory details.

1. Child care programs often fail to provide an ideal environment for children.

_____

_____

_____

_____

_____

2. Computer skills are increasingly important.

_____

_____

_____

_____

_____

3. Modern technology is a mixed blessing.

_____

_____

_____

_____

_____

4. Sports heroes are overvalued in our society.

_____

_____

_____

_____

_____

5. Americans have less privacy than they once did.

_____

_____

PATTERNS FOR STRUCTURING SUPPORTING DETAILS

The specific sentences you use to support a topic sentence may be structured in a variety of ways. Two common ways to structure supporting details are to use patterns of coordination and subordination. **Coordinate details** are equally specific, whereas **subordinate details** are increasingly specific.

Coordinate Pattern	Subordinate Pattern
Topic sentence	*Topic sentence*
Supporting sentence	Supporting sentence
Supporting sentence	Supporting sentence
Supporting sentence	Supporting sentence
Supporting sentence	Supporting sentence

As these patterns suggest, in the coordinate pattern each sentence supports the topic sentence and is equally specific. In the subordinate pattern, although all the sentences support the topic sentence, each one is increasingly specific. Thus the first supporting sentence is more specific than the topic sentence, the second is more specific than the first, the third is more specific than the second, and so on.

Using the Coordinate Pattern

To develop the main idea of a paragraph using coordinate, or equally specific, details, you will need to think of a series of sentences (usually five to eight), each of which supports your topic sentence. The details in the following paragraph are coordinate:

[1] Mexico offers visitors a world of contrasts. [2] Its pyramids and ancient ruins give us a glimpse of the past while its modern cities provide us with the best of today's technology. [3] Its mountains offer cool weather and majestic peaks while, only a few miles away, its beaches tempt us with brilliant sun and white sand. [4] Its elegant restaurants serve the most sophisticated continental cuisine while, across the street or down the block, sidewalk vendors sell the simplest of native foods. [5] Thus the traveler to Mexico is faced with a series of delightful decisions.

In this paragraph, the topic sentence is supported by three equally specific, or coordinate, supporting details. This paragraph can be diagrammed as shown here:

| Topic sentence (sentence 1) |
| Coordinate detail (sentence 2) |
| Coordinate detail (sentence 3) |
| Coordinate detail (sentence 4) |
| Concluding sentence (sentence 5) |

EXERCISE

5.3   Write a paragraph describing a place you know well—a place where you have lived or worked or visited often—using coordinate details. Use the block form in the following diagram to write your rough draft, writing a different sentence in each block.

| Topic sentence |
| Coordinate detail |
| Coordinate detail |
| Coordinate detail |
| Concluding sentence |

Expanding Coordinate Details

If you want to write a longer paragraph, you may simply expand your coordinate details by adding related but more specific details to support them. This pattern is illustrated for you in the following paragraph. This paragraph contains three major coordinate details, each of which is further supported by a more specific detail. As you read the paragraph, try to decide which sentences express the major coordinate points and which express the more specific details.

> [1]My father's death, which occurred when I was nine years old, had several important effects on me. [2]First of all, I felt great sadness and loneliness. [3]For the first few months, my loneliness was so great that I often dreamed that my father would miraculously return. [4]In addition, throughout the rest of my childhood, I was afraid of losing someone else whom I loved. [5]Whenever my mother was away from home, I was always nervous until she returned. [6]The loss of my father also caused me to develop a greater sense of responsibility. [7]For example, I believed that with my father gone I was responsible for helping my mother with her chores. [8]My father's death, therefore, left me lonely, frightened, and responsible—a young child with adult feelings.

In this paragraph, the main idea is stated in sentence 1: the major coordinate details are stated in sentences 2, 4, and 6; the more specific supporting details occur in sentences 3, 5, and 7; and sentence 8 briefly summarizes the paragraph. This paragraph pattern can be diagrammed as shown here:

| Topic sentence (sentence 1) |
| Coordinate detail (sentence 2) |
| Supporting detail (sentence 3) |
| Coordinate detail (sentence 4) |
| Supporting detail (sentence 5) |
| Coordinate detail (sentence 6) |
| Supporting detail (sentence 7) |
| Conclusion (sentence 8) |

A variation of this pattern is illustrated in the following paragraph, which also contains three major coordinate details. However, in this pattern, each coordinate detail is supported by not one but two specific details. As you read the paragraph, try to determine which sentences contain the major coordinate details and which contain the more specific supporting details.

> [1]The older woman who returns to school faces a number of problems. [2]For one thing, upon enrolling in college, she immediately becomes a minority. [3]She is no longer surrounded by her peers—other women who have shared experiences—but by young people, many of whom are the ages of her own children. [4]Very often, the only person in a class who is her age is the instructor (and even he or she may be much younger). [5]In addition, an older woman who reenters the

academic world assumes the double burden of managing a household while being a student. [6]She may still have children at home or a husband who makes demands on her time. [7]If she is divorced or widowed, she faces problems such as managing finances, maintaining a car, and mowing the lawn. [8]Finally, a woman middle-aged or older who decides to complete her education faces the challenge of developing a new image of herself—one that is not related to her roles as wife and mother.[9]This problem may prove to be the most difficult of all, for it is not easy to assume a new identity, especially if the former one has been comfortable and secure. [10]To make the transition from housewife to student, a woman must think of herself as an individual rather than as a person whose identity depends on her relationships to other people. [11]Although her maturity may well prove to be an asset as she continues her studies, the older coed initially finds herself in a challenging situation.

In this paragraph, the main idea is stated in sentence 1; the major coordinate details are stated in sentences 2, 5, and 8; more specific supporting details are stated in sentences 3 and 4, 6 and 7, and 9 and 10; and the concluding statement comes in sentence 11. This paragraph can be illustrated as shown here:

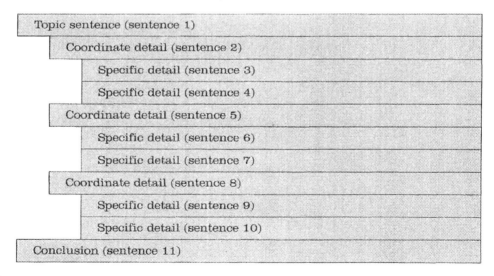

Topic sentence (sentence 1)

   Coordinate detail (sentence 2)

      Specific detail (sentence 3)

      Specific detail (sentence 4)

   Coordinate detail (sentence 5)

      Specific detail (sentence 6)

      Specific detail (sentence 7)

   Coordinate detail (sentence 8)

      Specific detail (sentence 9)

      Specific detail (sentence 10)

Conclusion (sentence 11)

EXERCISE

5.4   Write a paragraph telling why you want a college degree. Structure your paragraph according to one of the patterns given for expanded coordinate details. Use two or three coordinate details, developing each with one or more specific details. Use the following block form, writing a different sentence in each block. (*Note:* You may not need to use all of the blocks.)

(Topic sentence)

(Coordinate detail)

(Specific detail)

(Specific detail)

(Coordinate detail)

(Specific detail)

(Specific detail)

(Coordinate detail)

(Specific detail)

(Specific detail)

(Conclusion)

Using the Subordinate Pattern

To develop a topic sentence using the subordinate pattern, you must write a series of sentences that express increasingly specific details. In this pattern, each detail is more specific than and subordinate to the one before it.

[1]Global warming is increasingly viewed as a very real threat rather than an academic theory or the ranting of alarmists. [2]Last summer most of the states in the United States experienced temperatures that were above normal. [3]The Southwest especially suffered from intense heat and drought most of the summer. [4]In Texas, for example, the temperature hovered around 110 degrees for weeks, and there was no rain for nearly two months. [5]As a result of these experiences, many people are now taking global warming seriously for the first time.

In this paragraph the main idea, which is stated in sentence 1, is a general statement about global warming. Sentence 2 is more specific, narrowing to the experience of the United States with global warming last summer. Sentence 3 is still more specific, focusing on the Southwest—a particular region of the United States. Finally, sentence 4 is limited to the effects in a single state. Sentence 5 concludes the paragraph by reinforcing the topic sentence. A diagram of this pattern is shown here:

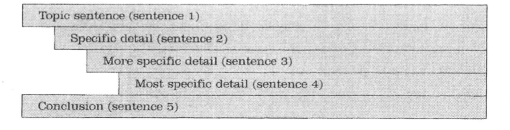

Topic sentence (sentence 1)

Specific detail (sentence 2)

More specific detail (sentence 3)

Most specific detail (sentence 4)

Conclusion (sentence 5)

EXERCISE

5.5　Write a paragraph about some characteristic of your generation. Develop your paragraph with details that are increasingly specific. Use the following block form to write your rough draft, placing a different sentence in each block.

```
┌─────────────────────────────────────────────────────────────┐
│ Topic sentence                                                │
│                                                               │
│   ┌───────────────────────────────────────────────────────┐  │
│   │ Specific detail                                        │  │
│   │                                                        │  │
│   │   ┌──────────────────────────────────────────────────┐ │  │
│   │   │ (More specific detail)                           │ │  │
│   │   │                                                  │ │  │
│   │   │   ┌────────────────────────────────────────────┐ │ │  │
│   │   │   │ (Most specific detail)                     │ │ │  │
│   │   │   │                                            │ │ │  │
│   └───│───┘                                            │ │ │  │
│ ┌─────────────────────────────────────────────────────┐   │  │
│ │ (Conclusion)                                          │   │  │
│ │                                                       │   │  │
│ └───────────────────────────────────────────────────────┘   │
└─────────────────────────────────────────────────────────────┘
```

You will find these patterns helpful not only in structuring details but also in generating ideas—that is, in thinking of additional details. These patterns are therefore strategies for gathering as well as organizing information because they encourage you to write more detailed, better-developed paragraphs. These patterns can also be used when you write longer compositions

EXERCISE

5.6

To test your knowledge of the relationship between topic sentences and supporting details, read the following two paragraphs and answer the questions that follow each.

PARAGRAPH A

How do you write a rough draft? There is no simple way to do it; there are several approaches, including no doubt some which no one has tried yet. You will find some writers who say they begin by writing and rewriting their introduction until they get their thesis, purpose, and plan stated clearly and their relationship with their readers established. They believe that once they get the opening in reasonably good shape they can write the rest of the paper relatively easily. You will find other writers who state that they try to write the end of their paper first in the belief that it is easier to write the rest once they know the final idea they want to lead up to. You will find still others who say that they begin anywhere they can in the hope that once they start writing they can more easily pull their best ideas from the unconscious. They are all right—up to a point. Writers write rough drafts just about any way they can.

—Thomas E. Pearsall and Donald H. Cunningham. *The Fundamentals of Good Writing*

1. What is the main idea of this paragraph?

   _____

   _____

2. In the following spaces, rewrite in your own words the major supporting ideas.

   a. _____

   _____

   b. _____

   _____

   c. _____

   _____

PARAGRAPH B

   Against Britain's armies of well-trained regulars, the Patriots seemed ill-matched. For one thing, the soldiers of the Continental Army had little experience in military tactics and fighting in open battle. Their training had been limited largely to frontier warfare against the Indians and the French. Their officers, too, had little experience compared to British officers. What is more, the Continental Army was loosely organized. Patriots had joined up, not because they had been ordered to do so, but of their own free will. Such volunteers felt free to return to their homes whenever their short terms of service were finished. As a result, the leaders of the army could hardly tell from day to day how many troops were under their command. Also, the colonies had no real navy. Against the strongest navy in the world the Americans could send not one first-class fighting ship.

—Howard B. Wilder et al., *This Is America's Story*

1. What is the main idea of this paragraph?

_____

_____

2. This paragraph includes both coordinate and more specific support-ing details. How many major coordinate details does it include?

_____

3. What are the coordinate details?

_____

_____

_____

_____

4. What more specific details support the first coordinate detail?

_____

_____

_____

_____

5. What more specific details support the second coordinate detail?

_____

_____

_____

_____

RELEVANT AND IRRELEVANT DETAILS

In general, good writing is detailed writing. The more specific details you use to support your main ideas, the easier it will be for a reader to under-stand your paragraph. However, you should be sure that the details you include in a paragraph actually support the main idea of that paragraph.

Inexperienced writers often include details that do not clearly relate to the topic sentence they are trying to develop, as in the following paragraph:

[1] Two benefits of using a computer are its speed and accuracy. [2] A computer can perform repetitive functions with great accuracy. [3] For example, a robot can be used to perform a task on an assembly line.

[4]A person might get tired of doing the same thing for eight hours a day, but a computer-driven robot never gets tired. [5]However, robots cannot solve problems the way humans can. [6]On the other hand, humans often miss work because of illness.

This paragraph has a number of specific details, but few of them directly support the topic sentence, sentence 1. The writer gets sidetracked and begins writing about robots versus humans, failing to address the issues of accuracy and speed on which the topic sentence focuses. The details correspond loosely to the topic stated in the topic sentence, but they do not clearly develop the assertion that the two main benefits of a computer are its speed and accuracy

In writing a paragraph, be sure that each detail you include directly supports—is relevant to—your topic sentence. Details that do not support the main idea will distract and confuse your readers. In contrast, a paragraph that includes details that clearly support the topic sentence is unified and communicates clearly. In order to check a paragraph for unity, you can turn the topic sentence into a question and then see if each detail answers this question. If a detail does not answer the topic sentence question, it is probably irrelevant—off the subject—and should be omitted. For example, if you turn the topic sentence of the paragraph about computers into a question (*How are a computer's speed and accuracy beneficial?*), you can see that sentences 3, 4, 5, and 6 are irrelevant.

EXERCISE

5.7

The following paragraphs are not unified because each includes a sentence that does not develop the topic sentence. In each paragraph, determine which sentence should be omitted by turning the topic sentence into a question and then seeing if the other sentences answer this question. Underline the sentence that is irrelevant.

PARAGRAPH A

Students need to know the process for appealing a grade. This process usually begins with a conference with the teacher who gave the grade that is being appealed. Often this conference can resolve the problem. If so, the process is over. However, if a student still wants to appeal his or her grade after talking with the teacher, making an appointment with the department chair or program director should be the next step. Department chairs are often busy people with very little time to spare. When the student meets with the chair, the chair may make a decision about the grade that is acceptable to the student or may convince the student that the grade in question is appropriate. However, if the student is not satisfied with the outcome of this meeting, he or she may appeal to the dean or the academic vice president. At this point, the appeal is usually made in writing and may or may not include a conference.

PARAGRAPH B

The term *rhetoric* has several different meanings. In the ancient Greek and Roman civilizations, rhetoric was the main discipline studied in school. Being able to construct effective arguments and deliver clear, convincing speeches was considered a valuable skill. Only males were given an education in these societies. Rhetoric was understood to be the study and practice of effective discourse. Today, however, the term *rhetoric* is often applied to highly emotional discourse, both oral and written. It is even used to describe discourse that is considered dishonest or to mean effective but empty and bombastic speaking and writing.

CHAPTER REVIEW

- Topic sentences should be supported and developed by specific details.
- Details may be factual or sensory.
- Coordinate and subordinate patterns are useful ways of structuring supporting details.
- Supporting details must be directly relevant to the topic sentence if the paragraph is to be unified.

WRITING ASSIGNMENT

Write a unified paragraph on one of the topics given in Exercise 5.1 or 5.2. Decide in advance whether you will use a coordinate or subordinate pattern for your paragraph, and be sure to include both factual and sensory details.

PARTICIPATING IN THE ACADEMIC COMMUNITY

Working with a partner or peer group, evaluate the paragraphs you have written. Is the topic sentence clear and well supported by specific details? To determine if the paragraph is unified, turn the topic sentence into a question and then read each sentence aloud to be sure it answers that question.

Use the suggestions you receive from your classmates to revise your paragraph.

Moving from Paragraph to Essay

As a college student, you are frequently required to read and write compositions longer than a paragraph, such as reports and essays. Because the basic structure of reports and essays is similar to that of paragraphs, your knowledge of paragraph structure will be helpful to you as you begin to work with these longer compositions.

This chapter focuses on the **essay** because it can serve as a pattern for all types of discourse. As a college student, you will be asked to write various types of reports, book reviews, case studies, essay exams, and research papers. Although each of these types of academic discourse has its own distinguishing characteristics, especially in terms of format, all are related to the essay. An essay is, very simply, the elaboration of a single idea. Other types of academic discourse may not look like an essay, but they nearly all consist of a central idea that is developed and supported by the writer's arguments and evidence just as an essay is. If you can write a well-constructed, well-developed essay, you can write almost any type of academic discourse.

Most essays, like most paragraphs, consist of an introduction, a body, and a conclusion. However, whereas a paragraph consists of a series of related sentences, an essay is composed of a series of related paragraphs. A good essay is composed of well-developed paragraphs that develop the main idea, or **thesis**, of the essay.

Many readers and writers make the mistake of ignoring the structure of the paragraph once it is part of an essay. Although the paragraphs that make up the body of an essay may not be able to stand alone as compositions, they often have essentially the same structure as paragraphs that are meant to stand on their own. Therefore, as you read and write essays, you will continue to use your knowledge of paragraphs.

The essay illustrated in the following diagram consists of five paragraphs: an introductory paragraph, three body paragraphs, and a concluding paragraph. Of course, the number of paragraphs varies widely from one essay to another. Some essays are brief; others are quite long. But the five-paragraph essay serves as a convenient model.

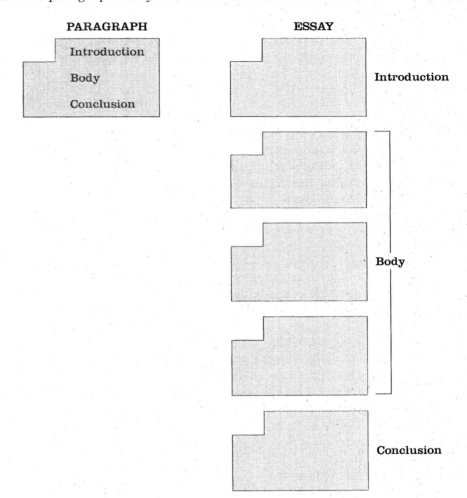

INTRODUCTION: STATING THE THESIS

Essays, like paragraphs, develop one main idea. The main idea of an essay is called a **thesis statement**, and it is usually expressed at the end of the introduction. Like the main idea of a paragraph, a thesis is a general statement. It is usually more general than the topic sentence of a paragraph but not as general as the thesis of a book.

Topic Sentence of a Paragraph

My sixth-grade teacher was a strict disciplinarian.

Thesis of an Essay

Discipline problems created a poor environment for learning in my high school.

Thesis of a Book

One of the major problems with the U.S. system of education is its failure to deal effectively with discipline problems.

Notice that the topic sentence of the paragraph is limited to a particular person (sixth-grade teacher) and to a specific aspect of that person (role as disciplinarian). The paragraph that develops this topic sentence will not merely describe the sixth-grade teacher but will focus on how he disciplined the class. In contrast, the thesis of the essay is broad enough to include a discussion of several problems that contributed to a lack of discipline in the high school, but it is limited to a particular high school at a particular time and to the experience of one person. The essay that develops this thesis will not discuss every aspect of the writer's high school experience—just the problems associated with discipline in the school. The thesis of a book, however, is much broader, allowing for a complex, complete discussion of how a lack of discipline affects the entire school system of the United States.

A broad, vague, overly general statement is inappropriate as the thesis of an essay. In fact, many times, the same idea that served as the topic sentence of a paragraph can be used effectively as the thesis of an essay. If you narrow your main idea so that your focus is fairly limited, you will have less difficulty writing your essay and will write a better essay.

Writers usually place their thesis at the end of their introduction because this is where readers expect to find it. The introduction of an essay may consist of a single paragraph or of several paragraphs, depending on the length of the essay. Whatever its length, the introduction usually concludes with a statement of the writer's main idea.

Writing Introductions

An introduction serves as a contract between a writer and his or her readers. In the introduction, a writer makes specific commitments that must then be fulfilled. The most important of these is the thesis statement, which commits the writer to a specific focus. In effect, it provides the reader with an accurate expectation of what the writer plans to do—the main idea that the writer plans to develop.

In general, a good introduction accomplishes three purposes:

1. It attracts the reader's interest.
2. It provides the reader with background information.
3. It focuses the reader's attention on the main idea of the essay.

The following paragraph could serve as an introduction to an essay on the discipline problems that affected one person's high school education:

> From 1982 to 1986, I attended an inner-city high school in Chicago. The school was located in an area that was rapidly changing from residential to commercial. It was an old, respected school that had educated the children of the families in the neighborhood for over fifty years. Many of the teachers were dedicated, competent professionals who had taught in this school all of their professional lives. Others were inexperienced, young teachers who were encountering their first students. However, neither the experienced nor the inexperienced teachers were able to handle the undisciplined, unmotivated students who attended the school in the 1980s. As a result, discipline problems created a poor environment for learning in the high school.

Notice that the writer devotes several sentences to background information, supplying the reader with a context for what is to follow. The sentence about the problems the teachers had in controlling the students serves as a transition, focusing the reader's attention on the thesis statement that follows. The writer and the reader are now ready to explore this thesis statement in the body of the essay.

As a writer, you want your introduction to be not only clear but also interesting. A dull or trite introduction can discourage a reader from continuing to the main part of the essay. Beware, however, of attempts at cuteness and cleverness; they often fail, resulting in an introduction that is not only unclear but also embarrassingly inappropriate.

SUGGESTIONS FOR WRITING EFFECTIVE INTRODUCTIONS

- Be clear and direct. Clarity is more important than cleverness.
- Provide the background information your reader needs to understand your subject.
- Avoid trite expressions, such as *in the world today* or *for as long as man has existed.*
- End your introduction with a clear statement of your thesis.

EXERCISE

6.1   Narrow each thesis statement so that it can be developed adequately in a brief essay.

1. Some students prefer a different grading system.

_____

_____

2. Technology is frustrating.

_____

_____

3. Experience is the best teacher.

_____

_____

BODY: DEVELOPING THE THESIS

The body of a unified, coherent essay consists of a number of related paragraphs that develop the thesis. The individual sentences within each paragraph support the main idea (topic sentence) of the paragraph, and the paragraphs support the main idea (thesis) of the essay, as shown in the following diagram:

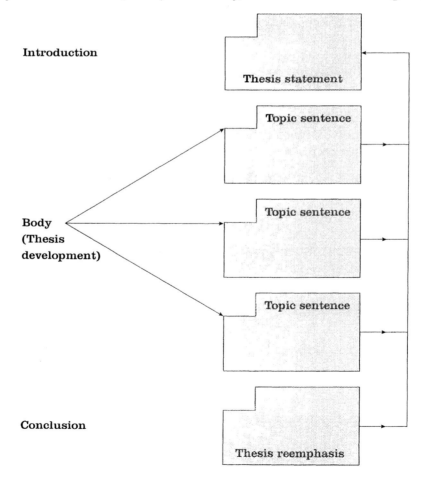

A writer develops the topic sentence of a paragraph by discussing, explaining, and expanding the idea that it expresses. A writer develops the thesis of an essay in the same way. Both topic sentences and thesis statements are general statements that must be supported by specific facts, details, and examples. In an essay, a writer usually devotes a paragraph to each major supporting point. Each of these supporting points is directly related to the thesis and helps develop it. But each major supporting point is also developed individually as a paragraph.

Writing Body Paragraphs

The paragraphs you write in the body of your essay should be well structured and well developed. Most, if not all, of these paragraphs should begin with a topic sentence, which is then supported and developed by five to eight sentences. These sentences should be less general (more specific) than the topic sentence but should all relate directly to the topic sentence.

The primary difference between an independent paragraph and one that is in the body of an essay is that body paragraphs require conclusions less often. Whereas you will frequently include a concluding sentence if you are writing an independent paragraph, you will seldom need to include one in the body paragraph of an essay. If you do include a conclusion in a body paragraph, it should function primarily as a transition to the next paragraph.

Remember that all paragraphs need not only a main idea but also lots of supporting details. These details can be arranged in a variety of ways—in order of importance, in chronological order, and so on (see Chapter 8). Remember also the patterns of subordination and coordination that you learned in Chapter 5. These patterns are useful in structuring body paragraphs in an essay. You may also want to consult the chapters in Part Two (Chapters 10 through 18) for additional patterns of development that can be used for body paragraphs.

SUGGESTIONS FOR WRITING EFFECTIVE BODY PARAGRAPHS

- Keep your thesis in mind at all times; each paragraph in the body of your essay should support and develop your thesis.
- Structure each paragraph so that it has a topic sentence (stated or implied) that is fully developed by supporting details.
- Avoid paragraphs of only one or two sentences. Such paragraphs are usually underdeveloped or unnecessary.
- Vary the structure of the paragraphs in the body of your essay so that the topic sentence is not always the first sentence.
- Vary the number of paragraphs in your essays. Every essay does not have to have exactly five paragraphs.

CONCLUSION: REEMPHASIZING THE THESIS

The conclusion of an essay, like the conclusion of a paragraph, gives the reader a sense of completion. Conclusions usually refer to the introduction or at least reemphasize in some way the thesis stated in the introduction. Often the conclusion briefly summarizes the thesis and the major supporting points. A good conclusion always confirms the readers' understanding of what they have read by reminding them of the writer's purpose. Like an introduction, a conclusion often provides readers with an overview. The following paragraph would effectively conclude the essay on discipline problems in the Chicago high school:

> Recently, I visited my parents in Chicago and drove past my old high school. Now a warehouse for textbooks, the building looks abandoned and dilapidated. Crude, obscene messages remain scrawled on the walls, and many of the windows are broken or missing. Evidently, the discipline problems finally defeated the valiant but discouraged teachers. I am glad the school is now closed, for learning had become impossible in that environment.

Conclusions should not be cute or trite or obvious. The best conclusions are appropriate, clearly written, and straightforward. They do not strain for an effect they cannot achieve (such as humor, cleverness, or brilliance). If you have not written a good essay, your conclusion cannot save it; however, a good essay can be damaged by an ineffective or inappropriate conclusion.

Writing Conclusions

Just as an introduction can be viewed as a contract between you and your reader, a conclusion reassures your reader that you have fulfilled your contract. Your closing paragraph should leave your reader with a sense of completion—with the feeling that you have done what you intended to do and have finished what you had to say. Several types of conclusions accomplish this purpose:

1. *Restatement of main idea.* You may choose to reemphasize or reinforce the main idea in your conclusion. If you choose this type of conclusion, however, be sure not to merely repeat your thesis. You should vary the wording so that your conclusion is not too similar to your introduction, and you should also try to get beyond your thesis statement—to express an appropriate conclusion and to give your reader a sense of closure.

2. *General impression.* If your essay is basically a description of an experience or of a person, place, or thing, an effective conclusion might consist of a statement of the dominant impression you have attempted to convey. For example, if your essay about your high school is largely a description of what occurred to you when you were there, you might conclude with what you remember most clearly about the whole experience.

3. *Evaluation.* An essay may also conclude with a judgment or opinion based on the information presented. For example, you might end an essay on your high school by evaluating whether the experience was essentially negative or positive.

4. *Recommendation.* An essay can be concluded with a suggestion for some action the writer feels should be taken. This type of conclusion is especially appropriate if the main idea is a controversial statement or one that is persuasive in nature. For example, you might conclude your essay about your high school's discipline problems by recommending that a new administration be hired or a new school board be elected.

5. *Prediction.* Even though a conclusion is the final part of an essay, it can be used to make a prediction on the basis of the major points made in the essay. This prediction should be closely related to the content of the essay, giving a reasonable explanation of what may happen. For example, you might predict in the conclusion to your essay about your high school's problems that the school will be closed in the near future.

6. *Implications.* In a conclusion you can discuss the implications of the arguments and evidence you have presented. In other words, you can explain why what you've written is important.

Regardless of the type of conclusion you choose for your essay, the conclusion should be a clear signal to your reader that you have completed what you had to say. Following are suggestions that will be helpful to you in writing conclusions.

SUGGESTIONS FOR WRITING EFFECTIVE CONCLUSIONS

- Do not contradict the point you have made.
- Do not introduce a new topic or new information.
- Do not conclude with a cliché (such as *You can't teach an old dog new tricks*).
- Do not apologize for lack of knowledge, ability, or resources.
- Do not use obvious transition words or phases such as *in conclusion, in summary,* and *as I have attempted to show.* You may, however, use less obvious transition words, such as *therefore, finally,* and *consequently.*
- Do make your conclusion brief and to the point.
- Do make the tone (serious, humorous, clever, straightforward, and so on) consistent with the overall tone of your essay.

FROM PARAGRAPH TO ESSAY

Read the following paragraph, which focuses on a common myth about college students. Note especially the topic sentence and the major supporting points.

Although most people think the college years are carefree and irresponsible, many college students are depressed, overwhelmed, and in debt. Separation from friends and family may cause severe depression in some students; others may suffer depression because they have reached a time in their lives when, for the first time, they feel they must solve their own problems and make their own decisions. Others are simply overwhelmed by new pressures on their time and tougher competition in their courses. And, increasingly, college students are in debt—sometimes seriously in debt. The happy-go-lucky college student is all too often simply a myth.

EXERCISE

6.2   Answer the following questions about the paragraph you have just read.

1. What is the main idea of the paragraph?

_____

_____

2. Is the main idea expressed in a topic sentence? _____

3. If so, underline the topic sentence.

4. What are the major supporting points developed in the paragraph?

a. _____

b. _____

c. _____

Now read the following essay, which has the same main idea as the paragraph you have just read. As you read, notice that the main difference between the paragraph and the essay is that the writer uses different paragraphs for each of the three major supporting points in the essay and that she uses many more details and examples to support each major point.

[1]College students are often stereotyped as irresponsible, carefree, happy-go-lucky young people who are still supported by their families. It is commonly thought that their parents pay most of their bills; their teachers provide them with interesting, stimulating lectures; and student-life organizations or social clubs arrange for them to have active, exciting social lives. But this pretty picture often conflicts with

the real situation in which most college students find themselves. For many students, their college years are not filled with checks from home, supportive professors, and endless parties. In reality, many college students are depressed, overwhelmed, and in debt.

2Depression is as common among college students as it is among the general population. Antidepressants, such as Prozac and Zoloft, are routinely prescribed by college medical personnel in an effort to deal with the large numbers of students who suffer from depression. Some students experience only mild depression as a result of being away from home for the first time, but others suffer from severe, debilitating forms of depression. Although depression is often genetic in origin, it can also be situational. And the situation in which college students often find themselves—on their own without familiar support systems and facing much tougher academic competition than they are accustomed to—can easily lead to depression.

3Nearly all college students feel overwhelmed at one time or another, but many of them experience this feeling all the time. They may feel overwhelmed because they are trying to work 40 hours a week and take five courses each semester; because their courses are demanding; or because they are trying to pay their own bills, do their own laundry, and manage their own lives for the first time. Or they may even be overwhelmed by the number and variety of social activities from which they may choose. This sense of being overwhelmed creates a lot of anxiety and stress. Rather than setting priorities or getting help from a counselor, a student may simply become too overwhelmed to function effectively. In fact, the stress caused by having too much to do often leads students to give up and drop out of school.

4Perhaps the most serious problem facing many college students today is the amount of debt they have incurred. For a long time, students have gone into debt to finance their education by taking out government-financed student loans. These loans can add up to $50,000 or $60,000 over the four or five years that most people spend in college. However, many students today are not only going into debt as a result of student loans but also running up enormous credit card debts. Whereas student loans usually have relatively low interest rates and many lenders allow borrowers to defer repayment until they have finished their degree, credit card companies charge very high interest rates and insist on monthly payments from the time the debt is incurred. Many students attempt to avoid going too deeply in debt by working while they are in school. In fact, some students hold two or more jobs. Unfortunately, even if they do manage to hold down their debts, these students often drop out of school because they are overwhelmed by having too much to do.

⁵Being a college student may be a wonderful experience for a minority of privileged young people who have strong academic backgrounds and parents who are able and willing to pay their bills. But for most people, it is a struggle. After years of dealing with depression, stress, and indebtedness, most students understand the real cost of an education.

EXERCISE

6.3   Answer the following questions about the essay you have just read.

1. What is the main idea of the essay?

   _____

   _____

2. Is the main idea expressed in a thesis statement? _____

3. If the main idea is expressed in a thesis statement, underline it.

4. What are the major supporting points developed in the essay?

   a. _____

   b. _____

   c. _____

5. Does each of these major supporting points serve as a topic sentence of a paragraph? _____

6. Underline each of the topic sentences.

7. Compare these topic sentences with the three major supporting points of the original paragraph. Are they the same? _____

8. List several details the writer uses in the essay but not in the paragraph.

   a. _____

   b. _____

   c. _____

▦ CHAPTER REVIEW

- A good essay is composed of well-developed paragraphs that, in turn, develop the main idea of the essay.

- A good essay consists of three major parts: introduction, body, and conclusion.

- The introduction of an essay usually concludes with the thesis statement.
- The body of a unified, coherent essay consists of a number of related paragraphs that develop the thesis.
- The conclusion of an essay, like that of a paragraph, gives the reader a sense of completion, usually reemphasizing in some way the thesis stated in the introduction.

WRITING ASSIGNMENT

Write a paragraph about a topic that interests you, or choose a paragraph you wrote for a previous assignment. Then expand the paragraph into a fully developed essay, restructuring and adding details as needed.

PARTICIPATING IN THE ACADEMIC COMMUNITY

Meet with a group of your classmates to read and evaluate your essays. Identify the thesis statement and major supporting points in each essay.

Gathering Information

Your own experiences and knowledge will serve as the basis for many of your writing assignments. However, some writing assignments will require other sources. For example, you might use your textbooks as a source in a writing assignment or find information in newspapers or magazines. Still other assignments will require library research. Increasingly, the Internet is also used as a source of information. But in this chapter you will learn how to gather information from interviews and observation—two common types of field research used extensively by many writers.

INTERVIEWING

Many writers find interviews can be productive sources of information. In effect, when a writer interviews a subject, he or she questions the subject for the purpose of obtaining certain information. You might think of an interview as a structured, focused conversation.

Interviews may serve as a writer's only source; for example, character sketches are often based on a single interview. However, most writers use interviews to support and develop their own ideas. In fact, an interview can strengthen almost any type of writing assignment.

The key to a good interview is preparation. In **preparing for an interview**, follow these steps.

- *Interview a person who has experience and/or knowledge of your subject.* The person need not be an expert but should have first-hand knowledge or experience to share with you. For example, if you are writing a paper on welfare reform, you might interview a government official, a caseworker, or a welfare recipient to get a particular point of view.

- *Find out as much as possible about the person you are interviewing prior to the interview.* The more you know about this person, the better you will be at interviewing him or her, so find out as much as you can before the interview.

- *Make a list of questions you want to ask the person you are interviewing.* Don't depend on coming up with questions during the interview or think that you can just listen to what the interviewee chooses to say. You need a list of specific questions to which you can refer. Thus armed, you won't forget to ask an important question or not be able to think of questions that will keep the interview going.

- *Don't include questions that permit the person you are interviewing to respond with a simple "yes" or "no."* Your questions should invite a lengthy, thoughtful response or, at least, some useful information. For example, don't ask, "Do you like your work?" but "What do you like about your work?"

Once you have prepared carefully, you are ready for the interview. **Conducting a successful interview** is not difficult if you follow these suggestions:

- *Tape the interview if possible; otherwise, take careful, extensive notes.* You should ask your interviewee in advance for permission to record the interview. If he or she agrees, be sure to use a tape recorder that functions properly and that you know how to operate. If you cannot record the interview, be sure to take extensive notes. Be especially careful to write down accurately phrases or sentences you think you might want to quote. It is also a good idea to read such statements back to the interviewee to be sure you quoted him or her correctly.

- *Don't be too rigid about keeping to your list of questions.* Although it is important to have a list of questions, don't insist that the interviewee answer each and every one. If the person you are interviewing wants to talk about something that interests him or her, listen carefully. Often, unsolicited comments and even digressions that occur during an interview provide you with the most valuable material.

When you have completed the interview, be sure to thank the person you interviewed and ask if you may call if you have additional questions. Then you are ready to transcribe what you have recorded or read what you have written. Be sure to do this right away while your memory of what was said is fresh.

Keep in mind the following suggestions when **writing your account of the interview**:

- *Identify the person you interviewed.* Someone who consents to an interview is, in effect, providing you with a source of additional material, which you can then use to develop your writing assignment. In this respect, an interview is like a book or an article. It is a source you may use but that you must identify and credit. If you fail to acknowledge your source each time you use material from an interview, you are guilty of plagiarism—an offense that has severe academic and even legal consequences.

Therefore, each time you use material from an interview, whether it is quoted or summarized, you are expected to identify the person whose thoughts and words you are using. You may do this initially by simply stating the person's name and position (or by pointing out why this person is a credible source). For example, you might introduce material from an interview with the following statement:

> **Example:** On May 20, 2002, I spoke with Jason Precourt, a receptionist at the Bellevue Emergency Room. Jason pointed out that. . .

You should also include in your Works Cited (your list of sources that appears at the end of your paper) the following information about your interview: (1) name of person interviewed, (2) the words *Personal interview*, and (3) the date of the interview. Below is an example of how this information is presented and punctuated in a list of works cited:

Precourt, Jason. Personal interview. 20 May 2002.

- *Distinguish clearly between your ideas, opinions, and statements and those of the person you interviewed.* It is important to let your reader know when you are using ideas or information you gained from the person you interviewed. The best way to keep your reader informed about your use of material from your interview is simply to use the person's name repeatedly in the context of your paper.

> **Example:** Precourt added that . . .
>
> **Or:** According to Precourt, . . .

If you do not mention the subject's name in the context of the paper, you must include a parenthetical citation at the end of any material you have used from the interview. (See Appendix A)

> **Example**: The emergency room is busiest on Saturday evenings from 10:00 until about 1:00 a.m. (Precourt).

- *Be sure to quote your source accurately.* Refer to your recording or to your notes frequently, and contact the interviewee if you are in doubt.

Interview Notes and Reports

In writing a paper about how to increase school spirit, a student named Denise interviewed ex-students as well as current students at her university. As you can see in the sample interview printed below, Denise found out about the experience and background of her interviewee, she remembered to ask questions that would not allow the interviewee to answer just "yes" or "no," and she took good notes she could use later.

Interviewee—Jennifer (not presently enrolled)

Date—April 24, 2002

1. What could Texas A&M University-Commerce do to make student life better and increase student pride?

   "Have a concert or some other kind of cool event once a week on the lawn outside the Student Union Building."

2. What activities do other universities have that you would like at TAMU-C?

   "An on-campus coffee house that is open really late on weekends where you could go and maybe hang out and maybe get burgers or some sort of entertainment."

3. When you were enrolled, did you attend student activities or sports events? Why or why not?

   "No, because I usually never heard of them until I read about them in the school newspaper, and then they were over."

Using the information she gained from this interview, Denise wrote the following paragraph:

This semester, I have been concerned about how Texas A&M University-Commerce can increase school spirit and school pride. The university already provides many wonderful activities. However, attendance is often low, and students do not take advantage of the opportunities provided for them. Jennifer, an ex-student of TAMU-C, stated in an interview that she rarely attended campus activities: "I usually never heard of them until I read about them in the school newspaper, and then they were over." It seems that word of events on campus does not get circulated very well. One solution to this problem is to publicize more effectively the TAMU-C web page and to be sure the list of activities and school information is kept current on this site. Another solution would be to provide a hotline with an automated message that is updated several times a week so a student can call and hear announcements, activities, and school information. These solutions would cost little after the initial set-up and would enable students to check the Internet or call the hotline to find out the time, place, and other details about upcoming events. Indeed, these efforts on the part of TAMU-C might keep students like Jennifer enrolled in the university.

—Denise Bryson-Harley (student)

Note that Denise clearly identifies Jennifer and explains that she is an ex-student. She also accurately quotes Jennifer's reason for not participating in campus events. Finally, Denise draws a logical conclusion about the effect of campus participation on keeping students in school.

EXERCISE

7.1   Following the guidelines above, interview a classmate about a problem you perceive on your own campus and then report on your interview to your peer response group or your class.

EXERCISE

7.2   Write a paragraph based on the interview you did for Exercise 7.1. Be sure to quote the person you interviewed at least once.

OBSERVING

Observations are another productive source of information. But observing something casually is not the same as a focused, structured observation. Like interviews, successful observations require forethought and preparation. You need to plan your observation carefully in advance (where you will position yourself, exactly what you are looking for, how long you will remain, etc.) and to take careful notes on what you see. An observation is usually most productive when you determine in advance a purpose or a focus. Although an unstructured observation can sometimes provide you with an idea about a topic, the most useful observations are those guided by a particular purpose. For example, you might observe the seating patterns in your cafeteria to determine if students tend to congregate on the basis of ethnicity, age, style of dress, or type of haircut. Or you could observe the students in a computer lab to determine how they react when problems occur.

Whatever your purpose, you should follow these guidelines when you observe:

1. *Position yourself so you can see clearly and yet are not in the midst of what you are observing.* It is best to have some distance between yourself and whatever you are observing, yet you want to be close enough to have a good, clear view of what is going on.

2. *Take detailed, objective notes on everything you observe.* Don't try to interpret what you are seeing at this point. Simply record as many details as possible.

3. *Don't forget to use all your senses.* Although observations usually depend primarily on visual information, remember you also have other senses that can relay equally important information. Remember that an observation may include what you are hearing, smelling, and feeling as well as what you are seeing.

4. *When you use the information from your observation in a writing assignment, be sure to identify clearly the place or event you observed.* Make it clear to your reader that the information you are including is based on a careful, structured observation of a certain place or event rather than simply the result of a casual glance.

You may want to repeat your observation several times to verify what you observed or to gain additional information.

Observation Notes

Below are the notes a student named Christie took while she was observing the *Atalanta*, the private railroad car of Jay Gould, a wealthy railroad tycoon.

From the outside

—wooden car, painted red, with metal strappings

—sits on 7 wood blocks

—is tied to concrete slab by steel cables

—has steel posts welded to axles and set in concrete

From the inside

—original cast-iron boiler and pipe heater extend along baseboard from one end of car to the other

—original glass icebox in kitchen

—rich mahogany and maple wood inside (varnish has melted and bubbled from heat)

—in observation room and dining room are stained and leaded glass windows

—brass hardware (railings, bathroom hooks, places for light fixtures)

—on bottom of dining room light fixture is jaybird sketched into glass

—bathtub very small (32 inches in length)

—seats very low and beds very short

Notice that Christie observed carefully from both the outside and the inside of the railroad car. Notice also that she recorded both factual details (32 inches in length) and descriptive details (the wood bubbled from the heat). In her report below, you will see how Christie used these observation notes in her finished paper.

EXERCISE

7.3

Observe a specific place or event on your campus (e.g., a parking lot, popular hangout, particular area of the library, computer lab, social event, or busy classroom or office). Observe this place at three different times on the same day or on three different days. Be sure to take detailed notes of what you observe.

EXERCISE

7.4

Write a paragraph about the place or event you observed. Be sure your paragraph has a focus (or main point) and that the details you choose reinforce this focus.

COMBINING INTERVIEWS AND OBSERVATIONS

When possible, it is a good idea to combine these two methods of field research. Because one complements the other, your report or essay will be more interesting if you use both interviews and observations. Both methods provide you with an abundance of specific details, which you can then use to develop your paper. In the following report, Christie uses both interviews and observations to explore the history of the old railroad car she saw on a brief vacation to Jefferson, Texas.

Atalanta: Goddess of Speed

The *Atalanta*, Jay Gould's private railroad car, which was built in 1888, was a marvel of engineering for its day. It is 88 feet long and has four staterooms, a lounge, a dining room, a kitchen, a butler's pantry, and a bathroom. An interesting museum car today, the *Atalanta* was once a comfortable and elegant setting for the travels of Gould and his family.

Visitors to the restored car in Jefferson, Texas, can see that it still has its original cast-iron boiler and the original pipe heater extending along the baseboard from one end of the car to the other. The car had both electric and gas lighting. The original glass icebox can still be seen in the kitchen. Although most cars built at the same time were not made of wood, Gould's car was made of wood inside and outside. Today visitors can see how the varnish on the rich mahogany and maple wood inside the car has bubbled from the heat.

A close examination of the restored car shows that life on this rolling mansion was not just comfortable, however. It was also elegant. Formal dress was required in the dining room. All the hardware in the car—railings, bathroom hooks, places for light fixtures—is made of brass, and the original mother-of-pearl buttons used to call the porter or cook are still in place. The original light fixture for the formal dining room is still there, and on the bottom a jaybird is sketched into the glass.

Atalanta's owner, the prominent railroad tycoon Jay Gould, had visited Jefferson in 1882 but left in disgust because he failed to gain permission for his railroad to pass through the town, which was then booming because it had water passage to the Gulf of Mexico. Before he left town, however, Gould signed the Excelsior House register with "End of Jefferson, Texas" in bold letters and told people in the lobby that "Jefferson would see the day when bats would roost in its belfries and grass would grow in its streets" (Terry).

The *Atalanta* was used by Jay Gould until his death in 1892. After his death, the *Atalanta* rode the rails for a few more years because it became the private car of his son, George Jay Gould, and his daughter, Helen Gould. However, from the 1930s until the car was restored and moved to Jefferson, it was used as a private residence by people not connected to the family (Terry).

The restoration of the *Atalanta* began in 1954, when the Jessie Allen Wise Garden Club of Jefferson found it in an old East Texas oil field (Terry). The *Atalanta* at this time looked nothing like a railroad tycoon's opulent coach. After the *Atalanta* anchored in Jefferson, the thirty-five members of the Garden Club went to work. They began paint scraping, brass polishing, window cleaning, and roof patching. The furnishings and restoration were based on research of the original designs. Mrs. Lois Mueller, a current Garden Club member, recalls that after the restoration project began, someone bought an elegant old suitcase at an auction, not knowing that it contained Gould memorabilia: pictures of the Gould family, personal letters, diaries, account statements for Lyndhurst (the Gould home in Tarrytown, New York), stock certificates from the Audubon Society, and newspaper clippings of the Gould family (Mueller). These artifacts can now be seen as well as the car itself.

It is quite ironic that after all this time the *Atalanta* has found its way back to Jefferson. Ironically, too, the car—originally named for the Greek goddess of speed—is sitting on seven wooden blocks and rooted by steel cables in a concrete slab. Where the middle wheels should be, steel posts are welded to the axles, which are also set in concrete. It doesn't look as if Jay Gould's private railroad car is going anywhere now.

Works Cited

Mueller, Lois. Personal Interview. 5 April 2001.

Terry, Lucille. Personal Interview. 5 April 2001.

As you can see, this paper is filled with detailed information that resulted not only from Christie's own observations but also from the knowledge of the two Jefferson citizens whom she interviewed.

CHAPTER REVIEW

- Field research is a productive method of gathering information.
- When you conduct an *interview*, you should
    1. Be thoroughly prepared.
    2. Tape or take extensive, careful notes of what is said.
    3. Report what you learn from the interview accurately.
    4. Give the interviewee credit for his or her contributions.

■ When you conduct an *observation*, you should

1. Prepare carefully.
2. Pay close attention to details (both factual and descriptive).
3. Record accurately everything you observe.

WRITING ASSIGNMENT

Select an issue on your campus or in your community and write a report on this issue using both interview(s) and observation(s). Possible topics include inadequate medical facilities, a controversial charity or organization, a practice such as tattooing or body piercing, or an event that is objected to by certain people. Be sure to acknowledge the material you derived from your interview(s) by (1) indicating the person's name when you quote or summarize what the person told you and by (2) including an appropriate citation in your list of Works Cited at the end of your paper.

PARTICIPATING IN THE ACADEMIC COMMUNITY

Read your report aloud to your class or to your peer response group. Afterward, answer any questions your class members may have about your essay or the interview and observation processes.

CHAPTER

8

Achieving Coherence

For your writing to communicate clearly to your audience, your sentences and paragraphs must be linked so they cohere, or hold together. That is, your ideas must be logically arranged and connected. A paragraph or an essay is coherent if the different ideas in it function as a unit, or as a unified whole, and not as a series of individual, unconnected sentences or paragraphs. In this chapter, you will learn more about **coherence**—about how ideas relate to one another and about the transitions that writers use to communicate these relationships to their readers.

ARRANGING IDEAS

One of the primary ways writers achieve coherence is by using logical patterns of **arrangement** that are familiar to their readers. As discussed in Chapters 4 and 5, the most common pattern is general to specific, in which a writer begins with a general idea and then supports this idea with specific details. But additional patterns are often needed. Three of the most frequently used patterns are **time order, space order**, and **order of importance**. As you read this chapter, you will find that you are actually already familiar with these patterns, but the following explanations and exercises will help you see how writers use them to communicate effectively.

Time Order

For example, many essays and paragraphs are arranged in chronological, or time, order—most narratives (compositions that tell a story, relate a series of events, or describe a process) are arranged in chronological order—that is, they are arranged in the order in which the events of the narrative occurred. Compositions arranged in chronological order often include references to specific times or dates. Or they include transition words such as *first, then, next,* and *last* to indicate the passage of time. As you read the following paragraph, notice not only the time order in which the events are arranged but also how the bolded words and phrases make this order clear to the reader:

> [1]The **beginning** of each school term marks a period of rebirth for college campuses. [2]**Before the term begins**, the campus is strangely vacant and quiet. [3]**Then** students begin to move into the dorms, carrying suitcases, trunks, and boxes from their cars to their assigned rooms. [4]Shouts of laughter, yells of greeting, and squeals of excitement ring across the campus as students resume their interrupted relationships and establish new ones. [5]**Meanwhile**, maintenance crews move busily around the campus trimming, repairing, painting, and generally refurbishing the campus and buildings. [6]**A few days later**, teachers arrive, coming to their offices to plan for their classes, going to the library to complete a last bit of research, exchanging stories with colleagues. [7]**Finally, on the day classes begin**, commuting students flood the campus, fighting for parking spaces, joining resident students as they scurry to classes, and generally adding to the growing sense of confused activity. [8]**A new semester has begun**, and the campus is alive **once more**.

The writer of this paragraph begins with events that occur before the new semester starts and ends with the actual beginning of the semester, thus using chronological order to structure the paragraph.

EXERCISE

8.1

Each of the following groups of sentences may be rearranged in a paragraph based on time order. Study each group of sentences, looking for the logical time sequence and for transition clues. Then number the sentences in what you believe is the appropriate order. (The topic sentence, the first sentence in the paragraph, has been identified for you.)

PARAGRAPH A

TS: __1__ I was impressed by a television commercial I saw when I was little.

_____ The camera then moved slowly up the Native American's body, showing his clothes and markings.

_____ In the beginning of this commercial, the camera was focused on pieces of trash lying on the roadside—cans, bottles, candy wrappers, and cigarette butts.

_____ Then, the camera completed its journey, showing the pain and disturbance clearly visible in his face.

_____ With a pause after each item of trash, the camera slowly moved to a pair of moccasin-covered feet.

_____ When the camera reached the lower part of his face, I noticed the drops of tears rolling down his fleshy, strong cheeks.

_____ The Native American's tears were falling because of the contamination of the land.

—Dave McNish, student (adapted)

PARAGRAPH B

TS:__1__ Motion pictures became another form of entertainment for the American people.

_____ A second landmark was in 1927, when Al Jolson's *The Jazz Singer* successfully introduced motion pictures with sound.

_____ The widespread popularity of television after World War II reduced the number of moviegoers.

_____ Pioneered in America by Thomas Edison, the earliest motion pictures were different from those we see today.

_____ However, through the years to the present, "going to the movies" has continued to be the favorite recreation of millions of Americans.

_____ Then, during the 1930s, pictures in color added to the enjoyment of moviegoers.

_____ In the thirties and forties, as many as 100 million people went to the movies each week.

_____ In 1915, the success of *Birth of a Nation* (which has recently been criticized for its racism) encouraged the building of silent-movie theaters in cities and towns throughout the country.

—Adapted from Howard B. Wilder et al., *This Is America's Story*

EXERCISE

8.2   Write a paragraph in which you narrate your typical morning or evening routine. Use time order to arrange your details and appropriate transition words to help your reader follow the sequence of events or steps in your routine.

Space Order

Many compositions, especially those that describe places or people, are arranged in space order—that is, the objects or details are arranged in the order in which they are observed in space. In a description of a room, for example, the writer may describe objects from left to right, from floor to ceiling, or from the outside walls to the center of the room. In describing a landscape scene, the writer could move visually from far to near or from near to far.

Compositions arranged in space order often include references to directions, such as *right, left, up, down, east, west, under, over, beyond, in front of, behind,* and so on. The following paragraph illustrates space order. As you read this paragraph, pay particular attention to the order in which the author describes the spatial view. The bold words and phrases indicate this order.

> [1] The view **from the front door** was breathtaking. [2] Immediately **in front of** the house, **to the west**, was a small dirt road, and **beyond this road** the land dropped sharply so that the entire valley was visible. [3] This broad valley was cut **down the center** by the Snake River, a curving blue-white scar **across the pale green sagebrush** that covered most of the valley. [4] **On the far side of the valley**, sandstone cliffs rose abruptly from the gently rolling valley floor. [5] **Rising above the cliffs** were the **distant mountains**, majestic peaks crowned with snow and ice.

As shown by the transition words, this paragraph is arranged in space order, moving from the house to the most distant view from the front door.

EXERCISE

8.3

Each of the following groups of sentences may be rearranged in a paragraph based on space order. Study each group of sentences, looking for the logical spatial sequence and for transition clues. More than one arrangement may be possible for the sentences in each group, but in Paragraph A the best order is from the house outward, and in Paragraph B the best arrangement is from bottom to top. Number the sentences in the clearest, most logical order. (The topic sentence, the first sentence in the paragraph, has been identified for you.)

PARAGRAPH A

TS: __1__ Skillful landscaping distinguishes the professor's white stucco house.

_____ A low trellis separates these flowers from the evenly manicured lawn, which is broken only by a circular planter.

_____ In front of the brick wall of the courtyard is a carefully shaped box hedge.

_____ This circular planter is filled with more geraniums and centered with a fountain.

_____ At the edge of the street, this lawn drops sharply three feet to a street-level sidewalk.

_____ Directly in front of the house is a small brick courtyard in which cacti and yucca plants have been attractively arranged.

_____ Next to this hedge grow rows of brightly colored flowers—red geraniums and white periwinkles.

PARAGRAPH B

TS: __1__ College Hall was one of the oldest and most used buildings on campus.

_____ The maps that covered the dusty chalkboards of classrooms on that floor reflected the history courses that occupied them.

_____ Above, on the second floor, was the English Department, one of the largest departments on campus.

_____ The third floor of the building housed the overflow from the English Department plus the Sociology Department.

_____ On the first floor, the History Department coexisted peacefully with the Dean's office.

_____ On this top floor were also most of the classrooms used by the English and Sociology Departments.

_____ Two programs related to the English Department, the computer lab and writing center, were also on this floor.

EXERCISE

8.4   Write a paragraph in which you describe a room or building you see daily. Arrange the details of the place you are describing in an appropriate spatial order.

Order of Importance

The details in a composition may also be arranged according to their order of importance. Writers may begin with the most important supporting point and end with the least important. Or they may begin with the least important and end with the most important, allowing them to build to a high point, or climax. In either arrangement, writers may help their readers by emphasizing the major points with transition words such as *first, second*, and *finally* or with transition phrases such as *more important* and *most important*. As you read the following paragraph, notice not only the transition words that are in bold type but also how the details are arranged to indicate their relative importance to the writer:

¹Several considerations should influence your choice of a career. ²**First**, you should choose a career that will provide the lifestyle you want. ³If living in an expensive house and driving a big car are your goals, you should not decide to be a schoolteacher or a paramedic. ⁴Although it is possible to make a good living in these professions, most teachers and paramedics make rather modest salaries, especially at the beginning of their careers. ⁵**Second, and more important**, you should choose a career for which you have an aptitude. ⁶Even though you may love art, if you have no talent as an artist, you will not be successful. ⁷**Finally, and most important**, you should choose a career you will enjoy. ⁸Deciding to be a mechanic because you are good at repairing

cars is not wise if you do not find car maintenance interesting or enjoyable. [9]Becoming a lawyer is a mistake if you do not enjoy writing briefs or researching legal issues. [10]You will spend countless hours working at whatever career you choose. [11]Those hours will be more rewarding and less tiring if they are spent in work you enjoy.

To emphasize the writer's most important point, the reasons in this paragraph are arranged from least important to most important.

EXERCISE

8.5   Each of the following groups of sentences may be rearranged in a logical paragraph based on the order of importance. Study each group of sentences, looking for the most logical order and for transition clues that indicate that order. Number the sentences so they are arranged in order of importance. (The topic sentence, the first sentence in the paragraph, has been identified for you.)

PARAGRAPH A

TS: __1__ During the Middle Ages, England had a very strict class structure based on the manor, a self-supporting landed estate.

_____ Above the serfs and below the lord was a large group of freemen, including tenants, shop owners, craftsmen, clergymen, soldiers, and lesser nobles.

_____ Finally, at the very top of the class structure was the king, to whom the nobleman owed his allegiance.

_____ The least important member of the class system was the serf, a servant who was bound to the soil of the manor and to the nobleman who owned it.

_____ Near the top of the hierarchy was the lord who owned the estate.

PARAGRAPH B

TS: __1__ All organisms can be classified on the basis of their specializations into more or less well-defined categories.

_____ Within a phylum, the next highest rank is the class.

_____ Within the living world as a whole, the highest taxonomic rank usually recognized is the kingdom.

_____ Using criteria of likenesses and differences among and within groups, one may recognize orders within a class, families within an order, genera within a family, and species within a genus.

_____ The species normally is the lowest unit.

_____ The next highest rank within the kingdom is the division, or the phylum.

—Adapted from Paul Weisz, *The Science of Biology*

EXERCISE

8.6   Write a paragraph in which you discuss three to five goals you hope to accomplish in the next ten years. Arrange these goals according to their order of importance.

CONNECTING IDEAS

Arranging your ideas in familiar and logical patterns is one important way of achieving coherence in your writing. Readers and writers generally agree that certain arrangements, or patterns, are logical. For example, it is logical to discuss how to dress for an interview before discussing what to say (time order), to describe the front of a house before describing the rear of the house (space order), and to consider the most important reason for choosing to attend a certain college after you have considered the less important reasons (order of importance). But readers often need help to see your logic as a writer. Even though you arrange your ideas in a familiar, logical pattern, a reader may not perceive the pattern or the logic. Thus, a second important method of achieving coherence is to use various types of transition to connect your ideas clearly and logically.

Transition can be defined as the clues, or signals, a writer provides to help a reader see the connections between ideas. If the connections among your ideas are quite clear, transitions are less necessary; if these connections are less obvious, clear transitions become essential. Good writers are sensitive to the needs of their readers and give them as much assistance as possible.

The three basic methods of connecting ideas are (1) **repetition of key words and ideas**, (2) **repetition of structure**, and (3) use of **transition words and phrases** to indicate the appropriate relationships.

Repetition of Key Words and Ideas

One of the most common means of achieving coherence is to repeat key words and ideas. This repetition reinforces the main idea and connects supporting details to the main idea and to one another. In writing, you may reinforce, clarify, or elaborate a key word or idea by (1) repeating the same word, (2) using a more specific word or phrase for the same idea, (3) using a word or phrase with a similar meaning (a synonym), or (4) substituting a pronoun. Here are examples of each of these types of repetition:

1. *Repetition of exact word*: The *sea* can be beautiful, but the *sea* can also be dangerous.

2. *Repetition through more specific words*: In literature, *birds* often appear as symbols. For example, the *robin* may symbolize hope and the *raven* death.

3. *Repetition through synonyms*: The candidate made an *attempt* to convince voters, but his *try* was unsuccessful.

4. *Repetition through pronouns*: The *professor* started her lecture on the Constitution, but *she* was unable to finish it before the bell rang.

Much of the coherence of the following paragraph comes from the effective use of various types of repetition to reinforce the main topic, *dangerous chemicals*. Key words and phrases that repeat or reinforce this topic have been highlighted for you. In addition, marginal notes indicate how the author has used repetition to make the paragraph cohere, or "stick together."

Topic sentence (1)

Key phrase (1)

Repetition through pronoun (2)

Repetition through synonym (2)

Repetition through pronouns (3)

Repetition through more specific phrase (4)

Repetition through pronouns (4, 5)

Repetition through related word (synonym) (5)

Repetition through pronoun (6)

Repetition through exact word (7)

Repetition through pronoun (8)

1 For the first time in the history of the world, every human being is now subjected to contact with dangerous chemicals from the moment of conception until death. 2 In the less than two decades of their use, the synthetic pesticides have been so thoroughly distributed throughout the animate and inanimate world that they occur virtually everywhere. 3 They have been recovered from most of the major river systems and even from streams of groundwater flowing unseen through the earth. 4 Residues of these chemicals linger in soil to which they may have been applied a dozen years before. 5 They have entered and lodged in the bodies of fish, birds, reptiles, and domestic and wild animals so universally that scientists carrying on animal experiments find it almost impossible to locate subjects free from such contamination. 6 They have been found in fish in remote mountain lakes, in earthworms burrowing in soil, in the eggs of birds—and in man himself. 7 For these chemicals are now stored in the bodies of the vast majority of human beings, regardless of age. 8 They occur in the mother's milk, and probably in the tissues of the unborn child.

—Rachel Carson, *Silent Spring*

As you read the preceding paragraph, did you notice that the writer reinforced the key words *dangerous chemicals* with all four types of repetition of key words and ideas? If she had used only one type of repetition—through exact words or through pronouns, for example—the paragraph would be repetitious and dull. To see how different the effect would have been, reread the paragraph and substitute the exact word *chemicals* for each boxed word. You will discover that it is not just repetition but repetition with variation that provides the most effective transition.

8.7   The coherence of the following paragraph comes primarily from the effective use of repetition. Study the paragraph and underline all the words and phrases that refer to the subject *language*.

> Americans speak many languages. There is English, of course, which most of us speak more or less well. But there are other languages that many of us also speak. Spanish, Chinese, and Japanese, for example, are increasingly spoken in this country. In addition, there are different dialects spoken in the major geographical regions of the country. Southern English is not the same language as the Northeastern and Midwestern varieties of English. And Cajun English differs from every other language spoken in this country. Then there are the jargons that characterize different language communities. For example, lawyers speak their own version of English, whereas teenagers, truck drivers, and musicians speak still others. Thus, our "official" language has many variations.

Repetition of Structure

Repetition of structure can also improve coherence. When writers present information in obviously similar, or parallel, structures, they help their readers focus on their ideas and on the relationships among those ideas. In contrast, when writers present related details and ideas in forms that have different, or nonparallel, structures, the awkward presentation of those ideas may keep readers from understanding them. For example, which of the following sentences is easier to read and understand?

1. A successful pilot must have education, experience, and is courageous.

2. A successful pilot must have education, experience, and courage.

Do you agree that the second sentence is clearer? The first sentence is awkward because the writer has not used parallel forms in a situation in which the reader expects similar forms or structures to be repeated. In contrast to the first sentence, which shifts from noun forms (*education* and *experience*) to an adjective (*courageous*), the second sentence clearly emphasizes three necessary attributes of a pilot by repeating them in parallel noun forms.

As a writer, you can add coherence by repeating parallel (1) word forms, (2) phrases, (3) clauses, and (4) sentences. As a reader, you can use such repetition of structure to help you identify important supporting details and their relationships to one another. Following are examples of the four major types of structural repetition:

1. *Repetition of word form*: The coach *fired* the punter, *traded* a running back, and *hired* a new wide receiver. (repetition of verbs of similar structure)

2. *Repetition of phrases:* The child looked everywhere for the missing ball—*in the closet, behind the door,* and *under the bed.* (repetition of phrases of similar structure)

3. *Repetition of clauses:* It was obvious *that I had failed* and *that she had succeeded.* (repetition of clauses of similar structure)

4. *Repetition of sentences: I was tired. I was hungry. I was lost.* And, suddenly, *I was afraid.* (repetition of sentences of similar structure)

Now read aloud the following paragraph. As you read, notice how the writer repeats similar structures to make his paragraph more coherent, more readable, and more rhythmic. As you read the paragraph, notice especially the repetition of the word *it* and the repeated structure of *it* plus a verb, which occurs throughout the paragraph. The repeated, parallel structures have been underlined and noted for you in the margins.

Repetition of
phrases
  from dawn
  to dusk
  to dawn

Repetition of
sentences
  It trembles
  It moves
  It is

Repetition of *who*
clauses
  who gaze
  who jump
  who lumbers
  who cross
  . . .smash,
  . . .shortchange,
  . . .get jammed up

¹In New York from dawn to dusk to dawn, day after day, you can hear the steady rumble of tires against the concrete span of the George Washington Bridge. ²The Bridge is never completely still. ³It trembles with traffic. ⁴It moves in the wind. ⁵Its great veins of steel swell when hot and contract when cold; its span often is ten feet closer to the Hudson River in summer than in winter. ⁶It is an almost restless structure of graceful beauty which, like an irresistible seductress, withholds secrets from the romantics who gaze upon it, the escapists who jump off it, the chubby girl who lumbers across its 3,500-foot span trying to reduce, and the 100,000 motorists who each day cross it, smash into it, shortchange it, get jammed up on it.

—Gay Talese, "New York"

By repeating the same structures, the writer is able to emphasize the various activities of the different people who use the bridge. Indeed, his repetition of structure creates a rhythm that reminds us of traffic rushing back and forth across the bridge. By repeating similar structures but varying the content of those structures, you can make your writing clearer and more interesting for your reader. Moreover, you can improve the sound and rhythm of your writing and learn to be more aware of the rhythms in your reading.

EXERCISE

8.8   The following paragraph also makes effective use of repetition of structure. Read the paragraph aloud and listen to its rhythm. Then reread the paragraph and look for structures that are repeated. Finally, fill in the blanks in the outline that follows the paragraph.

> On Wednesday morning at quarter past five came the earthquake. A minute later the flames were leaping upward. In a dozen different quarters south of Market Street, in the working class ghetto and in the factories, fires started. There was no opposing the flames. There was no organization, no communication. All the cunning adjustments of a twentieth century city had been smashed by the earthquake. The streets were humped into ridges and depressions, and piled with the debris of fallen walls. The steel rails were twisted into perpendicular and horizontal angles. The telephone and telegraph systems were disrupted. And the great water mains had burst. All the shrewd contrivances and safeguards of man had been thrown out of gear by thirty seconds' twitching of the earthcrust.
>
> —Jack London, "San Francisco Earthquake"

1. Repetition of phrases

    a. In _____

    b. in _____

    c. in _____

2. Repetition of sentence structures and *no* phrases

    a. There _____

    b. There _____

3. Repetition of sentence structures

    a. All _____

    _____

    _____

    b. All _____

    _____

    _____

4. Repetition of sentence structures, phrases, and word forms

    a. The streets _____

       and _____

    b. The steel rails _____

    _____

    c. The _____ and _____

    _____

    d. And _____

    _____

Transition Words and Phrases

One of the most effective ways of achieving coherence is the use of specific transition words and phrases to indicate relationships within and among sentences and paragraphs. These words and phrases signal changes and thus alert readers to "shift gears" or to take a new direction. For example, the word *however* signals contrast, and the words *next* and *then* signal progression.

Transition within the following paragraph is clear because signal words indicate specific relationships among ideas. As you read the paragraph, be sure you understand the appropriateness of each transition word. The transition words have been bolded, and the relationships that they indicate have been noted in the margin.

	Bessie Delaney was one remarkable woman. In 1918, she was
Cause	turned down by New York University's dentistry program **because**
Contrast	she was a woman. **However**, she enrolled at Columbia University in
	1919 to pursue her dream of becoming a dentist. She also encountered
Cause	prejudice in that program not only **because** she was a woman but also
Cause	**because** she was an African American. Bessie would never have
Condition	reached her goal of becoming a dentist **if** she had not been both brave
Addition, contrast	**and** determined. **Nevertheless**, Bessie studied hard **and** didn't give up.
Result	**As a result**, she graduated from Columbia University in June of 1923.
Time clue	**After** practicing dentistry for many years, she died in 1995 at the age
	of 104.

—Based on Sarah Delaney and Elizabeth A. Delaney, *Having Our Say*

As readers, we know to expect a contrasting idea when we see the word *nevertheless*, a similar—or additional—idea when we see *and*, and a condition when we see *if*. As writers, we can use transition words such as these to guide our readers from one idea to another. However, be careful not to rely too heavily on transition words, and be sure to use these words carefully to indicate the appropriate relationships among ideas. If you arrange your sentences and paragraphs so one idea follows another in a logical progression, your transition words will serve primarily to reflect and reinforce the natural order and connections among your ideas.

The following lists suggest some of the most common transition words and phrases. Notice they are divided into categories that not only reflect the relationships they share but also suggest the order of arrangement or method of development.

Time Order		
after	meanwhile	when
afterward	next	whenever
as	now	while
before	sometime(s)	finally
first, second, etc.	soon	gradually
last	then	immediately
later	until	suddenly

Space Order		
above	under	at the top
around	outside	at the bottom
before	upon	to the north
behind	where(ever)	to the south
in	in front	to the east
out	in back	to the west
outside	to the left	up / down
over	to the right	through

Order of Importance		*Addition*	
first, second, etc.	foremost	in addition	also
especially	primarily	moreover	too
less (important)	more (important)	furthermore	and
least (important)	most (important)		

Example	*Cause*	*Result*
for example	because	accordingly
for instance	for	as a result
to illustrate	hence	consequently
such as	since	therefore
that is	so	thus

Comparison	Contrast	
and	but	although
also	yet	even though
as	however	though
just as	nevertheless	whereas
like	on the contrary	while
likewise	on the one hand	instead
similarly	on the other hand	rather
too	in contrast	still

Summary	Emphasis	Condition
in conclusion	surely	if
finally	certainly	as if
in short	undoubtedly	unless
in brief	indeed	
in other words	in fact	

EXERCISE

8.9 For practice in using transition words, read the following paragraph carefully and then use the preceding lists to help you choose appropriate transition words to fill in the blanks. (The relationship is indicated in parentheses under each blank.) Be sure to read the paragraph completely before you start to fill in the transition words.

Some influences on consumer behavior can be directly observed and measured. _____ others must be inferred. _____, the
                    (contrast)   **(example)**
impact of a retailer placing a large "sale" sign in the window of his or her store can be an important influence in triggering the start of the purchase decision process for consumers walking by the store. Many of these consumers will notice the sign _____ quickly begin the problem recognition stage,
                              (addition)
stopping and entering the store to obtain information about the sale item. The sign is, _____, a very direct influence on consumer behavior.
            (result)
—Thomas C. Kinnear and Kenneth L. Bernhardt, *Principles of Marketing*

UNIFYING IDEAS

In addition to arrangement, repetition, and transition, another method of achieving coherence in writing is **unity**. That is, each of your major points should relate clearly to your main idea (your topic sentence or your thesis), and each detail should be clearly connected to the point it is intended to develop.

In the following paragraph, for example, the bolded sentence introduces an irrelevant idea that destroys the unity of the paragraph:

> [1]Several important advances toward democracy have occurred under trees. [2]King John signed the Magna Carta under the giant Arkenwyke Yew at Runnymede, England. [3]To save their charter from their cruel governor, the people of Hartford, Connecticut, hid it in what has come to be known as the Charter Oak. [4]**My own grandfather was born under an oak tree as his family traveled to California.** [5]Finally, it was under an elm tree, later known as the Washington Elm, that George Washington accepted the command of the Revolutionary Army that fought for the colonies' independence.

The writer of the bolded sentence may have thought that the detail about his grandfather belonged in the paragraph because the event it describes, like the other relevant events, occurred under a tree. However, unlike the other supporting sentences in the paragraph, this sentence does not develop the paragraph's main idea that *Several important advances toward democracy have occurred under trees.* Therefore, this irrelevant sentence should be omitted from the paragraph (see also pages 57–59).

EXERCISE

8.10   Read the following paragraph. Then underline the irrelevant sentence that destroys the unity of the paragraph.

> Each day, a similar drama occurs in my history class. Just before class, all the students are chatting to their friends. Once the professor enters the room, however, it becomes silent, except for the rustle of paper as the students prepare to take notes. The professor soon begins to lecture, stopping only occasionally to write on the board. Most students write busily, trying to get as much information as possible in their notes. However, not all students take notes. One guy stares at the blonde who sits next to him. And another sits with his head on his desk, asleep because he stayed too late at a fraternity party the night before. He belongs to the Beta Fraternity, but the most popular fraternity on campus is the Kappa Alpha. Soon the bell rings, and once again the classroom is filled with the bustling and buzzing of students as they leave for their next classes.

ACHIEVING COHERENCE IN ESSAYS

Thus far in this chapter, you have practiced arranging and connecting ideas within paragraphs. However, arrangement, transition, and unity are just as important—if not more important—in essays. That is, good writers connect their ideas effectively *between* paragraphs as well as *within* paragraphs.

The same principles for arranging and connecting ideas that apply to paragraphs also apply to essays. Thus, you may organize entire essays as well as paragraphs according to time order, space order, or order of importance. Moreover, you should use repetition of key words, repetition of structure, and transition words to connect ideas in essays just as in paragraphs.

As you read the following essay-length passage from an American government textbook, notice the annotations. Then answer the questions that follow the essay.

Presidential Leadership in Congress

Thesis
Key word *way(s)*

1The job of president is ever-expanding, a trend that makes it more and more difficult for any one individual to govern well enough to meet the rising expectations of the American public. Yet ability to govern comes down to a president's ability to get his programs through Congress. According to one political scientist, **a president has three ways to improve his role as a legislative lobbyist to get his favored programs passed**.

Transition/key word
Repetion of structure
Repetition of structure

2The first way involves the traditional political avenue of using jobs, or other special favors or rewards, **to win support.** Invitations to the White House and campaign visits to districts of members of Congress running for office are two ways **to curry favor with legislators**. Inattention to key members can prove deadly to a president's legislative program. House Speaker Thomas P. O'Neill reportedly was quite irritated when the Carter team refused O'Neill's request for extra tickets to Carter's inaugural. This did not exactly get the president off to a good start with the powerful Speaker.

Transition/key word

3A second political way a president can bolster support for his legislative package is to call on his political party. As the informal leader of his party, he should be able to use that position to his advantage in Congress, where party loyalty is very important. This strategy works best when the president has carried members of his party into office on his coattails, as was the case in the Johnson and Reagan landslides of 1964 and 1984, respectively. In fact, many scholars regard LBJ as the most effective legislative leader. Not only had he served in the House and as Senate majority leader, but he also enjoyed a comfortable Democratic Party majority in Congress.

Transition/key word

4The third way a president can influence Congress is a less "political" and far more personalized strategy. A president's ability to lead and to get his programs adopted or implemented depends on many

Repetition of structure

factors, including **his personality, his approach** to the office, others' perceptions of **his ability** to lead, and **his ability** to mobilize public opinion to support his actions. Many call this **his "style."**

Clue to order of importance

[5]Frequently, the difference between great and mediocre presidents centers on their ability to grasp **the importance of leadership style. Truly great presidents**, such as Lincoln and Franklin D. Roosevelt, understood that the White House was a seat of power from which decisions could flow to shape the national destiny. They recognized that their day-to-day activities and how they went about them should be designed to bolster support for their policies and to secure congressional and popular backing that could translate their intuitive judgment into meaningful action. Mediocre presidents, on the other hand, have tended to regard the White House as "a stage for the presentation of performances to the public" or a fitting honor to cap a career.

—Adapted from Karen O'Connor and Larry J. Sabato, *The Essentials of American Government: Continuity and Change*, 3rd ed.

The introduction to this passage clearly states the writers' thesis, and each of the three body paragraphs develops one of the main points of the essay. Each of these main points is arranged logically and introduced with a clear transition that not only connects each main point to the thesis but also shows the clearly unified relationships among the main points in the essay. As shown in the annotations, further coherence is given to the essay through effective repetition of structure, key words, and ideas.

EXERCISE

8.11

Answer the following questions about the essay you have just read, referring back to the essay as necessary.

1. What is the thesis, or main idea, of the essay?

   _____

   _____

2. What are the three main supporting points of the essay?

   a. _____

   b. _____

   c. _____

3. What method of arrangement have the writers used for the three main points of the essay (time order, space order, order of importance)?

   _____

4. What words provide clues to the primary method of arrangement in the essay?

_____

_____

5. What words and phrases provide transitions between paragraphs?

_____

_____

_____

6. What other method(s) of achieving coherence have the writers employed?

_____

_____

7. Which of the following passages would be more clearly relevant to the essay and why? That is, which idea could be included in the passage without marring its unity?

   a. As commander-in-chief, the president also has authority over the various military branches. In this capacity, he can (within the limitations outlined by the Constitution) simply command support from the military branches.

   b. A president can also gain favor with members of his party in Congress by promoting laws that aid constituents traditionally supportive of the party and its issues. For example, a Democratic president can win points with his party by promoting laws favorable to labor.

▓ CHAPTER REVIEW

- Coherence in writing is achieved through effective arrangement, repetition, and use of transitions.
- Three useful patterns of arrangement are time order, space order, and order of importance.
- Three effective ways of connecting ideas are repetition of key words and ideas, repetition of structure, and use of transition words and phrases.
- Logical arrangement, effective transitions, and unity of ideas are important not only within paragraphs but also between paragraphs in essays.

▚ WRITING ASSIGNMENT

Select one of the paragraphs that you wrote for Exercise 8.2, 8.4, or 8.6 and develop it into an essay. Be sure to arrange your major points in logical order, to include various types of transition, and to avoid irrelevant ideas so your essay will be unified and coherent.

▚ PARTICIPATING IN THE ACADEMIC COMMUNITY

With a classmate, exchange drafts of the essays you wrote for the previous assignment. Underline examples of effective coherence (repetition of key words, repetition of structure, and transition words) in each other's papers, and identify irrelevant ideas that should be omitted or places where additional transitions should be used.

Revising Your Essay

An essential part of the writing process is rewriting. In fact, many writers believe that rewriting is the most important part of writing. This chapter focuses primarily on revising, or "reseeing," what you have written in terms of focus and unity, content and development, and organization and coherence. Revising consists primarily of **adding, deleting**, or **changing** what you have written. For example, you may need to add specific details or clearer transitions. You may need to delete unnecessary sentences or phrases that are repetitious or do not support your thesis. Or you may need to sharpen your focus, clarify your thesis, or change your conclusion to meet the needs of your audience.

You should always begin to rewrite by focusing on these important elements. However, rewriting also involves editing and proofreading—making sure your writing is as clear and correct as possible. This chapter includes suggestions for editing and proofreading; in addition, Part Three provides instruction to help you edit and proofread your writing.

REVISING FOR FOCUS AND UNITY

You actually begin to revise, or resee, your writing when you first begin to think about what you are going to write. In the prewriting stage, you consider various topics and purposes, rejecting some immediately and exploring others until you find a good starting point for writing. As you write your first draft, you may find that your initial focus continues to change and develop—that you are actually revising your original ideas and discovering more clearly your focus, or what you want to write about. Hence, this first draft is often called a *discovery draft*.

After brainstorming and then freewriting about her hometown of Biloxi, Mississippi, Karen wrote the following discovery draft:

> In Biloxi, my hometown, tourists, sunbathers, and fishermen leave the harbors in route to the Barrier Island. They make their living by shrimping and oystering.
>
> Sunbathing at any of the islands and boating is a popular activity along the coast. Yahats of all sizes travel to the islands for beach and sun. During the summer, the heat blisters the sand and bakes the decks. ~~On a boating trip, the salty air may blow, but it does not stop the The warm salty water off the coast of the islands also attracts boaters. The water is salty, but many sunbathers like to swim.~~ As the sunbathers swim in the salty water, they baste in the sun. ~~The salty water attracts the sun so a high sun protection must be used.~~ After about 2 hours the sunbathers turn a rosy red color. One can find the rosy red humans spread out on the white sandy beaches or on top of yahats and shrimp boats. <u>These tourists also like to go out on the gambling boats along the Biloxi shore.</u>
>
> —Karen Mikovich Freeman, student

In this first draft, Karen tried to focus on the tourists who are sunbathing and boating—but her false starts, repetitions, and strike-throughs show that she isn't going anywhere with this topic. Actually, it is not until the last sentence of her discovery draft that Karen found her subject: the gambling boats on the Biloxi shore.

In her next draft, then, Karen sharpened her focus by limiting her topic to the gambling cruise ships that had recently been approved for the Mississippi Gulf Coast. She also discovered her initial purpose: to inform readers about the new tourist attraction in Biloxi. However, even at this early stage in her writing process, Karen decided to delete a couple of sentences from her draft:

> A taste of Las Vegas has settled in the backyard of the Mississippi Sound. Gambling ships are now allowed to cruise along the coast. Two years ago, ships were not allowed to pass through the Sound area. Many conflicts occurred between citizens of the coast about these gambling ships. ~~The citizens couldn't agree about the gambling issue.~~ Turmoil arose between political leaders and church organizations. Political leaders stressed that ships would boost the economy and tourism of the surrounding area. Church organizations stressed moral values of individuals who gamble along the coast.

Despite efforts to sink operations in the Sound, the House of Representatives approved a bill to allow any vessel of 150 feet or more to conduct gambling operations in the Sound. ~~The Sound is a 8 to 12 mile-wide stretch of water between the beach along U. S. 90 and the barrier islands.~~ This particular bill would allow vessels to operate anywhere in the Sound as long as the boat is moving.

The gambling boats have certainly changed the Biloxi-Gulfport coast.

—Karen Mikovich Freeman, student

EXERCISE

9.1   Writers delete words and sentences for several reasons. For example, the deleted material may be irrelevant, repetitious, or awkward.

1. Why do you think Karen made the first deletion?

_____

_____

2. Why do you think she made her second deletion?

_____

_____

REVISING FOR CONTENT AND DEVELOPMENT

One of the most common problems writers have is lack of adequate development. Adding specific examples, details, and facts to your essay during the revision stage can greatly improve your writing. In her next draft, therefore, Karen not only revised her essay to clarify her focus and organization but also added more specific supporting details to develop her focus, as described in the annotations.

A Taste of Las Vegas

[1] A taste of Las Vegas has settled in the backyard of the Mississippi Sound. The Sound is an 8- to 12-mile-wide stretch of water between the Biloxi and Gulfport coastline and the barrier islands. After much disagreement about gambling in this area, tourists now ride the gambling ships that cruise the Sound on daily excursions and make an important contribution to the economy of the Biloxi area.

Added definition of Mississippi Sound.

Added thesis sentence.

Started new paragraph and added topic sentence about conflict over gambling.

[2] **Two years ago, a debate began about whether gambling ships should be allowed in the Sound**. Many conflicts occurred between citizens over the decision of legalized gambling. In particular, turmoil arose between political leaders and church organizations. Political leaders stressed that ships would boost the economy and tourism of the surrounding area. Church organizations, on the other hand,

Clarified position of churches and added details about conflict.

stressed the immorality of gambling and tried to block gambling ships along the Mississippi Gulf Coast with state and federal regulations. Many Baptist and Catholic organizations were especially concerned with the gambling issue.

Kept paragraph/ topic sentence about bill.

Added detail about ships that can offer gambling.

[3]**Despite the churches' efforts to sink gambling operations, the state House of Representatives approved a bill to allow any vessel of 150 feet or more to conduct gambling operations in the Sound**. This particular bill would allow vessels to operate anywhere in the Sound as long as the boat is moving. Cruise ships as small as 150 feet with a passenger capacity of two hundred can now offer the full array of casino games.

Added paragraph/topic sentence about area economy.

Deleted repetitious sentence.

[4]**The gambling cruise ships have certainly improved the economy of the Mississippi Gulf Coast**. The ships depend on the citizens and tourists of the area for financial support of their industry. ~~To keep the ships of entertainment alive, their financial needs must be met by the community and tourists of the area~~. Furthermore, the tourists who arrive from the surrounding states show that casino gambling is popular and profitable in the area. For example, hotels and restaurants in the Biloxi-Gulfport area have shown an increase in service since the ships arrived.

Clarified conclusion and purpose.

[5]The gambling ships make a significant contribution to the economy of the community. Therefore, I hope the public will continue to support legalized gambling in Mississippi because it will bring more tourists to this area.

—Karen Mikovich Freeman, student

EXERCISE

9.2

Answer the following questions about the focus, content, and development of Karen's essay.

1. What is Karen's thesis statement? _____

_____

_____

2. What detail does Karen add to paragraph 2? _____

_____

3. What detail does Karen add to paragraph 3? _____

_____

4. Explain why Karen deleted the third sentence in paragraph 4?

_____

_____

5. The introduction and conclusion of this draft clarify Karen's purpose and suggest her audience.

   a. What is her purpose? _____

   _____

   b. Who is her audience? _____

   _____

6. What additional changes, additions, or deletions would you suggest Karen make in revising her essay?

   _____

REVISING FOR ORGANIZATION AND COHERENCE

If you begin your paragraph or essay with a logical plan, you may not have to make major changes in your organization. However, if you simply write ideas down in the order in which you think of them, you may later realize these ideas must be rearranged in a more logical order. One of the most effective ways to evaluate the organization of an essay is to create an outline using the thesis of the essay and the topic sentence of each paragraph. For example, Karen's essay could be outlined as follows:

Thesis: After much disagreement about gambling in this area, tourists now ride the gambling ships that cruise the Sound on daily excursions and make an important contribution to the economy of the Biloxi area.

Topic sentence paragraph 2: Two years ago, a debate began about whether gambling ships should be allowed in the Sound.

Topic sentence for paragraph 3: Despite the churches' efforts to sink gambling operations, the state House of Representatives approved a bill to allow any vessel of 150 feet or more to conduct gambling operations in the Sound.

Topic sentence for paragraph 4: The gambling cruise ships have certainly improved the economy of the Mississippi Gulf Coast.

Conclusion: Therefore, I hope the public will continue to support legalized gambling in Mississippi because it will bring more tourists to this area.

This outline allowed Karen to determine that her essay was arranged in chronological (or time) order and thus would be logical to her readers. It also revealed that her essay was unified because each paragraph clearly related to the thesis she stated in her introduction (paragraph 1).

EXERCISE

9.3   Further evaluate the organization and coherence of Karen's essay by answering the following questions:

1. Identify at least five transition words or phrases Karen uses to reinforce her organization (see pp. 94–95 for a chart of common transition words and phrases):

   _____

   _____

   _____

   _____

   _____

2. Repetition of key words is a major way to ensure coherence when you write. Which key terms does Karen repeat throughout her essay?

   _____

3. Would you suggest additional changes in the organization or coherence of her essay?

   _____

STRATEGIES FOR REVISING

The drafts of Karen's essay illustrate several areas writers may need to pay special attention to when revising their writing—focus and unity, content and development, organization and coherence. In addition, it is helpful for writers to use specific strategies when revising their own writing. The following sections provide you with guidelines for revising your work with the aid of your peers or on your own.

Revising in Groups

One of the most helpful strategies for revising your writing is to work with a group of peers who read and respond to one another's paragraphs or essays. For peer group sessions to be successful, however, you and your classmates need to keep in mind the responsibilities you have in preparing for and participating in the sessions.

1. As a participant in a group, you and your peers have a responsibility to one another—as well as to yourselves and your instructor—to come to class with complete drafts for discussion.

Peer Revision Guide

Writer's Name: _____

Names of Peer Reviewers: _____

INSTRUCTIONS TO PEER REVIEWERS: First, read through the following questions. Then, give the writer time to read his/her essay (or paragraph) aloud while you listen carefully (and follow along on a copy if available). After the writer finishes reading, take a few minutes to respond individually to each question on this guide. Then use these questions as the basis for a discussion about the essay. Be sure to give the writer an opportunity to respond and to ask you questions.

1. What do you like best about the essay (or paragraph)?

2. What is the writer's main idea (topic sentence for paragraphs, thesis sentence for essays)? Underline the main idea if you have a copy of the paper. How can this main idea be made clearer?

3. Does the essay (or paragraph) include clear subtopics or major supporting points? What are these supporting points? List these points below and put a plus or a minus beside each to indicate whether or not it clearly supports the paper's main idea. Does the writer need another major supporting point? If so, what would you suggest?

4. What specific supporting examples, details, and facts has the writer used? In the following space, list three of the most effective of these. Where does the writer need additional examples, details, and facts? What suggestions do you have for additional support?

5. What principle of organization has the writer used in arranging the major supporting points (time, space, order of importance)? Can you suggest a better method of organization or arrangement?

6. What transitions has the writer used? (If you have a copy of the paper, circle these transitions.) Where does the writer need additional transitions? (Insert arrows at these points.) What additional suggestions do you have for improving the coherence and unity of the paper?

7. How effective are the introduction and the conclusion? Does the introduction capture the reader's attention and indicate the writer's purpose? Does the conclusion bring the writer's main points together and refer back to the thesis or topic sentence? How can the introduction and conclusion be improved?

8. If you could give the writer only one suggestion for improving this paper, what would it be?

2. You and your peers are responsible for respecting one another and one another's writing during the session. On the one hand, you should be encouraging rather than overly critical of your peers' efforts; on the other hand, you will not be able to help your peers revise their writing effectively if you do not provide them with specific and honest suggestions for improvement. Just telling classmates their drafts are fine is cheating them of the serious response you owe them (*all* writing can be improved in some way).

3. You have a responsibility to share the allotted time fairly among the members of the group. In a forty-minute session, for example, a group of four students can spend only ten minutes on each draft. You may even want to appoint one member as timekeeper to let you know if you are spending too long on one student's writing.

Revising Independently

Receiving feedback about your writing from your peers can be very helpful. However, you won't always have the opportunity to participate in a peer revision group, and even when you do have this opportunity, you must make the final decisions on your own. Therefore, you should find the following suggestions for independent revision helpful:

1. *Allow some time to pass between writing your draft and revising it.* If you try to make revisions immediately after you finish your draft, you will be so close to your writing you will not see problems in it. You need some distance to "resee" your writing and make effective revisions.

2. *Pretend you are a reader who is seeing the draft for the first time.* In order to revise effectively, you must be able to switch roles from that of the writer to that of the reader, looking at your writing from the point of view of someone who doesn't have the knowledge or experience you had in writing it.

3. *Reread your draft several times, selecting a different focus for each reading.* Most of us have trouble keeping several tasks in mind at the same time. Therefore, you may find it helpful to read your essay once to be sure everything in it relates to your focus as stated in your thesis, once to be sure you have included specific support for each major point, once to be sure that your organization is clear, and once to be sure you have included effective transitions.

4. *Read your draft aloud.* Sometimes hearing your words aloud will bring to your attention problems in focus, content, organization, development, and coherence that you would not have otherwise noticed.

5. *Ask a tutor (or your instructor) to respond to your draft.* If your college or university has a writing lab, a tutor will be happy to read and respond to your draft. Also, most instructors will take the time to answer specific questions before you submit your essay for evaluation.

EXERCISE

9.4

Work both independently and with a group of your peers to revise a paragraph or an essay you have written recently. Which method(s) of revising do you find most helpful? Why?

EDITING AND PROOFREADING

After you have made whatever revisions are needed in the larger areas of focus and unity, content and development, and organization and coherence, it is time to edit and proofread your essay. In the earlier stages of your revision process, you were concerned primarily with what you had to say, or with substance; at this point in your revision process, you will concentrate more on how you express your ideas, or on style and correctness. That is, you will edit and proofread your draft for problems in sentence style; for major sentence structure errors; and for errors in grammar, usage, punctuation, spelling, and capitalization.

The following suggestions will help you edit and proofread your writing more effectively:

1. *Ask a friend or tutor to read your draft aloud while you follow along on another copy.* Often when you read your own writing—even orally—you read incorrect sentences correctly without realizing it. Hearing another person read *exactly* what is on the page often helps you identify these problems.

2. *Read your draft aloud yourself.* When a friend or tutor is not available to read your draft orally for you, it is still a good idea to read it aloud yourself. Hearing your essay orally—whoever reads it—will not only help you identify and correct errors in grammar, usage, and sentence structure but also give you a sense of the essay's natural rhythms and help you smooth out rough places in your style.

3. *As you read your draft, use a pencil or your finger to point to each word.* This process slows your reading and forces you to notice each word and mark of punctuation. Therefore, you are more likely to notice errors.

4. *Read your draft backward, beginning with your last sentence and concluding with your first sentence.* Because the reading process involves predicting, you often read into your essay what you meant to write or what you think you wrote rather than what is actually on the page. Reversing the order in which you read your sentences helps you interrupt this process of prediction and see problems more clearly.

5. *Reread your draft several times, focusing on only one or two editing or proofreading concerns at a time.* Because it is difficult to keep several language tasks in your mind at the same time, your proofreading will be more effective if you read your essay once for sentence fragments and run-ons, a second time for grammatical problems such as errors in subject-verb agreement and tense, a third time for errors in punctuation and capitalization, and a fourth time for errors in spelling and word usage.

EXERCISE
9.5

Edit and proofread the following paragraph from a student essay. Use the questions following the paragraph to guide your editing.

Newman states that "all branches of knowledge are connected together, because the subject matter of knowledge is intimately united in itself. . ." (42). This statement suggests that each discipline of the academic world will lend itself to the others. The disciplines are all related, each one will help support the next. Learning math will assist a student in science and computer science classes. The basics of english will prepare a student to construct better papers and organize thoughts for other colledge courses. For example, in english I have already learned new methods to decipher main ideas from what I read, which has carried over into history and will assist me in all future classes.

1. This paragraph includes a major sentence structure error—a comma splice (a type of run-on sentence). Locate this error and correct it below (see Chapter 21):

_____

_____

_____

2. Underline the error in capitalization in this paragraph. Write the correction below.

_____

3. Circle the misspelled word in this paragraph. Write the correct word below.

_____

(*Note:* Part Three of this text provides specific instructions for identifying and correcting errors in your writing.)

CHAPTER REVIEW

- Rewriting includes three functions: revising, or "reseeing," the larger elements as well as editing and proofreading for problems in style and correctness.
- Revision involves adding, deleting, or changing what you have written.
- Good writers initially concentrate on focus and unity, content and development, and organization and coherence when they revise.
- Two effective methods of revision are revising in groups and revising independently.
- Editing and proofreading involve rereading your writing to correct problems in sentence style, sentence structure, grammar, and usage.

WRITING ASSIGNMENT

After you have met with the members of your peer response group, determine which of their suggestions you want to use in revising your paragraph or essay. In addition, use the suggestions given in this chapter to help you revise, edit, and proofread.

PARTICIPATING IN THE ACADEMIC COMMUNITY

Select a paragraph or essay you have written recently and discuss this essay with a group of your classmates. Members of the group should suggest revisions in focus, development, organization, coherence, and unity as well as identify errors in sentence structure, usage, spelling, and punctuation.

PART 2

Methods of Development

Several methods of development provide you with strategies for organizing and presenting your ideas in paragraphs and essays. Methods of development such as narration and description go back to the beginning of speech and the stories of hunting and fighting told around ancient campfires. Other methods of development, such as definition and comparison, originated over two thousand years ago with the ideas of the Greek philosopher Aristotle. Still others, such as process and cause and effect analysis, appear to be more modern in nature. And the ability to use persuasion, to use evidence and emotion to convince others to act or believe as you wish, is timeless.

In Part Two, you will see how other writers have used various methods of development in their writing and learn how to use these methods yourself. As you concentrate on each chapter, remember that many paragraphs and essays use these methods in combination. However, each writing example in this unit is clearly based on a primary method of development. Learning to understand and use these strategies can be extremely helpful to you in generating and organizing ideas for writing. Indeed, you will often be required to use certain methods of development—such as example, classification, definition, comparison and contrast, and cause and effect—in answering essay examination questions for classes such as history, sociology, and biology.

Description

Description is one of the most common methods of development in both paragraphs and essays. You can describe how a person looks, how a glass of lemonade tastes, how a headache feels, how cinnamon rolls smell, or how a rock concert sounds. Description can be part of many types of writing—fiction, poetry, history, science, biography, and business. Description is used heavily in technical manuals and advertising copy, but it can also be found in the most sophisticated novel and the simplest story, in the most formal speech and the most casual conversation. Although many works are primarily descriptive, description is also used to support other methods of development, especially narration.

To describe someone or something effectively, you must be a good observer. You must see people, places, objects, and events with a sharp eye and be able to relate your impressions clearly. Thus, writing an effective description involves more than using many adjectives and adverbs. It requires noticing, selecting, and ordering images and details so they communicate effectively to a reader.

UNDERSTANDING DESCRIPTION

In the following paragraph, Sandra Cisneros provides an effective description of a house in which she lived as a child. In her description, she enables you to share her experience—to see and feel what she saw and felt:

> **But the house on Mango Street is not the way they told it at all.** It's small and red with tight steps in front and windows so small you'd think they were holding their breath. Bricks are crumbling in places, and the front door is so swollen you have to push hard to get in. There is no front yard, only four little elms the city planted by the curb. Out back is a small garage for the car we don't own yet and a small yard that looks smaller between the two buildings on either side. There are stairs

in our house, but they're ordinary hallway stairs, and the house has only one washroom. Everybody has to share a bedroom—Mama and Papa, Carlos and Kiki, me and Nenny.

—Sandra Cisneros, *The House on Mango Street*

Qualities of Effective Description

As illustrated in Cisneros's paragraph, effective description includes the following qualities:

1. *A clear purpose and main idea.* The main idea of a description may be stated, or it may be implied. In either case, however, it holds the description together and gives it meaning. In her topic sentence, which is set in bold type, Cisneros suggests that her feelings about the house on Mango Street are negative. However, it is through her details, especially through her emphasis on the smallness of everything in or around the house, that Cisneros achieves her purpose of creating an impression of stuffiness and confinement.

2. *Sensory details.* Writers most often use details that appeal to the sense of sight, but good description also appeals to the other four senses— to hearing, taste, smell, and touch. In describing the red color of the house, the small "tight steps," the "small garage," and the "small yard that looks smaller between the two buildings on either side," Cisneros appeals primarily to the sense of sight. However, she also appeals to the sense of touch in describing the soft, crumbling brick and the front door that is "so swollen you have to push hard to get in."

3. *Factual details.* Factual details give exact information about a subject. For example, Cisneros tells us that there are "only four little elms" by the curb in place of a yard and that there is "only one washroom" to support her impression that the house is small. Working together, factual and sensory details can provide strong support for the main idea of a description.

4. *Effective comparisons.* Using comparisons that create images in the reader's mind is also an effective way to develop a main impression. Cisneros describes the windows as being "so small you'd think they were holding their breath" to emphasize the impression of tightness and confinement. (*Note:* Many comparisons begin with *like* or *as*.)

5. *A clear and consistent method of arrangement.* Finally, good description consistently uses a clear method of arrangment, such as space order, time order, or order of importance. Cisneros arranges the details in her paragraph according to space order, beginning with the front ("tight steps in front," "front door," "front yard"), moving to the back ("Out back"), and then moving from the outside to the inside ("ordinary hall stairs," "only one washroom," "share a bedroom").

EXERCISE

10.1   Read the following paragraphs, and answer the questions that follow each. The main idea may be stated or implied.

PARAGRAPH A

Desert landscapes frequently appear stark. Their profiles are not softened by a carpet of soil and abundant plant life. Instead, barren rocky outcrops with steep, angular slopes are common. At some places the rocks are tinted orange and red. At others they are gray and brown and streaked with black. For many visitors desert scenery exhibits a striking beauty; to others, the terrain seems bleak. No matter which feeling is elicited, it is clear that deserts are very different from the more humid places where most people live. As we shall see, arid regions are not dominated by a single geologic process. Rather, the effects of . . . running water, and wind are . . . apparent. Because these processes combine in different ways from place to place, the appearance of desert landscapes varies a great deal as well.

—Edward J. Tarbuck and Frederick K. Lutgens, *Earth Science,* 7th ed.

1. What is the main idea of the paragraph? _____

_____

2. To what sense(s) do most of the details appeal? _____

3. What are some of the most effective factual and sensory details?

_____

_____

PARAGRAPH B

It was a nice piece of toast, with butter on it. You sat in the sun under the pantry window, and the little boy gave you a bite, and for both of you the smell of nasturtiums warming in the April air would be mixed forever with the savor between your teeth of melted butter and toasted bread, and the knowledge that although there might not be any more, you had shared that piece with full consciousness on both sides, instead of a shy awkward pretense of not being hungry.

—M. F. K. Fisher, *The Art of Eating*

1. What is the main idea of the paragraph? _____

_____

2. To what sense(s) do most of the details appeal? _____

3. What are some of the most effective factual and sensory details?

_____

_____

EXERCISE

10.2   Using each of your five senses, write below descriptive details about a particular fruit. Consider more unusual fruits such as mangoes and avocados as well as the more common apples, oranges, and peaches. Be sure to have the fruit in front of you as you describe it so you can see, touch, smell, taste, and hear it.

Sight _____

Touch _____

Smell _____

Taste _____

Hearing _____

Working in pairs, read aloud the sensory details you have written and ask your partner to try to guess what fruit you described.

WRITING DESCRIPTIVE PARAGRAPHS

Whether your descriptive paragraph describes a place, a person, an object, or an action, you should try to include the qualities of effective description you studied in the previous section: a clear main idea or overall impression, specific sensory and factual details, effective comparisons, and a clear and consistent method of arrangement. Your method of arrangement will vary according to the subject you choose and the point of view that you take toward your subject. For example, in describing a fishing pier, you could arrange details in space order from the back of the pier to the docks on the edge of the sea; in time order based on the view at different times of the day; or in order of importance from the deserted warehouses to the bustling unloading docks.

Describing a Place

In the following paragraph about his parents' kitchen, Alfred Kazin states his main idea clearly in a topic sentence (which is in bold type) and arranges his details in space order, moving outward from the table in the center of the room. Words that provide spatial cues are highlighted with color bars:

The kitchen held our lives together. My mother worked in it all day long, we ate in it almost all meals except the Passover *seder*, I did my homework and first writing at the kitchen table, and in winter I often had a bed made up for me on three kitchen chairs near the stove. On the wall just over the table hung a long horizontal mirror that sloped to a ship's prow at each end and was lined in cherry wood. It took up the whole wall, and drew every object in the kitchen to itself. The walls were a fiercely stippled whitewash, so often rewhitened by my father in slack seasons that the paint looked as if it had been squeezed and cracked into the walls. A large electric bulb hung down the center of the kitchen at the end of a chain that had been hooked into the ceiling; the old gas ring and key still jutted out of the wall like antlers. In the corner next to the toilet was the sink at which we washed, and the square tub in which my mother did our clothes. Above it, tacked to the shelf on which were pleasantly arranged square, blue-bordered white sugar and spice jars, hung calendars from the Public National Bank on Pitkin Avenue and the Minsker Progressive Branch of the Workmen's Circle; receipts for the payment of insurance premiums, and household bills on a spindle; two little boxes engraved with Hebrew letters. One of these was for the poor, the other to buy back the Land of Israel.

—Alfred Kazin, "Brownsville: The Kitchen," *A Walker in the City*

Kazin uses effective factual details ("square tub") and sensory details ("fiercely stippled whitewash," "blue-bordered white sugar and spice jars"), and he makes an effective comparison when he describes "the old gas ring and key" that "jutted out of the wall like antlers."

Describing a Person

In the following paragraph, N. Scott Momaday describes his Kiowa grand-mother as he remembers her. Although a paragraph describing a person could also be organized by space order, moving from the person's feet to her head, or vice versa, Momaday's paragraph is organized by order of importance. That is, in describing the "several postures that were peculiar" to his grandmother, he builds to the most important posture: that of prayer. As you read this paragraph, notice the boldfaced statements that suggest Momaday's main idea that he remembers his grandmother most clearly at prayer. Notice also the highlighted phrase that suggests that the posture of prayer is the most important to her as well.

> **Now that I can have her only in memory, I see my grandmother in the several postures that were peculiar to her:** standing at the wood stove on a winter morning and turning meat in a great iron skillet; sitting at the south window, bent above her beadwork, and afterwards, when her vision failed, looking down for a long time into the fold of her hands; going out upon a cane, very slowly as she did when the weight of age came upon her; **praying. I remember her most often at prayer.** She made long, rambling prayers out of suffering and hope, having seen many things. I was never sure that I had the right to hear, so exclusive were they of all mere custom and company. The last time I saw her she prayed standing by the side of her bed at night, naked to the waist, the light of a kerosene lamp moving upon her dark skin. Her long, black hair, always drawn and braided in the day, lay upon her shoulders and against her breasts like a shawl. I do not speak Kiowa, and I never understood her prayers, but there was something inherently sad in the sound, some merest hesitation upon the syllables of sorrow. She began in a high and descending pitch, exhausting her breath to silence; then again and again—and always the same intensity of effort, of something that is, and is not, like urgency in the human voice. Transported so in the dancing light among the shadows of her room, she seemed beyond the reach of time. But that was illusion; I think I knew then that I should not see her again.
>
> —N. Scott Momaday, *The Way to Rainy Mountain*

In this paragraph, Momaday appeals to the senses of sight ("the light of a kerosene lamp moving upon her dark skin," "long, black hair . . . drawn and braided," "dancing light among the shadows of her room") and sound ("high and descending pitch," "urgency in the human voice"). He also makes an effective comparison in the "long, black hair" that "lay upon her shoulders and against her breasts like a shawl."

Describing an Object

The following paragraph has personal relevance for Scott Russell Sanders. However, it also has many qualities in common with the kind of technical description you might be asked to write in a business course. Like a technical description, which would give the exact length and width of the hammer, this description is specific and concrete. Unlike a technical description, however, Sanders's details appeal strongly to the senses.

Early in the paragraph, Sanders describes how the hammer looks ("scratched and pockmarked," "dull sheen") and how it feels ("about the weight of a bread loaf"). Then he provides additional details in space order, moving from the head of the hammer to its handle. Notice also the effective comparison of the hammer to "an old plowshare" and of its sheen to "fast creek water in a shade."

> **The hammer had belonged to him [Sanders's father] and to his father before him.** The three of us have used it to build houses and barns and chicken coops, to upholster chairs and crack walnuts, to make doll furniture and bookshelves and jewelry boxes. The head is scratched and pockmarked, like an old plowshare that has been working rocky fields, and it gives off the sort of dull sheen you see on fast creek water in the shade. It is a finishing hammer, about the weight of a bread loaf, too light, really, for framing walls, too heavy for cabinet work, with a curved claw for pulling nails, a rounded head for pounding, a fluted neck for looks, and a hickory handle for strength.
>
> —Scott Russell Sanders, "The Inheritance of Tools"

Although the first sentence of this paragraph does not fully state the main idea, it combines with details such as the hammer's strength and its comparison to an "old plowshare" to imply the hammer is a treasured family heirloom.

Describing an Action

Although a paragraph describing an action is similar to a narrative (indeed, narration and description are often used together), the following paragraph by Mark Twain is primarily descriptive. As suggested in the boldfaced sentence, this paragraph describes the "oppressiveness," or the foreboding and frightening atmosphere, that foreshadows the thunderstorm that Tom Sawyer, Huck Finn, and Joe Harper experience while camping in the woods. The paragraph creates a feeling of awe and fear in the presence of nature's power. Because it describes the chronological development of the thunderstorm, the paragraph is appropriately developed according to time order (see highlighted words and phrases).

About midnight Joe awoke, and called the boys [Huck and Tom]. **There was a brooding oppressiveness in the air that seemed to bode something.** The boys huddled themselves together and sought the friendly companionship of the fire, though the dull dead heat of the breathless atmosphere was stifling. They sat still, intent and waiting. The solemn hush continued. Beyond the light of the fire everything was swallowed up in the blackness of darkness. Presently there came a quivering glow that vaguely revealed the foliage for a moment and then vanished. By and by another came, a little stronger. Then another, then a faint moan came sighing through the branches of the forest and the boys felt a fleeting breath upon their cheeks, and shuddered with the fancy that the Spirit of the Night had gone by. There was a pause. Now a weird flash turned night into day and showed every little grass blade, separate and distinct, that grew about their feet. And it showed three white, startled faces, too. A deep peal of thunder went rolling and tumbling down the heavens and lost itself in sullen rumblings in the distance. A sweep of chilly air passed by, rustling all the leaves and snowing the flaky ashes broadcast about the fire. Another fierce glare lit up the forest and an instant crash followed that seemed to rend the treetops right over the boys' heads. They clung together in terror, in the thick gloom that followed. A few big raindrops fell puttering upon the leaves.

—Mark Twain, *Tom Sawyer*

Twain uses verbs ("followed"), adjectives ("waiting," "fleeting"), and prepositional phrases ("About midnight") as well as transition words ("then," "how") to indicate the passing of time. In addition, he uses effective descriptive details that appeal not only to sight ("light of the fire" and "quivering glow") but also to sound ("faint moan came sighing" and "peal of thunder went rolling and tumbling").

Writing Topic Sentences for Descriptive Paragraphs

Each of the preceding descriptive paragraphs has a stated or implied topic sentence that includes both a topic and an assertion (see Chapter 4, pages 35–36. The topic sentence of Kazin's paragraph about his family's kitchen can be analyzed in this way:

Topic	Assertion
The kitchen	held our lives together.

The rest of the paragraph clearly supports this topic sentence, not only describing the kitchen itself but also suggesting family activities that occurred there.

Kazin's topic sentence clearly states his paragraph's topic ("the kitchen") and his assertion ("held our lives together"). In their partially implied topic sentences, Momaday asserts that his memories of his grandmother (topic) focus most often on her prayer (assertion), and Sanders suggests that his father's hammer (topic) reminds him of the strength, the work, and the closeness he and his father had shared (assertion).

The assertion in a descriptive paragraph often suggests an impression, effect, or feeling that the writer wants to create. For example, Kazin's description of his family's kitchen and Sanders's description of his father's hammer suggest feelings of love and closeness, whereas Momaday's description of his grandmother at prayer and Twain's description of the thunderstorm create feelings of awe, wonder, or fear.

EXERCISE

10.3   For each of the following topics, write a topic sentence that includes both a topic and an assertion. Then list two or three sensory or factual details that you could use to support that topic sentence.

▶ **Example:**   *Topic:* Ringing of the office telephone

Topic sentence: <u>The ringing of the office telephone is</u>
<u>annoying.</u>

Sensory and factual details: <u>Rings at least four times</u>
<u>before I can reach it. Ringing is loud and harsh and</u>
<u>seems to go on forever. A bright light flashes every time</u>
<u>the phone rings.</u>

1. *Topic:* A hamburger

   Topic sentence: _____

   _____

   Sensory and factual details: _____

   _____

   _____

2. *Topic:* The wind blowing

   Topic sentence: _____

   _____

   Sensory and factual details: _____

   _____

   _____

3. *Topic:* One of the rooms in your house

   Topic sentence: _____

   _____

   Sensory and factual details: _____

   _____

   _____

EXERCISE

10.4   The Italian artist Giorgio de Chirico painted *Mystery and Melancholy of a Street* in 1914, while he was living in Paris. Study this painting and write a topic sentence in which you describe the overall feeling it gives you. Then develop your topic sentence into a paragraph, being sure to include specific supporting details from the painting to support your impression.

Mystery and Melancholy of a Street, 1914 (oil on canvas) by Giorgio de Chirico (1888–1978). Copyright 2003 Artists Rights Society (ARS), New York/SIAE, Rome. Private Collection/Bridgeman Art Library.

Using Transitions in Descriptive Paragraphs

Written by a first-year college student, the following paragraph combines the description of a place with an event that occurred at that place. As you read this paragraph, notice how the highlighted words and phrases indicate space order.

Student Paragraph

Yellowstone National Park is filled with a fabulous array of underground streams and geysers. These natural springs are not only beautiful, but fascinating as well. As I began my hike through the park, I noticed in front of me the constant gurgling and popping of the boiling spring water. The steam from these underground streams created a musical effect as they poured into the sky. As I stood amidst the geysers admiring their beauty, the ground suddenly began to shake beneath my feet. I quickly turned around, just in time to see the eruption of Old

Faithful, the grandfather of all geysers. Water and steam shot up 150 feet into the sky, creating an awesome display.

—Byron Black, student

This paragraph includes not only a clear topic sentence (bolded) and sensory details ("gurgling and popping," "musical effect," etc.) but also effective transitions. Although Byron uses *as* to show the events occurring in time, his transitions (*through, in front of, into,* etc.) indicate space order, which is the primary pattern of organization for the paragraph. The following chart lists words that indicate space order, which is common in descriptive writing:

above	in, into	at the top
amid	inside	at the bottom
around	out, outside	in front
before	over	in back
behind	through	to the left
beneath	under	to the right
between	up, upon	to the east (west)
down	within	to the north (south)

See Chapter 8, pages 94–95, for a list of transition words that show time order and order of importance. Remember to use transitions to help readers follow the arrangement of ideas in your descriptions.

EXERCISE

10.5   Select a place, person, object, or action you would like to describe. Then fill in the following plan to help you write a paragraph about this topic:

1. *Topic:* _____

    Assertion: _____

    Topic sentence: _____

    _____

2. What method of arrangement will you use to arrange your details?

    _____

3. Write several details that support your topic sentence. Be sure to include both factual and sensory details. (If possible, include details that appeal to more than one of the five senses.)

    _____

    _____

    _____

4. Now, go back and review your details to be sure they all develop your topic and assertion. Cross out any irrelevant details. Then decide on the method you want to use to arrange your details (space order, time order, order of importance). Number your details to fit this arrangement, and write here the transition words you might use to connect these details.

_____

_____

5. Finally, use the information you have generated in this exercise to write a paragraph about your chosen topic.

WRITING DESCRIPTIVE ESSAYS

Although a descriptive essay can explore a topic more fully than a descriptive paragraph can, it includes the same basic elements. The main idea of a descriptive essay occurs in a thesis statement in the introduction rather than in a topic sentence, but specific factual and sensory supporting details arranged in a logical order with effective transitions are just as important in an essay as in a paragraph.

In the following essay written for an English composition class, Sherri George describes her visit to St. Simons Island in Georgia, where she had lived as a child. Although this essay is primarily descriptive, it also contains some narration. Such a combination of description and narration is quite common in both personal and academic writing.

As you read the essay, notice that George uses past tense in the introduction and conclusion of her essay but switches to present tense in the body of the essay. Although a writer should keep the use of tense consistent during the same time frame, changing tenses is acceptable when the time of action actually changes or when a writer is trying to recreate another time or a feeling of direct experience, as George does in presenting the feelings of discovery she and her sons had on their visit to St. Simons Island.

St. Simons Island, Georgia

[1] It has been said, "You can never go home again, and you can't relive your childhood through your children." Five years ago for one week I did both. I took my two boys on vacation to St. Simons Island, Georgia, my childhood hometown. One of several islands that make up the Golden Isles of Georgia, St. Simons Island is a small island, just barely finding a spot on the map, off the southeastern tip of Georgia's coast. It is south of Savannah, Georgia, north of Jacksonville, Florida,

and nestled deep within my heart of memories. On this visit, I recaptured the feeling of being home and relived many moments of my own discoveries as I watched my boys make these same discoveries.

²Leaving the mainland, we cross the salt-water marsh and intracoastal waterway to reach the island. The tide is coming in, filling the marsh with the damp, salty smell of the ocean. It has a peculiar smell to the boys' senses, but to me it smells like coming home. Anticipation grows as we cross the two "singing bridges," or drawbridges that raise and lower to let the shrimp boats and barges pass under. When the car crosses the bridge, it makes a singing, humming sound on the tires. We are almost on the island now.

³The giant oak trees are the first welcoming sight. These trees have stood like sentries on guard for generations. Their branches are dripping with Spanish moss, reaching out like a canopy over the road. The moss is colored like cold ashes left from a fire. It is thick and hangs off the branches like an old sea captain's beard. The road bends and narrows, and the oak trees crowd each side of the road, making a first-comer think of southern plantations and mint juleps.

⁴We come to the red light marking the center of town. The heartbeat of St. Simons is the downtown ending at the pier. Main Street is only four or five blocks long, full of character and adventure. The hardware store, office supply, drugstore, and Roberta's Dress Shop have been there seemingly forever. The smell of coffee comes from the coffee and tea shop. T-shirts are hung in nearly every shop window. Everything we see beckons us to stop and shop, but we are headed to the pier.

⁵When we finally arrive at the pier, it looks, smells, and feels the same as it did when I was a little girl. The pier juts out over the greenish gray ocean for half the length of a football field. Thick barnacle-covered beams hold the pier steady against the tide. The roof covers the first one-third of the pier, so we can escape the sun or occasional rain shower. A long wooden bench lines the pier railing. The bench is perfect for romantic couples sitting, looking out over the ocean, or for the more serious business of fishing and crabbing. The signs of both are everywhere. Sweethearts' initials are carved in the railing posts. The railing is lined with fishing poles, bait buckets, crab lines, ice chests, and bushel baskets to put your catch of crabs in. The smell of fish carcasses, day-old chicken necks for crab bait, and tanning lotion mingles with the ocean breeze. To my boys, who have never seen the ocean before, everything is new, fresh, and exciting. They hurry from one fisherman to the next crabber and back again. They stick their curious noses in every bucket and ask a thousand questions. To me, however, these sights and sounds are familiar because I spent hours on this pier while growing up.

⁶That week in St. Simons, with my boys, I did go home again. I relived a part of my childhood through my children. I watched their excited faces and knew how they felt with each new discovery. I discovered for myself that although I had left the island, the island would never leave me.

—Sherri George, student

EXERCISE

10.6

1. What is the thesis, or main idea, of George's descriptive essay? (*Hint:* Reread the introductory and concluding paragraphs to identify the writer's topic and assertion.)

   _____

   _____

2. What is the method of arrangement used in this essay?

   _____

3. What are some of the most effective details in the essay?

   Factual details: _____

   _____

   Sensory details that appeal to sight: _____

   _____

   _____

   Sensory details that appeal to senses other than sight: _____

   _____

   _____

4. What are some effective comparisons used in the essay? (*Hint:* Comparisons often use *like.*)

   _____

   _____

CHAPTER REVIEW

- Effective description has a clear sense of purpose.
- A good descriptive paragraph or essay has a main idea, which may be implied or stated in a topic sentence or thesis statement.

- The main idea in a descriptive paragraph or essay includes both a topic and an assertion about that topic.
- Effective description includes both factual and sensory details.
- Sensory details appeal to the five senses: sight, hearing, taste, smell, and touch.
- Good description often includes comparisons, many of which use the word *like* or *as*.
- Descriptive paragraphs and essays may be organized according to space order, time order, or order of importance.

WRITING ASSIGNMENT

Rewrite the paragraph you wrote for Exercise 10.5, developing it into an essay. Be sure your essay contains a clear thesis (topic and assertion), a clear and consistent method of arrangement, and specific factual and sensory details.

PARTICIPATING IN THE ACADEMIC COMMUNITY

After you finish a draft of your descriptive essay, meet with a group of your classmates to read one another's essays. Use the Chapter Review to make suggestions for improvement. First, check each essay to be sure it has a thesis statement that states the main idea clearly. Second, read each essay to be sure it has specific factual and sensory details that support the thesis. Third, determine how the supporting details are arranged (space, time, importance), and then evaluate the effectiveness of that arrangement.

Narration

Most simply, **narration** is a story. Stretching back into ancient times when the only entertainment was telling stories around a campfire, narration is probably the oldest and is certainly the best known of all methods of development. We have all had experiences with stories—listening to them, telling them, watching them on television or movie screens—even before we learned to read and write.

Narration, however, is useful not only for entertaining readers but also for informing them. It is often combined with other methods of development, especially description, process, and example. Because narration may also be used to illustrate a point or explain a process, it is often used in academic writing. For example, you may use narration in your sociology class to provide an instance of racial discrimination, in your earth science class to describe how a hurricane forms, or in your history class to relate the events at the Battle of Gettysburg.

UNDERSTANDING NARRATION

In the following story, N. Scott Momaday narrates the events the Kiowa (Native Americans of the southern plains) believe led to the creation of the constellation of the Big Dipper.

> Eight children were there at play, seven sisters and their brother. Suddenly the boy was struck dumb; he trembled and began to run upon his hands and feet. His fingers became claws, and his body was covered with fur. Directly there was a bear where the boy had been. The sisters were terrified; they ran, and the bear after them. They came to the stump of a great tree, and the tree spoke to them. It bade them climb upon it, and as they did so it began to rise into the air. The bear came to kill them, but they were just beyond its reach. It reared against the

tree and scored the bark all around with its claws. **The seven sisters were borne into the sky, and they became the stars of the Big Dipper.**

—N. Scott Momaday, *The Way to Rainy Mountain*

Stories like this one that provide a people's explanation for objects and events in nature are called *myths*. Myths are among the oldest of narratives.

Qualities of Effective Narration

Like Momaday's paragraph, good narration includes the following qualities:

1. *A clear purpose and main idea.* Although some stories are written primarily for entertainment, the purpose of most narratives is to make a point or reveal a truth about life. This point may be stated in a topic sentence or thesis statement, as in the first sentence of Annie Dillard's paragraph on the death of a moth (p. 133), or it may be implied, or suggested, by the events of the narrative. Although the last sentence of Momaday's paragraph seems to be simply a description of the final event in his narrative, this sentence actually suggests the significance of the story itself: to explain the origin of the Big Dipper. Like Momaday's paragraph, most narratives in academic and literary writing do more than entertain. They illustrate a point, develop a theme or an idea, explain a process, or provide information.

2. *Use of descriptive details and dialogue.* The use of vivid details makes a narrative come alive, but these details should contribute clearly to the main point, help set the context, or move the narrative along to its climax (or high point of action). For example, in Momaday's paragraph the details of the brother's transformation into a bear, especially the description of his sharp claws, lead naturally to the sisters' terror, and their flight leads directly into the climax of their own miraculous escape and transformation into the stars of the Big Dipper. Well-chosen dialogue can also make a narrative more effective, as in the inner dialogue Lizzie Means records in the student paragraph on pages 135 and 136.

3. *An appropriate and consistent point of view.* Point of view should remain consistent throughout a narrative. By using the third-person point of view in his story, Momaday suggests the events he narrates are important not only to him but also to Native Americans in general and to his own Kiowa tribe in particular. The third-person point of view (*he, she, they*) is probably the most common approach in both literary and academic narratives. However, as shown in Lizzie's paragraph, the first person (*I, we*) can also be appropriate and effective in a narrative paragraph.

4. *Consistent use of tense.* Verb tenses (past, present, future) in narratives should remain consistent, changing only if there is an actual change in the time during which the events occur. Momaday consistently uses the past tense to narrate the events of this story, which is believed to have occurred many ages ago.

5. *Clear chronological organization and effective transitions.* A narrative tells what happened—that is, it relates a sequence of events, usually in chronological order (time order), or in the order in which they occurred. Momaday's narrative, for example, follows the order of events beginning with the brother and sisters' playing together, then moving to the brother's transformation into a bear and the sisters' terror and flight, and culminating in the sisters' escape and transformation into the stars of the Big Dipper. Momaday's narrative is so clear and simple that he needs few transition words, but he does provide time clues in the words *suddenly, directly*, and *as they did so*.

EXERCISE

11.1   Read the following paragraph about the assassination of President John F. Kennedy. Then answer the questions that follow it.

> When they arrived at Love Field, Congressman Henry Gonzalez said jokingly. "Well, I'm taking my risks. I haven't got my steel vest yet." The President, disembarking, walked immediately across the sunlit field to the crowd and shook hands. Then they entered the cars to drive from the airport to the center of the city. The people in the outskirts, Kenneth O'Donnell later said, were "not unfriendly nor terribly enthusiastic. They waved. But were reserved, I thought." The crowds increased as they entered the city—"still very orderly, but cheerful." In downtown Dallas enthusiasm grew. Soon even O'Donnell was satisfied. The car turned off Main Street, the President happy and waving, Jacqueline erect and proud by his side, and Mrs. Connally saying, "You certainly can't say that the people of Dallas haven't given you a nice welcome," and the automobile turning on to Elm Street and down the slope past the Texas School Book Depository, and the shots, faint and frightening, suddenly distinct over the roar of the motorcade, and the quizzical look on the President's face before he pitched over, and Jacqueline crying, "Oh, no, no ... Oh, my God, they have shot my husband," and the horror, the vacancy.
>
> —Arthur M. Schlesinger, Jr., *A Thousand Days*

1. The main idea in this narrative paragraph is implied rather than stated. Underline the phrases that most clearly suggest this main idea; then express it in a sentence of your own.

_____

_____

2. Circle transition words and other phrases that show chronological order in the narrative.

3. Schlesinger's choice of details emphasizes the irony, or apparent unexpectedness and lack of appropriateness, of the shooting. What are two details that suggest the contrast between what the participants expected and what actually happened?

_____

_____

4. Schlesinger's narrative builds suspense to a high point, or climax. What is this climax?

_____

5. How does the use of dialogue contribute to the overall effect of the paragraph?

_____

6. Is the point of view first person or third person? Why is this choice effective in this paragraph?

_____

_____

WRITING NARRATIVE PARAGRAPHS

You may write a narrative paragraph as a complete composition or as part of a longer essay. The following narrative paragraph by Annie Dillard is part of a larger narrative but stands alone effectively.

One night a moth flew into the candle, was caught, burnt dry, and held. I must have been staring at the candle, or maybe I looked up when a shadow crossed my page; at any rate, I saw it all. A golden female moth, a biggish one with a two-inch wingspan, flapped into the fire, dropped her abdomen into the wet wax, stuck, flamed, frazzled and fried in a second. Her moving wings ignited like tissue paper, enlarging the circle of light in the clearing and creating out of the darkness the sudden blue sleeves of my sweater, the green leaves of jewelweed by my side, the ragged red trunk of a pine. At once the light contracted again and the moth's wings vanished in a fine foul smoke. At the same time her six legs clawed, curled, blackened, and ceased, disappearing utterly. And her head jerked in spasms, making a spattering noise; her antennae crisped and burned away and her heaving mouth parts crackled like pistol fire. When it was all over, her head was so far as I could determine, gone, gone the long way of her wings and legs. Had she been new, or old? Had she mated and laid her eggs, had she done her work? All that was left was the glowing horn shell of her abdomen and thorax—a fraying, partially collapsed gold tube jammed upright in the candle's round pool.

—Annie Dillard, "The Death of a Moth," *Holy the Firm*

Notice that Dillard states her main point clearly in the bolded topic sentence at the beginning of the paragraph, organizes the sequence of events in clear chronological order, and uses vivid descriptive details in narrating the sequence of events. She also uses effective transitions, such as *when, at once*, and *at the same time* (see highlighted words and phrases), and maintains consistency in point of view (first person) and tense (past). Finally, Dillard employs vivid action verbs ("flamed," "frazzled," "curled," "crisped").

Writing Topic Sentences for Narrative Paragraphs

Although the topic sentence of a narrative paragraph may be implied, many writers—student writers as well as professional writers such as Dillard—find it helpful to state a topic sentence near the beginning of the paragraph. Remember that a good topic sentence includes both a topic (what you are writing about) and an assertion (the point you are making) (see pages 122 and 123). The following exercise gives you practice in writing topic sentences for narrative paragraphs.

EXERCISE

11.2

For each of the following topics, write a topic sentence you could develop into a narrative. (Be sure your topic sentence includes both a subject and a point, or an assertion.) Then, in the space provided, list the major events to be included in the narrative.

1. An experience that helped you to grow up (or find your identity)

Topic sentence: _____

_____

*Major events:*_____

_____

_____

_____

2. A historical event

   Topic sentence: _____

   _____

   *Major events:*_____

   _____

   _____

   _____

3. An emotional experience, such as becoming angry

   Topic sentence: _____

   _____

   *Major events:*_____

   _____

   _____

   _____

Using Transitions in Narrative Paragraphs

The following paragraph was written as a composition assignment by a first-year college student. Notice that the student, Lizzie, stated her point clearly in her topic sentence, included specific details arranged in chronological order, and used effective transitions.

Student Paragraph

"Just because I am capable of doing the same work as the men on this ranch," I thought to myself as I climbed out of bed, "does not mean I want to or should feel obligated to do so." Shivering, I shoved my legs through a pair of old Wranglers and contemplated why I was here. "Shouldn't we draw the line somewhere? I mean really, what girl should have to endure this kind of manual labor?" I shook as I brought one foot and then the other out from under my canvas bed roll, taking care to avoid agitating the tender blisters my boots had rubbed on my heels the day before. "Surely this is a man's work. I shouldn't be here. I shouldn't be doing this," I thought. Then the sound of a spoon beating on a tin can pierced the early morning silence. Frustrated, I rolled my eyes and crawled out of my tipi into the still, cool Texas morning. While walking the twenty yards from my tipi to the camp, I noticed that the bunkhouse was still. The cowboys had probably been up for some time now. The campfire was slowly burning, and our cook stood at the chuck wagon kneading a batch of fresh dough. I reached the campfire just as the morning's first pot of coffee was being pulled from the glowing coals. Feeling no obligation to wait to see if my father, the cook, or the older cowboys would like a cup, I poured one for myself and then sat on a warm log close to the fire. Tired and achy from yesterday's work, I sipped the steaming coffee and let myself drift in and out of consciousness, hypnotized by the bright colors of the cooling coals. Burning first a fire red, then an icy blue, and finally a bronzing gold, the coals would begin to die down before a rushing wind would sweep by, turning them into fire red once again. The caffeine in the coffee began to revive me, and soon I felt quite awake—awake enough to face another day of hard, unwelcome labor on the ranch.

—Lizzie Means, student

One of the major strengths of this narrative is its vivid sensory details, as shown in the description of the fire. Another strong point in the paragraph is Lizzie's effective use of transition words—highlighted for easier identification—to clarify the chronological organization. To help you in writing your own narrations, several transition words indicating time order are listed here:

after	for a minute	sometime(s)
as, just as	immediately	soon
at the same time	later	suddenly

by the time	last	then
before	meanwhile	until
eventually	next	when
finally	now	whenever
first, second, etc.	often	while

EXERCISE

11.3   Think of something that happened to you that caused you to have a strong emotional feeling, such as anger. Then, write a sentence in which you identify this event. (*Note:* You may be able to use some of your ideas from Exercise 11.2.)

1. I was angry when _____

_____

2. Now list what happened—the specific events that led to your anger.

_____

_____

_____

_____

_____

_____

_____

3. Now, think for a moment about what happened to you and why it made you angry. Was it the only time this sort of thing made you angry, or do you frequently respond with anger when something similar happens? Do you think your anger was justified, or were you later sorry that you became angry? Can you reach some conclusion, or generalization, about this incident and why it made you angry? Write your generalization here.

_____

_____

_____

4. Rewrite your conclusion and use it as the topic sentence for a paragraph in which you tell what happened when you became angry. Be sure to include effective transitions.

11.4   A fable uses a brief narrative to illustrate a moral, or lesson, about life. The moral of one of Aesop's most famous fables, "The Miller, His Son, and Their Donkey," is "The person who tries to please everyone will please no one." Early-twentieth-century painter Arthur Rackham illustrated this fable with the following series of silhouettes. Use Aesop's moral as your topic sentence and Rackham's illustrations to help you relate the story of the fable.

WRITING NARRATIVE ESSAYS

Narration is used as the primary method of development in essays as well as in paragraphs. For an essay examination in your history class, for example, you might be asked to relate the sequence of events leading up to the Revolutionary War. For a case study in your sociology class or education class, you might be asked to observe and write a narrative of the activities of an emotionally disturbed child. Or as illustrated in the following student essay, you might simply be asked to write a personal experience narrative for your composition class.

As you read the essay below, notice that Liz provides background information in her introductory paragraph. Also, try to identify the main point of the narrative and other qualities of effective narration you have already studied:

The River

1It was late spring, and my family and I were on our way to meet friends at my favorite campground in Arkansas: Camp Albert Pike. Since I was a child, I had always looked forward to these trips with great anticipation. This particular trip, however, would teach me something important about life.

2By the time we reached the campgrounds, it was just turning dark. Our friends had already spent the day on the river and were just about to eat supper. My father and I listened to the stories of an exciting day that the adventurous part of our group had spent on the river. We then planned to go tubing as soon as possible the next day. To our dismay, however, we awoke the next morning to the sudden and spontaneous flashes of lightning. This light was the only tear in the thick blankets of rain that covered the morning sky. The loud booming of thunder crashed in my ears like a band of cymbals. We would have to wait patiently before we would be able to go tubing.

3I spent most of the day in that old familiar cabin. The pot-bellied stove in the corner, the soft warm bed, and the ceiling fan that made a slight tink-tink-tink sound when it ran all gave me such a comforting glow inside. A friend finally mentioned that he thought the rain had died down enough that he could take us down the river, where the group had gone only the day before. Looking out the window at the strength of the river and the still threatening skies, I had very strong doubts as to whether I really wanted to take part in the "fun."

4My father must have read my mind, because just as I was about to try and get out of this, he turned to me and said, "Don't even think of trying to back out, young lady; you got us into this, and we've come too far to back out now." At this time, all the others turned to me and began giving me their reassurances as to the condition of the river and my ability to tame it.

5We drove up the river until we came to the spot where we were to put the tubes into the water. All of a sudden, the sky began to fall down on us. The rain felt like bricks, and we found ourselves in the midst of a terrible storm. Despite this and the extreme cold temperature of the river, our friends decided to go ahead and tube back to the cabin and safety. The whole thought of this was terribly frightening, but instead of taking the most logical route back, I allowed our friends (who, I might add, were mostly in their 50s and should have known better) to persuade me to follow them down the river.

6To fully understand what I was about to do, it is important to remember that at the river's calmest state, there are huge boulders scattered throughout, averaging about four feet tall and approximately five feet wide. These rocks were almost fully covered by raging water from the earlier rain. As I went over the first rapid, I felt my heart pounding harder than ever before, and I was gasping for breath. It was then that I fully realized my foolishness. The next few rapids went by fine, but as I approached one farther down the river, I noticed that there was quite a bit of bare rock showing above the water. For an instant, I thought that I had fully cleared the rapid safely, until I felt the tube begin to slip out from under me. Somehow, the tube had gotten hung on the rock, and I had been thrown into the water, helpless.

7From this point on, my legs often got caught in the rocks so that at one time I was stuck with water rushing over my head. I tried to remain calm as I attempted to reach the side of the river. I reached for tree limbs above my head, only to have them break off in my hands. I looked farther ahead and saw a huge rock coming up to my right. I realized that if I could hang on to that, I could probably get over to the side, and that's just what I did. After I realized I was safe, I turned around to see just exactly how far I had been dragged. My heart sank to my stomach. The rushing water overpowered the boulders, and at that moment I felt that I was extremely lucky not to have been seriously injured. Despite bruised legs and some cuts here and there, I had come out of it fairly unscathed (only a few scars remain). Later, we found out that at the time this event was happening, a tornado was tearing down everything in its path less than a mile away.

8Even though I cannot look back on this experience as a pleasant one, it taught me many things. I learned that I should listen to what my instincts and common sense tell me, for they are usually right. I also learned that I have the ability to keep my head in very stressful and frightening situations. But most important, I learned that at any time our lives can be taken from us. This experience has shown me just how precious life can be.

—Liz Doughty, student

EXERCISE

11.5

1. What is the main point, or thesis, of this narrative essay? (*Hint:* Read the introduction and conclusion carefully.)

_____

_____

_____

2. What are the major events in the narrative? Write these events in the space provided. (*Hint:* Look for a major event in each paragraph of the body of the essay.)

Paragraph 2: _____

Paragraph 3: _____

Paragraph 4: _____

Paragraph 5: _____

Paragraph 6: _____

Paragraph 7: _____

3. What is the climax, or high point, of the story?

   _____

   _____

4. Circle ten transition words or phrases that indicate time order in the essay.

5. What is the effect of the dialogue in paragraph 4?

   _____

   _____

6. What are three of the most effective sensory details in the essay?

   _____

   _____

   _____

7. What point of view (first person or third person) and tense (present or past) does Liz use?

   _____

CHAPTER REVIEW

- A narrative is a story, a retelling of a sequence of events or of "what happened."
- Effective narration has a clear point, which may be implied or stated in a topic sentence or thesis sentence.
- Good narration is usually organized in chronological (time) order and includes clear transitions.
- Good narration includes specific, relevant details and may include dialogue.
- In narration, point of view and tense should be consistent.

WRITING ASSIGNMENT

Write a narrative essay based on one of the topics from Exercise 11.2, or revise the paragraph you wrote for Exercise 11.3 by expanding it into an essay, adding additional details and, if relevant, dialogue. As you write your essay, keep in mind the qualities of effective narration listed in the Chapter Review.

PARTICIPATING IN THE ACADEMIC COMMUNITY

Plan a classroom presentation day in which you and your classmates read your narratives aloud to the rest of the class. After the readings are completed, vote on the essays that best fulfill each of these qualities:

- the most interesting narrative
- the narrative that makes its point most effectively
- the narrative that makes the most important point

Award first, second, and third places in each category.

CHAPTER

12

Process

A **process** is a series of actions that brings about a particular end or result. When you are writing about a process, you will be more successful if you analyze it, or divide it into its various steps or stages. Because good process writing gives a detailed description of the actions involved, this method of development has elements in common with descriptive writing. Process writing is even more closely linked to narration, however, because it is structured chronologically, or in time order.

Although process writing has elements in common with description and narration, it is nevertheless a unique kind of writing. It differs from both description and narration in that it focuses on a sequence of actions that does not occur just once but is repeatable and even somewhat predictable—such as changing a tire, baking a cake, or bathing a baby.

UNDERSTANDING PROCESS WRITING

As illustrated in the following examples, process writing is divided into two general types. The first **instructs** the reader about how to complete, or duplicate, a specific process; the second **explains** how a process is completed so the reader can understand the process itself more fully.

Instructions for Completing a Process

Freewriting is the easiest way to get words on paper and the best all-around practice in writing that I know. To do a freewriting exercise, simply force yourself to write without stopping for ten minutes. Sometimes you will produce good writing, but that's not the goal. Sometimes you will produce garbage, but that's not the goal either. You may stay on one topic, you may flip repeatedly from one to another: it doesn't matter. Sometimes you will produce a good record of your stream of consciousness, but often you can't keep up. Speed is not the goal, though sometimes the process revs you up. If you can't think of anything to write, write about how that feels or repeat over and over "I have nothing to write" or "Nonsense" or "No." If you get stuck in the middle of a sentence or thought, just repeat the last word or phrase till something comes along. The only point is to keep writing.

—Peter Elbow, *Writing with Power*

Explanation for Understanding a Process

When the grave is finished, the wasp returns to the tarantula to complete her ghastly enterprise. First she feels it all over once more with her antennae. Then her behavior becomes more aggressive. She bends her abdomen, protruding her sting, and searches for the soft membrane at the point where the spider's leg joins its body—the only spot where she can penetrate the horny skeleton. From time to time, as the exasperated spider slowly shifts ground, the wasp turns on her back and slides along with the aid of her wings, trying to get under the tarantula for a shot at the vital spot. During all this maneuvering, which can last for several minutes, the tarantula makes no move to save itself. Finally the wasp corners it against some obstruction and grasps one of its legs in her powerful jaws. Now at last the harassed spider tries a desperate but vain defense. The two contestants roll over and over on the ground. It is a terrifying sight and the outcome is always the same. The wasp finally manages to thrust her sting into the soft spot and holds it there for a few seconds while she pumps in the poison. Almost immediately the tarantula falls paralyzed on its back. Its legs stop twitching; its heart stops beating. Yet it is not dead, as is shown by the fact that if taken from the wasp it can be restored to some sensitivity by being kept in a moist chamber for several months.

—Alexander Petrunkevitch, "The Spider and the Wasp"

Qualities of Effective Process Writing

As illustrated in the paragraphs by Elbow and Petrunkevitch, good process writing has the following characteristics:

1. *A clear purpose and main idea.* The general purpose of process writing is either to give instructions that the reader can follow or to explain a process so a reader can understand it. In the first paragraph, composition specialist Peter Elbow shows that freewriting is "the easiest way to get words on paper" by giving instructions on how to freewrite. In the second paragraph, naturalist Alexander Petrunkevitch explains for his readers the

natural process in which the wasp attacks and captures a spider to provide food for her young.

2. *Inclusion of all steps, details, and definitions necessary for duplicating or understanding the process.* The process may be rather simple, as in freewriting, or quite complex, as in the wasp's paralyzing of the spider. In either case, however, good process writing includes all the essential steps of the process. Good process writing also includes all details necessary for describing those steps—but no irrelevant or distracting details. Some necessary details are those that explain reasons for certain steps in the process and explanations of options that may occur during the process. Thus, Elbow describes results that may occur in addition to just getting words down on paper, and he explains what to do if the writer "gets stuck." In addition, good process writing defines or explains the significance of any terms that may be unfamiliar or confusing to readers. For example, Petrunkevitch explains that the membrane for which the wasp searches is "the only spot where she can penetrate the horny skeleton."

3. *A chronological sequence and clear transitions.* For readers to be able to understand or reproduce a process, the description must follow a clear chronological sequence. Thus, Petrunkevitch cannot describe the wasp thrusting her sting into the soft spot of the spider before he describes her preparations for this sting. In addition, writers can help their readers to understand the processes they are describing by providing clear transitions. For example, Petrunkevitch begins his paragraph with what the wasp does *first*, proceeds to what she does *then*, and concludes with those events that occur *finally* or *at last*.

EXERCISE

12.1   The following paragraph describes how stalactites are formed. Read this paragraph and then answer the questions that follow it.

Of the various **dripstone**, or cave deposit, features found in caverns, perhaps the most familiar are stalactites. These iciclelike pendants hang from the ceiling of the cavern and form where water seeps through cracks above. When water reaches air in the cave, some of the dissolved carbon dioxide escapes from the drop and calcite, or a crystalline form of natural calcium carbonate that forms limestone, begins to precipitate. Deposition occurs as a ring around the edge of the water drop. As drop after drop follows, each leaves an infinitesimal trace of calcite behind, and a hollow limestone tube is created. Water then moves through the tube, remains suspended momentarily at the end, contributes a tiny ring of calcite, and falls to the cavern floor. The stalactite just described is appropriately called a *soda straw*. Often the hollow tube of the soda straw becomes plugged or its supply of water increases. In either case, the water is forced to flow, and hence deposit, along the outside of the tube. As deposition continues, the stalactite takes on the more common conical shape.

—Edward J. Tarbuck and Frederick K. Lutgens, *Earth Science*, 7th ed.

1. What process is described in this paragraph?

   _____

2. Does this paragraph give instructions for completing a process or explain a process so readers can understand it?

   _____

3. List the four or five major steps in this process.

   (1) _____

   (2) _____

   (3) _____

   (4) _____

   (5) _____

4. Circle the transitions in the paragraph.

5. The authors of this paragraph define three terms that might be unfamiliar to readers. Identify two of these technical terms and provide their definitions.

   Term: _____ *Definition*: _____

   _____

   Term: _____ *Definition*: _____

   _____

EXERCISE

12.2

Following are a topic sentence and a brainstorming list of steps for the process of making maple syrup. However, several of these steps are out of order. Number the steps in a logical sequence.

Topic Sentence: Since colonial days New England farmers have been making maple syrup from the sap of the sugar maple tree.

_____ When the water is gone, only pure maple syrup is left in the containers.

_____ First, they drill a two-inch hole into the trunk about three or four feet from the ground.

_____ The syrup is then strained, graded according to color, and bottled for shipment to grocery stores and supermarkets.

_____ In late winter or early spring, they begin tapping the maple trees.

_____ After the sap is collected each day, the farmers take the containers to the "sap house," where the water is boiled away into steam.

_____ They then insert a spout into the hole and attach a container to the spout to catch the sap.

WRITING PROCESS PARAGRAPHS

The subject of a process paragraph should be limited enough to allow it to be developed clearly in a single paragraph. For example, describing the complete process of redecorating a room is too broad for a paragraph. The simpler process of painting a door would be more appropriate for a paragraph.

The outline that follows lists the major steps in the process of _making a vegetable garden_:

1. Select and prepare the ground.
2. Select and buy the plants.
3. Set the plants in the ground.
4. Care for the garden as the plants grow.
5. Harvest the vegetables and enjoy eating them.

The entire process of making a garden would be appropriate for an essay. As shown in Keith's paragraph below, however, the more limited task of actually setting the plants in the ground is a better topic for a paragraph.

Writing Topic Sentences and Using Transitions in Process Paragraphs

Ideally, a process paragraph begins with a topic sentence that includes both the topic the writer wants to discuss and the assertion, or point, the writer wants to make. Thus, Keith begins his paragraph with this sentence: "Setting plants in a garden" (topic) "involves four important steps" (assertion).

Student Paragraph

Setting plants in a garden involves four important steps.

First, plan carefully where the plants will go in the garden. Be sure to keep plants of the same type in the same section of the garden so they do not block one another from the sun. For example, keep viney plants such as zucchini, squash, and cucumbers in the same area. Second, be sure to space the plants according to the instructions on the plastic stick that comes in the plant box. If you ignore this information, your plants may grow too close together and may not mature enough to produce fruit. Third, place your plants in the ground carefully. For each plant, dig a hole deep enough to hold the complete root structure. Then put the plant in the hole and cover the plant to the base of the stem, making sure all the roots are covered. Fourth, after you finish setting your plants, water your garden until it is well soaked, with some water still standing on the soil.

—Keith Casey, student

As shown by the highlighted words, Keith uses clear transitions to show the sequence of setting plants. He also divides this process into four primary steps and describes each.

EXERCISE

12.3

1. Reread Keith's paragraph and list the four steps for setting out plants:

    (1) _____

    (2) _____

    (3) _____

    (4) _____

2. Why is the first step important?

    _____

    _____

3. What may happen if a gardener ignores the second step?

    _____

    _____

As you write your own process narratives, you will find the following list of transition words helpful in indicating order and sequence:

after	for a minute, etc.	often
as, just as	immediately	sometime(s)

at the same time	later	soon
by the time	last	then
before	meanwhile	until
finally	next	when(ever)
first, second, etc.	now	while

EXERCISE

12.4   Use the following questions to help you plan a paragraph describing a simple process, such as doing a push-up, shampooing your hair, shaving, painting your fingernails, cleaning a windshield, or putting up a wallpaper border.

1. What specific process will you explain?

   _____

2. Will your purpose be to provide instructions so the reader can perform the process or to explain the process so the reader can understand how it works?

   _____

3. After considering your main point, write a topic sentence.

   _____

   _____

4. List the steps needed to complete this process.

   (1) _____

   (2) _____

   (3) _____

   (4) _____

Review these major steps to be sure you have listed them in the correct time order. If necessary, renumber the steps so they are arranged in the correct order.

Now write a paragraph based on the plan you have made; add details as necessary to develop your plan. Be sure to include effective transitions to show the relationships among the steps in your process. When you have finished your paragraph, look back at the qualities of effective process writing listed on pages 144–145. Use this list to help you evaluate and revise your paragraph.

EXERCISE

12.5   Instructions for completing a process often include visual illustrations. The illustrations that follow accompany instructions for replacing ceramic tiles in a kitchen or bathroom. Study both the introductory information and the illustrations and write a paragraph in which you give your reader instructions for replacing tiles.

YOU WILL NEED: hammer, small chisel, tile adhesive, sponge
TIME REQUIRED: 45–60 minutes to replace 1–3 tiles

Step One   Step Two

Step Three   Step Four

—Adapted from *Better Homes and Gardens*
New Complete Guide to Home Repair and Improvement, p. 41

WRITING PROCESS ESSAYS

A process essay is similar to a process paragraph in that it can either give instructions for duplicating a process or an explanation of how a process works. In an essay, however, the writer may discuss a more complex process. For example, your political science professor might assign an essay examination question asking you to explain how a bill becomes law, or your computer science instructor might ask you to write instructions for installing a program.

In the following student essay, Andy responded to an assignment from his English teacher to describe a familiar process. Notice that this essay includes the same qualities of effective process writing as the paragraphs you have studied in this chapter—a clear main idea statement (thesis), effective supporting steps and details, a logical arrangement (often including identifiable major steps) and clear transitions. Indeed, Andy explains the process of making chili so well you could actually make it yourself.

Texas Chili

[1] Some people identify Texas with cowboys, horses, oil, or even J. R. Ewing—but not me. I think of the great food of Texas, and that food is chili. A staple dish in my household, chili is a dish with a long history. From the pioneer days of the early West to today, chili remains a favorite among many in the West, but particularly in Texas. My chili recipe is based on the contributions of friends, relatives, and a hometown chili parlor. Prepared with its own special ingredients, my Texas Chili will make your guests' eyes and mouths water and leave them with a satisfied appetite.

[2] First, you will need to get the equipment and ingredients you will need to make Texas Chili. Several pieces of equipment are necessary: an electric skillet (with cover), a small wooden spatula, a can opener, a set of measuring spoons, a measuring cup, a glass plate, a microwave, 4–6 medium-sized bowls, and 4–6 spoons. A lengthy but appetizing set of ingredients is also vital to this heavenly dish: 1 pound of lean ground beef, two 16-oz. cans of Del Monte whole peeled tomatoes, 4 tablespoons of Gebhart chili powder, 1 tablespoon of garlic powder, 2 teaspoons of ground black pepper, 1 teaspoon of ground cayenne pepper, 2 teaspoons of ground cumin, 1 teaspoon of table salt, and 1/2 cup of water. Now that the equipment and ingredients are clear, let's really get started.

[3] When you have obtained all of the specified equipment and ingredients listed above, the next step is to prepare your ingredients. Measure each individual dry ingredient and pour it into a separate small bowl. Open the cans of tomatoes and leave them in their cans. Measure the water and leave it in the measuring cup until you need it. If the beef is frozen, defrost it in the microwave for approximately 8 minutes. When it is thawed, unwrap it and place it on a glass plate. Now, place all the measured ingredients, the ground beef, and the tomatoes on the counter and place the electric skillet next to them. Plug the skillet in and turn the dial to 225 degrees. You are now ready to begin the actual cooking.

[4] When the temperature light goes off the electric skillet, or when the inside of the skillet feels warm to a quick touch, it's time to start cooking the beef. Place the ground beef in the skillet and break it apart with the spatula until it covers the bottom of the skillet. Stirring with the spatula every 30 seconds, cook the ground beef approximately

6 minutes, or until each piece of beef turns gray inside and out. At the moment the ground beef reaches this stage, pour the garlic powder over the ground beef and stir with the spatula until the garlic is dissolved (approximately ten times around the skillet). When this step is completed, there will be a strong "sinus-healing" smell that will tickle the inside of your nose. The garlic makes its presence known.

⁵After the garlic powder is dissolved, add the tomatoes and remaining spices. Pour the tomatoes, including the juice, into the skillet. Using the spatula, cut up the tomatoes into small pieces and stir them around until they are evenly distributed in the skillet along with the ground beef and garlic powder. At this point, add the chili powder and cayenne pepper to the mixture and stir with the spatula to dissolve these spices. Next, pour the table salt, ground black pepper, and ground cumin into the skillet and stir until these ingredients are also dissolved in the mixture. Add the water to the skillet mixture and stir it approximately twenty times around. After these ingredients are combined, the chili will appear a dark red color and will provide a mixed aroma of sweet-smelling tomatoes and spicy hot chili powder along with its cayenne cousin. Now, raise the heat to 350 degrees by turning up the dial on the skillet.

⁶In the final stage of cooking, the chili will start to boil. This is easy to see because the chili will resemble a miniature lava pool, with its dark red mixture giving off steam by its bubbling and belching. Let the mixture boil (and belch) for 3 minutes, stirring with the spatula every 15 seconds. Then, turn the dial on the skillet to "simmer" and put the cover on top of the skillet. Let the chili simmer for 8 minutes, stirring with the spatula every minute and reapplying the cover each time. At the end of 8 minutes, turn the dial on the skillet to "off" and take the cover off the skillet. The finished product will be a thick, spicy-smelling red mixture filled with chunks of beef halfway submerged in a hot tub of spicy juices.

⁷The chili is now ready to eat! This recipe serves four Texas-sized portions or six regular portions. Ladle the chili in bowls, and then tell everyone to use a big spoon and dig in. This chili is spicy and even hot at times, but its combination of sweet and sour flavors is both unique and delicious. A bottle of Corona, twenty crackers, and a big pickle are optional.

—Andy Savage, student

EXERCISE

12.6   1. What process is described in this essay?

_____

2. What is the thesis, or main idea, of this process essay? Underline the thesis, and then rewrite it here.

_____

_____

3. What is the purpose of this essay? That is, does it give instructions for completing a process or explain a process so readers can understand it?

_____

_____

4. List the five major steps of the process described in this essay.

(1) _____

(2) _____

(3) _____

(4) _____

(5) _____

5. This essay uses transition effectively to move from one major stage to the next. Circle two or three transitions in each paragraph.

6. This essay is an excellent example of a process essay that combines description with process narration. What are some of the most effective sensory details (appealing to taste, touch, sight, smell, and hearing) in the essay?

_____

_____

What are some of the factual details?

_____

_____

CHAPTER REVIEW

- A process is a series of actions that brings about a particular end or result.
- Process writing often uses narration, description, and cause and effect; however, it is unique in that it focuses on a typical, representative, or repeatable action or process.
- Process writing may either give instructions so readers can duplicate a process or provide an explanation of a process so readers can understand how it works.

■ A good process paragraph or essay includes all of the following elements:

1. A clear main point that implies the writer's purpose
2. All essential steps and details for completing or understanding the process
3. A clear chronological sequence
4. Effective transitions
5. Definitions of unfamiliar terms

▓ WRITING ASSIGNMENT

Write a process essay on a topic involving from three to five major steps or stages. You may either give instructions for completing a specific process or explain how a particular process works. For example, you might explain how to complete a process necessary for college, home, or work, such as applying for financial aid, taking notes in class, studying for an examination, changing a tire, changing the oil in your car, doing a load of laundry, or applying for a job. Or, you might—like Andy—give directions for preparing one of your favorite foods.

Begin your essay with an introductory paragraph that explains your purpose and gives your thesis. Focus a separate paragraph on each major step, being sure to arrange these steps in chronological order and to provide transitions to help your readers move from one step to the next. Include all the relevant details necessary for your reader to follow your instructions or understand the process being explained, and explain any terms that might be unclear or confusing to your readers.

▓ PARTICIPATING IN THE ACADEMIC COMMUNITY

When you have finished your process essay, work with a partner from your class to evaluate and revise your work. Does your partner's essay exhibit all of the qualities of effective process writing listed in the Chapter Review? Is the process clear to you? Do you understand the process, or could you perform it yourself from your partner's description?

Example

Writers frequently develop their main ideas by using **examples**, or the method of exemplification. Indeed, whatever the primary method of development, a writer nearly always finds it helpful—even necessary—to use examples for support. But exemplification is used not just as a secondary means of development but also as the primary method of development in both paragraphs and essays.

Examples are frequently employed in academic writing. Your history textbook gives examples of inventions that brought about the Industrial Revolution, your sociology textbook gives examples of gender discrimination, and your biology textbook gives examples of mammals. In writing an explanation of stress for your psychology class or a personal essay on the same topic for your English composition class, you may want to give examples of the stress you have observed and experienced.

UNDERSTANDING EXAMPLES

Two major types of exemplification exist. In the first type, several brief examples are given to support the main idea (topic sentence or thesis sentence). In the second type, one extended example develops the main idea. As you read the two paragraphs that follow, notice that the first one uses several brief examples and the second one uses one extended example. The topic sentences of these paragraphs are set in bold type.

Brief Example

There is even a geography of smells. Certain places have an aroma that becomes an integral part of their profile; for me, there will always be a Baltimore smell. For a colleague, there will always be the smell of the manicured cemetery across the road from his home in Champlain, New York. Sri Lanka is known for the fragrance of palm oil, Jakarta for the pervasive aroma of cloves. The smells of cheap gasoline and inferior cigarettes will forever recall the Soviet Union. You can often tell where in the world you are simply by breathing. This is particularly true of the Third World and in any place where primary crops are processed.

—George J. Demko, *Why in the World: Adventures in Geography*

Extended Example

Bees are filled with astonishments, confounding anyone who studies them, producing volumes of anecdotes. A lady of our acquaintance visited her sister, who raised honeybees in northern California. They left their car on a side road, suited up in protective gear, and walked across the fields to have a look at the hives. For reasons unknown, the bees were in a furious mood that afternoon, attacking in platoons, settling on them from all sides. Let us walk away slowly, advised the beekeeper sister, they'll give it up sooner or later. They walked until bee-free, then circled the fields and went back to the car, and found the bees there, waiting for them.

—Lewis Thomas, "Clever Animals"

Qualities of Effective Exemplification

A paragraph or essay developed by examples should have the following characteristics:

1. *A clear purpose and main idea.* Like other types of writing, an exemplification paragraph or essay should have a clear main idea, usually stated in a topic sentence or thesis statement. In the paragraphs by Demko and Lewis, the topic sentence states the main idea of the paragraph and prepares the reader for the supporting example, or examples, to follow.

2. *One extended example or several brief examples that support the main idea.* Supporting examples, whether one fully developed example or several shorter ones, should illustrate the main idea. Each example in the paragraph from Demko's *Why in the World* clearly shows how particular smells are associated with specific places, and the extended example from Thomas's essay "Clever Animals" directly supports the main idea that bees are astonishing, "confounding anyone who studies them" and "producing volumes of anecdotes."

3. *A logical arrangement.* Examples may be arranged in various ways, such as in the order in which they occur in space or in time, in the order of increasing or decreasing importance, or in other logical orders. Demko arranges his examples from the more personal smells he and his colleague associate with particular places to smells associated with Third World countries. Lewis gives a chronological account of his acquaintance's visit to her beekeeper sister and of the events that occurred, from leaving the car on the road to the encounter at the hive and finally to the surprising return to the care. Indeed, as shown in Lewis's paragraph, a narrative or an anecdote (a brief, illustrative story) is often used as an extended example.

EXERCISE

13.1

The two paragraphs that follow are taken from a college history textbook. Read each paragraph; then answer the questions that follow it.

PARAGRAPH A

Though often thought of as outposts of rugged individualism, many early agricultural settlements depended heavily on family and kinship networks and communal cooperation. Sugar Creek on the Sangamon River in central Illinois exemplified this cooperative spirit. The white settlers who arrived in 1817 named the settlement for its sugar maples, tapped first by the Kickapoos and then by the American settlers. Although the settlement was based on private land ownership, most newcomers over the next decade were members of kin networks who assisted each other in clearing land and turning temporary dwellings into permanent cabins. Whether raising hogs or children, Sugar Creek families depended on kin and friends for support. In crises, too, they rose to the occasion. When, someone "would be sick with chills or jaundice, or something else," Sugar Creek farmer James Megredy recalled, "his neighbors would meet and take care of his harvest, get up wood, or repair his cabin, or plant his corn." Neighbors set up a "borrowing system" whereby scarce tools and labor constantly circulated through the neighborhood. Settlers who came without previous ties, if they stayed, did not long remain strangers.

—Mary Norton et al., *A People and a Nation,* 5th ed.

1. Underline the topic sentence that states the main idea of this paragraph. Then restate the main idea in your own words.

_____

_____

_____

2. Is the paragraph developed by several brief examples or one extended example?

_____

3. Write the example(s) here.

_____

_____

_____

PARAGRAPH B

   Dorothea Dix described the nether [lower] world she had uncovered in her investigation of the treatment of the insane in the previous two years. She reported appalling conditions in Massachusetts towns: men and women in cages, chained to walls, in dark dungeons, brutalized and held in solitary confinement. In a surprise visit to a Newburyport almshouse in the summer of 1842, Dix expressed her surprise at the comfortable conditions for the "one idiotic" and seven insane inhabitants. On the grounds she discovered, however, one man residing in a shed whose door opened to the local "dead room" or morgue; the man's only companions were corpses. Shocked, she heard from an attendant about another insane inmate whom no one spoke of: "a woman in a _cellar_."

—Mary Norton et al., _A People and a Nation_, 5th ed.

1. Underline the sentence that best states the main idea of this paragraph. Then restate the main idea in your own words.

_____

_____

_____

2. Is the paragraph developed by several brief examples or one extended example?

_____

3. Write the example(s) here.

_____

_____

_____

WRITING EXAMPLE PARAGRAPHS

   In writing an example paragraph, you should apply each of the three qualities of effective exemplification: (1) begin your paragraph with a topic sentence that clearly states your main idea; (2) use one extended example or several shorter ones that clearly support your main idea; and (3) arrange your examples logically.

Writing Topic Sentences and Using Transitions in Example Paragraphs

In addition to beginning an example paragraph with an effective topic sentence (see pages 35–36 and 122), you should also include clear **transitions** that reinforce your method of arrangement. The following paragraph, for instance, is organized according to order of importance. The topic sentence is in bold type, and the transition words that indicate examples or order of importance are highlighted with color bars.

Student Paragraph

A college freshman who displays good study habits will be a successful student. First, a responsible college freshman will make sure she gets to class on time every day. My roommate Pam, for instance, gets to her classes ten to fifteen minutes early. She wants to be prepared for the daily lecture or any pop quizzes. Even more important, Pam pays close attention to her teacher so she can take good study notes. She also tries to catch key words and hints that he may give during lectures that might help her with her homework or tests. Finally, and most important, a successful student like Pam always begins her assignments early and spends plenty of time on them. She sets aside certain hours to do her homework, and she disciplines herself so that she never turns in a late or a sloppy assignment. As a result of these good study habits, Pam and students like her make good grades.

—Jill Kerr, student

Jill begins her paragraph with a topic sentence stating her main point: that good study habits (topic) help a student succeed in college (assertion). She then illustrates her point by providing examples of study techniques her roommate has used to become a successful student. The organization of Jill's paragraph is also effective, moving from less important to more important examples of study habits. Finally, Jill uses effective transitions between her supporting examples. The following list shows

not only the transition words Jill uses but also other transitions you will
find helpful in writing example paragraphs and essays:

also, and	furthermore	moreover
another	in addition	next
finally	less important	one of
first, second, etc.	least important	such as
for example	more important	that is
for instance	most important	to illustrate

EXERCISE

13.2   Write a topic sentence for each of the following subjects. Then list three
examples to support this topic sentence.

1. Your favorite type of movie

    Topic sentence: _____

    _____

    Examples: a. _____

                 b. _____

                 c. _____

2. Friends (or family members) who have influenced you

    Topic sentence: _____

    _____

    Examples: a. _____

                 b. _____

                 c. _____

3. Problems on your college campus

    Topic sentence: _____

    _____

    Examples: a. _____

                 b. _____

                 c. _____

EXERCISE

13.3   Select the topic that interests you most in Exercise 13.2. Then use the topic sentence and examples you wrote for that exercise and the following questions to plan a paragraph on this topic.

1. What is the topic? _____

2. What is your topic sentence? (*Note*: You may want to revise the topic sentence you wrote for Exercise 13.2.)

_____

_____

3. Decide on the order in which you want to arrange your examples. Then rewrite these examples in the order you have chosen and add details to support each example.

Example 1: _____

Details: _____

_____

Example 2: _____

Details: _____

_____

Example 3: _____

Details: _____

_____

Use this plan to write a paragraph developed by examples. You may develop your paragraph by using three brief examples or by developing one example fully. In either case, be sure to use clear transitions. You may find especially helpful the transition words listed earlier.

EXERCISE

13.4   The following set of photographs portrays examples of common human emotions. Select three examples of emotions shown in these photographs and write a paragraph about the way these human faces reveal the emotion represented. Include in your paragraph a clear topic sentence and specific details showing how the photographs illustrate each of the three emotions you have selected.

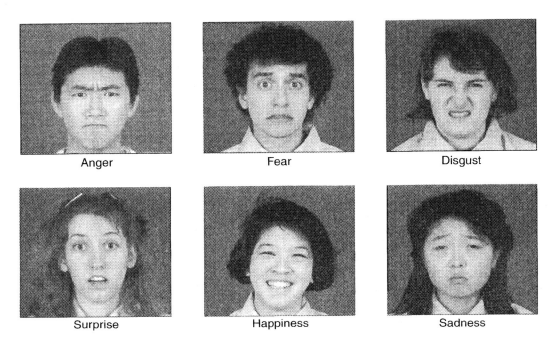

Anger   Fear   Disgust

Surprise   Happiness   Sadness

—Adapted from Lester Lefton, *Psychology*, 6th ed., p. 332
Photos: Copyright Matsumoto and Ekman 1988.

WRITING EXAMPLE ESSAYS

While examples occur to some degree in nearly all writing, they are often used as the primary method of development in essays as well as paragraphs. Like a paragraph, an essay may develop one long example or use several briefer examples. Each paragraph within an essay may develop a single example or include several examples. The possible variations are nearly endless. As you read the following student essay, notice the different ways Christie uses examples. Notice also that her essay includes a clear main idea (thesis statement), a logical arrangement of the primary supporting examples, and effective transitions.

Who's in Charge—Man or Machine?

[1] As I dialed the number to order a compact disc I'd seen advertised on television, I was hoping that I would get an answer. After all, it was fifteen minutes after 5 o'clock, and I had some questions about the free gift that I would receive for purchasing *George Strait's Greatest Hits*. "Hello," I said when I heard the click of a phone being picked up. "I am calling about the George Strait CD, and I have some questions about . . ." While I was trying to blurt out my question, I heard this

strange monotone thanking me for calling and telling me what a great deal this offer was. The voice was slow and had an eerie similarity to Darth Vader's voice from *Star Wars*. The voice continued to brag about the George Strait CD but with about the same enthusiasm I'd have if I were eating oatmeal in a prison. "Dang computers!" I screamed as I slammed down the phone. I'm not much on ordering over the phone, but when I do, I at least want to talk to a real person since I'm sending in real money.

[2]This instance with telephone ordering is just one of many negative experiences I have had with computers. In my opinion, the world is becoming so computerized that there is real danger of the human element being lost. Many businesses, such as colleges, banks, and car manufacturers, are relying more and more on computers rather than on people.

[3]First, computer error occurs frequently on college campuses. For example, when I was a senior in high school, I was also enrolled in History 121 at East Texas State University. After I finished the semester, I couldn't wait to get my grade. I knew I had a B for sure, and I thought I had a chance for an A. I was horrified, however, when my grade report said that I had made a D. That couldn't be right, I thought. The lowest grade I'd made all semester was a 79 on the first and hardest test we had had. My other grades were A's, and I thought I had done well on the final. I called my instructor to check on the grade and try to get it changed. He said I had made a B and that he was sure he had turned in a B. The secretary or the computer had made a mistake. I'm sure that some person had entered the grade wrong, but with the over-reliance on computers, no one wanted to take the responsibility for the error.

[4]Even more frightening is the fact that banks have become almost completely computerized. While this computerization has some advantages for bankers and their customers, my family recently had an experience that shows some of the problems that can be caused by computers in banks. My grandmother has had a life insurance premium automatically deducted from her account each month for several years. After she died last year, we told the bank so there would be no more automatic withdrawals. The lady at the bank said there would be no charge to stop payment. The computer, however, automatically made a $15.00 stop check charge. The account was low since no new deposits had been made since my grandmother's death, so the $15.00 deduction made the account $.88 overdrawn, which caused the computer to go crazy and charge $42.00 in overdraft and nonsufficient fund penalties. The problem was quickly remedied, however, when we talked to a real person at the bank, and all charges were refunded.

[5]Finally, and most disturbing of all, manufacturers of various products are also relying more and more on computers not only to run

their businesses but also to produce their products. I hear on television every day that more and more people are laid off from factories because of new engineering and computerized machines doing the work of many people. The factories and manufacturing companies would rather pay for an expensive computerized system than keep human workers to do the same job and provide them benefits and insurance. Car manufacturers are particularly guilty of this practice. For example, the plant for the Saturn car uses many computer robots, and the plant that makes the Ranger pickups is almost completely run by computers. I can see how a company may want to save money in the long run, but this isn't just cutting costs. These are men's and women's lives.

⁶I do believe that the world is becoming too computerized and that the human element is being lost. Many people don't even talk to other people over the telephone anymore. They talk through the Internet, by e-mail, and over fax machines. We are taking computers to the extreme when they start replacing people.

—Christie Welch, student

This essay is a variation of the five-paragraph pattern you studied in Chapter 6. The first paragraph provides an extended example that captures the interest of the reader and introduces the subject of the essay: the relationship of human beings to computers. The second paragraph, like many introductory paragraphs, places this example in context and states the thesis of the essay, even listing in a logical order the three main examples to be developed (i.e., reliance of colleges, banks, and manufacturers on computers more than human beings). Moreover, each paragraph in the body of the essay begins with a transition that not only connects each main point to the thesis but also shows the relationships among the main points in the essay.

EXERCISE

13.5   Answer the following questions about the essay you have just read, referring to the essay as necessary.

1. Why does Christie use an example in her introduction?

    _____

    _____

2. Underline the thesis statement; then rewrite it here.

    _____

    _____

3. Reread the body paragraphs and indicate whether each is based on several brief examples or on one extended example.

Paragraph 3: _____

Paragraph 4: _____

Paragraph 5: _____

4. List the specific example(s) you believe are most effective in the essay.

_____

_____

_____

_____

5. What method of arrangement does Christie use for the three main points of the essay (time order, space order, order of importance)?

_____

6. What transitions between paragraphs provide clues to the primary method of arrangement in the essay?

_____

_____

7. Individual paragraphs in an essay may be arranged according to a different method of arrangement than that used for the essay itself. What method of arrangement is used in paragraphs 1, 3, and 4?

_____

CHAPTER REVIEW

- An exemplification paragraph or essay should have a clear purpose.
- A paragraph or essay developed by example should have a clear main idea (topic sentence or thesis statement).
- Each example in a paragraph or essay should clearly support the main idea.
- The main idea of an exemplification paragraph or essay may be supported by several brief examples or one extended example.
- The examples should be logically arranged and clearly connected with effective transitions.

WRITING ASSIGNMENT

Expand the paragraph you wrote for Exercise 13.3 into an essay. You may use each of the examples from your original paragraph as the basis for one of your body paragraphs, adding details to each example, or you may expand one of your examples into an essay. Whatever your method of expansion, be sure to arrange your example(s) in a logical order and use appropriate transitions.

PARTICIPATING IN THE ACADEMIC COMMUNITY

When you have completed a draft of your essay, meet with a group of your classmates to evaluate one another's essays. Read each essay aloud. After each essay is read, use the guidelines in the Chapter Review to identify the strong points and weak points of each essay and to make suggestions for improvement. If possible, suggest ways to improve the development of the supporting example(s).

Comparison and Contrast

In its broadest definition, **comparison** involves showing both similarities and differences between people, places, objects, or actions. Thus, you may compare two computers, cars, or houses—looking at differences as well as similarities—before deciding which to buy. In academic writing assignments, however, instructors often distinguish between the processes of comparing and contrasting, using *comparing* to mean "showing similarities" and *contrasting* to mean "showing differences." Thus, your biology professor might ask you to compare two mammals to identify the similarities that place them in the category of mammal, or your history professor might ask you to contrast two presidents. As these examples suggest, **comparison/contrast** is an extremely useful method of development in academic writing.

UNDERSTANDING COMPARISON AND CONTRAST

Both paragraphs and essays can be developed by comparison, contrast, or a combination of the two. This chapter will help you recognize effective comparison and contrast writing in your reading, understand how comparison and contrast are organized, and learn how to use this method in your own writing.

The first of the following paragraphs emphasizes similarities, whereas the second focuses on differences.

Paragraph A: Comparing

Barbiturates and tranquilizers are both sedatives. They relax or calm people; and when taken in higher doses, they often induce sleep. *Barbiturates* decrease the excitability of neurons throughout the nervous system. They calm the individual by depressing the central nervous system. The use of barbiturates as sedatives, however, has diminished; they have largely been replaced by another class of drugs— tranquilizers. *Tranquilizers* are a group of drugs that also sedate and calm people. With a somewhat lower potential for abuse, they are sometimes called minor tranquilizers. Valium and Librium are two of the most widely used tranquilizers prescribed by physicians for relief of mild stress. Although tranquilizers are less dangerous than barbiturates, they have also been widely abused by all segments of society because of their availability.

—Adapted from Lester A. Lefton, *Psychology*, 6th ed.

Paragraph B: Contrasting

Moving from Detroit, Michigan, to Hobbs, New Mexico, was not easy because I had to get used to the differences in climate, size, and attitudes toward time. Even though the weather in Michigan is not ideal, it was what I had known all my life, and I was used to the dampness and the cold in winter and the dampness and the heat in the summer. Detroit is a large, industrial city that never sleeps. In this busy city, time is a valuable commodity, seldom wasted. Thus, everyone in Detroit is on the move—in a hurry, rushed, afraid of being late. Hobbs differs from Detroit in each of these three areas. In the dry climate of Hobbs, any moisture evaporates immediately, and it is sometimes difficult to tell winter from summer because the two seasons are so much alike. Unlike its large city neighbor to the north, the small town of Hobbs never wakes up. It is so quiet that I felt at first as though I were living on the fringe of civilization. But the biggest difference between the two places was the attitude toward time. I don't mean just the fact that Detroit is on Eastern Standard Time and Hobbs is on Mountain Standard Time. I mean fast versus slow. In contrast to Detroit, no one in Hobbs really cares what time it is. No one seems concerned about getting places on time, much less early. But now that I have lived in Hobbs for a year, I find that I too am slowing down. Moreover, I have found that I haven't left civilization. I've just moved to a different type— a drier, smaller, quieter, slower one.

Qualities of Effective Comparison and Contrast

Effective comparison/contrast paragraphs and essays have several qualities in common:

1. *A clear sense of purpose.* Like other types of writing, comparison and contrast writing should have a clear sense of purpose. Most of the comparison and contrast writing you will write or read in your college classes will be either informative or persuasive, but you may occasionally encounter comparison and contrast writing that is intended to entertain. Lefton's paragraph about sedatives is not only informative but also mildly persuasive, concluding that barbiturates are more dangerous than tranquilizers. The paragraph about Detroit and Hobbs uses a rather humorous style to explain the differences to which the writer had to adjust.

2. *Two related and limited subjects.* Comparison and contrast writing presents two subjects that can be effectively compared or contrasted. These subjects should also be narrow enough to be developed into a paragraph or essay that is supported with specific details and examples. For instance, because barbiturates and tranquilizers are both sedatives, they clearly have a basis for comparison. Even though Detroit and Hobbs have many differences, these subjects also have a clear basis for contrast because they are both cities. The two subjects in both of these paragraphs are clearly limited and defined.

3. *A stated or clearly implied main idea.* Effective comparison and contrast writing has a clear main idea (usually stated in a topic sentence or thesis statement) that specifies the subjects and their relationship. The main idea usually indicates whether these subjects are primarily similar or different. The topic sentence of the first example paragraph about barbiturates and tranquilizers points out similarities. The topic sentence of the second paragraph explains that life in Hobbs, New Mexico, is quite different from life in Detroit, Michigan.

4. *Effective supporting points and details for both sides of the comparison/contrast.* The number of points to be compared or contrasted and the details and examples used to support each subject should be fairly balanced. Lefton provides effects and uses (and abuses) of both barbiturates and tranquilizers, and the writer of the paragraph about Detroit and Hobbs gives details about living in both cities. Moreover, both writers provide specific examples and details to support their points. Lefton lists Valium and Librium as examples of tranquilizers, and the writer of the paragraph contrasting Detroit and Hobbs gives specific details about the climate, size, and attitudes toward time in both cities. For example, Detroit is described as primarily cold and damp, whereas Hobbs is hot and dry.

5. *A logical organizational structure.* As shown in the next section, a balanced presentation of the two subjects of a comparison or contrast and of the major points and details supporting each subject may be achieved by either of two organizational structures.

Arrangement in Comparison and Contrast Writing

The most common patterns of arrangement for supporting points and details in a comparison/contrast paragraph or essay are the **subject-by-subject** (or block) **method** and the **point-by-point** (or alternating) **method.**

Subject-by-Subject (Block) Method

In the subject-by-subject method used in the sample paragraphs on pages 167–168, the writer presents first one subject and then the other of the comparison or contrast. The following outline illustrates how the details contrasting Detroit and Hobbs are arranged in this subject-by-subject method:

Topic sentence: Moving from Detroit, Michigan, to Hobbs, New Mexico, was not easy because I had to get used to the differences in climate, size, and attitudes toward time.

Subject A: Detroit, Michigan
   Point 1: Climate
   Point 2: Size
   Point 3: Attitudes toward time

Subject B: Hobbs, New Mexico
   Point 1: Climate
   Point 2: Size
   Point 3: Attitudes toward time

Point-by-Point (Alternating) Method

In the point-by-point method, the writer discusses the first point for both subjects of the comparison or contrast, then the second point for both subjects, and so on. Using the point-by-point method, the same contrasting information about Detroit and Hobbs would be organized like this:

Topic sentence: Moving from Detroit, Michigan, to Hobbs, New Mexico, was not easy because I had to get used to the differences in climate, size, and attitudes toward time.

Point 1: Climate
   Subject A: Detroit
   Subject B: Hobbs

Point 2: Size
   Subject A: Detroit
   Subject B: Hobbs

Point 3: Attitudes toward time
   Subject A: Detroit
   Subject B: Hobbs

Although the subject-by-subject structure is sometimes easier for writers to use, the point-by-point pattern may be more effective in longer paragraphs and essays because it is often easier to read.

EXERCISE

14.1   Read the following paragraphs and answer the questions that follow about each paragraph's meaning and structure.

PARAGRAPH A

Some people say the business about the jolly fat person is a myth, that all of us chubbies are neurotic, sick, sad people. I disagree. Fat people may not be chortling all day long, but they're a hell of a lot *nicer* than the wizened and shriveled. Thin people turn surly, mean, and hard at a young age because they never learn the value of a hot-fudge sundae for easing tension. Thin people don't like gooey soft things because they themselves are neither gooey nor soft. They are crunchy and dull, like carrots. They go straight to the heart of the matter while fat people let things stay all blurry and hazy and vague, the way things actually are. Thin people want to face the truth. Fat people know there is no truth. One of my thin friends is always staring at complex, unsolvable problems and saying, "The key thing is. . . ." Fat people never say that. They know there isn't any such thing as the key thing about anything.

—Suzanne Britt, "That Lean and Hungry Look"

1. Underline the sentence that best states Britt's main idea. Does this main point emphasize similarities or differences?

_____

2. Does Britt organize her paragraph according to the subject-by-subject (block) method or the point-by-point (alternating) method?

_____

3. Complete the following outline of the paragraph.

	Thin people	**Fat people**
Point 1: General attitude	_____	_____
Point 2: Food preference	_____	_____
Point 3: Amount of directness	_____	_____
Point 4: View of truth	_____	_____

PARAGRAPH B

For me there were none of the gradations between public and private so normal to a maturing child. Outside the house was public society; inside the house was private. Just opening or closing the screen door behind me was an important experience. I'd rarely leave home all alone or without reluctance. Walking down the sidewalk, under the canopy of tall trees, I'd warily notice the—suddenly—silent neighborhood kids who stood warily watching me. Nervously, I'd arrive at the grocery store to hear there the sounds of the *gringo*—foreign to me—reminding me that in this world so big, I was a foreigner. But then I'd return. Walking back toward our house, climbing the steps from the sidewalk, when the front door was open in summer, I'd hear voices beyond the screen door talking in Spanish. For a second or two, I'd stay, linger there, listening. Smiling, I'd hear my mother call out, saying in Spanish . . . : 'Is that you, Richard?' All the while her sounds would assure me: *You are home now; come closer; inside. With us.*

—Richard Rodriguez, *Hunger of Memory*

1. Underline the sentence that best states Rodriguez's main idea. Does this main point emphasize similarities or differences?

   _____

2. Does Rodriguez organize his paragraph according to the subject-by-subject (block) method or the point-by-point (alternating) method?

   _____

3. Complete the following outline of the paragraph.

	Public	**Private**
Point 1: Location	_____	_____
Point 2: Attitude	_____	_____
Point 3: Language	_____	_____

EXERCISE

14.2 Narrow each of the following topics to two subjects that can be effectively compared; then list three points of comparison, or similarities, for each subject.

▶ **Example:** Two courses

Limited subjects: A. <u>freshman composition</u>   B. <u>freshman history</u>

Point 1:   listening (in student   listening (to lecture)
                    groups)

Point 2:	writing (essays)	writing (essay examinations)
Point 3:	reading (student essays)	reading (professional essays)

1. Two people (parents, friends, politicians, etc.)

Limited subjects: A. _____ B. _____

  Point 1:   _____   _____

  Point 2:   _____   _____

  Point 3:   _____   _____

2. Two places (rooms, buildings, vacation spots, etc.)

Limited subjects: A. _____ B. _____

  Point 1:   _____   _____

  Point 2:   _____   _____

  Point 3:   _____   _____

3. Two things (cars, computers, animals, plants, etc.)

Limited subjects: A. _____ B. _____

  Point 1:   _____   _____

  Point 2:   _____   _____

  Point 3:   _____   _____

EXERCISE

14.3 In the space below, contrast the same narrowed subjects that you compared in Exercise 14.2. List three points of contrast, or difference, for each subject.

▶ **Example:** Two courses

Limited subjects:	A. <u>freshman composition</u>	B. <u>freshman history</u>
Point 1:	student centered	teacher centered
Point 2:	emphasizes discussion	emphasizes lecture
Point 3:	focuses on current issues	focuses on past events

1. Two people (parents, friends, politicians, etc.)

Limited subjects: A. _____ B. _____

  Point 1:   _____   _____

Point 2:   _____   _____
Point 3:   _____   _____

2. Two places (rooms, buildings, vacation spots, etc.)

   Limited subjects: A. _____ B. _____

   Point 1:   _____   _____
   Point 2:   _____   _____
   Point 3:   _____   _____

3. Two things (cars, computers, animals, plants, etc.)

   Limited subjects: A. _____ B. _____

   Point 1:   _____   _____
   Point 2:   _____   _____
   Point 3:   _____   _____

WRITING COMPARISON/CONTRAST PARAGRAPHS

You will be able to write better comparison and contrast paragraphs if you pay particular attention to three important elements of each paragraph: (1) the topic sentence, (2) the organization, and (3) the transitions.

Writing Topic Sentences in Comparison/Contrast Paragraphs

The topic sentence of a comparison/contrast paragraph usually identifies the two subjects and indicates whether the paragraph will focus on their similarities, differences, or both. For example, the following topic sentences provide clear main ideas for paragraphs comparing or contrasting your composition and history classes:

COMPARISON: My composition and history classes have several similarities.

CONTRAST: My composition and history classes are different in several ways.

Notice that the assertion, or the main point, in these topic sentences is based on whether the two subjects are similar or different. The major sup-

porting points in paragraphs developing these topic sentences would focus
on these similarities or differences.

14.4   In Exercises 14.2 and 14.3, you narrowed three broad topics and listed both
similarities and differences for each of these topics. For each topic, write
below one topic sentence that compares your two subjects and another topic
sentence that contrasts them.

1. People

   Narrowed topic: _____ and _____

   Comparison topic sentence: _____

   _____

   Contrast topic sentence: _____

   _____

2. Places

   Narrowed topic: _____ and _____

   Comparison topic sentence: _____

   _____

   Contrast topic sentence: _____

   _____

3. Things

   Narrowed topic: _____ and _____

   Comparison topic sentence: _____

   _____

   Contrast topic sentence: _____

   _____

Using Transitions in Comparison/Contrast
Paragraphs

Because of the complex relationships among subjects in a comparison/con-
trast paragraph, you need to be especially careful to use appropriate transitions to guide your readers. Although both methods of organizing a
comparison or contrast paragraph require effective transitions, you will

need to use more transition words with the point-by-point method than with the subject-by-subject method. For example, notice the transition words that Janna uses in the following paragraph contrasting point by point how a wealthy man and a poor man are treated by the legal system:

Student Paragraph

In the legal system, people are often judged by their financial status. In two parallel cases, a wealthy man and an indigent man were charged with the same type of crime: robbery. The wealthy man had the financial resources to hire three attorneys and an investigator to work on his case. However, the indigent man had only one court attorney appointed to his case and did not have the money to hire a private investigator. The wealthy man had actually committed the crime of breaking into a store and stealing money from it, but his case was dismissed because he had money to buy his freedom. The poor man, on the other hand, was convicted of robbery and spent three years in jail even though he was innocent. As these instances show, the legal system in the United States is often unfairly biased to the "haves" over the "have-nots."

—Janna Hammons, student

In this paragraph, Janna uses the point-by-point method of organization. She discusses first the financial resources of both the wealthy man and the poor man and then the legal results for both men. Notice that for each point, she uses a transition to move from one subject to the other. Thus, she uses the transition word *however* to show the contrast between the financial resources of both men and the transition phrase *on the other hand* to show the contrast between the results of the cases for the two men. If she had used the subject-by-subject method, she would have needed to discuss both the financial resources and legal results for first one man and then the other.

The following chart lists several helpful transition words:

Comparison			
and	both	in the same way	neither
also	both . . . and	just as . . . so	similarly
as	either	like	too
as well as	in addition	likewise	

Contrast			
but	in contrast	conversely	unlike
although, [even] though	on the contrary	nevertheless	whereas
however	on the other hand	or, nor	while, yet

EXERCISE

14.5 Rewrite Janna's paragraph using the subject-by-subject method of organization. Be sure to provide appropriate transitions.

EXERCISE

14.6 Select one of the narrowed topic sentences you wrote in Exercise 14.4 and write a paragraph comparing or contrasting two people, places, or things. Determine the organizational arrangement (subject by subject or point by point) you want to use and the major supporting points you want to include. (Refer to Exercises 14.2 and 14.3.) Use the planning space below:

Relationship (comparison or contrast): _____

Topic sentence: _____

_____

Arrangement: _____

SUBJECT-BY-SUBJECT PLAN

Subjects: _____

Side A: _____

    Point 1: _____

    Point 2: _____

    Point 3: _____

Side B: _____

    Point 1: _____

    Point 2: _____

    Point 3: _____

POINT-BY-POINT PLAN

Subjects: _____

Point 1: _____

    Side A: _____

Side B: _____

Point 2: _____

  Side A: _____

  Side B: _____

Point 3: _____

  Side A: _____

  Side B: _____

WRITING COMPARISON/CONTRAST ESSAYS

In addition to writing comparison and contrast paragraphs that can stand alone or function as part of a longer composition, you will occasionally need to write an entire essay that is developed primarily by comparison and contrast. For example, your history professor might ask you to compare Presidents Franklin Roosevelt and Woodrow Wilson, your psychology professor might ask you to compare long-term and short-term memory, or your literature professor might ask you to compare two poems or characters.

Expanding the sample paragraph on p. 168, the following student essay focuses on the relationship between Detroit and Hobbs. As you read this essay, look for (and underline) the thesis sentence that states the writer's main point, and pay particular attention to the essay's organization and use of transition.

Moving from Detroit to Hobbs

[1] I was born in Detroit, Michigan, and had lived there all of my life until I married and moved with my husband to Hobbs, New Mexico. The morning my parents took us to the airport, they cried as if I were leaving the country and moving to a foreign land. Although I felt some apprehension, I thought that surely there could not be much difference between one state or city and another. I felt confident that my life would be much the same. It did not take me long to discover, however, that moving from Detroit to Hobbs was not easy because I had to get used to differences in climate, size, and attitudes toward time.

[2] First, I had to get used to the change in climate. Even though the weather in Michigan is not ideal, it was what I had known all my life. I was used to the dampness and the cold in the winter and the dampness and heat in the summer. I accepted mildew and frizzy hair as facts of

life. In Hobbs, however, any moisture that accidentally occurs immediately evaporates. Even in the early morning there is no dew on the grass, and a rainfall is a major event, celebrated and talked about for days. Fog and mist are absolutely unheard of. Day after day the sun shines brightly, even relentlessly, drying out everything. In fact, it is sometimes difficult to tell winter from summer because the two seasons are so much alike.

³My next problem was adjusting to life in a small town. Detroit is a large, industrial city that never sleeps. In contrast, Hobbs never wakes up. It is so quiet and small that I felt at first as though I were living on the fringe of civilization. Instead of several major newspapers, a variety of local radio and television channels, and a choice of big-name entertainers and shows, Hobbs has one daily newspaper, a small radio station, and a few movies. By ten o'clock at night almost everyone is at home. And everyone knows everyone else. In Detroit, I could go all over the city and never see anyone I knew, but in Hobbs I rarely see anything but familiar faces. A stranger in town is the source of real excitement—a cause for speculation and curiosity. In Hobbs I don't dare go to the supermarket (there are only a few) with my hair in curlers, for I am sure to see people I know. In Detroit I could be anonymous when I chose; in Hobbs I am part of a small, even intimate, community.

⁴But the biggest problem I had was the difference in time. I don't mean just the fact that Detroit is on Eastern Standard Time and Hobbs is on Mountain Standard Time. I mean fast versus slow. Everyone in Detroit is on the move—in a hurry, rushed, afraid of being late. In Hobbs, on the other hand, no one really cares what time it is. No one seems concerned about getting places, on time, much less early. For example, soon after we arrived in Hobbs, we were invited to a party. Conditioned by years of living in Detroit, where everyone strives to be punctual, my husband and I arrived at the party on time. The door was opened by a surprised hostess, who, dressed in a robe, was straightening the living room and preparing some last-minute snacks for the party. She graciously invited us in and explained that the other guests would be arriving soon. ("Soon" turned out to be almost an hour later.) We sat uncomfortably in the deserted living room as the hostess finished dressing and preparing the food. When the other guests finally arrived, an hour after the appointed time, the party began, although guests continued to arrive late into the evening. I now realize that when people in Hobbs say a party begins at a certain time, they don't really mean at that exact time. The attitude toward time is so relaxed that it is almost impossible to be *late*. People just aren't terribly concerned with being punctual.

⁵I have now lived in Hobbs for a year, and I find that I am slowing down, too. I don't drive as fast as I did; I don't worry if I am a few

minutes late; and I certainly don't arrive at parties on time. I am also getting used to the climate. On a recent trip back to Detroit I was terribly conscious of the humidity and nearly froze because the weather was so cold and damp. Moreover, I have discovered that moving to Hobbs has not meant that I left civilization. I've just moved to a different type of civilization—one that is drier, smaller, quieter, and slower.

—Jeanette Gregory, student

EXERCISE

14.7

1. Are the subjects of this essay (Hobbs and Detroit) compared or contrasted? That is, does the writer show similarities or differences?

_____

2. What is the thesis sentence of this essay?

_____

_____

3. What organizational pattern does this essay follow? That is, is it organized by the subject-by-subject method, discussing first one subject and then the other, or by the point-by-point method, alternating information about Hobbs and Detroit as each point is discussed?

_____

4. Is each of the main points in the body of the essay introduced in a topic sentence? If so, underline these topic sentences. Then write the writer's main points about Hobbs and Detroit here.

_____

_____

_____

5. Circle transition words that show the relationship between these two cities.

6. What conclusion does the writer draw about Detroit and Hobbs?

_____

_____

▦ CHAPTER REVIEW

- ■ To compare is to show similarities between two subjects; to contrast is to show differences between two subjects.

- Comparison and contrast writing, like any other type of writing, should have a clear purpose.

- Two limited and related subjects are essential to effective comparison and contrast.

- The main point of a comparison/contrast paragraph or essay should be expressed in a topic sentence or a thesis statement that identifies the subjects and indicates whether they will be compared or contrasted.

- Comparison and contrast paragraphs and essays should have clearly identified and balanced supporting points.

- Comparison and contrast paragraphs and essays should be structured according to the subject-by-subject or the point-by-point pattern and should include effective transitions.

- Each side of a comparison or contrast paragraph or essay should be supported with specific details and examples.

WRITING ASSIGNMENT

Choose one of the following options and write an essay comparing or contrasting two people, places, actions, or objects.

OPTION A: Develop the paragraph you wrote in Exercise 14.6 into a comparison and/or contrast essay. (Or, if you prefer develop another one of your topics from Exercise 14.2, 14.3, or 14.4 into an essay.)

OPTION B: Select two comparable subjects and compare and/or contrast these subjects in an essay. For example, you might compare or contrast two presidents, two ancient cities, two weather events, two computers, or two college classes. Be sure, however, that you limit your subjects, or choose subjects narrow enough that you can develop them fully in an essay.

Before you write your essay, decide on the arrangement that you want to use and list your major points and examples.

PARTICIPATING IN THE ACADEMIC COMMUNITY

When you have finished your draft, meet with a small group of your classmates for a peer evaluation of your essays. If you have access to computers during class, send your essay file to the other members of your group; if you do not have access to computers, make multiple copies of your essay so each group member will have a copy. Then adapt the questions from Exercise 14.7 to guide your discussion of one another's essays.

CHAPTER

15

Classification

When you organize information by placing items into groups with other items that have similar characteristics, you are classifying. **Classification** is used not only by writers but also by other people who want to organize information clearly. Scientists classify plants, sociologists classify families, and political scientists classify types of government. Students classify their professors according to the subjects they teach (history professors, English professors, psychology professors), and at the end of each semester, teachers often classify students according to their performance in class (A students, B students, and so on).

UNDERSTANDING CLASSIFICATION

Because classifying means organizing items into categories, only plural subjects can be classified. For example, you can classify students, colleges, computers, pizzas, cars, and televisions, but you can't classify a single student, college, computer, pizza, car, or television show. The following paragraph is an example of classification:

> **There are three kinds of book owners**. The first has all the standard sets and best-sellers—unread, untouched. (This deluded individual owns woodpulp and ink, not books.) The second has a great many books—a few of them read through, most of them dipped into, but all of them as clean and shiny as the day they were bought. (This person would probably like to make books his own, but is restrained by a false respect for their physical appearance.) The third has a few books or many—every one of them dog-eared and dilapidated, shaken and loosened by continual use, marked and scribbled in from front to back. (This man owns books.)
>
> —Mortimer Adler, "How to Mark a Book"

Qualities of Effective Classification

The following qualities are present in effective classification paragraphs and essays:

1. *A clear purpose.* Although classification writing can persuade or entertain, most academic classification is informative in purpose. For example, the sample paragraph informs readers that three kinds of book owners exist, then identifies and discusses them.

2. *A single basis, or criterion, of classification.* To develop a system of classification, the writer must first determine a basis for classifying—that is, a *criterion* on which to base the classification. Although Adler could have classified book owners according to the money they spend on their books or the types of books they own (literary, scientific, religious), he chose to focus on the criterion of how much (and how well) book owners use their books. Only one basis of classification should be used at a time.

3. *Completeness of classification.* The important point in classification is not *how many* categories you have but *how clearly and fully* the items being classified fit into the chosen categories. Ideally, each item within a subject area should fit into one—and only one—category. Thus, Adler believes all book owners fit into one of the three categories he describes: those who possess books but do not read them, those who respect the physical appearance of the books more than the ideas inside them, and those who have truly come to "own" their books through continual use.

4. *A clear main idea.* Good classification writing includes a stated or implied main idea that provides the subject of the paragraph or essay and may include either the basis of classification or the categories of the classification (or both). The first sentence in Adler's paragraph states his main idea, identifying the subject as "book owners" and pointing out that book owners are of "three kinds." The remainder of the paragraph implies Adler's basis of classification (how book owners use their books) and provides the three specific categories of owners: nonreading book owners, overly respectful book owners, and true book owners.

5. *Logically arranged subtopics supported with specific examples and details.* The categories of a classification paragraph or essay function as major supporting points, or subtopics. Thus, the paragraph about book owners includes the three subtopics of nonreading owners, overly respectful owners, and true owners. These subtopics are arranged logically in order of importance from the least important to the most important type. In addition, effective classification paragraphs and essays also include specific details, examples, and explanations as well as clear transitions. For example, the model paragraph provides clear descriptions and explanations of each type of book owner and clear transitions between subtopics.

EXERCISE

15.1   Each of the following groups has one item that doesn't belong. First, identify the basis of classification into which most of the items fit and write it in the space provided. Then circle the item that does not fit this classification system.

▶ **Example:** Restaurants

  a. Chinese

  b. Mexican

  ©. fast-food

  d. Italian

  Basis of classification: national, or ethnic, background

1. TV shows

  a. situation comedies

  b. dramas

  c. soap operas

  d. popular shows

  Basis of classification: _____

2. Types of government

  a. democracy

  b. American

  c. monarchy

  d. dictatorship

  Basis of classification: _____

3. Learning styles

  a. visual (sight)

  b. auditory (hearing)

  c. successful

  d. tactile (touch)

  Basis of classification: _____

EXERCISE

15.2   For each of the following subjects, determine a basis of classification; then list the categories into which the subject can be divided.

▶ **Example**   Pollution

         Basis of classification: <u>where pollution occurs</u>

         Categories: <u>air, water, land</u>

1. Jobs

     Basis of classification: _____

     Categories: _____

2. Music

     Basis of classification: _____

     Categories: _____

3. Colleges

     Basis of classification: _____

     Categories: _____

4. Movies

     Basis of classification: _____

     Categories: _____

WRITING CLASSIFICATION PARAGRAPHS

Once you understand how to classify items, you are ready to employ this method of development in your writing. Although classification is also used to develop essays, you will find it much easier to begin by writing a classification paragraph.

Writing Topic Sentences and Using Transitions in Classification Paragraphs

The point, or main idea, developed in a classification paragraph is usually stated in a topic sentence. Whether this main point—the topic and the assertion—is stated or implied, however, it should be clear to the reader. Beginning with a clearly stated point is particularly important in academic writing, as shown in the following paragraph in which Lue answers her biology teacher's question about the major classes of trees. Notice the bold-faced topic sentence.

Student Paragraph

According to what happens to their leaves in winter, most trees can be categorized into one of two types: those that

keep their leaves and those that lose them. Trees that fit into the first category, or those that keep their leaves throughout the year, are called evergreens or coniferous trees. These trees produce seeds in cones and have needle-shaped leaves. This type of trees includes pines, firs, and cedars. The second group of trees, those that lose their leaves in the winter, are called deciduous trees. They bear seeds that are encased in a fruit or berry, and their leaves are usually broad and flat. Elms, maples, and oaks, for example, are deciduous trees.

—Lue Kernes, student

In this student paragraph, the topic sentence states (1) the subject to be classified, (2) the basis of classification, and (3) the categories that result. In this topic sentence, the subject for classification is "trees," the method of classification is "what happens to their leaves in winter," and the categories are "those that keep their leaves" and "those that lose them." In addition, Lue's paragraph uses several transition words, which are highlighted to help you identify the categories of classification and the supporting examples. These transitions and other helpful words for writing classification paragraphs are listed here:

Transition Phrases	*Verbs*
the first category (class, etc.)	include(s)
the second group (kind, etc.)	fit into (are divided into, etc.)
another type (method, etc.)	can be categorized (classified,
a final category (finally)	etc.)
for example, for instance	

EXERCISE

15.3   Each item in this exercise includes (1) the subject to be classified, (2) the basis of classification, and (3) the categories. Use this information to write a topic sentence in the space provided. (Your topic sentence should include the subject, the basis of classification, and/or the categories.)

▶ **Example**

Subject: restaurants
Basis of classification: type of napkins

Categories: those that provide cloth napkins,
                       those that provide paper napkins, and
                       those that provide no napkins

Topic sentence 1: Restaurants can be classified according to the type of napkins they use. (basis of classification)

Topic sentence 2: Restaurants can be classified according to whether they have cloth napkins, paper napkins, or no napkins. (categories)

1. Subject: sports
   Basis of classification: player participation
   Categories: individual or team
   Topic sentence: _____

2. Subject: literary works
   Basis of classification: genre
   Categories: fiction, poetry, drama
   Topic sentence: _____

3. Subject: economic systems
   Basis of classification: the way wealth is divided
   Categories: capitalist, socialist, communist
   Topic sentence: _____

EXERCISE

15.4

Classify the students who attend your school according to how they dress, their study habits, or some other basis of classification. Write here both the basis for your classification and the names of your categories. Then, for each category, list appropriate subcategories or examples. (*Note*: You may have two or four categories instead of three.)

Basis of classification: _____

Category 1: _____

    a. _____

    b. _____

Category 2: _____

    a. _____

    b. _____

Category 3: _____

    a. _____

    b. _____

Write a topic sentence in which you state your subject, the basis of your classification, and the categories you have identified.

_____

_____

Now, write a paragraph in which you develop this topic sentence by briefly describing and providing examples for each of the categories of students you have identified.

WRITING CLASSIFICATION ESSAYS

Classification may be used as the primary method of development in essays as well as in paragraphs. In a classification essay, the subject to be classified as well as the basis of classification and/or the categories of the classification are usually stated in the thesis statement. A successful classification essay also includes clear transitions. The ideas in a classification essay are more fully developed than those in a classification paragraph. Indeed, classification essays—as well as classification paragraphs—often employ other methods of development, such as the use of example, comparison/contrast, and definition.

As you read the following student classification essay on types of shoppers, look for the various qualities of effective classification:

Types of Shoppers

¹Shoppers come in all shapes, sizes, and personalities. Having worked for nine years at a fast-food restaurant and for the past two years as a clerk and cashier in the dry goods department at Wal-Mart, I have had an opportunity to observe customers carefully. Based on their attitudes and actions, today's shoppers can be categorized into easy-to-please, hard-to-please, or impossible-to-please customers.

²The first category is made up of congenial, easy-to-please individuals. These shoppers are friendly and appreciative no matter what the circumstance. These shoppers do not get upset if they have to wait for service or if it takes the clerk a while to find particular items. Recently the Wal-Mart store where I work was out of some material that

an elderly woman needed, but she simply asked me when the next shipment would be in, smiled, and went on her way.

[3]The second group is that of hard-to-please shoppers. These individuals complain not only about the products but also about the service. These customers often cannot find what they want, and they usually think the service is too slow. Yesterday, for instance, a younger woman had me take down several bolts of material for her to examine before she finally found something that "would do." Then she complained that I was too slow in cutting the material she wanted.

[4]Finally, the third category is composed of rude, impossible-to-please shoppers. Like the hard-to-please shoppers, these individuals find fault with everything from product to service to price. But people in this category are much ruder in their remarks and actions. For example, this morning when I started ringing up the items a woman had laid on my counter, she rudely barked, "Don't ring up any more until I am finished," and this afternoon a man threw his items down on the counter and stalked out when I asked to see an identification card to approve his check.

[5]If it takes all kinds of people to make up the world, those different kinds of people also shop at Wal-Mart! A clerk or cashier at Wal-Mart will encounter some customers who are easy to please, others who are hard to please, and still others who are impossible to please.

—Kimberly Mitchell, student

EXERCISE

15.5

1. Underline the thesis sentence. Then restate it here in your own words.

_____

_____

2. What is the general subject classified in this essay?

_____

3. What is the basis of classification used in this essay?

_____

_____

4. The author divides her subject into three primary categories, which she presents in order from the most likable to the least likable. What are these three categories?

   a. _____

   b. _____

   c. _____

5. Circle the transition words used to identify these three categories.

6. What methods of development besides classification are used in this essay? Identify two of these methods and give an example of each.

Method 1: _____

Example: _____

Method 2: _____

Example: _____

CHAPTER REVIEW

- The purpose of classification is to organize items with similar characteristics into categories.

- An effective classification paragraph or essay has a clear purpose and a clearly stated or implied main idea (topic sentence or thesis statement) that usually includes the subject to be classified and either the basis of the classification or the categories of the classification.

- Good classification writing uses only one basis of classification at a time, and the categories of the classification include all items to be classified.

- Good classification writing includes logically arranged subtopics connected with clear transitions.

- Good classification writing includes specific examples and details.

- Classification writing may include other methods of development (example, comparison and contrast, and so forth).

WRITING ASSIGNMENT

Look back at Exercise 15.4. Review your topic sentence and rewrite it as the thesis of an essay on that subject. Be sure your thesis includes the subject to be classified and the basis of classification or the categories within the classification.

Thesis sentence: _____

_____

_____

On a separate sheet of paper, write a topic sentence for each of the categories you created for your paragraph in Exercise 15.4, skipping some space between the sentences. In this space, add supporting examples for each of your categories. Finally, use this plan to write a classification essay.

▦ PARTICIPATING IN THE ACADEMIC COMMUNITY

Before writing your essay, share your plan with a small group of your classmates. Evaluate one another's thesis sentences to be sure each thesis clearly states the subject to be classified as well as the basis of classification and/or the categories to be included. Check to see if each category follows the basis of classification. Finally, review the topic sentence and supporting examples for each category to be sure they also fit the category clearly.

Cause and Effect

Another method of developing a main idea is to explore its causes and effects. Whereas process writing focuses on how something is done, **cause and effect** writing focuses on *why* something exists or occurs and on *what results.* You use cause and effect thinking in many academic classes as well as in your everyday life. In your American history class, you may analyze the causes of the Civil War; in an environmental sciences class, you may speculate on the possible effects of global warming; and in your sociology class, you may consider both the causes and effects of divorce. Like the other methods of development, cause and effect is not just a way of writing but also a way of thinking.

UNDERSTANDING CAUSE AND EFFECT

A cause and effect paragraph or essay can focus on causes, effects, or both. The important thing is to explore the relationship between cause and effect. Thus, a writer can begin with a cause and explain its effect or with an effect and explore its cause. As illustrated here, writers can move in one direction or the other:

CAUSE → EFFECT ▸ EXAMPLE: Smoking often causes lung cancer.
                      (cause)   (effect)

EFFECT → CAUSE ▸ EXAMPLE: Lung cancer is one effect of smoking.
                      (effect)   (cause)

The following paragraphs are developed primarily by cause and effect. Isak Dinesen moves from cause to effect; James Thurber begins with the effect and then discusses the cause.

Cause to Effect

Once I shot an Iguana. I thought that I should be able to make some pretty things from his skin. A strange thing happened then, that I have never afterwards forgotten. As I went up to him, where he was lying dead upon his stone, and actually while I was walking the few steps, he faded and grew pale, all colour died out of him as in one long sigh, and by the time that I touched him he was grey and dull like a lump of concrete. It was the live impetuous blood pulsating within the animal, which had radiated out all that glow and splendour. **Now that the flame was put out, and the soul had flown, the Iguana was as dead as a sandbag**.

—Isak Dinesen, "The Iguana," *Out of Africa*

Effect to Cause

I passed all the other courses that I took at my university, but I could never pass botany. This was because all botany students had to spend several hours a week in a laboratory looking through a microscope at plant cells, and I could never see through a microscope. I never once saw a cell through a microscope. This used to enrage my instructor. He would wander around the laboratory pleased with the progress all the students were making in drawing the involved and, so I am told, interesting structure of flower cells, until he came to me. I would just be standing there. "I can't see anything," I would say.

—James Thurber, "University Days," *My Life and Hard Times*

Qualities of Effective Cause and Effect Writing

The qualities of good cause and effect writing found in the paragraphs by Dinesen and Thurber are listed for you here:

1. *A clear purpose.* The purpose of cause and effect writing may be to inform or persuade. In explaining the causes of his failure in biology, Thurber informs and perhaps justifies the result to his audience—and maybe to himself. In describing the effects of killing the iguana, however, Dinesen subtly argues against shooting an animal to use its skin for decoration. In achieving its purpose, cause and effect writing often employs narration, as well. For example, Dinesen narrates the events that lead to the death and dullness of the iguana, and Thurber narrates the events that resulted from his inability to see through a microscope.

2. *A main idea that indicates the causal relationship.* As shown in the bolded sentences, both Dinesen and Thurber include topic sentences that state the causal relationships developed in their paragraphs: Dinesen begins with the shooting of the iguana, which causes the effect she will describe in detail; Thurber begins with his failure in botany and then discusses in detail the causes of this effect. However, a cause and effect paragraph may also divide its focus evenly between causes and effects, or it may move from a cause to an effect that then causes another effect, and so on.

3. *Specific details that develop the causal relationship stated in the main idea.* By including specific descriptions of the effect of shooting the iguana—and its loss of color at death—Dinesen re-creates the experience for her readers and leads them to her implied conclusion that the death of the iguana was a waste—even useless and cruel—because the beautiful skin colors that would have made "pretty things" disappeared with its life. In developing his paragraph, Thurber shows that his inability to see plant cells through a microscope led to his instructor's anger and to the ultimate effect of Thurber's failure. Thus, the details in cause and effect writing may develop a single cause and/or effect, as in Dinesen's paragraph, or multiple causes and/or effects, as in Thurber's.

4. *Logical and relevant support.* Supporting details for cause and effect writing should always be logical and relevant. Writers should avoid oversimplifying events or relying on coincidental occurrences and should limit support to logical and/or proven cause and effect relationships. For example in Paragraph C in Exercise 16.1, we deleted from the original the fact that the 1989 World Series was being played in Candlestick Park when the Loma Prieta earthquake hit because that detail was coincidental rather than causal.

5. *Effective organization and transition that reinforce causal relationships.* The organization should clearly move from cause to effect, as in Dinesen's paragraph, or from effect to cause, as in Thurber's paragraph. Although logical connections between events and feelings are the basis of strong cause and effect writing, transition words that clearly show causal relationships can certainly clarify those relationships. For example, Thurber clearly suggests that he failed botany *because* of his poor laboratory performance. The relationship between Thurber's poor performance and his grade is present even without the word *because*, but the transition provides a valuable clue to this relationship for the reader.

EXERCISE

16.1   Read the following cause and effect paragraphs and answer the questions that follow each.

PARAGRAPH A

The impact of Alzheimer's disease on the patient is enormous; the disease severely damages the quality of life. At the beginning patients are not necessarily stripped of their vigor or strength, but they slowly become confused and helpless. Initially, they may forget to do small things. Later, they may forget appointments, anniversaries, and the like. The forgetfulness is often overlooked at first. Jokes and other coping strategies cover up for memory losses and lapses. The memory losses are not always apparent; some days are better than others. Ultimately, however, the disorder grows worse. Alzheimer's patients start to have trouble finding their way home and remembering their own name and the names of their spouses and children. Sometimes fast retrieval is impaired more than general accumulated knowledge. Patients' personality also changes. They may become abrupt, abusive, and hostile to family members. Within months, or sometimes years, they lose their speech and language functions. Eventually, they lose all control of memory and even of basic bodily functions.

—Lester A. Lefton, *Psychology*, 6th ed.

1. As stated in the topic sentence, what is the main idea of this paragraph?

_____

_____

2. Does the development and support in this paragraph focus *primarily* on (a) causes, (b) effects, or (c) both causes and effects?

_____

3. Does the organization of this paragraph move from cause to effect or effect to cause?

_____

PARAGRAPH B

The Dust Bowl was an ecological disaster. In the 1920s farmers on the southern plains had bought tens of thousands of tractors and plowed millions of acres. Then, in the 1930s, the rain stopped. Soil that had been plowed was particularly vulnerable to the drought that gripped the plains. Strong winds caused enormous dust storms; from 1935 through 1938, 241 dust storms hit the southern plains. Farmers shuttered their homes against the dust as tightly as possible, but, as a woman in western Kansas recounted in 1935, "those tiny particles seemed to seep through the very walls. It got into cupboards and clothes closets; our faces were as dirty as if we had rolled in the dirt; our hair was gray and stiff and we ground dirt between our teeth." Farm animals lacked all protection. The photographer Margaret Bourke-White observed that "cattle quickly become blinded. They run around in circles until they fall and breathe so much dust that they die."

—Mary Norton et al., *A People and a Nation*, 5th ed.

1. As stated in the topic sentence, what is the main idea of this paragraph?

_____

_____

2. Does the development and support in this paragraph focus *primarily* on (a) causes, (b) effects, or (c) both causes and effects?

_____

3. Does the organization of this paragraph move from cause to effect or effect to cause?

_____

PARAGRAPH C

The most tragic result of the violent shaking was the collapse of some double-decked sections of Interstate 880, also known as the Nimitz Freeway. The ground motions caused the upper deck to sway, shattering the concrete support columns along a mile-long section of the freeway. The upper deck then collapsed onto the lower roadway, flattening cars as if they were aluminum beverage cans. Other roadways that were damaged during the earthquake included a 50-foot section of the upper deck of the Bay Bridge, which is a major artery connecting the cities of Oakland and San Francisco. The vibration caused cars on the bridge to bounce up and down vigorously. A motorcyclist on the upper deck described how the roadway bulged and rippled toward him: "It was like bumper cars—only you could die! . . ." Fortunately, only one motorist on the bridge was killed.

—Edward J. Tarbuck and Frederick K. Lutgens, *Earth Science*, 7th ed.

1. What is the main idea of this paragraph?

_____

_____

2. Does the development and support in this paragraph focus *primarily* on (a) causes, (b) effects, or (c) both causes and effects?

_____

3. Does the organization of this paragraph move from cause to effect or effect to cause?

_____

WRITING CAUSE AND EFFECT PARAGRAPHS

You may write a cause and effect paragraph that functions independently or as part of an essay. In either case, it should have a clear main idea, logical organization, specific and relevant support, and effective transitions.

Writing Topic Sentences and Using Transitions in Cause and Effect Paragraphs

As in other types of paragraphs, the main idea of a cause and effect paragraph is usually stated in a topic sentence. Ideally, the topic sentence states the basic relationship between causes and effects and indicates whether the paragraph will focus on causes or effects. In the following paragraph, for example, Davy moves from effect to cause, explaining the causes of his poor performance in elementary school:

Student Paragraph

My poor performance in elementary school was caused by weaknesses in the education I had received in the second and third grades. Because my class had twenty-nine students to one teacher for both of these years, I didn't get the help and attention that I needed. More important, however, I didn't learn because my second and third grade teachers were both poor educators. My second grade teacher, Mrs. Myers, expected me and the rest of the class to understand everything the first time it was explained. I was also afraid of her because she lost patience easily and even threw erasers at us. My third grade teacher Mrs. Kivell wasn't interested in teaching the basics of reading, writing, and arithmetic. Instead, she just taught arts, crafts, and foreign holidays. As a result of these factors, I performed very poorly in school until I attended a high school that had smaller classes and concerned, dedicated instructors.

—Davy Moseley, student

As Davy's topic sentence suggests, his focus is primarily on the causes of his poor performance in elementary school. He gives two primary causes, class size and poor teachers, and then provides supporting details and examples.

In addition to providing a clear topic sentence and support, Davy also uses effective verbal clues to show the relationships within his paragraph. Notice how the highlighted words clarify the cause and effect relationships in the paragraph. The following list shows several additional transition words and phrases you can use to show cause and effect relationships in your own writing:

accordingly	for	so
as a result	hence	so that
because	in order that	therefore
consequently	since	thus

In addition to these transition words, you can also use the nouns *causes, reasons, results*, and *effects* and the verbs *caused* and *resulted* to show causal relationships.

EXERCISE

16.2   The terrorist attack on America on September 11, 2001, had many far-reaching effects on our nation and on its citizens. Write a paragraph in which you discuss the effects of this attack in one of the specific areas listed below:

air travel   health of rescue workers

disaster planning   immigration

the economy   the military

President George W. Bush   patriotism

families of the victims   tourism

EXERCISE

16.3   For each of the following topics, list three causes and three effects. Decide whether a paragraph on this subject would be more effective if it moved from cause to effect (developing the effects) or from effect to cause (developing the causes), and write this relationship in the space provided. Then write a topic sentence that expresses this causal relationship.

Causes   **Effects**

1. Stress _____

    a. _____   a. _____

    b. _____   b. _____

    c. _____   c. _____

This paragraph will develop (causes or effects): _____.

This paragraph will move from _____ to _____

Topic sentence: _____

_____

2. Drug or alcohol abuse_____

    a. _____   a. _____

    b. _____   b. _____

    c. _____   c. _____

    d. _____   d. _____

This paragraph will develop (causes or effects): _____.

This paragraph will move from _____ to _____

Topic sentence: _____

_____

3. Divorce

    a. _____   a. _____

    b. _____   b. _____

    c. _____   c. _____

    d. _____   d. _____

This paragraph will develop (causes or effects): _____.

This paragraph will move from _____ to _____

Topic sentence: _____

_____

Now select one of these topics and use your plan to write a cause and effect paragraph.

WRITING CAUSE AND EFFECT ESSAYS

The principles that apply to writing cause and effect paragraphs also apply to writing cause and effect essays. A cause and effect essay will move either from cause to effect or from effect to cause. Although an essay may provide a detailed analysis of a single cause and a single effect, most cause and effect essays are developed by focusing either on several effects of one cause or on several causes of one effect. As you read the following essay by Greg

Rogers, determine whether it moves from a single effect to a discussion of several causes or from a single cause to a discussion of several effects.

Starting Out Right

[1] Teenagers should be encouraged to have a part-time job while attending high school. I have held many jobs, but the most important to me was my first job as a dishwasher at an Italian restaurant in Seattle. Because of this job, I learned about responsibility, money values, and human relationships.

[2] One result of my job is that it taught me responsibility. A job and responsibility go hand in hand. Indeed, in most cases, people get paid on the basis of how much responsibility they can handle. Responsibility means being accountable for one's actions or duties, including being at work on time. Before I got my first job, I didn't own a watch, much less keep track of time. This job forced me to get a watch and keep my eye on it. The duties I had to perform included taking out the trash to the large trash can in back. Another one of my duties was to sweep and mop the floor of the entire restaurant. Grotesque is the only way to describe the floor after a booming Friday night. Pizza sauce and pasta covered the fake marble tile floor, and it was my job to scrub the tile until it didn't look fake. Because I began to take great pride in my work, I worked really hard to make the place look good. I came to feel that my work was a mirror of me as a person. Therefore, with this job, I became more responsible.

[3] Another effect of my job was that it helped me to learn more about the value of money. I had to work two weeks before I could get my first pay check, and I was counting every minute. I calculated all the hours that I would have on my check about a hundred times to make sure I knew how much it would be. When that long-awaited Friday came, I got up early, went to school, and went straight to work from there. As I ran inside, the owner met me at the counter with a strange grin, thanked me for my hard work, and handed me an envelope containing my first check. I was excited, but I composed myself and thanked her. All that night at work, I thought of how I was going to spend my hard-earned money. After all the empty trips back from the mall, you'd think I would have narrowed what I wanted to buy down to about ten items, but no, I wanted it all. The next morning I woke my mom up fifteen minutes before the mall opened, and after ten minutes of tormenting this poor woman, she was up and out of her room— mad as hell, but up nonetheless. I started out with two hundred dollars. As we traveled this mecca of material objects in the mall, I found myself saying, "I wouldn't throw my money away for that." I said that more and more times the longer we stayed. I went home that night with a very tired mom and one hundred ninety-eight dollars and fifty cents.

The only things I had bought were two Orange Juliuses that my mom and I had enjoyed very much. Although I don't think I realized it until much later, I learned a lesson that day. If your money is hard earned, it's hard spent also.

⁴A final outcome of my job was that I learned about relationships with others from this first job. The restaurant was like a home away from home, but with better food. One night after work, my bike was stolen, and I was very upset at myself because I had been careless and immature and had forgotten to lock it up. Knowing that I was upset, Frank, a cook, told me to wait around a while after work. Then he told me to get into his Jeep. I thought he was going to give me a ride to my house near his, but he drove past my house, turned down another street, and stopped in front of a local pawnshop. I didn't know what was going on, so I stayed in the Jeep while he went inside. I sat there clueless until Frank came outside and told me to come in. I opened the door and scanned left to right for Frank, but before I saw him, my eyes locked on my bike. "That's mine!" I yelled. Frank stood next to the bike, smiling from ear to ear. He paid the twenty-five bucks for the bike, and we took it outside. Drunk with relief and happiness, I thanked him. Then he said, "Kid, you can't give people a chance to rip you off." As I rode home, I thought that what Frank did was one of the nicest things anyone had done for me. After that I locked my bike up every day and paid Frank back the twenty-five dollars. I've learned that a job is not just a job; it's also relationships with the people you work with.

⁵I loved working at this first job. It taught me how to conduct myself responsibly in a job, how to manage the money I earned, and how to get along with and learn from other people. Every day I went to work and worked hard because everyone around me also worked hard. I may have only made three dollars and eighty-five cents an hour, but I learned a lot about work and the real world from the good people I worked with.

—Greg Rogers, student

EXERCISE
16.4

1. What is the thesis of this essay?

_____

_____

2. Does this essay move from cause to effect or from effect to cause?

_____

3. Does the body of the essay (its development) focus primarily on causes or effects?

_____

4. What are the three major supporting points (causes or effects) of this essay?

   a. _____

   b. _____

   c. _____

5. Circle transition words in the essay used to show cause and effect relationships.

6. What are some of the most effective supporting details and examples in the essay?

   _____

   _____

   _____

7. Although this essay is developed primarily by cause and effect, it also employs other methods of development. What are two of these methods, and in what paragraph(s) are they used?

   a. _____

   b. _____

▓ CHAPTER REVIEW

- Cause and effect writing focuses on why something occurs and on what results.

- The purpose of cause and effect writing may be to inform or persuade.

- Cause and effect writing includes a clear main idea (topic sentence or thesis statement) that states the causes and/or effects to be developed.

- Supporting details in cause and effect writing should clearly develop the causal relationship being discussed; details should never be coincidental or oversimplified.

- The organization of cause and effect writing may move from cause to effect or from effect to cause.

- Good cause and effect writing includes not only logical organization but also effective transitions.

▓ WRITING ASSIGNMENT

Write a cause and effect essay on one of the following topics:

Stress	Dropping out of high school
Drug or alcohol abuse	Pollution

Divorce   Credit card debt

Success (or failure) in college or a job   Violence in schools

Your thesis sentence should express the relationship between cause and effect found in the topic and clarify your purpose and focus. You will probably have a more coherent essay if you focus on either effects, discussing several effects of a single cause, or on causes, discussing several causes of a single effect. Be sure you include in your essay specific, relevant evidence to support the causal relationship you are analyzing. (*Note:* Because you listed causes and effects for some of these topics in Exercise 16.3, you may find that you have already done some helpful planning for your essay.)

PARTICIPATING IN THE ACADEMIC COMMUNITY

Make a 3 to 5 minute presentation to your class in which you summarize the content of your essay. Begin with your introduction and thesis statement; then summarize the causes and/or effects that you discuss. (You may want to follow a brief outline that you write on the chalkboard, print on a transparency to be used on an overhead projector, or post on class computers.)

CHAPTER

17

Definition

Definition is not really a different method of development as much as it is a combination of all the other methods. Your main concern in defining a subject is to tell what it is. You can give a brief definition as part of a longer composition, or you can devote your entire composition to defining a term or an idea. You can define a subject by describing, illustrating, comparing, or classifying it. You can even define a subject by telling a story about it or analyzing its causes or effects.

UNDERSTANDING DEFINITION

Clear definitions are essential to the process of communication. When you read a chapter in a textbook, you must understand the basic terminology in order to comprehend the ideas being expressed. For example, because your political science text will frequently refer to "governmental bureaucracy," you need to know that a *bureaucracy* is a set of complex agencies and departments that help a governor or president carry out law and policy. When you write a paragraph or an essay, you must be sure not only that you understand the words you are using but also that you define terms so your reader can understand how you are using them.

As you read the following two definition paragraphs, think about why they are successful definitions and try to identify other methods of development the writers use to develop their definitions.

> **Robotics is the science that deals with the construction, capabilities, and applications of robots.** Most robots are used to perform tedious, dangerous, or otherwise undesirable work in factories. . . . These industrial robots can work where humans cannot, and do not need protective devices. They never need time off; a typical industrial robot is up and running 97 percent of the time! And the

quality of work never suffers. Further, management never has to contend with sick, tired, or bored robots. The machines never complain, go on strike, or ask for higher wages.

—Steven L. Mandell, *Introduction to Computers*

Falling in love is an experience that almost everyone has at least once and usually several times. **To fall in love is to fall into a profound set of emotional experiences.** There may be a range of physical symptoms such as dry mouth, pounding heart, flushed face, and knotted stomach. The mind may race, and fantasy, especially about the loved one, is rampant. Motivation to work, play, indeed for anything except the lover, may fall to zero. As the love feelings develop, strong feelings of passion may occur. In fact, passionate love is essentially the same as romantic love, except that the focus is more specifically on the emotional intensity and sexual passion.

—Clyde Hendrick and Susan Hendrick, *Liking, Loving, and Relating*

Qualities of Effective Definition

The qualities of effective definition illustrated in the sample paragraphs defining robotics and falling in love are listed here:

1. *A sense of purpose and audience.* Writers need to have a clear sense of purpose and audience when they define a subject. Definition is most often used to inform, but it may also be used to persuade. For example, the writer of the paragraph on robotics seems to be addressing a scientific or business audience interested in technological efficiency, whereas the authors of the paragraph on falling in love are addressing a more general audience.

2. *A stated or clearly implied main idea.* A good definition paragraph begins with a topic sentence that introduces and makes an assertion about the subject. Often this main idea is stated in the form of a brief introductory definition. In the first example paragraph, the writer initially defines *robotics* by classifying it as a science and explaining that it "deals with the construction, capabilities, and applications of robots." The writer then explores other characteristics of robots, especially their capabilities and applications. In the second paragraph, falling in love is defined briefly in the first two sentences; the second sentence states the main point—that falling in love results in "a profound set of emotional experiences."

3. *Use of several methods of development in extended definitions.* When writers define a subject, they are free to use any methods of development that will help their readers arrive at a clear understanding of the subject. A writer may describe a subject (using both factual and sensory details), give an example of it, compare or contrast it with something else, or classify it. The main strength of the sample paragraph on falling in love is its extended development through various methods. The authors provide effective descriptive examples of how one feels (having "dry mouth, pounding heart, flushed face, and knotted stomach") and acts ("the mind may race, and fantasy, especially about the loved one, is rampant") when falling in love. The definition also includes effects ("motivation . . . may fall to zero" and "strong feelings of passion may occur") of falling in love.

Formal Definitions

When you look up a word in the dictionary, the definition you find is usually a formal definition. A **formal definition** places the subject (or term) into a category and tells how it differs from the other members of that class. For instance, we can define a *lullaby* by placing it in the general category of songs and specifying the characteristics that make it different from other songs. We might, therefore, arrive at the definition "a lullaby is a song used to encourage babies to sleep." A formal definition is more effective if the term is placed in a category that is not too broad. Thus, the category of *song* is much more effective than that of *music* for defining a lullaby.

Formal definitions are usually brief and to the point. In paragraphs and essays, therefore, they are most often used as part of an extended definition. Formal definitions are also used to define secondary terms within a composition.

EXERCISE

17.1

Read the following definition paragraph and answer the questions that follow it.

An earthquake is the vibration of the earth produced by the rapid release of energy caused when rock plates that are pressure balanced on either side of a fault zone slide past each other, releasing the stored energy in short bursts. This energy radiates in all directions from its source, the focus, in the form of waves analogous to those produced when a stone is dropped into a calm pond. Just as the impact of the stone sets water waves in motion, an earthquake generates seismic waves that radiate throughout the earth. Even though the energy dissipates rapidly with increasing distance from the focus, instruments located throughout the world record the event. On October 17, 1989, at 5:04 p.m. Pacific Daylight Time, for example, strong tremors shook the San Francisco Bay area. Millions of Americans and others around the world were just getting ready to watch the third game of the World Series, but instead saw their television sets go black as the shock hit Candlestick Park. Although this Loma Prieta earthquake was centered in a remote section of the Santa Cruz Mountains, about 16 kilometers north of the city of Santa Cruz, major damage occurred in the Marina District of San Francisco 100 kilometers to the north. Here, as many as 60 row houses were so badly damaged that they had to be demolished.

—Adapted from Edward J. Tarbuck and Frederick K. Lutgens, *Earth Science*, 7th ed.

1. This paragraph begins with a formal definition. Analyze the parts of this formal definition in the space provided.

   Term: _____ *Class*: _____

   Differentiation from others in class: _____

   _____

2. This paragraph uses at least four methods of development besides definition. In the spaces below, identify and give an example of two of these methods.

   Method 1: _____

   Example: _____

   Method 2: _____

   Example: _____

EXERCISE

17.2

Write formal definitions of the following terms.

1. *Term*: Cellular phone

   Class: _____

   How it differs from others in its class: _____

   _____

2. *Term*: University

   Class: _____

   How it differs from others in its class: _____

   _____

3. *Term*: Hero

   Class: _____

   How it differs from others in its class: _____

   _____

Informal Definitions

Sometimes writers prefer to use **informal definitions** rather than formal ones. You will often find words defined informally in your reading, especially in your textbooks. Informal definitions are particularly helpful for defining words in definition paragraphs and essays. As discussed in the following sections, informal definitions include restatement through synonyms; contrast, often using antonyms; brief examples and illustrations; and brief explanations.

Restatement and Synonyms

The simplest kind of informal definition provides a synonym for the word being defined. A **synonym** is a word that has the same, or approximately the same, meaning as the word being defined. Thus, the synonym restates the word's meaning in more familiar terms.

▶ **Example**   The millionaire was **magnanimous,** or generous, with his money.

The word *generous* is a synomym that restates the meaning of *magnanimous*, thus defining as well as emphasizing the meaning of the word.

Contrast and Antonyms

A word may also be defined through contrast, usually using an antonym and/or transition words that show contrast. An **antonym** is a word that means the opposite of the word in question.

▶ **Example**   Mark was **surly** rather than polite when he accepted the ribbon for being second in the race.

In this example, the words *rather than* indicate the contrast in meaning between *surly* and *polite*, thus helping the reader understand that *surly* means "rude." Other transition words that show contrast include *but, although*, and *however*.

Examples

Another way to define a word informally is to use an example, or examples, of the term to be defined.

▶ **Example**   I do not like **acrid** foods such as sour pickles and green persimmons.

Because sour pickles and green persimmons are both bitter in taste, the reader can infer that *acrid* means "bitter or sharp." Writers often use the transition words *for example* and *such as* to introduce examples.

Explanation

Finally, an informal definition may simply provide an explanation of the word's meaning in the context of its usage.

▶ **Example**   The boy's grandfather was so **parsimonious** with his monthly income that he even refused to buy enough to eat.

Here the explanation that the boy's grandfather was so parsimonious that he wouldn't buy enough to eat suggests that the word *parsimonious* means "thrifty" or "stingy" to the point of self-denial.

EXERCISE

17.3

Write the definition and the type of informal definition (synonym or restatement, antonym or contrast, example, explanation) for each of the bold-faced words in the following sentences.

1. The storekeeper was so **avaricious** that he tried to cheat his customers when he gave them change.

   Definition: _____

   Type of informal definition: _____

2. Although our last gardener was lazy, the present gardener is **diligent.**

   Definition: _____

   Type of informal definition: _____

3. **Clairvoyants**—such as fortune-tellers, seers, and prophets—do not always give accurate predictions.

   Definition: _____

   Type of informal definition: _____

Denotations and Connotations

When writers are defining a word—especially when writing an extended definition—they also need to be aware of the difference between a word's **denotation** and its **connotation.** The **denotation** of a word is its formal dictionary definition; the **connotation** of a word includes the personal and societal associations the word brings to mind. The word *fire*, for example, may suggest warmth and romance to a woman who received her engagement ring in front of the flickering fire of her fireplace but remind another woman of the raging fire that destoyed her home and all her family photographs.

EXERCISE

17.4   1. Write the denotation of the word *house*.

_____

2. Now, write two or three words that have similar denotations to *house* but that have different connotations. Beside each word, write the connotations, or associations, the word has for you.

a. _____

b. _____

c. _____

WRITING DEFINITION PARAGRAPHS

A definition paragraph may be a separate composition or a part of a longer composition. As illustrated in the following student paragraph, a good definition paragraph may combine formal and informal definitions. Also, a well-developed definition paragraph usually includes various methods of development. As you read Kristy's paragraph, see how many methods of development you can identify.

Student Paragraph

Known informally as "falling sickness," epilepsy is a nervous disorder in which the sufferer experiences a loss of sensory, motor, and mental functions. An attack of epilepsy, often called an epileptic seizure, occurs when certain nerve cells in the brain suddenly release a large burst of electrical energy. What causes this to occur in the brain? Many seizures seem to occur for no other reason than fatigue or emotional stress. The brain of an epileptic patient sometimes is unable to limit or control the large burst of electrical energy. Epileptic seizures can be of different types. In a Petit Mal ("small bad") seizure, a person usually goes blank for a few seconds, during which he or she is unaware of everything. During this type of seizure, the epileptic may appear to be dreaming. In the more serious Grand Mal ("large bad") seizure, the person usually falls down, and the entire body stiffens and then twitches or jerks uncontrollably. Often the person cries out as the larynx goes into spasm, the muscles contract rigidly, and the person's jaw clamps shut with tremendous pressure. It is not uncommon for the person to bite his or her tongue. As the seizure subsides, the person may fall into a deep sleep. This type of attack often lasts three to five minutes and leaves the victim disoriented or confused and perhaps with a severe headache. Most of the time, the person has no memory of the event. According to *The New Good Housekeeping Family Health and Medical Guide,* one million people in the United States suffer from recurrent seizures.

—Kristy Childers, student

Kristy's paragraph begins with a topic sentence that provides not only a formal definition of epilepsy but also an informal definition ("falling sickness"). Kristy focuses on the formal definition, which states that the condition is a nervous disorder. The methods of development she uses to expand this definition are cause and effect, classification, contrast, description, process, narration, and example.

Because definition involves so many methods of development, no one particular type of transition word is more helpful than another. However, in writing definition paragraphs and essays, you may find yourself overusing the verb *to be,* especially *is,* in defining terms. Following is a list of verbs you may find helpful in introducing definitions.

denotes	connotes	indicates
means	suggests	implies

EXERCISE

17.5

Write a paragraph on one of the following topics:

1. Select a word that means "a place to live" and write a paragraph defining that word. For example, you might define *house, home, residence, domicile, dwelling, shack, mansion, apartment,* and so on. Begin your paragraph with a clear topic sentence and use clear and varied introductory terms and transitions. You may want to include both formal and informal definitions, and you should pay particular attention to connotation as well as denotation. Also, be sure to use several methods of development, such as description, narration, comparison and contrast, and so forth. (*Hint:* Your brainstorming list from Exercise 17.4 may be helpful prewriting for this assignment.)

2. Choose a subject that particularly interests you and write a paragraph defining that subject. You may define an object, an emotion, an event, or a type of person. Once you have selected your subject, think about the different methods you might use to define it. Can you describe it, compare or contrast it with something or someone else, illustrate it, classify it, discuss its causes or effects, and so on? Decide which methods would explain your subject clearly to a reader and use at least two of these methods in your paragraph. Include a clear topic sentence and a formal and/or informal definition.

WRITING DEFINITION ESSAYS

In your academic classes, you may sometimes be asked to write an essay defining a particular term. For example, your sociology instructor might ask you to define *sexual harassment* or *discrimination;* your political science teacher might ask you to define *socialism* or *capitalism;* and your music appreciation teacher might ask you to define *rock* or *baroque* music. Each of these concepts is so complex you would need to define it in an essay rather than a paragraph.

In the following essay, Joe defines a musical instrument, the French horn.

The French Horn

[1] The French horn is a member of the brasswind family of musical instruments that has an attractive and interesting appearance, a unique shape, and a delightful mellow tone. The French horn resembles a large circular disk made of tubing that has a bright polish. The physical properties of the French horn are essential to the powerful sound that the horn produces.

[2] Physically, the horn is an attractive and interesting instrument. The horn has a finely polished surface, like chrome on a sports car. The horn has four valves at the top—three to the right side and one underneath the tubing for the thumb. The polish, interrupted only by a leather cord added by many musicians, looks as clear as a mirror. The cord is wrapped around the tubing and keeps the finish from being broken down by sweat from the player's hand. The cord starts right after a parallel spot above the thumb valve and continues to the shepherd's crook. The shepherd's crook that cradles the pinkie finger is found on many different instruments and gets that name from its resemblance to the crook of a shepherd's staff.

³ Physical shape and sound are closely related in the French horn. Thus, the most notable feature of the French horn is the bell at the end of the tubing where sound emanates. One of the qualities that makes a French horn different is that, unlike the bells in other brass instruments, this bell points back behind the horn player. The bell in the French horn is also quite large—about the diameter of a basketball. The horn player puts his or her hand into the bell to control the sound. The player can change positions of his or her hand, either by putting the hand palm up or palm down, and thus change the sound of the horn.

⁴ The sound of the French horn is peaceful and pleasant. To the sensitive listener, it creates an image of autumn with all the leaves in colors of red and yellow. The hearer can imagine trees standing in a peaceful state with small animals scampering about them. The long, slow passage of the wind can be heard from the beginning of the horn's whole notes. When the horn hits the high notes in a phrase, listeners may see a mental image of an eagle soaring through the air in search of prey. As the imaginary eagle drops toward a small brook, the horn hits a run of fast notes from high to low. About the time the imaginary eagle snags a small fish out of the water and soars back into the sky, the horn makes a leap to an upper note that plays clearly and triumphantly. The low notes are the stately ones, reminiscent of a steamboat on the Mississippi. The performance comes to an end by bringing thoughts of winter and a snowy sleep to the listener.

⁵ My knowledge of the French horn is firsthand, based not only on my general experience with French horns but also on my knowledge of my own new French horn. Because my French horn is new, it as yet has no dents or scratches and can therefore be distinguished from the older French horns in my college band. The valves of this particular instrument work as smoothly as the sighing of the autumn wind that the instrument recreates each time I play it.

—Joe Johnson, student

EXERCISE

17.6

1. What is the thesis statement of this essay?

   _____

2. This thesis is also a formal definition. Identify the elements of this formal definition.

   Term: _____ *Class:* _____

   Distinguishing characteristics: _____

   _____

   _____

3. What are the main points of the thesis statement developed in the essay?

   a. _____

   b. _____

   c. _____

4. This essay uses several methods of development. Indicate the method(s) of development used in each paragraph and provide supporting examples for each.

   Paragraph 2

   Method(s): _____

   Examples: _____

   Paragraph 3

   Method(s): _____

   Examples: _____

   Paragraph 4

   Method(s): _____

   Examples: _____

   Paragraph 5

   Method(s): _____

   Examples: _____

CHAPTER REVIEW

- A definition paragraph or essay should have a sense of purpose and audience
- A successful definition paragraph or essay should have a clear main idea (topic sentence or thesis statement).
- Extended definitions also employ other methods of development.
- A formal definition places a subject (or term) into a class and then tells how it differs from other members of that class.
- Informal definitions may be synonyms, antonyms, examples, or explanations.
- The meaning of a word includes its connotations (associations) as well as its denotations (formal dictionary definitions).

WRITING ASSIGNMENT

Write an essay in which you provide an extended definition of a quality or feeling (courage, love, hate, integrity, patriotism, prejudice, success, failure, etc.) or of a type of person (hero, friend, patriot, traitor, leader, etc.). Include a formal definition in your introduction, perhaps as a part of your thesis statement, but write about what the word means to you as well as its formal dictionary definition. That is, consider the word's connotations as well as its denotation. Develop your definition with at least two methods of development. Finally, include informal definitions of the word where you think they will add to your definition.

PARTICIPATING IN THE ACADEMIC COMMUNITY

Working with a group of four or five classmates, create a classroom publication of your definition essays to distribute to all members of your class. Your instructor will organize your groups based on the topics of your essays; for example, students who defined *success* or *failure* might form one group, whereas students who wrote about *patriots* and *patriotism* could constitute another group.

After your instructor has guided you through revising, editing, and proofreading your essays, decide on a title for your publication and on the best way to arrange the essays. Create a cover or title page and a table of contents, and make copies of your "book" for your class. Finally, congratulate yourselves on being published authors!

CHAPTER 18

Persuasion

The primary purpose of **persuasion** is to convince readers to agree with a particular position or point of view. In addition, persuasion often encourages readers to act in support of that position. To achieve these purposes, writers must provide effective support for their arguments.

In your classes, you will often be asked to take a position on a controversial issue and defend that position in writing. Your biology teacher might ask you to argue for or against stem cell research; your sociology professor might ask you to argue for or against capital punishment; and your journalism or computer science instructor might ask you to argue for or against censorship of information available on the Internet. As a student, you will also be required to evaluate persuasive writing to determine if an argument is logical, fair, and effective. For example, in your political science class, you might be asked to evaluate the contrasting arguments of a liberal and a conservative politician.

UNDERSTANDING PERSUASION

Persuasive writing differs from other types of writing in purpose more than in content. In attempting to persuade readers to accept a particular position or point of view, writers use many of the same methods of development already discussed in this unit. As illustrated in the following paragraph, one of the most common methods of development in persuasive writing is the use of examples and statistical evidence to support an argument:

> **We are encouraged by conservation success stories, of course, but only the most hopeful among us are optimistic about the long term.** Of earth's 9,000 species of birds, about 1,000 are already at risk. And while the old perils—habitat destruction, pesticide poisoning, shooting, oil spills, migrant-killing TV towers, and others—continue, we are adding new threats. Especially sinister are the gaseous byproducts of advanced technology—carbon dioxide, methane, nitrous oxide, CFCs—

the products responsible for acid precipitation, ozone depletion and the greenhouse effect, developments whose long-term impact on birds (and other life) we are beginning, nervously, to guess at. To what future will man's growing population and attendant technologies take us? Harvard biologist E. O. Wilson, in a recent interview, delivered a stark warning: "Humanity, in the desperate attempt to fit eight billion or more people on the planet and give them a higher standard of living, is at risk of pushing the rest of life off the globe."

—Alan Pistorius, "Species Lost," *Country Journal*

Qualities of Effective Persuasion

As illustrated in the paragraph by Alan Pistorius, the qualities of effective persuasion include the following:

1. *A sense of purpose and a clear main idea stating the writer's position.* Persuasive writing states the writer's position or solution to a problem with the overall purpose of convincing the audience to agree with the argument. To qualify as persuasion, the statement must be arguable and not a simple statement of fact. In the preceding paragraph, for example, the first sentence states Pistorius's position that "only the most hopeful among us are optimistic about the long term" outlook for many species— a statement with which some people would disagree. In persuasive paragraphs such as this one, the writer's position—or main idea—is often stated at the beginning of the paragraph. In a persuasive essay, however, the writer usually provides some background information or a statement of the problem before stating the thesis, which may appear at the end of the first paragraph or even in the second paragraph.

2. *Strong supporting evidence.* The success of persuasive writing depends on the quality of the writer's support for his or her argument. That is, a writer who convinces readers to agree with his or her position must provide strong reasons and evidence. For example, Pistorius supports his position about the danger of extinction with statistics about the number of birds at risk (1,000), with examples of dangers to different species (habitat destruction, pesticide poisoning, carbon dioxide, etc.), and with a statement from an authority in the field (E. O. Wilson).

3. *Recognition and refutation of opposing arguments.* To persuade readers—especially those who disagree—writers cannot ignore opposing arguments. Instead, a writer should recognize the strongest arguments against his or her point of view and refute, or argue against, each of these arguments. In his first sentence, Pistorius recognizes that there are some "conservation success stories" but nevertheless argues that the evidence he has provided suggests a bleak outlook for many species.

4. *A clear and logical structure.* Although the structure of a persuasive argument may vary, the sample paragraph suggests a helpful pattern for writing essays as well as paragraphs. This pattern is outlined here:

a. Background and statement of persuasive claim
b. Evidence to support the argument
c. Recognition and refutation of opposing arguments
d. Conclusion

Each of these structural divisions is included in condensed form in Pistorius's paragraph. In an essay, however, the first paragraph or two would provide background and state the writer's position (main idea), the next two or three paragraphs would give support for the writer's argument, another paragraph or two would recognize and refute opposing arguments, and the final paragraph would conclude the essay. (This structure is illustrated in Mike Burton's essay on pages 228–230).

EXERCISE

18.1

Select three arguable topics and write them in the spaces labeled Topic A, Topic B, and Topic C. For each topic, write an assertion that states your position on that topic. Possible topics include abortion, stem cell research, capital punishment for minors, stricter immigration enforcement, AIDS testing of health care employees, drug testing in the workplace, and gun control.

TOPIC A: _____

Assertion: _____

TOPIC B: _____

Assertion: _____

TOPIC C: _____

Assertion: _____

EXERCISE

18.2

On a separate sheet of paper list three arguments for and three arguments against your position for each of the topics you selected. Discuss one or more of these topics with a group of your classmates, and then review your assertions about these topics. Do you agree with your original position on each topic, or do you need to revise one or more of your position statements?

Using Persuasive Appeals

In order to persuade readers to agree with a particular position on an issue, writers need to think carefully about how they will appeal to their audience and what support they will use. Depending on who their audience is, writers may want to appeal to their readers' **reason, emotions,** or sense of the writer's **character.** If you are arguing, for example, that taxes in your community need to be raised so better lighting can be added at the city park, you will make different persuasive appeals to different audiences. You could appeal to the emotions of parents who are worried about the safety of their children, but you would want to appeal to the reason of other taxpayers and local government officials, arguing that better lighting in the city park could actually save money by reducing crime in the area.

Martin Luther King, Jr.'s "Letter from Birmingham Jail" is an extremely effective argument that uses all three persuasive appeals. As you read the paragraphs from his letter in the following sections, keep in mind that King wrote them in 1963, when he was in jail for "parading without a permit" in Birmingham, Alabama. In his letter, King was directly addressing eight Birmingham clergymen who "deplored" the demonstrations in their city, but indirectly he was addressing all humanity for the purpose of gaining equal rights and justice for African Americans and, indeed, for all people.

Reason

An appeal to reason presents representative, fair, and logical evidence. As illustrated in the following paragraph, this appeal often relies on an accepted truth, such as the idea that some laws are just while others are unjust. Once this accepted truth, or premise, is established, the writer can then develop an argument based on this premise.

> You express a great deal of anxiety over our willingness to break laws. This is certainly a legitimate concern. Since we so diligently urge people to obey the Supreme Court's decision of 1954 outlawing segregation in the public schools, at first glance it may seem rather paradoxical for us consciously to break laws. One may well ask: "How can you advocate breaking some laws and obeying others?" The answer lies in the fact that there are two types of laws: just and unjust. I would be the first to advocate obeying just laws. One has not only a legal but a moral responsibility to obey just laws. Conversely, one has a moral responsibility to disobey unjust laws. I would agree with St. Augustine that "an unjust law is no law at all."
>
> —Martin Luther King, Jr., "Letter from Birmingham Jail"

From the premise that some laws are just and others are unjust, King reasonably concludes that "one has a moral responsibility to disobey unjust laws."

Emotion

In using an emotional appeal, a writer uses language, examples, and descriptions that make readers react to the argument with their personal feelings. When presented fairly and honestly, as it is in the following paragraph by King, an appeal to the reader's emotions is an effective and justifiable type of persuasion.

> We have waited for more than 340 years for our constitutional and God-given rights. The nations of Asia and Africa are moving with jetlike speed toward gaining political independence, but we still creep at horse-and-buggy pace toward gaining a cup of coffee at a lunch counter. Perhaps it is easy for those who have never felt the stinging darts of segregation to say, "Wait." But when you have seen vicious mobs lynch your mothers and fathers at will and drown your sisters and brothers at whim; when you have seen hate-filled policemen curse, kick, and even kill your black brothers and sisters; when you see the vast majority of your twenty million Negro brothers smothering in an airtight cage of poverty in the midst of an affluent society; when you suddenly find your tongue twisted and your speech stammering as you seek to explain to your six-year-old daughter why she can't go to the public amusement park that has just been advertised on television, and see tears welling up in her eyes when she is told that Funtown is closed to colored children, and see ominous clouds of inferiority beginning to form in her little mental sky, and see her beginning to distort her personality by developing an unconscious bitterness toward white people; when you have to concoct an answer for a five-year-old son who is asking, "Daddy, why do white people treat colored people so mean?" . . .—then you will understand why we find it difficult to wait. There comes a time when the cup of endurance runs over, and men are no longer willing to be plunged into the abyss of despair. I hope, sirs, you can understand our legitimate and unavoidable impatience.
> —Martin Luther King, Jr., "Letter from Birmingham Jail"

King's emotional appeal in this paragraph is effective because it is based on actual experiences and human feelings with which readers can identify. However, writers should be careful not to misuse the emotional appeal by unjustly exaggerating or misrepresenting events or situations.

Character

The final persuasive appeal is based on the credibility, or believability, of the character of the writer. Your argument will be more persuasive if you convince your readers you are a fair, honest, and ethical person. You can do this in part by using solid and logical evidence to support your argument and by maintaining fairness in your appeals to your readers' emotions and reason. In the following paragraph, King enhances his own credibility by comparing his beliefs to those of other respected individuals:

> But though I was initially disappointed at being categorized as an extremist, as I continued to think about the matter I gradually gained a measure of satisfaction from the label. Was not Jesus an extremist for love: "Love your enemies, bless them that curse you, do good to them that hate you, and pray for them which despitefully use you." Was not Amos an extremist for justice: "Let justice roll down like waters and righteousness like an ever-flowing stream." Was not Paul an extremist for the Christian gospel: "I bear in my body the marks of the Lord Jesus." Was not Martin Luther an extremist: "Here I stand; I cannot do otherwise, so help me God." And John Bunyan: "I will stay in jail to the end of my days before I make a butchery of my conscience." And Abraham Lincoln: "This nation cannot survive half slave and half free." And Thomas Jefferson: "We hold these truths to be self-evident, that all men are created equal. . . ." So the question is not whether we will be extremists, but what kind of extremists we will be. Will we be extremists for hate or for love? Will we be extremists for the preservation of injustice or for the extension of justice? In that dramatic scene on Calvary's hill three men were crucified. We must never forget that all three were crucified for the same crime—the crime of extremism. Two were extremists for immorality, and thus fell below their environment. The other, Jesus Christ, was an extremist for love, truth, and goodness, and thereby rose above the environment. Perhaps the South, the nation, and the world are in dire need of creative extremists.
>
> —Martin Luther King Jr., "Letter from Birmingham Jail"

EXERCISE

18.3   Both of the following persuasive paragraphs focus on the controversy of handgun control. As you read these paragraphs, identify in each the writer's position on the topic and the primary appeal (reason, emotion, or character). (*Note*: The writer's position is clearly stated in one of these paragraphs and clearly implied in the other.)

PARAGRAPH A

Gun control is not an easy issue. But, for me, it is a fundamental issue. My family has been touched by violence; too many others have felt the same terrible force. Too many children have been raised without a father or a mother. Too many widows have lived out their lives alone. Too many people have died.

— Edward M. Kennedy, "The Need for Handgun Control," *Los Angeles Times*

1. What is the writer's position on the topic?

_____

2. What is the writer's primary appeal?

_____

PARAGRAPH B

It is clear, I think, that gun legislation simply doesn't work. There are already some 20,000 state and local gun laws on the books, and they are no more effective than was the prohibition of alcoholic beverages in the 1920s. Our most recent attempt at federal gun legislation was . . . intended to control the interstate sale and transportation of firearms and the importation of uncertified firearms; it has done nothing to check the availability of weapons. It has been bolstered in every nook and cranny of the nation by local gun-control laws, yet the number of shooting homicides per year has climbed steadily since its enactment, while armed robberies have increased 60 percent.

—Barry Goldwater, "Why Gun-Control Laws Don't Work," *Reader's Digest*

1. What is the writer's position on the topic?

_____

2. What is the writer's primary appeal!

_____

Evaluating Evidence

To persuade readers to agree with a position, a writer must present convincing evidence. That is, a writer must use enough relevant, reliable evidence to prove the persuasive point to the audience. As you plan your persuasive paragraph or essay, be sure to use only your strongest support.

Using Effective Evidence

Effective support for persuasive writing includes relevant **examples**, accurate **facts and statistics**, and **reliable sources**.

1. *Examples.* Relevant examples provide effective support for an argument. If possible, choose examples that will have a strong impact on read-

ers, and remember that two or three examples are often more persuasive than one.

> ARGUMENT: [G]raphic violence . . . [is] especially damaging for young children because they lack the moral judgment of adults . . . [but] are excellent mimics.
>
> EXAMPLE: One 5-year-old boy from Boston recently got up from watching a teen-slasher film and stabbed a 2-year-old girl with a butcher knife. He didn't mean to kill her (and luckily he did not). He was just imitating the man on the video.
>
> —Tipper Gore, "Curbing the Sexploitation Industry," *Raising PG Kids in an X-Rated Society*

2. *Facts and statistics.* Both facts and statistics are effective in persuasive writing because they provide objective evidence that can be proved (or disproved). Statistics are a particular kind of fact based on numerical evidence. In the following example, the statement that 1,000 species are at risk is a statistic; the statement that habitat destruction, pesticide poisoning, and so forth are perils (dangers) for nonhuman species is factual because it can be proved or disproved. Both statements support Alan Pistorius's argument that the earth has been made unlivable for many forms of life. Be sure the factual evidence you use clearly supports your argument.

> ARGUMENT: Modern man has made the Earth unlivable for many other species. . . .
>
> FACT/STATISTIC: Of earth's 9,000 species of birds, about 1,000 are already at risk. And . . . the old Perils—habitat destruction, pesticide poisoning, shooting, oil spills, migrant-killing TV towers, and others—continue. . .
>
> —Alan Pistorius, "Species Lost," *Country Journal*

3. *Reliable sources.* Persuasive writing often uses support from reliable sources. Support from a respected and believable authority in the field can be convincing evidence. For example, Martin Luther King, Jr.'s quotation from St. Augustine, a respected fifth-century scholar and author, lends strength to his persuasive argument.

> ARGUMENT: One has a moral responsibility to disobey unjust laws.
>
> AUTHORITY: I would agree with St. Augustine that "an unjust law is no law at all."
>
> —Martin Luther King, Jr., "Letter from Birmingham Jail"

Avoiding Ineffective Evidence

When writers plan support for their arguments, they should be careful to avoid unreliable and ineffective evidence. The four general types of unreliable and illogical support that should be avoided are **oversimplification, irrelevant evidence, unfairly emotional words**, and **distorted or suppressed evidence**.

1. *Oversimplification.* Oversimplification is poor reasoning that weakens a persuasive argument. Oversimplification occurs when a writer draws a conclusion based on insufficient evidence. Concluding, for example, that all women are bad drivers because three women in one town received traffic tickets in one day is oversimplifying the issue and drawing a hasty conclusion. Similarly, writers may make an illogical assumption that one thing causes another simply because these two events occur one after another—as in the superstition that a black cat crossing a road causes an accident that occurs afterward. Writers also oversimplify many situations by assuming that only two choices are possible when several choices may actually exist. Advertisers of a particular brand of toothpaste, for example, would have us believe that the only alternative to using their product is to have cavities, when actually several other products can also prevent cavities. Sometimes writers also make comparisons that can be misleading. Comparing life to a chess game is interesting but does not make a logical point. Finally, writers are guilty of circular reasoning—and of proving nothing—when they make a statement such as "Alcohol is intoxicating because it makes you drunk."

2. *Irrelevant evidence.* Politicians are frequently guilty of using irrelevant evidence. One candidate may criticize another candidate for gambling or failing to serve in the military, even though such accusations are irrelevant to the political issues being discussed in the campaign. If the accuser has no supporting evidence, he or she may simply hint that the candidate is a racist or an adulterer. If a reporter asks a politician a direct question about his or her opinion or vote on a particular issue, the politician may simply change the subject and give an irrelevant response.

Of course, politicians aren't the only people who use irrelevant evidence. A beginning writer may be tempted to make a statement because "everybody believes it" rather than search for evidence to support the truth. Another example of irrelevant evidence is quoting someone simply because he or she is famous. To be a reliable authority, the person must have expertise or experience on the subject.

3. *Overly emotional words.* In choosing words, writers should consider the connotations (personal associations) as well as denotations (dictionary definitions). Thus, if a writer wanted to present a positive picture of a celebrity, she would call him *famous*; if she wanted to present a negative picture of the individual, she would call him *notorious*. However, a writer should be careful not to use words just for their emotional impact—either positive or negative. That is, while the emotional appeal is valid, writers should not substitute emotion for reason. In particular, writers should be careful about *name calling* (*conspirator, racist, chauvinist,* etc.) or about using *glittering generalities* (*American way of life, decent standard of living*). Such words and phrases have lost much of their meaning from having been used too frequently and thoughtlessly.

4. *Distorted or suppressed evidence.* Finally, good persuasive writing does not distort or suppress evidence. One kind of distortion is taking a quotation out of context. A second kind of distortion is misrepresenting an opposing point of view before refuting it. And finally, suppression of evidence occurs when the opposing view is completely ignored. All of these problems in reasoning ultimately weaken the writer's persuasive argument.

EXERCISE

18.4   Each of the following items is an example of weak reasoning. Write in the blank the kind of weak reasoning it illustrates: oversimplification, irrelevant evidence, overly emotional words, or distorted or suppressed evidence.

1. Let's go see the new movie at the Majestic. Everybody says it's great.

   _____

2. He doesn't go to church on Sundays, so he must be an atheist.

   _____

3. Mayor Beech is a self-seeking individual who has sold the city out to special-interest groups and racketeers.

   _____

4. Try our new cigarettes. They give you only a fresh menthol taste.

   _____

5. All foreign cars have bad engines. I know because I have owned two foreign cars, and the engines blew up in both of them.

   _____

WRITING PERSUASIVE PARAGRAPHS

The topic sentence of a persuasive paragraph states the writer's position, or main idea. Because you do not have as much space for supporting evidence in a paragraph as you do in an essay, you should be especially careful to select the most persuasive evidence. As you read Davy's paragraph, notice both his organization and the types of evidence he uses.

Student Paragraph

Unless Congress reinstates the support price for the sale of fluid milk, many more family dairy farms will go out of business. Opponents of a dairy support price argue that other businesses don't receive help from the government and that such help is expensive to taxpayers. It is true that few other businesses receive government help, but all business people except farmers can set their own prices to be sure they make a profit. As President John F. Kennedy observed many years ago, "The American farmer is the only person in society who buys at retail, sells at wholesale, and pays the freight both ways." The milk company that buys the dairy farmer's milk sets the price the farmer receives as well as the price the farmer must pay the company to haul his milk. Because fluid milk will spoil, the dairy farmer is forced to take whatever price is offered regardless of expenses. The American dairy farmer is at a disadvantage both within the United States and with other countries because the governments of most other countries continue to help their dairy farmers. In addition, the actual price of fluid milk in the 1990s declined or remained the same while other farm expenses went up. For example, a tractor that cost a farmer $15,000 in the late 1970s costs over $50,000 today. Yet, fluid milk that sold for about $14.00 (per hundred pounds) in the late 1970s and for $16.00 in the late 1980s sold for only $13.00 in the mid-to-late 1990s. As a result of these relatively low milk prices, many dairy farmers have gone out of business. For example, in one major dairying county in Texas, 250 of the county's 500 dairy farms went out of business during the late 1990s. Thus, possible money from taxes is being lost, and a business important to the health of America's citizens—especially to its children—is being destroyed. If the trend continues, several results will occur. Americans will be forced to rely more and more on dairy products from other countries or the production of dairy products by large companies. In either case, the price of dairy products is likely to go up as the quality goes down. Ultimately, the taxpayers must pay a higher price than they would have if they had supported a reasonable governmental price floor to keep small dairy farms in business. Therefore, I encourage you to write your national legislators and urge them to keep the dairy support price.

—Davy Moseley, student

After beginning with the topic sentence that states his position, Davy gives necessary background about the practice of supporting dairy prices. Then he recognizes and refutes the opposing argument that dairies should not receive government aid because other businesses in the United States do not receive such help. Davy continues by providing evidence for the necessity of the dairy support price and to encourage readers to act in support of his position.

Davy uses several kinds of evidence in his paragraph, including a quotation from President Kennedy, an example of the increased cost of tractors, and statistics about the price of fluid milk and the declining number of dairies. Although a persuasive paragraph or essay can include many types of development, the most common methods of development are probably the use of comparison and contrast to present opposing arguments, examples to provide evidence for the writer's argument, and cause and effect to speculate about results. Some of the transition words used in these methods of development, which are highlighted in Davy's paragraph, include the following:

Contrast	*Example/Addition*	*Cause/Effect/Condition*
although	and, also	as a result
but	first, second, etc.	because
however	for example	consequently
in contrast	for instance	for, hence, if
nevertheless	finally, last	since, so
on the other hand	such as	therefore
yet	ultimately	thus

EXERCISE

18.5   Write a persuasive paragraph on one of the following topics. State your position in your topic sentence, and use fair, reasonable, and effective reasons and evidence to support that claim. Do not forget to refute the opposing argument.

1. Physical education activity courses should (or should not) be required for college graduation.

2. A foreign language should (or should not) be required for college graduation.

3. The Internet should (or should not) be regulated.

4. Minors should (or should not) be allowed to purchase _____.

5. Candidates should (or should not) use negative advertising.

WRITING PERSUASIVE ESSAYS

The purpose of a persuasive essay, like that of a persuasive paragraph, is to convince your reader to agree with your position and, perhaps, to take action accordingly. However, a persuasive essay requires much fuller development than a persuasive paragraph. Thus, you have space in the introductory paragraph of an essay to provide background before stating your position in your thesis. You can also provide more detailed support of your position and a fuller refutation of the opposing position in an essay. Moreover, in developing your argument, you may use completely different methods of development in different paragraphs. As you read the following essay, look for the thesis; different types of appeals, reasons, evidence, and methods of development; and the refutation of the opposing argument.

¿Que Es el Problema?

[1] What is bilingualism? It is a method of teaching in which students for whom English is a second language are given the opportunity to learn in their native language. Bilingual education (bilingualism) uses three methods; *transition*, which helps students move from their native language to English; *enrichment*, which uses their native language to enrich their studies; and *maintenance*, which allows students to continue to learn in their native language throughout their school careers. Of these three types of bilingual education, the maintenance method is the least effective. Indeed, this approach creates several problems. Bilingual maintenance programs in schools in the United States cost additional taxes, separate students for whom English is a

second language from other students, and may even keep these students from becoming productive and successful citizens.

[2]The first problem with the maintenance method is that it is expensive. In contrast to the transition and enrichment programs, which provide extra instruction for only three to five years, the maintenance program requires extra funding for the entire thirteen years that the student is in school. Thus, the maintenance program is approximately three times as expensive as the other methods of bilingual education. With an average teacher's salary of $30,000, the difference in expenses for the school with between one and three teachers would be $60,000. Although a district can often put in a single classroom several students whose native language is Spanish, an even greater problem arises when a district has only two or three French, German, or Japanese students because ideally each group would be placed in a separate classroom. Of course, extremely small bilingual classes are even more expensive to teach than average-sized classes.

[3]Another problem with the bilingual maintenance program is that it separates students in the program from the rest of the student body for their entire school career. School teaches students not only writing and arithmetic but also how to get along with other people and other cultures. Keeping students in the maintenance program requires that they interact only with people from their same culture. Some may argue that this isolation is only in the classroom because students are able to interact with other students at lunch and playtime. However, students are much more likely to socialize with those whom they know from their classroom experiences. The placement of English-as-a-second-language students in separate classrooms may make other children see them as different and ignore or even ridicule them. At my own high school, the Spanish-speaking students always ate at a table by themselves, usually speaking Spanish, and the English-speaking students also ate by themselves. The maintenance program is governmentally supported segregation.

[4]Perhaps the greatest argument against the maintenance program, however, is that it often keeps its students from becoming productive and successful members of society. For example, if children are taught entirely in Spanish, they will never be able to compete in the job market in an English-speaking country. They will have difficulty completing job applications in English, will have trouble communicating on the job, and are likely to remain in a lower-paid position while those who have a better command of the English language are promoted.

[5]Supporters of the bilingual maintenance program offer two opposing arguments. First, these supporters argue that English-as-a-second-language students will be more successful in school if they are

taught in their native languages. Certainly, these students might initially succeed better in their native languages, but the negative long-term career effects outweigh the short-term classroom effects. Besides, a good bilingual transition program can prepare students to succeed in an English-speaking classroom as well as an English-speaking society. Second, supporters of the maintenance program argue that if students are taught in English, they will soon forget their native language and will lose their cultural heritage. Certainly, students should have the right and ability as well as the desire to hold on to their cultural heritage, but the classroom is not the only, or even the best, place to promote cultural values. English-as-a-second-language students can continue to speak their native language in their homes and communities, thus truly becoming bilingual by using two languages.

⁶Certainly, the public schools have a responsibility to establish reasonable bilingual programs, such as transition or enrichment programs, that allow English-as-a-second-language students to succeed in school. However, the various costs of the bilingual maintenance program are too high. This program costs the taxpayers more money, it separates bilingual students from other cultures, and, most important, it keeps these students from competing and succeeding in the job market. We must help English-as-a-second-language students become less dependent and more independent and truly bilingual.

—Mike Burton, student

EXERCISE

18.6

1. What is the writer's thesis?

_____

_____

2. What are the three reasons the writer gives to support his thesis?

a. _____

b. _____

c. _____

3. Identify and give an example of the primary appeal used in this essay.

Appeal: _____

Example: _____

Does the writer of this essay use any other appeals? If so, what?

_____

4. List two types of evidence used in this essay and an example of each.

   First type of evidence: _____

   Example: _____

   Second type of evidence: _____

   Example: _____

5. The writer of this essay recognizes and refutes two opposing arguments. Identify each of these opposing arguments and the refutation the writer uses for each.

   First opposing argument: _____

   Refutation: _____

   Second opposing argument: _____

   Refutation: _____

6. Identify the method(s) of development used in each paragraph in the body of this essay.

   Paragraph 2: _____

   Paragraph 3: _____

   Paragraph 4: _____

   Paragraph 5: _____

7. In your opinion, what is most effective about the writer's conclusion?

   _____

   _____

CHAPTER REVIEW

- Persuasive writing attempts to convince readers to agree with the writer's position, or argument.

- In persuasion, a writer's topic sentence or thesis should be an arguable statement and not a statement of fact.

- Effective persuasive arguments appeal to the reader's reason, emotion, and sense of the writer's character.

- Good support for a persuasive claim should be reasonable, fair, and effective; types of support include examples, facts and statistics, and reliable sources.

- Good persuasive writing avoids oversimplification, irrelevant evidence, overly emotional words, and distorted or suppressed evidence.

- Good persuasive writing recognizes and effectively refutes opposing arguments.
- Good persuasive writing includes the following:
  1. Background and statement of the writer's position on the subject
  2. Strong evidence for the writer's position
  3. Recognition and refutation of the opposing argument(s)
  4. A conclusion that restates the writer's position

WRITING ASSIGNMENT

In Exercises 18.1 and 18.2, you brainstormed about three arguable topics, identifying reasons or evidence to support each side of the argument and concluding with a persuasive position statement about the topic. Select one of these topics and develop your thesis into a persuasive essay. Use the following space to plan your essay:

PARAGRAPH 1

Background: _____

_____

Thesis statement: _____

_____

PARAGRAPH 2

Reason 1: _____

Evidence: _____

PARAGRAPH 3

Reason 2: _____

Evidence: _____

PARAGRAPH 4

Reason 3: _____

Evidence: _____

PARAGRAPH 5

Opposing argument(s): _____

_____

Refutation of opposing argument(s): _____

_____

PARAGRAPH 6

Conclusion: _____

_____

▨ PARTICIPATING IN THE ACADEMIC COMMUNITY

Arrange a classroom debate on a controversial topic. Each of the two teams should include two or three students who have written about the same topic. Team members might begin by arguing the position opposite to their own, and then switch to their preferred positions. Remember, just as persuasive writing is more effective if the writer recognizes the opposing arguments, effective debaters must know about and be able to argue both sides of an issue.

PART 3

Writing and Editing Sentences

As a student, you have repeatedly studied the sentence—its structure, its elements, even its definition. But at this point in your education, you may find you still need to know more about sentences. You may need the skills to analyze sentences—to take them apart, understand how they work, and put them back together in different ways. The ability to analyze sentences enables you to be a better editor and proofreader of your own writing.

In Chapter 9 you learned the importance of revising what you write so the content and organization accurately reflect your ideas and communicate clearly to your readers. But experienced writers also edit and proofread what they have written. Chapters 19–22 emphasize how to write effective sentences and how to edit them to make them more readable, more interesting, more graceful, and, ultimately, more correct. Chapters 23–27 focus on errors in sentence structure and usage, while Chapter 28 deals with matters of style. Finally, Chapters 29 and 30 provide instruction in punctuation, capitalization, and spelling.

Simple Sentences

To become a strong academic writer, you need a good basic knowledge of sentence structure. Because academic writing is nearly always directed at readers who value standard rules of sentence structure and punctuation, you must be able to write sentences that measure up to their expectations.

In terms of their structure, sentences are usually defined as *simple, compound,* or *complex.* Many of the sentences you write are probably simple, but that does not mean they are elementary or simple-minded, merely that they consist of a single subject–verb relationship. In fact, all writers produce an abundance of simple sentences not only because they are easy to read but also because they can be forceful and direct. Because sentence variety is a goal of most experienced writers, simple sentences are also used to provide contrast with longer, more structurally complicated sentences.

ESSENTIAL ELEMENTS OF THE SENTENCE

Writers produce an almost endless variety of sentences. But every complete sentence, regardless of how it varies from other sentences, has two essential parts: a **subject** and a **verb.** The subject of a sentence is what you are writing about, and the verb makes a statement or asks a question about the subject. Although a sentence may have other elements, it must have a subject and verb. The following sentence has only these two essential elements:

Maria smiled.

Most sentences, however, are longer and more detailed. Notice in the following sentence pairs that the essential elements (subject and verb) remain the same even though more details are added. (The subject is underlined once and the verb twice.)

▶ Examples

The car rolls.

The battered old car rolls down the hill.

Several stood.

Several of the construction workers stood with their backs to us.

The wind is blowing.

The hot, dry wind is constantly blowing the fine sand into our faces.

EXERCISE

19.1 Underline the subject once and the verb twice in each of the following simple sentences.

1. The judge allowed the trial to be televised.

2. Each year, the threat of global warming increases.

3. The tornado caused massive destruction.

4. My new computer is still sitting on the floor.

5. The cup of coffee sat on the edge of her desk.

6. The student wearily dropped her backpack onto a chair.

The preceding sentences are all examples of **simple sentences.** That is, they all have a single subject–verb relationship: The verb of each sentence makes a statement about the subject of the sentence. Even in a sentence in which the subject or verb is *compounded* (composed of two or more parts), the sentence is still a simple sentence if both the verbs are making the same statement about both of the subjects.

▶ Examples

Compound verb:	Maria smiled and nodded.
Compound subject:	Maria and John smiled.
Compound subject and verb:	Maria and John smiled and nodded.

All three examples are still simple sentences because they have only one subject–verb relationship. But if the sentence is changed so it expresses two subject–verb relationships, the sentence is no longer simple but compound:

▶ **Example**

Compound sentence: <u>Maria</u> <u><u>smiled</u></u>, and <u>John</u> <u><u>nodded</u></u>.

In Chapter 21, you will learn how to write and punctuate compound sentences.

> *Punctuation Note:* As illustrated in the previous examples, a comma is used with *and* when separating the two parts of a compound sentence but no comma is used with *and* when connecting compound subjects or compound verbs. You will learn more about writing and punctuating compound sentences in Chapter 21.

EXERCISE

19.2   Write five simple sentences, including at least one with a compound subject or verb. Underline the subject once and the verb twice in each sentence.

1. _____
   _____

2. _____
   _____

3. _____
   _____

4. _____
   _____

5. _____
   _____

Subjects

Because your subject is what you are talking about, it is often a word that names someone or something. We call such words **nouns.** Look at the following list of nouns:

1. computers   4. Miquel
2. dog   5. advise
3. actress

Using English As a Second Language: Articles

In English, an article (*a*, *an*, or *the*) is frequently used with a common noun. Although there are no definite rules about the use of articles, the following guidelines may help you decide when to use an article and which one to use.

- Use *a* with singular countable nouns that begin with a consonant sound (e.g., *book, car, uniform*).

- Use *an* with singular countable nouns that begin with a vowel sound (e.g., *orange, uncle, hour*):

- Use *the* with a specific singular countable noun (*the mayor's car*) or with a generalized singular countable noun (I like to go to *the theater*).

- Use *the* with plural countable nouns (*books, cars, oranges*) and with uncountable nouns (e.g., *machinery, furniture, pride, ice*).

- Use no article with abstract nouns (Jill is fascinated by *nature*.)

Note: An article is generally not used with a singular proper noun (e.g. *Mike, Korea, Harvard, New York*) but is used with plural proper nouns (e.g., *the Johnsons, the Alps, the British Isles*).

If you are not sure about whether to use an article or which one to use, ask a native speaker.

EXERCISE

19.3   Each of the nouns listed above can function as the subject of a sentence. Write five simple sentences, each using one of these nouns as a subject. (If English is a second language for you, refer to the note above on using articles.)

1. _____

_____

2. _____

_____

3. _____

_____

4. _____

_____

5. _____

_____

Pronouns are words that refer to nouns. Like a noun, a pronoun can function as the subject of a sentence. For example, the following pronouns could refer to the nouns listed earlier.

1. computers—they   4. Miguel—he
2. dog—it   5. advise—it
3. actress—she

EXERCISE

19.4   Rewrite the five sentences you wrote in Exercise 19.3, using an appropriate pronoun as the subject of each sentence.

1. _____
   _____

2. _____
   _____

3. _____
   _____

4. _____
   _____

5. _____
   _____

EXERCISE

19.5   Many of the subject nouns and pronouns are deleted from the following passage. Replace the blanks with appropriate nouns or pronouns so each sentence has a subject that makes sense. Any word that makes sense in the context is acceptable. Do not worry about right or wrong answers. If the word you choose is appropriate for the context, it is correct.

He was raised by his aunt and uncle, who was his father's brother.

_____ had been staying with them when his parents died, and he
        (1)

simply stayed on. _____ slept in a narrow bed in a small and dingy
                          (2)

room. _____ lived in a sunless groundfloor apartment in an old
             (3)

five-story red-brick building where his uncle collected the rents for the owner no one ever saw. The _____ was the talk of their Brooklyn
(4)
neighborhood. There was something wrong with it; _____ had gone
(5)
awry from the very beginning. The furnace was whimsical and tended to die when it was most needed; valves stuck, _____ leaked, faucets
(6)
gushed unevenly when turned on, or gave off explosions of air; electrical _____ shorted mysteriously; _____ of brick worked loose
(7)   (8)
and tumbled to the sidewalk; the tar paper covering of the roof, no matter how recently replaced, became warped, then buckled and cracked. But the rents were low, the _____ were always filled, and his uncle, who
(9)
earned an erratic livelihood from the badly organized and decrepit Hebrew bookstore he operated in the neighborhood, was kept very busy. Often his _____ himself fired up the furnace on those early winter mornings
(10)
when the janitor was in a drunken stupor from which he could not be roused. _____ came and went. His uncle's _____ was not
(11)   (12)
an easy one.

—Adapted from Chaim Potok, *The Book of Lights*

Verbs

In addition to a subject, each complete sentence must have a verb—a word or phrase that makes a statement or asks a question about the subject. The verb of a sentence may be a single word (such as *drink*) or a verb phrase (such as *will be drinking*). Each verb has many forms. The form of a verb changes most often to indicate **tense**—the time at which the stated action or being takes place. Look at the following examples of the tenses of the verb *dance:*

> I **dance** each day to keep in shape. (present)
> I **danced** for several hours last night. (past)

I **will dance** with you later. (future)

I **have danced** with her before. (present perfect)

I **had danced** for hours. (past perfect)

I **will have danced** every dance. (future perfect)

I **am dancing** too much. (present progressive)

I **was dancing** energetically. (past progressive)

I **will be dancing** in the chorus. (future progressive)

I **have been dancing** with him. (present perfect progressive)

I **had been dancing** for many years. (past perfect progressive)

I **will have been dancing** for twenty years next month. (future perfect progressive)

Most native speakers of English do not have to think consciously about using the appropriate tense—the one that communicates the intended relationship between the time of the action expressed in the sentence and the actual time at which the sentence is written or spoken.

▶ **Examples**

I **danced** all night. (past tense, occurring in the past at a specified time)

I **have danced** to that song before. (present perfect, occurring at some time in the past)

I **am dancing** too much. (present progressive, occurring at the present time)

Choosing the appropriate verb tense is part of a writer's responsibility, a responsibility that is often challenging for non-native speakers of English. Within the range of what is considered correct are many choices, but each choice conveys a different meaning. (See also forms in Chapter 26.)

Writers also use helping verbs (such as *should, would, could, might, may, can, must,* and *do* or *did*) to make other distinctions about verbs. Readers use these helping verbs as clues to interpret a writer's meaning.

▶ **Examples**

I **may** dance.
I **might** dance ⟶ possibility

I **must** dance.
I **should** dance ⟶ obligation

I **can** dance.
I **could** dance. ⟶ ability

I **would** dance. ─────── condition

I **will** dance. ─────── intent

I **do** dance ╮
                  ├──→ emphasis
I **did** dance. ╯

EXERCISE

19.6

The following four sentences have no main verb. Using the clues provided in each sentence, fill in an appropriate form of the verb *speak*.

1. Every day as he walks to work, Michael _____ to her.

2. Yesterday, as he walked to work, Michael _____ to her.

3. Tomorrow, as he walks to work, Michael _____ to her.

4. By then, Michael _____ to her.

EXERCISE

19.7

The main verbs have been deleted from each of the sentences in the following passage. Supply a verb for each sentence. Be sure to choose a verb that makes sense in the context of the paragraph. (Hint: Use past tense.)

In March there _____ a death on the island. Like most deaths
                 (1)

on Yamacraw, it _____ with unforeshadowed swiftness; there was
                  (2)

no lingering or gradual wasting away or bedside farewells. A heart attack

_____ Blossom Smith on a Saturday, an islander raced to Ted Stone's
     (3)

house, and Stone immediately _____ for a rescue helicopter from
                                (4)

Savannah. Blossom was _____ to an open field near the nightclub,
                        (5)

where half the island gathered around her wailing and praying. The

helicopter appeared, _____ rapidly and efficiently, received the
                       (6)

motionless Blossom into the dark angel with the rotating wings,

_____into the sky in a maelstrom of debris and air, and then
   (7)

_____ over the top of trees. It _____ all very quick, very
   (8)   (9)

impressive, and very futile. Blossom _____ that night in Savannah
(10)

surrounded by strangers and the ammonia smells of a death ward.

—Pat Conroy, *The Water Is Wide*

EXERCISE

19.8   Following are two lists of verbs. One consists of five present tense verbs, and the other consists of the same verbs in the past tense. Use each verb in a sentence that provides the appropriate context for the tense.

Present Tense Verbs	Past Tense Verbs
1. walks	2. walked
3. is singing	4. was singing
5. eat	6. ate
7. does believe	8. did believe
9. can study	10. could study

▶ **Example:**   He **reads** his lesson every day.

He **read** that novel last weekend.

1. _____

2. _____

3. _____

4. _____

5. _____

6. _____

7. _____

8. _____

_____

9. _____

_____

10. _____

_____

BASIC PATTERNS OF THE SIMPLE SENTENCE

All English sentences are derived from three basic patterns. A knowledge of these three patterns will enable you to analyze the structure of any sentence you read or write:

> **Pattern 1:** Subject–Verb (S–V)
> **Pattern 2:** Subject–Verb–Object (S–V–O)
> **Pattern 3:** Subject–Linking Verb–Complement (S–LV–C)

Pattern 1: Subject–Verb (S–V)

This pattern has only the two essential elements of a sentence: a subject and a verb. However, it may also have modifying words and phrases that describe and/or limit either the subject or the verb. Remember also that the verb of a sentence may be a verb phrase (a verb plus one or more helping verbs).

► Examples

Students study. (S–V)

Students will be studying. (S–V phrase)

Many students in Dr. Goff's chemistry class study together in the evening. (S–V plus modifying words and phrases)

Although the subject and verb in this pattern usually occur in the order shown (subject preceding verb), the order may be inverted without affecting the pattern.

► Examples

In the stacks, on the top floor of the library, study the most industrious, dedicated students.

(The subject of this sentence is *students,* and the verb is *study.* Even though the word order has been inverted, the pattern is still S–V.)

Did the biology <u>students</u> <u><u>study</u></u> for their test?

(Because this sentence is a question, the word order is inverted: The subject *students* comes between the auxiliary verb *did* and the main verb *study*.)

There <u><u>are</u></u> two <u>books</u> on the table.

(Because the sentence begins with *there*, the word order of the subject and the verb is reversed.)

Sentences with inverted word order offer writers additional options for subtle differences in meaning. *The moon we could not see* is not the same as *We could not see the moon.* As a writer, you need to be aware of the options that inversion of word order offers. As a reader, you need to be aware that such sentences are more difficult to read than sentences in normal word order. A knowledge of basic sentence patterns will help you analyze and understand such sentences.

EXERCISE

19.9   Write three sentences that follow the subject–verb pattern. Include one sentence that has inverted word order.

1. _____

_____

2. _____

_____

3. _____

_____

Pattern 2: Subject–Verb–Object (S–V–O)

This pattern has a third major element—an **object** (often called a **direct object**)—in addition to the essential subject and verb. An object completes and receives the action expressed by the verb. Like a subject, an object is a noun or a noun substitute, such as a pronoun.

▶ **Examples**

Her husband washed the dishes. (S–V–O)

Her husband was washing the dishes. (S–V phrase–O)

Silently but efficiently, her husband washed the dirty dishes. (S–V–O plus modifiers)

The elements in this pattern, like those in the S–V pattern, usually occur in normal order (S–V–O); however, the word order can also be inverted.

▶ **Examples**

<pre>
       O   S   V
</pre>
That book he had not read.

<pre>
           O   S   V
</pre>
This solution she had not considered.

Pronouns as Objects

Personal pronouns, which refer to people or things, assume different forms depending on their function in the sentence. The object form of a personal pronoun should be used when the pronoun is functioning as the object of a verb. Compare the contrasting examples of subject and object forms given here:

▶ **Examples**

He caught the frisbee. (personal pronoun as subject)

The frisbee hit **him.** (personal pronoun as object)

I met Shawn at the party. (personal pronoun as subject)

Shawn met **me** at the party. (personal pronoun as object)

She sent her accountant for a file. (personal pronoun as subject)

Her accountant sent **her** to the bank. (personal pronoun as object)

They visited their friends. (personal pronoun as subject)

Their friends visited **them.** (personal pronoun as object)

In the first example, the subject form of the pronoun (*he*) is used because the pronoun is functioning as the subject of the sentence. But in the second example, the object form (*him*) is used because the pronoun is functioning as the object of the sentence. The following chart lists both the subject and object forms of the personal pronouns:

	Subject Forms	*Object Forms*
First-person singular	I	me
Second-person singular	you	you
Third-person singular	he, she, it	him, her, it
First-person plural	we	us
Second-person plural	you	you
Third-person plural	they	them

Be sure to use the subject form of the pronoun if you are using it as a subject and the object form if you are using it as an object. (*Note:* Some sentences also include an **indirect object**—the one to or for whom the direct object is intended.)

▶ **Examples:**   S V IO   O
                   I sent **him** a letter.

Him is the indirect object—the one to whom the letter (the direct object) is sent. Pronouns that function as indirect objects are in the objective case.

EXERCISE

19.10   Write three sentences that follow the S–V–O pattern. Use a pronoun as the object of one sentence, and include an indirect object in one sentence.

1. _____

   _____

2. _____

   _____

3. _____

   _____

Pattern 3: Subject–Linking Verb–Complement (S–LV–C)

Like the S–V–O pattern, this one also has three elements: subject, linking verb, and complement. A **complement,** like an object, completes the meaning of the verb. However, in this pattern the verb is a **linking verb,** and the complement refers to the subject. In fact, the complement is often called a *subject complement.* A noun or pronoun renames the subject; an adjective describes the subject.

▶ **Examples:**   NOUN
                   Marcus is my friend. (S–LV–C)

                   ADJECTIVE
                   Marcus is friendly. (S–LV–C)

Both of these sentences follow the S–LV–C pattern, but the first has a noun complement (*friend* renames *Marcus,* telling who he is), and the second has an adjective complement (*friendly* describes *Marcus,* telling something about him). Both complements refer to the subject *Marcus* even though they are part of the verb. A complement, in fact, is necessary to complete the meaning of the linking verb.

Linking Verbs

A linking verb connects the subject to the subject complement. The verb *to be* (*am, is, are, was,* and *were*) is the most frequently used linking verb. (Because it is a highly irregular verb, we have listed its main forms on page 349.)

The following verbs may also function as linking verbs. Notice that each of these verbs could be replaced by some form of the verb *to be*.

Verb	Example of Verb in Sentence
act	The dog **acts** sick. (is sick)
appear	The plants **appear** healthy. (are healthy)
become	They **became** unhappy. (were unhappy)
fall	The gorilla **fell** ill. (is ill)
feel	I **feel** great. (am great)
get	My aunt **is getting** old. (is old)
go	The dog **went** crazy. (was crazy)
grow	The child **grew** sleepy. (was sleepy)
keep	My mother **keeps** healthy. (is healthy)
look	The winner **looked** happy. (was happy)
prove	That decision **will prove** a mistake. (will be a mistake)
remain	The mockingbird **remained** quiet. (was quiet)
run	That river **runs** deep. (is deep)
seem	You **seem** sad. (are sad)
smell	That onion **smells** terrible. (is terrible)
sound	That piano **sounds** off-key. (is off-key)
stay	The door **stays** open. (is open)
taste	The apple **tastes** sour. (is sour)
turn	The leaves **were turning** brown. (were brown)

Although each of these verbs could be replaced by a form of the verb *to be,* they are essential to good writing because they are more specific, concrete ways of expressing the overused verb *to be.*

Pronouns as Complements

Personal pronouns as well as nouns can function as complements. When a personal pronoun is used as a complement, it takes the subject form rather than the object form.

▶ **Examples**

Personal pronoun as subject:	**She** is a good student.
Personal pronoun as object:	Her teacher entered **her** in a contest.
Personal pronoun as complement:	In fact, the winner of the contest was **she**.

EXERCISE

19.11 Write three sentences that follow the S–LV–C pattern. Be sure to include linking verbs other than the verb *to be* in one of your sentences and to use one personal pronoun as a complement.

1. _____

_____

2. _____

_____

3. _____

_____

▨ CHAPTER REVIEW

- A simple sentence, like any sentence, has two essential elements: a subject and a verb.
- A simple sentence may have a compound subject and/or a compound verb.
- Subjects are usually nouns or pronouns.
- A verb has various forms that indicate tense—the time at which the stated action or being took place.
- Simple sentences can be classified according to the following patterns: subject–verb, subject–verb–object, or subject–linking verb–complement.

WRITING ASSIGNMENT

Rewrite a paragraph or an essay that you wrote for an earlier assignment, editing carefully. Focus especially on sentence structure. Have you used a variety of patterns for your simple sentences? Does each sentence have a subject and verb?

PARTICIPATING IN THE ACADEMIC COMMUNITY

Read a paragraph or essay that one of your classmates has just edited, focusing again on sentence structure. Does each sentence have a subject and verb? Does the writer use a variety of sentence patterns?

CHAPTER

20

Expanding the Simple Sentence

One of the most important ways to expand the basic elements of a simple sentence is by using modifiers—words and phrases that describe, limit, point out, identify, and make more specific the words they modify. Although modifiers are not an essential part of a sentence, they add information to the basic elements of the sentence. Without modifiers, writers could communicate only general ideas.

▶ **Examples**

> Armadillos dig. (basic elements unmodified)
>
> Two large armadillos dig ruthlessly in my yard every night. (basic elements modified)

Adding modifiers to the basic elements in the second example makes the sentence much more specific and vivid. We now know how many armadillos, the size of the armadillos, and how, where, and when they dig.

ADJECTIVES

Adjectives are modifiers of nouns or noun substitutes and can be divided into several types.

Indefinite Adjectives

Indefinite adjectives limit the nouns they modify, usually by restricting the amount or number. Look at the following list of frequently used indefinite adjectives:

some	every	much
many	each	most

other	all	another
few	any	several

Notice in the following sentences how the indefinite adjectives limit in some way the nouns they modify.

▶ Examples: **Some** restaurants stay open **all** night.

                Several photographers and a **few** reporters were seen at **each** meeting.

                Few policemen were at the **other** riot.

Notice also that an indefinite adjective always comes before the noun it modifies.

Demonstrative Adjectives

Demonstrative adjectives identify or point out. There are only four demonstrative adjectives—*this, that, these,* and *those*—and they always occur before the nouns they modify.

▶ Examples: **This** movie is as boring as **that** one.

                These sandwiches are stale and soggy.

                He selected **those** players for his team.

Descriptive Adjectives

As their name implies, **descriptive adjectives** describe the nouns they modify. They usually occur before the nouns they modify but may occur in a variety of positions.

▶ Examples: The **loud, rhythmic** music filled the room.

                Loud and **rhythmic,** the music filled the room.

                The music, **loud** and **rhythmic,** filled the room.

As a writer, you should be aware of the options you have in placing descriptive adjectives. Try to vary your basic sentence patterns by placing descriptive adjectives in different positions. Notice in the examples that the meaning, rhythm, and emphasis of each sentence are altered slightly by the changes in the placement of the adjectives.

Participles

Verb forms used as adjectives are called **participles.** For example, the verb *shake* has a present participle form, *shaking,* and a past participle form, *shaken.* Each of the participle forms can be used as part of a verb phrase that functions as the main verb of a sentence.

▶ **Examples:**   The old man **is shaking** his fist at us.

The medicine **was shaken** thoroughly.

As shown here, participles can also be used as adjectives:

▶ **Examples:**   The **shaking** child ran to her mother's waiting arms.

The child, **shaking,** ran to her mother.

Shaking and crying, the child ran to her mother.

The old man, pale and **shaken,** sat down carefully.

Shaken by the accident, the woman began to cry.

Notice in these examples the different positions a participle may take in relation to the word it modifies. In your own writing, try to achieve sentence variety by placing participles in different positions.

Using English as a Second Language: Adjective Order

Although the position of certain adjectives in relation to the words they modify can vary, the following list indicates the order in which adjectives usually occur in English sentences.

1. Articles, numbers, indefinite or demonstrative adjectives: *a, an, the, one, any*

2. Opinion: *beautiful, intelligent, weird, decaying*

3. Physical description (size, shape, age, color): *small, thin, young, tan*

4. Nation/religion: *French,   Chinese, Catholic, Muslim*

5. Material: *brick, wood, silk*

6. Function: *security* guard

7. Noun: *girl, house, shirt*

▶ **EXAMPLES:**

the ugly old brown Scottish castle

a large round straw hat

two brave young police officers

Introduction to Sentence Combining

In the following **sentence combining** exercises, you are given a series of short simple sentences. Using the first sentence as your base sentence, reduce the sentences that follow to modifiers that can be used to expand the base sentence.

▶ **Example:**   The wall stretched for miles.

The wall was granite.

The granite was gray.

The wall was thick.

The miles were endless.

Combinations:

The thick, gray granite wall stretched for endless miles.

Thick and gray, the granite wall stretched for endless miles.

The granite wall, thick and gray, stretched for endless miles.

Notice that several combinations are possible. There is no single correct combination. Try to think of as many combinations as you can; then choose the one you like best. You may want to say some of the combinations aloud before deciding on your choice. Try to vary the positions of your adjectives so they do not all come before the nouns they modify.

Punctuation Note: Descriptive adjectives that do not come before the nouns they modify are set off by commas.

> The quilt, **torn** and **ragged,** lay on the bed.

Coordinate (equal) adjectives in a series are separated by commas.

> The **torn, ragged** quilt lay on the bed.

However, if adjectives in a series are not coordinate, they are not separated by commas.

> The **careless young** man failed to signal as he turned.

To determine if adjectives are coordinate, insert the word *and* between them. If the resulting construction makes sense, the adjectives are coordinate.

> The **torn** and **ragged** quilt lay on the bed.

> The **careless** and **young** man failed to signal as he turned.

In the first sentence, the inclusion of *and* makes sense, so the adjectives are coordinate and should be separated by a comma.

> The **torn, ragged** quilt lay on the bed.

In the second sentence, the insertion of *and* does not make sense, so the adjectives are not coordinate and should thus not be separated by a comma.

> The **careless young** man failed to signal as he turned.

20.1

Using the first sentence as your base, reduce the sentences that follow to modifiers. Discuss punctuation possibilities with your instructor or classmates.

1. The groundhog peeked out of its hole.
   The groundhog was shy.
   The groundhog was shaggy.
   The hole was private.

   _____

   _____

   _____

2. The girl slept in the doorway.
   The girl was young.
   The girl was pretty.
   The doorway was cold.
   The doorway was dirty.

   _____

   _____

   _____

3. The dancers kept time to the music.
   The dancers were moving energetically.
   The music was loud.
   The music was pulsating.

   _____

   _____

   _____

4. The candle went out.
   The candle was sputtering.
   The candle was hissing.

   _____

   _____

   _____

5. The child looked into the box.
   The child was curious.
   The box was tiny.

The box was carved.
The box was wooden.

_____

_____

_____

EXERCISE

20.2

Replace the blanks in the following passage with appropriate adjectives.

It was a beautiful college. The buildings were _____ and covered
               (1)

with vines and the roads gracefully winding, lined with hedges and wild

roses that dazzled the eyes in the _____ sun. Honeysuckle and
                                (2)

_____ wisteria hung heavy from the trees and _____
   (3)   (4)

magnolias mixed with their scents in the _____ air. I've recalled it
                            (5)

often, here in my hole: How the grass turned _____ in the
                                   (6)

springtime and how the mockingbirds fluttered their tails and sang, how

the moon shone down on the buildings, how the bell in the chapel tower

rang out the precious short-lived hours; how the girls in _____
                                      (7)

summer dresses promenaded the _____ lawn. Many times, here at
                         (8)

night, I've closed my eyes and walked along the _____ road that
                                  (9)

winds past the girls' dormitories, past the hall with the clock in the tower,

its windows warmly _____ on down past the _____ white
                 (10)   (11)

Home Economics practice cottage, whiter still in the moonlight, and on

down the road with its sloping and turning, paralleling the _____
                                       (12)

powerhouse with its engines droning earth-shaking rhythms in the dark,

its windows _____ from the glow of the furnace, on to where the
           (13)

road became a bridge over a _____ riverbed, tangled with brush and
(14)

_____ vines; the bridge of rustic logs, made for trysting, but
(15)

virginal and untested by lovers; on up the road, past the buildings, with the

_____ verandas half-a-city-block long, to the sudden forking, barren
(16)

of buildings, birds, or grass, where the road turned off to the insane asylum.

—Ralph Ellison, *Invisible Man*

ADVERBS

Another way of expanding basic sentence patterns is by using **adverbs** to modify the verb of the sentence. Adverbs can also modify other modifiers (e.g., *She spoke **very** slowly*) or even entire sentences, but they usually give additional information about the verb of a sentence. Adverbs that modify verbs tell how (in what manner), when, or where.

> The student entered the classroom **late.** (when)
>
> They went **home** after the party. (where)
>
> The judge stood up **slowly** and **deliberately.** (how)

Adverbs do not necessarily occur either immediately before or after the verbs they modify, although they may occur in these positions. Notice that in the third example, the adverbs *slowly* and *deliberately* occur after the verb *stood up.* However, these adverbs could be shifted to the beginning of the sentence.

> **Slowly** and **deliberately,** the judge stood up.

Adverbs, especially those that end in *-ly,* can be shifted from one position in the sentence to another. However, when adverbs are placed at the beginning of the sentence rather than in their normal position after the verb, they are usually followed by a comma.

EXERCISE

20.3 Following is a series of short simple sentences. Using the first sentence as your base sentence, reduce the other sentences to adverbs and use them to expand the basic sentence. Remember to vary the placement of your adverbs. If you are adding *-ly* to a word that ends in *-y,* change the *y* to *i* before adding the *-ly* suffix.

1. The guitarist played.
   The playing was soft (ly).
   The playing was steady (ly).
   The playing was all evening.

   _____

   _____

   _____

2. The walrus waddled.
   The waddling was comical (ly).
   The waddling was clumsy (ly).
   The waddling was backward.

   _____

   _____

   _____

3. The plant grew.
   The growing was unexpected (ly).
   The growing was sudden (ly).

   _____

   _____

   _____

4. The wind blew.
   The blowing was constant (ly).
   The blowing was relentless (ly).
   The blowing was day and night.

   _____

   _____

   _____

5. Alice rode the motorcycle.
   The riding was fearless (ly).
   The riding was natural (ly).
   The riding was along the trail.

   _____

   _____

   _____

Replace each blank in the following passage with an appropriate adverb.

The stern of the vessel shot by, dropping, as it did so, into a hollow between the waves; and I caught a glimpse of a man standing at the wheel, and of another man who seemed to be doing little else than smoke a cigar. I saw the smoke issuing from his lips as he _____ turned his head
                                                                      (1)
and glanced _____ over the water in my direction. It was a careless,
               (2)
unpremeditated glance, one of those haphazard things men do when they have no immediate call to do anything in particular, but act because they are alive and must do something.

But life and death were in that glance. I could see the vessel being swallowed _____ in the fog; I saw the back of the man at the wheel,
              (3)
and the head of the other man turning, _____ turning, as his gaze
                                             (4)
struck the water and _____ lifted along it toward me. His face wore
                        (5)
an absent expression, as of deep thought, and I became afraid that if his eyes did light upon me he would nevertheless not see me. But his eyes did light upon me, and looked _____ into mine; and he did see me, for he
                         (6)
sprang to the wheel, thrusting the other man _____, and whirled
                                                 (7)
it round and _____, hand over hand, at the same time shouting
                (8)
orders of some sort. The vessel seemed to go _____ at a tangent to
                                                 (9)
its former course and leapt almost _____ from view into the fog.
                                       (10)

I felt myself slipping into unconsciousness, and tried with all the power of my will to fight above the suffocating blankness and darkness that was rising around me. A little _____ I heard the stroke of oars, growing
                            (11)

nearer and _____(12)_____, and the calls of a man. When he was

_____(13)_____ near I heard him crying, in vexed fashion, "Why in hell don't

you sing out?" This meant me, I thought, and _____(14)_____ the blankness

and darkness rose over me.

—Jack London, *The Sea Wolf*

PREPOSITIONAL PHRASES

Prepositional phrases provide a third way to expand basic sentences. A prepositional phrase consists of a preposition and its object (a noun or noun substitute). The prepositional phrase itself may be expanded by the addition of adjectives that modify the object of the preposition.

▶ **Examples:**   The nurse smiled **at the child.**
The nurse smiled **at the small, timid child.**

The fighter **in the corner** looked mean.
The fighter **in the far corner** looked mean.

We caught the bus **at the station.**
We caught the bus **at the central station.**

Common Prepositions			
aboard	behind	from	throughout
about	below	in	to
above	beneath	into	toward
across	beside	like	under
after	between	near	underneath
against	beyond	of	until
along	but	off	unto
amid	by	on	up
among	down	over	upon
around	during	past	with
at	except	since	within
before	for	through	without

Compound Prepositions		
according to	contrary to	instead of
along with	due to	on account of
as well as	in addition to	out of
because of	in place of	together with
		in spite of

Function

Prepositional phrases function in a sentence as either adjectives or adverbs, depending on whether they modify a noun or a verb. Those that function as adverbs give information (where, how, when, or why) about verbs.

▶ **Examples:**   The party was held **at the beach.** (where)

The stunned man wandered about **in a daze.** (how)

They arrived early **in the morning**. (when)

They came **for the homecoming party.** (why)

Prepositional phrases that function as adjectives modify nouns by telling which one(s).

▶ **Examples:**   The girl **in the red dress** raised her hand.

That book **of mine** caused a lot of trouble.

The room **on the second floor** is vacant.

In the preceding examples, the prepositional phrases function as adjectives because they modify nouns; they tell us which girl, which book, and which room. That is, they identify as well as describe the nouns they modify.

Using English as a Second Language: Prepositions of Place and Time

Students whose native language is not English often have difficulty figuring out which prepositions to use in particular situations. Although many rules and exceptions exist for using prepositions, the following chart provides examples of some of the more common prepositions of place and time:

Preposition	*Use*	*Example*
at (place)	refers to position	We saw them at church
in (place)	refers to position	I met him in class.
to (place)	refers to movement	Let's go to class.
at (time)	with time of day	He left at 5 o'clock at night.
on (time)	with dates and days of week	Mohammed arrived onMonday.
in (time)	with years, months, seasons	Bridgette was born in 1982.
by (time)	on or before	You must pay by noon at the latest.
until (time)	up to	You may keep the book until tonight.
during (time)	duration	I spoke with him during the break.
for (time)	length of time	Her speech lasted for ten minutes.

Placement

Most prepositional phrases that function as adverbs can be moved about freely.

▶ **Examples:** **During the morning,** the rain fell steadily.

The rain fell steadily **during the morning.**

Notice the slight difference in emphasis and style that results from the shift in the position of the prepositional phrase. The placement of adverbial prepositional phrases is another option that a writer has. However, prepositional phrases that function as adjectives are placed *immediately after* the nouns or pronouns they modify.

EXERCISE

20.5

In the following sentence-combining exercise, use the first sentence as your base sentence and reduce the others to prepositional phrases that modify a noun or verb in the main sentence. Remember to vary the placement of your adverb phrases but be sure each adjective phrase follows immediately the word that it modifies.

1. The picture hung.
   The picture was of the church.
   The church was on the hill.
   The hanging was in the office.

   _____

   _____

   _____

2. The wilting fern sat.
   The sitting was in a dusty corner.
   The corner was of the waiting room.

   _____

   _____

   _____

3. Marcelle went.
   The going was during her coffee break.
   The going was to the drug store.
   The going was for a few minutes.
   The going was for some aspirin.

   _____

   _____

   _____

4. The senator spoke to the crowd.
   The speaking was on Memorial Day.
   The senator was from Pennsylvania.
   The crowd was of retired citizens.
   The speaking was with great enthusiasm.

   _____

   _____

   _____

5. The father placed the small child.
   The placing was in her crib.
   The crib was beside the big bed.
   The placing was at night.

   _____

   _____

   _____

EXERCISE

20.6   Write appropriate prepositions in the blanks in the following passage.

The distance _____ the earth _____ the moon changes
            (1)   (2)

every day, even _____ minute _____ minute, because both
           (3)   (4)

the earth and the moon travel _____ oval orbits. Since the moon's
             (5)

orbit is not circular, but oval-shaped, the moon is closer _____ the
             (6)

earth _____ some times and farther away _____ other
    (7)   (8)

times. _____ the nearest approach to the earth, the moon
      (9)

is 360,000 km away. _____ its farthest point, the moon is
           (10)

404,800 km away. . . .

The moon does not actually change shape. It is the pattern

_____ reflected light that changes. The moon does not give off light
  (11)

_____ its own. It receives light _____ the sun, just as the
  (12)   (13)

earth and other planets do. The moon's barren surface reflects much

_____ the light into space and some _____ that light
          (14)   (15)

reaches the earth. One half of the moon is always lighted _____
                                                              (16)

the sun and one half is always dark, just as the earth is. But the same half

_____ the moon is not lighted all _____ the time because the
     (17)   (18)

moon is traveling _____ an orbit _____ the earth while the
                        (19)   (20)

earth travels around the sun.

—Adapted from William H. Matthews III et al., *Investigating the Earth*

APPOSITIVES

A final way that basic sentence patterns can be expanded is by the use
of appositives. An **appositive** is a noun or noun phrase (noun plus modifiers) that gives additional information about another noun. Unlike adjectives—which describe, limit, or identify nouns—an appositive explains or
defines a noun.

▶ **Examples:**   The picture, **a pastel watercolor,** was for sale.

   They served my favorite dessert, **raspberry sherbet.**

   An energetic person, Nora Smith is always up before dawn.

In the first two examples, the appositives follow the nouns they explain.
This is by far the most common position for an appositive. In the third sentence, however, the appositive comes before the noun it explains. In either
case, whether the appositive comes before or after the noun it explains,
it must be immediately adjacent to it.

An appositive is usually set off by commas. In instances in which the
appositive is essential to identify the noun it explains (e.g., *my friend Dale*),
commas may be omitted. But most of the time—in fact, any time the appositive could be omitted from the sentence without changing the meaning
of the sentence—it is set off by commas.

EXERCISE

20.7   Combine each sentence pair into one sentence by making one of the sentences an appositive that explains a noun in the other sentence.

▶ **Examples:**   The swing hung from a tree.

   The tree was an old live oak with low, gnarled branches.

Combination:

The swing hung from a tree, an old live oak with low, gnarled branches.

1. Dr. Singh performed the delicate operation.
   Dr. Singh is a renowned heart surgeon.

   _____

   _____

2. The plants were set in large clay pots around the patio.
   The plants were geraniums and periwinkles.

   _____

   _____

3. They liked the other car.
   The other car was a small Japanese model.

   _____

   _____

4. An aardvark was the main attraction at the zoo.
   An aardvark is one of the strangest looking animals in existence.

   _____

   _____

   _____

5. Kim is reading *The Scarlet Letter*.
   The Scarlet Letter is Nathaniel Hawthorne's most famous novel.

   _____

   _____

   _____

EXERCISE

20.8   This sentence-combining exercise contains a series of sentence groups that can be combined in various ways. Using the first sentence as your base sentence, reduce the sentences that follow to modifiers (adjectives, adverbs, or prepositional phrases) or appositives that can be used to expand the base sentence. Try to vary the position of the modifiers. If you are unsure of the correct punctuation, discuss the sentence with your instructor or classmates.

1. The cat stretched.
   The cat was fat.

The cat was sleek.
The cat was a Burmese.
The stretching was lazy (ly).

_____

_____

_____

2. The car rolled.
The car was a Mercedes.
The car was expensive.
The rolling was slow (ly).
The rolling was arrogant (ly).
The rolling was to a stop.

_____

_____

_____

3. I read the book.
The reading was reluctant.
The book was silly.
The book was repetitious.
The reading was to my son.

_____

_____

_____

4. The hotel sat.
The hotel was brick.
The brick was red.
The sitting was on a hill.
The hill was overlooking a cliff.
The sitting was precarious (ly).

_____

_____

_____

5. The dishes were stacked.
The dishes were dirty.
The stack was high.
The height was dangerous (ly).
The stacking was in the sink.

The sink was enamel.
The enamel was chipped.

_____

_____

_____

20.9   Using the first sentence as your base sentence, combine the following sentences. Then rewrite the sentences to create a paragraph about Santa Fe, New Mexico.

1. Santa Fe is a town.
   The town has a past.

   _____

   _____

   _____

2. It seems to belong.
   The belonging is to another time.
   The belonging is to another place.
   It is located in the hills.
   The hills are at the foot.
   The foot is of the mountains.

   _____

   _____

   _____

3. One immediately notices.
   What one notices is the age.
   The age is of the town.
   The age is obvious.
   One leaves the highway.
   The highway is modern.
   The highway is four-lane.
   The four-lane is wide.
   The highway leads to Santa Fe.

   _____

   _____

   _____

4. Some buildings date.
   The dating is back.
   The dating is to the 1600s.

   _____

   _____

   _____

5. Even the buildings are designed.
   The buildings are new.
   The designing is to look old.

   _____

   _____

   _____

6. Everything is built.
   The everything is new.
   The everything is old.
   The building is adobe.
   The adobe is sand colored.

   _____

   _____

   _____

7. Streets are narrow.
   Streets are unpaved.
   The unpaving is frequent (ly).

   _____

   _____

   _____

8. Dogs wander.
   The wandering is free (ly).
   The wandering is about the plaza.
   The plaza is central.
   The dogs ignore the traffic.
   The dogs ignore the tourists.

   _____

   _____

   _____

9. Women peddle their wares.
The women are Native American.
The women are wrapped.
The wrapping is in shawls.
The shawls are hand-woven.
The peddling is along the sidewalks.
The sidewalks encircle the plaza.

_____

_____

_____

10. They too ignore the traffic.
They too ignore the tourists.

_____

_____

_____

CHAPTER REVIEW

- One way to expand a simple sentence is to use indefinite, demonstrative, descriptive, or participial adjectives to modify nouns.

- A second way to expand a simple sentence is to use adverbs to modify the verb or other modifiers.

- A third way to expand a simple sentence is to add prepositional phrases.

- A fourth way to expand a simple sentence is to add an appositive, a noun phrase (noun plus modifiers) that gives additional information about the original noun.

WRITING ASSIGNMENT

Write a paragraph or essay describing a person, place, or thing. After you have written your first draft, go back and expand each of your sentences. Use each of the four methods of expansion discussed in this chapter at least once in your revision.

PARTICIPATING IN THE ACADEMIC COMMUNITY

Exchange your paragraph or essay with one of your classmates and identify the methods of expansion used in your partner's composition. Make suggestions about sentences that could be expanded further.

CHAPTER 21

Compound Sentences

In Chapter 19, you learned that a simple sentence consists of one subject-verb relationship and makes a single statement or asks a single question. Simple sentences are called **independent clauses** when they become parts of a compound sentence. Therefore, a compound sentence is a combination of two or more independent clauses—groups of words that have a subject and a verb and can function as a simple sentence.

▶ Examples

Independent clause (simple sentence):	The physician sat down.
Independent clause (simple sentence):	The patient remained standing.
Compound sentence:	The physician sat down, but the patient remained standing.

Notice that the two independent clauses (simple sentences) in the previous example are coordinate—that is, they are equal; each can function as a sentence on its own, each has a subject and verb, and each contributes equally to the meaning of the compound sentence. The diagram on the following page shows the essential parts of a compound sentence.

CONNECTING INDEPENDENT CLAUSES

To form a compound sentence, independent clauses must be connected clearly and correctly. To indicate the relationship between independent clauses in a compound sentence, writers often use a **coordinating conjunction** or a **conjunctive adverb**.

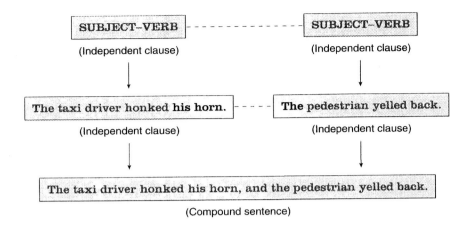

(Compound sentence)

Coordinating Conjunctions

The most common way to connect the independent clauses in a compound sentence is to use a **coordinating conjunction.** The following chart lists all of the coordinating conjunctions, categorizing them into groups according to the relationships they indicate:

Addition	Contrast	Alternate	Cause and Effect
and	but	or	for
both . . . and	yet	nor	so
		either . . . or	
		neither . . . nor	

Writers use coordinating conjunctions to express relationships between independent clauses and between other sentence elements (see Chapter 19), and readers use these same words as clues to understanding relationships within sentences they are reading. That is, a coordinating conjunction indicates the relationship between the elements it connects. For example, the meaning of each of the following sentences is completely altered when the coordinating conjunction is changed:

He was gaining slowly, **and** he kept trying. (addition)

He was gaining slowly, **but** he kept trying. (contrast)

He was gaining slowly, **so** he kept trying. (cause and effect)

Note: A strategy to help you remember the primary coordinating conjunctions is to think of the term FANBOYS: *for, and, nor, but, or, yet,* and *so.*

Conjunctive Adverbs

In addition to being connected by coordinating conjunctions, independent clauses in a compound sentence can also be connected by **conjunctive adverbs.** These words, like coordinating conjunctions, indicate relationships between independent clauses. The following chart lists some of the most common conjunctive adverbs and indicates the relationships they express:

Addition, Comparison	*Contrast*	*Time*	*Cause/Effect, Conclusion*	*Example*
also	however	finally	accordingly	for example
besides	in contrast	first, etc.	as a result	for instance
furthermore	instead	gradually	consequently	in fact
in addition	nevertheless	immediately	hence	that is
indeed	on the contrary	meanwhile	in conclusion	to illustrate
likewise	on the other hand	next	in summary	
moreover	otherwise	sometimes	of course	
similarly	rather	suddenly	therefore	
too	still	then	thus	

Conjunctive adverbs can express relationships similar to those indicated by coordinating conjunctions:

He was gaining slowly; **moreover,** he kept trying. (addition)

He was gaining slowly; **however,** he kept trying. (contrast)

He was gaining slowly; **therefore,** he kept trying. (cause and effect)

However, independent clauses joined by a conjunctive adverb are punctuated quite differently to clauses joined by a coordinating conjunction. The next section explains how to punctuate compound sentences.

PUNCTUATING COMPOUND SENTENCES

There are three ways to connect independent clauses and to punctuate correctly the resulting compound sentence.

1. *Use a coordinating conjunction and place a comma before the conjunction.*

   Some students want an education, **but** others simply want a degree.

2. *Use a conjunctive adverb and place a semicolon before the conjunction and a comma after it.*

   Some students want an education; **however,** others simply want a degree.

Punctuation Note: A conjunctive adverb may appear in a sentence in which it does not introduce an independent clause.

Some students, **however,** simply want a degree.

When used in this way, the conjunctive adverb is set off by commas but requires no semicolon because it is not introducing a second independent clause.

3. *Use no conjunction and place a semicolon between the two independent clauses.*

Some students want an education; others simply want a degree.

Notice that the independent clauses in a compound sentence are closely and logically related in thought. If the relationship between them is not apparent, the resulting sentence will be ridiculous.

Some students want an education; teachers deserve higher salaries.

If independent clauses are connected with just a semicolon and no connecting word or phrase that indicates their relationship, the two clauses must be clearly related in meaning. If a coordinating conjunction or a conjunctive adverb is used, the relationship can be less obvious but should, nevertheless, be clearly expressed by the connecting word.

Joan studied hard; _____ she failed the test.

A good choice for the connecting word in this example would be *however* because the relationship here is one of contrast. If a conjunctive adverb such as *moreover,* indicating addition, or *therefore,* indicating result or conclusion, were used, the sentence would not make sense because the relationship between the two clauses would not be logical.

EXERCISE

21.1

In this exercise, all of the coordinating conjunctions and conjunctive adverbs that connect the independent clauses have been omitted. Write in each blank an appropriate connecting word. In making your choice, consider the relationship between the two clauses and the existing punctuation. Remember that a comma is placed before a coordinating conjunction connecting two independent clauses and a semicolon is placed before a conjunctive adverb connecting two independent clauses.

Many of today's young students have an attention span that has been conditioned by years of watching television. They focus their attention on an issue for a very few minutes, approximately the length of a television

commercial; _____ they expect something different, _____
                    (1)   (2)

they grow bored. As a result, teachers must constantly arrange for a variety

of learning activities, _____ they lose the attention of their students.
                              (3)

Teachers, in effect, assume the role of entertainers; _____ students
                                                              (4)

assume the role of audience. One of the problems that arises from this

situation is that students who perceive themselves as an audience tend to be

passive. Learning requires active participation rather than passivity;

_____ these passive students are often nonlearners.
     (5)

EXERCISE

21.2

In this exercise, you are given one independent clause and a connecting
word, either a coordinating conjunction or a conjunctive adverb. Supply a
second independent clause that is related appropriately to the first.

1. Large cars usually use more fuel, **so** _____

_____

2. Large cars usually use more fuel; **however,** _____

_____

3. Large cars usually use more fuel; **for example,** _____

_____

4. The pilot needed to land the plane quickly, **for** _____

_____

5. The pilot needed to land the plane quickly; **consequently,** _____

_____

6. The pilot needed to land the plane quickly; **otherwise,** _____

_____

7. The rain fell steadily all day, **and** _____

_____

8. The rain fell steadily all day; **then** _____

_____

9. The rain fell steadily all day, **yet** _____

_____

10. The rain fell steadily all day; **therefore,** _____

_____

Punctuation Review

The three ways to connect independent clauses in compound sentences are reviewed for you below:

1. *Coordinating Conjunction and Comma*

Independent clause	, coordinating conjunction	independent clause

▶ **Examples**

| Carlos took five courses last semester | , and (addition) | he worked twenty hours each week. |
| Rachel likes most music | , but (contrast) | she doesn't like hard rock. |

2. *Conjunctive Adverb and Semicolon*

Independent clause	; conjunctive adverb,	independent clause

▶ **Examples**

| Carlos took five courses last semester | ; moreover, (addition) | he worked twenty hours each week. |
| Rachel likes most music | ; however, (contrast) | she doesn't like hard rock. |

3. *Semicolon*

Remember also that if two independent clauses are closely and obviously related, you may connect them by using just a semicolon.

| Independent clause | ; | independent clause |

▶ **Examples**

| Carlos took five courses last semester | ; | he also worked twenty hours each week. |

| Rachel likes most music | ; | she especially likes jazz. |

EXERCISE

21.3   Read each of the following pairs of independent clauses carefully to determine the relationship between them. Then, noting the punctuation that is given, write in each blank an appropriate connecting word.

1. The weather on the day of the election was cold and rainy, _____ a record number of voters went to the polls.

2. The price of oil declined; _____, the economy of the oil-producing states suffered.

3. The money was missing from the cash drawer, _____ the valuables had been taken from the safe.

4. The children behaved badly; _____, one refused to eat.

5. You may want the pecan pie for dessert, _____ you may prefer the cheesecake.

6. His handwriting was barely legible; _____, we could make out the words.

7. First, he opened the door carefully; _____ he peered inside the dimly lit room.

8. The weather was hot and humid, _____ everyone was terribly uncomfortable.

9. The commencement speaker was well prepared; _____, her talk was informative and entertaining.

10. Somehow they managed to move the huge chest, _____ they were not able to get it through the door.

EXERCISE

21.4   Combine the following pairs of independent clauses into compound sentences. Use each of the three ways of connecting independent clauses, and punctuate each sentence appropriately.

1. The red mustang swerved dangerously.
   The driver remained in control of the car.

   _____

   _____

   _____

2. The young widow lived alone.
   She was occasionally lonely.

   _____

   _____

   _____

3. The rain fell steadily all day.
   By evening the water had risen dangerously.

   _____

   _____

   _____

4. The Yomiko sisters resemble each other.
   They are not twins.

   _____

   _____

   _____

5. Hunting is not permitted in these parks.
   Many animals are shot every year

   _____

   _____

   _____

6. Rainfall is scarce in desert areas.
   Water is precious.

   _____

   _____

   _____

7. He must pay cash.
The restaurant does not take credit cards.

_____

_____

_____

8. This is not the first time.
It will be the last.

_____

_____

_____

9. The television commercial lasted only a few moments.
It seemed to last forever.

_____

_____

_____

10. The clouds were thick.
The eclipse was not visible.

_____

_____

_____

EXERCISE

21.5   Write the following types of compound sentences, punctuating each appropriately.

1. Three compound sentences in which the two independent clauses are connected by a coordinating conjunction:

a. _____

_____

b. _____

_____

c. _____

_____

2. Three compound sentences in which the two independent clauses are connected by a conjunctive adverb:

a. _____
_____

b. _____
_____

c. _____
_____

3. Three compound sentences in which no connecting word is used:

a. _____
_____

b. _____
_____

c. _____
_____

EXERCISE

21.6   The following paragraph includes some compound sentences that are not punctuated correctly. Edit this paragraph, supplying the correct punctuation for the compound sentences.

[1]Students often feel compelled to declare a major when they first arrive at college. [2]They are faced with countless forms that ask them to indicate their major and their parents often urge them to make this important decision as soon as possible. [3]In addition, their professor and classmates are constantly asking them what their major is. [4]Students feel they are remiss if they don't declare a major therefore they make this important decision without really knowing where their interests and talents lie. [5]Thus, they commit to a course of study but they soon realize they have made a mistake. [6]They discover they have chosen a

path that they do not wish to pursue yet they are reluctant to admit they have made a mistake. [7]Fortunately, a counselor, professor, or classmate usually comes to their rescue and helps them realize they need to reconsider their hasty decision.

CHAPTER REVIEW

- A compound sentence consists of two independent clauses (or simple sentences).
- There are three ways to connect the independent clauses in a compound sentence:
  1. Use a coordinating conjunction and a comma.
  2. Use a conjunctive adverb and a semicolon.
  3. Use just a semicolon.

WRITING ASSIGNMENT

Revise a paragraph or an essay you have previously written, combining some of the simple sentences into compound sentences.

PARTICIPATING IN THE ACADEMIC COMMUNITY

Working with a group of your peers, edit the paragraphs or essays you have revised, focusing on the correct punctuation of compound sentences.

Complex Sentences

Unlike a compound sentence, which consists of two independent clauses, a **complex sentence** is composed of two types of clauses: an independent clause and one or more dependent clauses. The independent clause expresses the main idea of the sentence, and the dependent clause expresses a supporting idea or detail. As shown in the following figure, the dependent clause functions as part of the independent clause:

The Complex Sentence

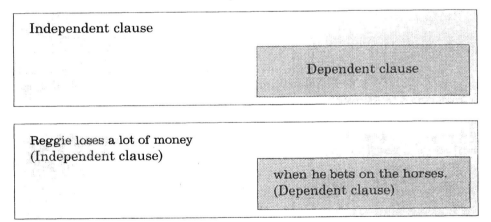

Independent clause

Dependent clause

Reggie loses a lot of money
(Independent clause)

when he bets on the horses.
(Dependent clause)

To understand dependent clauses, you must understand both phrases and independent clauses because a dependent clause has characteristics of both.

Phrases and Clauses

Phrase:	Does not have a	Functions as a	Cannot stand alone
to the theater	subject and verb	unit in a sentence	as a sentence

Dependent Clause: when he went to the theater	Has a subject and verb	Functions as a unit in a sentence (or independent clause)	Cannot stand alone as a sentence
Independent Clause: he went to the theater	Has a subject and verb	Does not function as a unit in another sentence (or in-dependent clause)	Can stand alone as a sentence

As the chart indicates, a dependent clause, unlike an independent clause, cannot function as a sentence even though it has a subject and a verb. A dependent clause is like a phrase in that it is part of an independent clause and functions as an adverb, an adjective, or a noun within the independent clause. Thus, the two clauses of a complex sentence are not equal (coordinate) as are the clauses of a compound sentence. In a complex sentence, the dependent clause *depends on*, or is subordinate to, the independent clause.

▶ **Examples**

Adverb clause: **Although the forests are old,** much of the undergrowth is recent.

Adjective clause: The actress **who appeared in the second act** had a shrill voice.

Noun clause: The jury concluded **that he was guilty.**

ADVERB CLAUSES

An **adverb clause** is a dependent clause that functions as an adverb within the independent clause in which it appears. An adverb clause usually modifies the verb of the independent clause. Listed here are some of the transition words, or subordinating conjunctions, commonly used to introduce adverb clauses:

after	because	rather than	when
as	before	since	whenever
as if	even if	so that	whereas
as soon as	even though	though	wherever
although	ever since	unless	whether
as though	if	until	while

The following complex sentences contain adverb clauses. Observe how the placement and punctuation of the adverb clause differ in the two sentences.

▶ **Examples**

At beginning of sentence: **Unless you save carefully,** you will run out of money.

At end of sentence: You will run out of money **unless you save carefully.**

Notice in the first sentence the adverb clause comes at the beginning of the sentence and is followed by a comma. In the second sentence, the adverb clause comes after the independent clause and is not separated from it by a comma. An introductory adverb clause is always followed by a comma; an adverb clause that occurs at the end of a sentence, however, requires no punctuation.

EXERCISE

22.1   Combine each of the following pairs of sentences into a complex sentence with an adverb clause. Vary the position of your adverb clauses and punctuate correctly. You may wish to refer to the list of transition words for adverb clauses provided earlier.

1. The desert is hot and dry.
   Many flowers grow there.

   _____

   _____

   _____

2. I looked out the rear window of the car. I came to a stop at the busy intersection.

   _____

   _____

   _____

3. The spectators were injured at an accident at the race track. No one was killed.

   _____

   _____

   _____

4. The Jacksons escaped from their burning house. Their three-year-old son was awakened by the heat.

   _____

_____

_____

5. I broke my leg. I went skiing in Colorado.

_____

_____

_____

EXERCISE

22.2   Write five complex sentences with adverb clauses. Be sure to vary the position of the adverb clauses you use. Punctuate your sentences correctly.

1. _____

_____

_____

2. _____

_____

_____

3. _____

_____

_____

4. _____

_____

_____

5. _____

_____

_____

ADJECTIVE CLAUSES

An **adjective clause** modifies a noun or a noun substitute within the independent clause in which it appears. Transition words (relative pronouns) used to introduce adjective clauses are listed here:

who	that	where
whom	which	when
whose		why

Adjective clauses needed to identify the words they modify are *essential clauses* and require no punctuation. *Nonessential adjective clauses* must be set off by commas. Both of the following sentences contain adjective clauses. As you read the sentences, notice the difference between them.

▶ **Examples**

Essential: The woman **who married Hitler** committed suicide to prevent capture by the Allies.

Nonessential: Eva Braun, **who married Hitler**, committed suicide to prevent capture by the Allies.

In the first sentence, the word *woman* is identified by the adjective clause *who married Hitler*, which is essential, or necessary, to complete the meaning of the sentence. In the second sentence, the adjective clause is not needed to identify Eva Braun; the clause is therefore nonessential.

EXERCISE

22.3   Combine each of the following pairs of sentences into a complex sentence with an adjective clause. Be sure to punctuate each sentence correctly. You may wish to refer to the list of transition words for adjective clauses provided earlier.

1. The city council supports a rapid-transit plan. The plan will reduce freeway traffic.

   _____

   _____

   _____

2. The citizens of Buffalo rallied to the defense of the man. The man was accused of stabbing his daughter's rapist.

   _____

   _____

   _____

3. The blue lake mirrored the snow-capped mountains. The lake was crescent-shaped.

   _____

   _____

   _____

4. I shopped at the new mall with my sister Myra. Myra lives in Anaheim.

   _____

5. Charles Lindbergh was received in New York with wild enthusiasm.
   He had accomplished a remarkable feat.

_____

_____

_____

EXERCISE

22.4   Write five complex sentences that include adjective clauses. Be sure to
include at least one sentence with an essential clause and one with a
nonessential clause. Punctuate your sentences correctly.

1. _____

_____

_____

2. _____

_____

_____

3. _____

_____

_____

4. _____

_____

_____

5. _____

_____

_____

NOUN CLAUSES

A **noun clause** functions as the subject, object, subject complement (see
p. 248), or object of a preposition within the independent clause of a complex
sentence. Transition words used to introduce noun clauses are listed here:

that	when	who
what	whenever	whoever

(Continued on next page)

whatever	where	whom
which	wherever	whomever
whichever	whether	why

The following four sentences illustrate the different kinds of noun clauses. Following each sentence is a second sentence in which a simple noun or pronoun has been substituted for the noun clause. By comparing these sentence pairs, you will be able to see more clearly how the noun clause functions within a complex sentence.

Types of Noun Clauses

1. **Subject: Whoever arrives early** can set up the tables and chairs. (**They** can set up the tables and chairs.)

2. **Direct object:** He knew **what she wanted to do**. (He knew her **plan.**)

3. **Subject complement:** The problem was **that we were already late**. (The problem was **our lateness.**)

4. **Object of preposition:** I will go to the play with **whoever asks me first**. (I will go to the play with **Fran.**)

Punctuation Note: Because a noun clause functions as an essential element within a sentence, it is not set off from the rest of the sentence by a comma or commas. If you are not sure whether a clause is a noun clause, substitute a noun or pronoun for the clause. If the substitution makes sense, the clause is functioning as a noun.

EXERCISE

22.5

Combine each of the following sentence pairs into a complex sentence with a noun clause. (You may use the transition words in parentheses.)

1. The patient knew something. (that)
   The operation might be fatal.

   _____

   _____

   _____

2. Please select something. (whichever)
   The dessert is your favorite.

   _____

_____

_____

3. The disposal of waste was the problem. (for which)
   They were seeking a solution.

_____

_____

_____

4. The candidate is someone. (whoever)
   Someone wins the primary.

_____

_____

_____

5. Please give the package to someone. (whoever)
   Someone answers the door.

_____

_____

_____

EXERCISE

22.6   Write five complex sentences with noun clauses.

1. _____

   _____

   _____

2. _____

   _____

   _____

3. _____

   _____

   _____

4. _____

   _____

   _____

5. _____

_____

_____

SIGNALING RELATIONSHIPS
IN COMPLEX SENTENCES

Good readers and writers are able to determine main ideas and supporting ideas within sentences and to understand the relationships between those ideas. One of the best ways to identify dependent clauses is to look for transition words that introduce them. The transition words also indicate the relationship in a complex sentence between the dependent clause and the independent clause of which it is a part.

In previous exercises, you have used transition words to connect independent and dependent clauses. The following chart not only lists the most common transition words used to introduce dependent clauses but also indicates the relationships shown by these words. Study the words carefully so you can use them appropriately to connect independent and dependent clauses.

Transition Words: Relationships

Place	*Contrast*		*Example*
where	although	whereas	such as
wherever	though	than	as
	even though	except	
	even if	except that	

Manner, *Condition*	*Time*	*Agent*	*Cause/Effect,* *Conclusion*
if	after	who	so that
unless	before	whom	in order that
as, as if	when	whose	because
lest	while	which	since
provided	until	that	
provided that	whenever	whichever	
in case	as long as	whoever	
just as	as soon as	whomever	
whether	as often as	whosoever	
how		whatever	

EXERCISE

22.7   Read each sentence carefully and then insert in the blank a transition word or phrase that shows the proper relationship between the main idea expressed in the independent clause and the supporting idea expressed in the dependent clause.

▶ **Example:**   The concert was canceled _____*because*_____ rain was forecast.

(The relationship here is one of cause and effect, so *because* is a good choice.)

1. _____ a left-handed child is forced to write with his or her right hand, the child may become confused.

2. The nurse ran into the patient's room _____ he could assist the doctor.

3. Most college students call their parents _____ they run out of money.

4. I wasn't sure _____ had given me the flowers until I read the card.

5. I don't know _____ the test is being given on Tuesday or Thursday.

6. _____ he is no longer a child, a teenager is not an adult.

7. The baby didn't know _____ the stove was hot.

8. _____ the car stopped, I crossed the street.

9. Cats can never be owned; they live with _____ takes care of them.

10. I hope _____ I have time to eat lunch _____ I have to go to my next class.

22.8

In the following paragraph, transition words used to introduce dependent clauses have been omitted. Read the paragraph carefully and write in the blanks appropriate transition words.

Young people _____ choose to teach today are a special breed.
              (1)

They are not primarily interested in money or prestige, for teaching affords

neither. _____ they wanted wealth, they would choose law or
          (2)

medicine or business as a career. These aspiring young teachers know

_____ teachers work long hours and receive little recognition and
   (3)

less pay. But they choose teaching _____ they want to serve society,
                                        (4)

or _____ they enjoy children, or _____ they love
     (5)   (6)

knowledge. _____ they make the decision to become teachers, they
              (7)

realize _____ they are giving up some important things, but they
           (8)

also know _____ they will realize important dreams and goals as
             (9)

teachers. Once upon a time young females became teachers _____
                                                            (10)

they had few other professional choices. Today teaching gives both males

and females _____ they value most—a sense of satisfaction.
               (11)

22.9

In this exercise, you are given an independent clause and a connecting word. Supply a dependent clause that fits the relationship indicated by the transition word and punctuate each sentence correctly.

1. They left the house before _____

   _____

2. They left the house so that _____

   _____

3. They left the house because _____

_____

4. Dr. Bell _____

performed the operation.

5. The woman who _____

won the prize.

6. We believe that _____

_____

7. We believe whoever _____

_____

8. Because _____

the child sleeps peacefully.

9. After _____

the child sleeps peacefully.

10. Whereas _____

the child sleeps peacefully.

PUNCTUATING COMPLEX SENTENCES

As explained earlier in this chapter, different types of dependent clauses require different punctuation. Review the following punctuation guide:

1. *An introductory adverb clause is set off by a comma:*
   Because the rain was coming down in torrents, the game was delayed.

2. *An adverb clause at the end of a sentence is not set off by a comma:*
   The game was delayed **because the rain was coming down in torrents**.

3. *A nonessential adjective clause is set off by commas:*
   Jim, **who is president of my fraternity**, is my best friend.

4. *An essential adjective clause is not set off by commas:*
   The man **who is president of my fraternity** is my best friend.

5. *A noun clause is not set off by commas:*
   Did you know **that I was here**?

EXERCISE

22.10   Edit the following complex sentences carefully by supplying punctuation where it is needed. Some sentences are correct.

1. When the party is over we'll have our meeting.

2. We took a vacation on Padre Island where there is a good beach.

3. I'll take you to Venice where you can ride in gondolas.

4. You have some very important decisions to make when you graduate.

5. Paul Farrell to whom my sister is engaged graduated from Yale.

6. The cook that the boss hired is very efficient.

7. Mrs. Thomas fired the secretary that Mr. Thomas liked so well.

8. Mr. Crockett who used to be a football player is enormous.

9. When I push this button the motor begins to run.

10. Because it was hot he opened the window.

11. This ball club never won a game until Jack was named manager.

12. When I married Sarah she weighed only ninety pounds.

13. His car skidded around the corner because the tires were slick.

14. When I came home late I entered quietly.

15. I bought him a card because it was his birthday.

16. That I lost my library card caused me many problems.

17. I discovered that I was overdrawn when I balanced my checkbook.

18. Although my sister loves to cook she hates to do the dishes.

19. The horse that broke through the fence did not hurt itself.

20. Your roommate wanted to know what time you got home.

21. Since I am a mountain man I like high places.

22. He visits his parents when he can.

23. The flight attendant who spilled my drink apologized profusely.

24. Their club president who was elected by only one vote resigned yesterday.

25. Although missing one class may not be serious missing a week of classes can hurt your grades.

EXERCISE

22.11   Each of the following pairs of sentences relating the Greek myth, or story, of Apollo and Daphne can be combined into a single complex sentence. Combine the sentence pairs, being sure to punctuate each new sentence appropriately. Remember to put main ideas in independent clauses and supporting ideas in dependent clauses. Then rewrite the sentences to create a paragraph.

1. One of Apollo's loves was Daphne.
   Daphne was the daughter of a river god. (adjective)

   _____

   _____

   _____

2. Cupid shot Apollo with a golden love arrow. (adverb)
   Apollo fell in love with Daphne.

   _____

   _____

   _____

3. Cupid shot Daphne with a leaden arrow. (adverb)
   Daphne did not fall in love with Apollo.

   _____

   _____

   _____

4. Daphne ran away. Apollo began to chase her. (adverb)

   _____

   _____

   _____

5. Apollo followed somewhere.
   The somewhere was wherever Daphne's footsteps led. (noun)

   _____

   _____

   _____

6. The wind caught Daphne's garments.
   The garments fluttered gracefully. (adjective)

   _____

   _____

   _____

7. Apollo was about to catch her. (adverb)
   Daphne called on her father to help her.

   _____

   _____

   _____

8. She was speaking. (adverb)
   Her body was transformed into a laurel tree.

   _____

   _____

   _____

9. Apollo decided something.
   He would make a memorial of the laurel. (noun)

   _____

   _____

   _____

10. Daphne could not be his wife. (adverb)
    She would henceforth be his tree.

    _____

    _____

    _____

EXERCISE

22.12   Edit the following paragraph, correcting the punctuation errors in the complex sentences.

[1] Although I had traveled widely in Europe and Mexico I had never been to Egypt. [2] When I arrived at the Cairo airport I immediately knew I had entered an exotic land that was very different from anything I had known before. [3] Most of the men

were dressed in long robes, and some wore long scarves wrapped around their heads. [4]Some of the women also wore long robes, and nearly all of them wore scarves on their heads. [5]In some cases these scarves also covered all but the center of their faces. [6]As we left the airport and headed toward the center of the city I was struck by the traffic which was incredibly hectic and noisy. [7]All the drivers seemed to use their horns at the slightest excuse. [8]When they were angry they honked. [9]When they were frustrated and impatient they honked. [10]They even honked when they wanted to express appreciation to another driver for letting them go first or squeeze through. [11]From time to time, I could see above all this confusion a minaret or mosque in the distance. [12]But I really knew that I had arrived in Egypt when we crossed the Nile and then, a few minutes later, caught sight of the pyramids at Giza. [13]At that moment I felt as if I had left the modern world and entered a much more ancient and exotic one.

CHAPTER REVIEW

- A complex sentence consists of an independent clause and one or more dependent clauses.
- A dependent clause cannot function alone as a sentence.
- Dependent clauses function as adverbs, adjectives, or nouns.
- The transition word that introduces a dependent clause indicates its relationship to the independent clause.

WRITING ASSIGNMENT

Edit a paragraph or essay you have previously written, changing some of the simple and compound sentences to complex sentences.

PARTICIPATING IN THE ACADEMIC COMMUNITY

Work with a group of your peers to review the paragraphs or essays you edited, focusing on the correct punctuation of the complex sentences you created.

Sentence Fragments and Run-On Sentences

Good writing is made up of well-constructed sentences that express complete thoughts. Sometimes, however, writers make major sentence errors that seriously detract from their writing. Two such errors are **sentence fragments** and **run-on sentences.** This chapter explains these errors and shows you how to identify and correct them in your writing.

SENTENCE FRAGMENTS

A fragment is an incomplete sentence that does not express a complete thought. To decide whether or not a group of words is a sentence or a fragment, ask yourself these three questions:

1. Does it have a *subject?*
2. Does it have a *verb?*
3. Does it express a *complete thought?*

If the answer to any one of these questions is no, the group of words is not a sentence but only a part of a sentence—a fragment.

Observe carefully the differences between the following fragments and complete sentences (in which subjects are underlined once and verbs are underlined twice):

FRAGMENT: The seven-foot basketball player. (subject but no verb)

FRAGMENT: Tripped and fell on the floor. (verbs but no subject)

FRAGMENT: The seven-foot basketball player running down the court. (subject but no verb)

FRAGMENT: As the seven-foot basketball <u>player</u> <u>was running</u> down the court. (dependent clause)

SENTENCE: The seven-foot basketball <u>player</u> <u>was running</u> down the court. (sentence with a subject and a verb)

SENTENCE: The seven-foot basketball <u>player</u> running down the court <u>tripped</u> and <u>fell</u>. (sentence with a subject, two verbs, and an *-ing* modifier)

Length doesn't determine whether a group of words is a sentence or a fragment. For instance, the sentence *The player tripped and fell* is much shorter than several of the fragments shown. Long fragments that contain several modifiers can easily fool you into thinking they are sentences. Therefore, in order to identify a fragment, you need to be able to analyze a group of words to determine whether it includes all the requirements for a complete sentence.

Many types of fragments exist, but five types occur often enough to need special explanation and practice. The five types of sentence elements commonly mistaken for complete sentences are (1) participial phrases, (2) appositive phrases, (3) prepositional phrases, (4) infinitive phrases, and (5) dependent clauses.

Participial Phrase Fragments

A participle is a verb form that may be used as part of a verb or as an adjective. Participles are sometimes mistaken for main verbs, and the phrases (see chart on phrases and clauses, p.282.) in which they appear are sometimes mistaken for complete sentences. **Participial phrase fragments** are of two types: **present participial phrase fragments** and **past participial phrase fragments**.

Present Participial Phrase Fragments

Present participles are *-ing* forms of verbs that must have a helping verb, such as *am, is, was, were,* or *has been,* to function as a verb in a sentence. Without such a helping verb, a participle or participial phrase is often a fragment, as shown here:

FRAGMENT: **Reading comic books all the time.**

The *-ing* form of a verb can be especially confusing when it is used with a noun or pronoun subject but without a helping verb, as shown in the following example:

FRAGMENT: Jim **reading comic books all the time.**

This structure is a fragment even though it contains a subject and a word that *looks* like a verb. You can correct this fragment by adding a helping verb, a form of the verb *to be*.

CORRECT: Jim was reading comic books all the time.

Or, you could add another verb to complete the sentence and use the *-ing* phrase as a modifier. In the following revised sentence, the participial phrase functions as an adjective modifying the subject of the independent clause to which it is attached:

CORRECT: **Reading comic books all the time,** Jim lived in a world of
                        fantasy.

Note: The -ing form of the verb may also function as a noun.

▶ **Example:**   Reading is my favorite hobby.

Past Participial Phrase Fragments

Past participles and past participial phrases without the helping verb *to have* or *to be* may also appear as fragments:

FRAGMENTS: **Hidden in the closet.**

                    The child **hidden in the closet.**

One way to correct this type of fragment is to add a helping verb to create a verb phrase.

CORRECT: The child **had hidden** in the closet. (verb phrase)

Another way to correct a past participial phrase fragment is to use the participial phrase as an adjective:

CORRECT: The child **hidden in the closet** was playing hide-and-seek.
                        (adjective)

Note: For a list of present and past participle verb forms, see the verb charts on pp. 343–346.

EXERCISE

23.1

The following five participial phrases are written incorrectly as sentence fragments. Write five complete sentences by adding an independent clause to each of these participial phrases. Be sure the phrase modifies the subject of your independent clause.

1. Waiting for the concert to begin.

_____

_____

2. Working on the project for weeks.

_____

_____

3. Expecting guests soon.

_____

_____

4. Carrying a heavy tray.

_____

_____

5. Forgotten in the confusion of the storm.

_____

_____

EXERCISE

23.2   The following five fragments include a subject and a participial phrase. Rewrite these fragments as complete sentences. You may add a new verb and use the participial as a modifier of the subject, or you may use a form of the verb *to be* to change the participle into a complete verb. Use each of these methods at least once.

1. The students wanting to know their grades.

_____

_____

2. The prisoner seeing no way out.

_____

_____

3. The teenager sneaking in her house through the back door.

_____

_____

4. The woman trapped inside the car.

_____

_____

5. The breeze blowing on the beach and the waves rolling on shore.

_____

_____

Appositive Phrase Fragments

An appositive or appositive phrase is a noun or noun phrase that explains the noun or pronoun it follows (see also p. 265). As shown below, neither an appositive nor an appositive phrase can stand alone as a sentence:

FRAGMENT: *The X-Files* was made into a movie. **A successful television series**.

"A successful television series" is an **appositive phrase fragment** explaining *The X-Files* and should be joined to the preceding sentence.

SENTENCE: *The X-Files*, **a successful television series**, was made into a movie.

As shown in this example, an internal appositive phrase is set off from the rest of the sentence by two commas. An appositive phrase at the beginning or end of a sentence is set off by one comma.

► **Example:**   I gave a party for Alvin, one of my best friends.

EXERCISE

23.3   Each of the following items includes both a complete sentence and an appositive or appositive phrase sentence fragment. Correct the sentence fragments by attaching them to the sentences, changing punctuation and capitalization as necessary. You may also need to rearrange word order.

1. We enjoy playing Parcheesi. A game from India.

_____

_____

2. The telephone can be both a blessing and a curse. An invention that has changed our lives.

_____

_____

3. Astronomers have recently photographed Saturn. The planet
   encircled by rings.

   _____

   _____

4. Thursday was named for Thor. The Norse god of thunder.

   _____

   _____

5. The Battle of Marathon was won by the Greeks. A famous battle,

   _____

   _____

Prepositional Phrase Fragments

Less frequently, but occasionally, a long prepositional phrase or series of
prepositional phrases is mistaken for a sentence.

FRAGMENT: **Without the professor's study questions**. (one long
prepositional phrase)

CORRECTED: **Without the professor's study questions**, Joel could not
prepare for the exam. (subject and verb added)

FRAGMENT: **In the summer around the old swimming pool in the field
behind our house**. (a series of prepositional phrases)

CORRECTED: **In the summer**, we meet **around the old swimming pool
in the field behind our house**. (subject and verb added)

Sometimes a prepositional phrase is attached to an element that can
function as a subject or verb in a sentence. The following example is a fragment because, although it has a word that can function as its subject
(*dancer*), there is no verb—only a series of prepositional phrases:

FRAGMENT: The young dancer **in the short, pink skirt with the
orange ribbon in her hair and purple scarf in her hand**.

CORRECTED: The young dancer **in the short, pink skirt with the
orange ribbon in her hair and purple scarf in her hand**
won the contest. (verb added)

To recognize **prepositional phrase fragments**, you need to know what words can function as prepositions. The following chart lists some common prepositions (see also p. 261):

about	before	except	of	to
above	behind	for	off	toward
across	below	from	on	under
after	beneath	in	onto	until
against	beside	inside	out	up
along	between	into	outside	upon
among	by	like	over	with
around	down	near	past	within
at	during	next to	through	without

EXERCISE

23.4   Rewrite the following prepositional phrase fragments by adding the essential elements they need to be complete sentences.

1. Without looking in the direction of the traffic on the street.

_____

_____

2. My broker at the respected firm of Smith, Hunter, and Kuhne

_____

_____

3. Out of the bushes to the right of the large oak tree.

_____

_____

4. Occasionally in the morning after a night out with my friends.

_____

_____

5. The fly in my cup of lukewarm coffee on the table before me.

_____

_____

Infinitive Phrase Fragments

The word *to* is often used as a preposition followed by the noun or pronoun that functions as its object. However, *to* plus a verb is an **infinitive** instead of a preposition:

▶ **Example:**   Arial wanted **to go** (infinitive phrase)
to the dance (prepositional phrase).

Infinitive phrases may be used either as modifiers or as noun substitutes in complete sentences. However, infinitive phrases that are not attached to a subject and a verb are **infinitive phrase fragments,** another type of fragment that you need to avoid.

FRAGMENT: **To get to work on time.**

SENTENCE
(infinitive   **To get to work on time,** Kayla drove ten miles an hour
as modifier):   over the speed limit.

FRAGMENT: **To dream the impossible dream.**

SENTENCES
(infinitives   **To dream the impossible dream** is the right of all
as nouns):   Americans. (subject)

The right of all Americans is **to dream the impossible
dream.** (subject complement)

23.5   Rewrite the following infinitive phrase fragments as complete sentences.

1. To move into the house by the time our lease is up.

_____

_____

2. To prepare for a successful career.

_____

_____

3. To have a happy marriage.

_____

_____

4. To try to make up for the eighteen years since I dropped out of college.

_____

_____

5. To make a good grade in the class.

_____

_____

The following paragraphs include eight fragments. Rewrite these paragraphs on a separate sheet of paper, correcting the fragments.

¹The American frontier, if we are to believe the tales that have been handed down, was populated with some amazing personalities. ²The heroes about whom we hear were always at least six feet tall and often reached the height of giants. ³Not only were these heroes large; they were also strong and clever. ⁴Eating enormous amounts of food, performing astounding feats of strength and courage, inventing miraculous methods of accomplishing difficult tasks, and doing an amazing amount of work. ⁵These heroes could out-run, out-jump, out-brag, out-drink, out-shoot, and out-fight anyone foolish enough to challenge them. ⁶These giants among men, our folk heroes. ⁷Superhumans created to populate and tame the rugged, often dangerous frontier.

⁸These folk heroes tell us something about the people who created them. ⁹Faced with countless dangers and constant weariness. ¹⁰The frontier settlers created mythical heroes. ¹¹Who were capable of facing dangers and doing work in unusual and often humorous ways. ¹²Many mythical supermen, such as Paul Bunyan and Pecos Bill, were entirely the products of the frontier imagination. ¹³Pioneers were even able to create the super folk heroine Swamp Angel, a female Paul Bunyan figure.

¹⁴However, the early Americans sometimes glorified actual people. ¹⁵Like Davy Crockett and John Henry. ¹⁶In an effort to transform them into larger-than-life heroes. ¹⁷Whether based on fact or fancy, these heroes were projections of the men who created them. ¹⁸Ordinary mortals needing to be superhuman in order to tame the frontier.

Dependent Clause Fragments

A dependent (subordinate) clause has a subject and a verb but does not express a complete thought. It cannot stand by itself as a sentence but must always be attached to an independent clause. The following diagrams illustrate a subordinate clause used correctly as part of an independent clause and one used incorrectly as a fragment unattached to an independent clause:

DEPENDENT CLAUSE AS PART OF
INDEPENDENT CLAUSE (CORRECT)

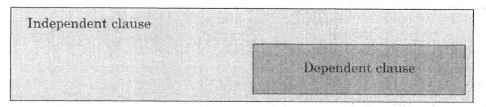

▶ **Example:**   She knew with certainty

that he was the prowler.

DEPENDENT CLAUSE AS FRAGMENT WITH
NO INDEPENDENT CLAUSE (INCORRECT)

No independent clause	Dependent clause

▶ **Example:**   **That he was the prowler.**

    When a dependent clause is attached to an independent clause, the dependent clause functions as an adverb, adjective, or noun in the independent clause. When one of these dependent clauses occurs by itself, the result is a **dependent clause fragment.**

ADVERB CLAUSE FRAGMENT:	**When Alonzo started college.**
SENTENCE WITH ADVERB CLAUSE:	**When Alonzo started college,** he had to learn to manage his time wisely.
ADJECTIVE CLAUSE FRAGMENT:	**Who makes the highest average.**
SENTENCE WITH ADJECTIVE CLAUSE:	The student **who makes the highest average** will win the scholarship.
NOUN CLAUSE FRAGMENT:	**That his examinations required essay answers.**
SENTENCE WITH NOUN CLAUSE:	Professor Yani explained **that his examinations required essay answers.** (direct object)

Each of the three types of dependent clause fragments illustrated in the previous examples may be corrected in one of two ways:

1. Attach the dependent clause fragment to an independent clause. (Example: **When Alonzo started to college,** he had to learn to manage his time wisely.)

2. Omit the subordinating word that makes the dependent clause subordinate. (Example: **When Alonzo started to college** = Alonzo started to college.)

The following chart provides a list of some of the subordinating conjunctions that introduce adjective, adverb, and noun dependent clauses (see also pp. 283, 285, and 287–288):

after	except	that	when	while
although	how	though	whenever	who
as	if	unless	where	whoever
because	provided	until	wherever	whom
before	since	what	which	whomever
even though	so that	whatever	whichever	whose

(See Chapter 22 for further explanation and practice with these three types of dependent clauses.)

EXERCISE

23.7   In the spaces provided, change each of the following dependent clause fragments into a complete complex sentence including both an independent clause and a dependent clause.

1. Which he couldn't understand.

_____

_____

2. Because the lights on the stage went out during the performance.

_____

_____

3. That we had made a mistake.

_____

_____

4. When the guests arrived.

_____

_____

5. Whom he remembered clearly.

_____

_____

EXERCISE

23.8   Rewrite the five sentences from Exercise 23.7 as complete sentences by omitting the introductory subordinating conjunction.

1. _____
2. _____
3. _____
4. _____
5. _____

EXERCISE

23.9   The following passage includes twelve fragments, each of which is a subordinate clause incorrectly written as a sentence. Rewrite the passage on a separate sheet of paper, connecting each fragment to a related independent clause.

[1]Almost every book on art includes a reproduction of the *Mona Lisa*. [2]Which is one of the most famous paintings in the world. [3]The *Mona Lisa* was painted by Leonardo da Vinci. [4]Who worked on it for four years (1503–1506). [5]The painting was never quite finished. [6]After he had worked for several hours. [7]Leonardo would sit down in front of the *Mona Lisa* to quiet his nerves. [8]Some people say. [9]That Leonardo did not finish the painting. [10]Because he wanted an excuse to keep it with him.

[11]On the face of the woman in the painting there is a mysterious smile. [12]Which has intrigued people for centuries. [13]Although no one knows the true explanation of the smile. [14]Several different legends have grown up about it. [15]One story says that the woman was smiling sadly. [16]When she sat for the portrait. [17]Because her child had died. [18]Another story, however, says that Leonardo hired musicians—flutists

and violinists—to play during the sittings. [19]So that he could capture the young woman's rapt expression.

[20]When Leonardo left Italy and moved to France. [21]He took the painting with him. [22]The French king persuaded him to sell the painting. [23]Which now hangs in the Louvre, an art museum in Paris.

RUN-ON SENTENCES

Two (or more) independent clauses that are incorrectly joined result in a **run-on sentence** (see also Chapter 21). The two basic types of run-on sentences are the **fused sentence** and the **comma splice**. A fused sentence is two complete sentences, or independent clauses, run together without any punctuation or conjunction to separate them:

▶ **Examples of Fused Sentences**

1. My sister is an **artist she** completely decorated her home.
2. The beef enchiladas were **spicy the tacos** were fresh.
3. My daughter likes rock **songs my son** likes classical music.
4. Our football boys played **hard they** lost by one point.
5. I'm really thankful for spring break this **year it** will give me a chance to catch up on my homework.

A comma splice is two complete sentences with only a comma to separate them:

▶ **Examples of Comma Splices**

1. My sister is an **artist, she** completely decorated her home.
2. The beef enchiladas were **spicy, the tacos** were fresh.
3. My daughter likes rock **songs, my son** likes classical music.
4. Our football boys played **hard, they** lost by one point.
5. I'm really thankful for spring break this **year, it** will give me a chance to catch up on my homework.

Correcting Run-On Sentences

Run-on sentences may be corrected in several ways, depending on the meaning and relationship of the two sentences involved. Here are five ways to correct run-on sentences:

1. *Write two separate sentences.* One of the most common ways to correct run-on sentences is to write them as two separate sentences.

RUN-ON: My sister is an **artist, she** completely decorated her home.

CORRECT: My sister is an **artist. She** completely decorated her home.

Correcting all fused sentences or comma splices in this way, how-ever, results in too many short, choppy sentences. Furthermore, you may need to show the relationship between the two independent clauses more clearly, as is possible with some of the other methods of correcting run-on sentences.

2. *Use a comma and a coordinating conjunction.* A second way to correct a run-on sentence is to insert a comma followed by a coordinating con-junction between the two independent clauses. The coordinating con-junction clarifies the relationship between the two clauses.

RUN-ON: The beef enchiladas were **spicy the tacos** were fresh.

CORRECT: The beef enchiladas were **spicy, and the tacos** were fresh.

The coordinating conjunctions are listed in the following chart:

and	or	both . . . and
but	nor	either . . . or
for	so	neither . . . nor
	yet	

3. *Use a semicolon.* A third way to correct a run-on sentence is to insert a semicolon between the independent clauses. A semicolon is particu-larly appropriate when the relationship between the two clauses is clear without a transition word, or when the two independent clauses are clearly balanced or parallel.

RUN-ON: My daughter likes **rock songs, my son** likes classical music.

CORRECT: My daughter likes **rock songs; my son** likes classical music.

4. *Use a semicolon and a conjunctive adverb.* A fourth method of correct-ing a run-on sentence is to use not only a semicolon but also a conjunctive adverb that shows the relationship between the two inde-pendent clauses.

RUN-ON: Our football boys **played hard, they** lost by one point.

CORRECT: Our football boys **played hard; however,** they lost by one point.

Notice that the conjunctive adverb is followed by a comma. The following chart lists some of the most common conjunctive adverbs and the relationships they indicate:

Addition, Comparison	Contrast	Time	Cause/Effect, Conclusion	Example
also	however	finally	accordingly	for example
besides	in contrast	first, etc.	as a result	for instance
furthermore	instead	gradually	consequently	in fact
in addition	nevertheless	immediately	hence	that is
indeed	on the contrary	meanwhile	in conclusion	to illustrate
likewise	on the other hand	next	in summary	
moreover	otherwise	sometimes	of course	
similarly	rather	suddenly	therefore	
too	still	then	thus	

5. *Change one of the independent clauses to a dependent clause.* A fifth, and final, way to correct a run-on sentence is to make one of the independent clauses a dependent clause. Sometimes this method is necessary to show the true relationship between the clauses in a run-on sentence.

RUN-ON: I'm really thankful for spring break this **year it** will give me a chance to catch up on my homework.

CORRECT: I'm really thankful for spring break this **year because it** will give me a chance to catch up on my homework.

Subordinating conjunctions that can be used to create a dependent clause include *although, because, since, if, before, after, when, while, unless,* and *until.* For a more complete list of subordinating conjunctions, see the charts on pages 283 and 308.

EXERCISE

23.10

Rewrite each of the following run-on sentences as a correctly punctuated sentence. Use a different method of correction for each sentence.

1. Eating at a restaurant is expensive, I learned to cook.

_____

_____

2. It has been raining all day it is very cold outside.

_____

_____

3. College students need to save money, they shouldn't lose credit hours when they transfer from a community college to a university.

_____

_____

_____

4. Change is sometimes very hard, for example it was difficult for my parents to sell their old home and move to a new one.

_____

_____

_____

5. Most sports require special equipment jogging is an exception.

_____

_____

_____

Punctuation Notes:

1. Notice that the little word *then* is a conjunctive adverb that should be preceded by a semicolon when it comes between two independent clauses. NEVER use the word *then* with just a comma to connect two independent clauses because the result is a run-on sentence.

   RUN-ON: Write a complete draft of **your paper, then** edit and proofread it.

   CORRECT: Write a complete draft of **your paper; then** edit and proofread it.

2. Although it should always be preceded by a semicolon when it separates two independent clauses, a conjunctive adverb is set off only with a comma, or commas, when it appears within a single independent clause.

   CORRECT: His **roommate, however,** was wide awake.

   His roommate was wide **awake, however.**

EXERCISE

23.11

Each of the following paragraphs contains run-on sentences—both fused sentences and comma splices. Rewrite each paragraph on a separate piece of paper, correcting all the run-on sentences.

Paragraph A

[1]I agree with John Henry Newman all branches of knowledge are connected. [2]Certainly, all sciences are related to one another, for instance medicine uses both plant life and animal life to make discoveries about diseases and to create new treatments. [3]Also, history helps explain literature, literature helps explain history. [4]Even today, studying one subject can help us to understand another subject better. [5]Also, knowledge of different subjects can help us in our careers, for example, the architect needs math to help him plan his blueprints the history teacher needs to understand English, art, and sociology to teach history.

Paragraph B

[1]Many people believe in the idea of a general studies program for the first two years of college I don't happen to be one of those people. [2]A general liberal arts education doesn't prepare students directly for their careers, it wastes their time and their money. [3]Students should be allowed to take and pay for the courses that will directly prepare them for their careers in life.

Paragraph C

[1]Ten years ago I dropped out of college I didn't have clear goals for my life and my career. [2]This time I don't intend to take any shortcuts, instead I intend to take all the liberal arts courses I can. [3]These courses will give me a good background in different areas then I can truly find the career area that interests me. [4]Also, I believe that knowing about areas other than my own field will give me more chances to get a good job.

▦ CHAPTER REVIEW

- A fragment is an incomplete sentence that does not express a complete thought.
- These are the five common types of fragments:
  1. Participial phrase fragments
  2. Appositive phrase fragments

    3. Prepositional phrase fragments

    4. Infinitive phrase fragments

    5. Dependent clause fragments

- A run-on sentence results from incorrectly joining two independent clauses.

- The two basic types of run-on sentences are fused sentences and comma splices.

- Run-on sentences may be corrected in five ways:

    1. Rewriting the independent clauses as two separate sentences

    2. Inserting a comma and a coordinating conjunction between the two clauses

    3. Inserting a semicolon between the two clauses

    4. Inserting a semicolon and a conjunctive adverb between the two clauses

    5. Changing one of the independent clauses to a dependent clause

WRITING ASSIGNMENT

Select a paragraph or essay that you are writing for one of your classes—perhaps your history class or this composition class—and edit it carefully for fragments and run-on sentences. Then rewrite the assignment with the corrected sentences.

PARTICIPATING IN THE ACADEMIC COMMUNITY

Compare your corrected versions of Exercises 23.9 and 23.11 with those of a small group of your classmates. (Remember that fragments and run-on sentences can be corrected in several different ways.) Or meet with a small group of your classmates to edit one of your writing assignments for major sentence errors.

Subject–Verb Agreement

The subject and verb of a sentence should agree in number. That is, if the subject is singular, the verb should be singular; if the subject is plural, the verb should be plural.

▶Examples: **She walks** to class. (singular subject *she* and singular verb *walks*)

They walk also. (plural subject *they* and plural verb *walk*)

He is an actor. (singular subject *he* and singular verb *is*)

They are pals. (plural subject *they* and plural verb *are*)

With the exception of the verb *to be,* verbs do not change their forms to indicate number except in the present tense.

▶Examples: **He walked** home. (singular subject and verb)

They walked home. (plural subject and verb)

AGREEMENT WITH REGULAR AND IRREGULAR VERBS

To master **subject–verb agreement**, you need to study the present tense of both regular and irregular verbs.

Agreement with Regular Verbs

Look carefully at the chart on the following page, which shows the different present tense forms of a typical regular verb. Notice that an *s* is added to the third-person singular form of a regular verb. (*Note*: Adding an *s* or *es* to a noun makes the noun plural. However, an *s* ending on a verb indicates that the verb is singular.)

The boy **walks** to school each day. (singular verb)

The three boys **walk** to school each day. (plural verb)

Present Tense of Regular Verb *To Walk*	
Singular	*Plural*
First person: *I walk*	First person: *we walk*
Second person: *you walk*	Second person: *you walk*
Third person: *he, she, it walks*	Third person: *they walk*

EXERCISE

24.1   Supply the correct third-person singular, present tense form of the verbs indicated in the sentences. Be sure all of your verbs end in an *s*.

1. In the end she always _____ her goals.
   (to reach)

2. He _____ at the library on weekends.
   (to work)

3. Here he _____ now, early as usual.
   (to come)

4. She _____ to be an accountant when she graduates.
   (to plan)

5. He _____ that hard work is always rewarded.
   (to believe)

Agreement with Irregular Verbs

Now examine carefully the present-tense forms of the three irregular verbs shown in the following chart. Note especially the third-person singular, present tense form of each of the verbs.

Present Tense of Three Irregular Verbs	
Singular	*Plural*
To be:	
First person: *I am*	First person: *we are*
Second person: *you are*	Second person: *you are*
Third person: *he, she, it* **is**	Third person: *they are*
To have:	
First person: *I have*	First person: *we have*
Second person: *you have*	Second person: *you have*
Third person: *he, she, it* **has**	Third person: *they have*

(Continued on next page)

To do:

First person: *I do*   First person: *we do*
Second person: *you do*   Second person: *you do*
third person: *he, she, it* **does**   Third person: *they do*

Notice that of these examples (*to be, to have, to do*) the verb *to be* is the most irregular. The other two verbs change their forms only in the third-person singular. Notice also that these irregular verbs also end in *s* in the third-person singular. In fact, the only exceptions to this pattern are the helping verbs *can, shall, may, will, ought,* and *must.* All other verbs end in *s* in the third-person singular present tense.

EXERCISE

24.2   Supply the correct present tense form of the irregular verbs indicated in the following sentences. Refer to the charts given earlier if you are in doubt.

1. You ＿＿＿＿＿＿＿＿ in a difficult situation.
   (to be)

2. ＿＿＿＿＿＿＿＿ she live in the dormitory?
   (To do)

3. They ＿＿＿＿＿＿＿＿ several reasons for voting as they did.
   (to have)

4. She ＿＿＿＿＿＿＿＿ a friend of mine.
   (to be)

5. In the morning, we ＿＿＿＿＿＿＿＿ an appointment with the dean.
   (to have)

6. It ＿＿＿＿＿＿＿＿ not matter where you park your car.
   (to do)

7. The books ＿＿＿＿＿＿＿＿ on reserve at the library.
   (to be)

8. ＿＿＿＿＿＿＿＿ he been absent before?
   (To have)

9. She ＿＿＿＿＿＿＿＿ more studying than he does.
   (to do)

10. ＿＿＿＿＿＿＿＿ they in the same class?
    (To be)

Noun and Pronoun Subjects

Thus far, the sentences in this chapter have used pronouns as subjects. Look now at the following sentences, which all have noun subjects.

▶ **Examples:**   **Sabrina** has a tough schedule this semester.

Jogging is a popular form of exercise.

Children play in the park around the corner.

Now fill in the blanks in the following sentences, substituting the appropriate pronoun subjects for the deleted noun subjects:

_____ has a tough schedule this semester.

_____ is a popular form of exercise.

_____ play in the park around the corner.

The pronoun *she* can replace the noun *Sabrina* in the first sentence; the pronoun *it* can be substituted for the noun *jogging* in the second sentence; and the pronoun *they* can be used instead of the noun *children* as the subject of the third sentence. All of these pronouns are third-person singular or plural.

If your noun subject is third-person singular, your verb must also be singular. And if you are using a present tense verb, be sure that the verb has an *s* ending. When you are in doubt about subject-verb agreement, substitute a pronoun for the noun subject; you are more likely to recognize errors in subject-verb agreement if the subject is a pronoun.

EXERCISE

24.3   In the following sentences, some of the subjects are nouns and some are pronouns. Supply the correct *present tense* form of the verbs indicated. If you are in doubt about the correct verb form, change the noun subject to a pronoun.

1. Many students _____ in computer courses each semester.
   (to enroll)

2. He _____ his lawn regularly.
   (to mow)

3. Smoking _____ not allowed in this building.
   (to be)

4. They _____ until late every night.
   (to work)

5. The English tutors _____ very helpful.
   (to be)

6. The desk _____ three drawers.
   (to have)

7. My room _____ as though a storm hit it.
   (to look)

8. A different lecturer _____ our class each Friday.
   (to visit)

9. Julia, Sam, and Tyrone _____ the same schedule.
   (to have)

10. My teacher _____ promptly at eight o'clock.
    (to arrive)

EXERCISE

24.4   The following sentences have plural subjects and plural verbs. In the space provided under each sentence, rewrite the sentence, changing the subject and verb so both are singular.

▶ **Examples:**   The **reports evaluate** the situation.

   The **report evaluates** the situation.

1. The secretaries take several breaks in the morning.

   _____

   _____

2. The computers badly need repairing.

   _____

   _____

3. The account books have many errors.

   _____

   _____

4. The salespeople are frequently late.

   _____

   _____

5. The phones ring almost constantly.

   _____

   _____

EXERCISE

24.5   Errors in subject–verb agreement are more difficult to identify when they occur in the context of a paragraph. Read the following paragraph carefully. In it are ten subject–verb agreement errors. Edit the paragraph by underlining the ten verbs that do not agree with their subjects in number. Then correct the errors you identified.

[1]Colleges and universities were once attended mainly by young, middle-class students who had just graduated from high school. [2]Today campuses across the United States are populated with a variety of different types of students, many of whom are not young, middle-class, or even American. [3]Some of these new students comes from lower economic backgrounds. [4]Government loans enables them to attend college when once they would have been forced to get a job. [5]In addition to students from lower economic backgrounds, U.S. colleges is also accepting increasing numbers of international students. [6]A student do not have to be an American citizen to attend a college or a university in this country. [7]One class may have students from several different countries. [8]Today students is also not necessarily young. [9]If an older person decide to start college, he may discover that many of his classmates are also middle-aged or even older. [10]Some of these students have been out of high school for ten to twenty years. [11]Others never completed high school. [12]Yet they seems capable of competing successfully with the young students. [13]In fact, an older student often has an advantage over the young people in his classes because he have more experience and motivation. [14]These new students who are poorer, older, or not American by birth add variety and interest to our campuses. [15]Although the new student have not replaced the traditional young high school graduate, he bring a new dimension to higher education in this country.

SPECIAL PROBLEMS WITH SUBJECT–VERB AGREEMENT

A subject and a verb must always agree in number, but in some cases the rule is difficult to apply. This section addresses some specific problems with subject–verb agreement.

Indefinite Pronoun Subjects

Some indefinite pronouns take a singular verb even though they appear to be plural in meaning. Following is a list of singular indefinite pronouns:

anybody	everything	either
anyone	nobody	neither
anything	none	someone
each	nothing	somebody
everybody	one	something
everyone	another	much

The following sentences have singular indefinite pronouns as subjects. Notice that in each of the sentences the verb is singular to agree with the singular subject.

▶ **Examples:**   Everyone **studies** before a test.

Nobody **likes** to study.

Neither of them **is going** to the library.

Much of the information **comes** from the textbook.

None of the students **listens** to the teacher.

Other indefinite pronouns, such as *few, many, both, some,* and *several,* are plural and, therefore, take plural verbs.

▶ **Examples:**   All of them **are** in the class.

Several **attend** the special study sessions.

Many **need** additional help.

A few of the indefinite pronouns can be either singular or plural, depending on their meaning. For example, *all* and *some* are usually considered plural, but if they refer to a mass instead of individual units, they are singular.

▶ **Examples:**   All of the class **has** that assignment. (singular)

All of the students **are** motivated. (plural)

Some of the material **is** boring. (singular)

Some of the students **are** bored. (plural)

In addition, the indefinite pronoun *none* is usually considered singular even though it means *no one.* However, usage appears to be changing regarding this pronoun, and many educated speakers and writers now use *none* as a plural as well as a singular pronoun.

▶ **Example:**   None of the tests **are** difficult.

See also Chapter 25, pp. 329–330.

EXERCISE

24.6   The following sentences have subjects that are indefinite pronouns. Provide the appropriate present tense verbs.

1. Each of us _____ the same course.
   (to want)

2. Few really _____ chicken livers.
   (to like)

3. Many Chinese restaurants _____ hot, spicy food.
   (to serve)

4. Nothing _____ my boss more than my being late.
   (to upset)

5. Somebody _____ the building at six o'clock each night.
   (to lock)

Compound Subjects

A compound subject is one in which two or more nouns or pronouns are joined by coordinating conjunctions (*and, or, nor*). Subjects joined by *and* are usually plural.

▶ **Example:**   The book and tape **are** both available.

Subjects joined by *nor* and *or* are usually singular.

▶ **Examples:**   The coach or the trainer **is** with the injured player.

Neither Mary nor Sue **plans** to graduate this semester.

However, if both subjects joined by *or* or *nor* are plural, then a plural verb should be used.

▶ **Example:**   Tapes or books **are** available.

If *or* or *nor* joins one singular subject and one plural subject, the verb agrees with the nearer subject.

▶ **Examples:**   The teacher or the students **are** always unhappy.

The students or the teacher **is** always unhappy.

24.7   Choose the correct present tense form of the verbs indicated in the following sentences.

1. Both my uncle and my aunt _____ to come to the wedding.
   (to plan)

2. The choir members and their director _____ to Russia each
   (to travel)
   summer.

3. The mare and colt _____ healthy.
   (to seem)

4. Neither my fears nor my anger _____ justified.
   (to be)

5. The veterinarian or his assistants _____ on the animals each
   (to check)
   evening.

Intervening Prepositional Phrases

Agreement problems often occur when a subject and a verb are separated by a prepositional phrase, as in the following example:

▶ **Example:**   One **of the boys** dates a computer science major.

The subject of this sentence is *one*, not *boys*; therefore, the verb is the singular *dates* rather than the plural *date*. In this type of sentence, it is important to distinguish between the subject of the main verb and any nouns or pronouns that may be part of the phrase that occurs between the subject and verb.

The following chart, which lists common prepositions, will help you to identify prepositional phrases that might cause difficulty in subject–verb agreement (see also p. 261):

about	before	except	of	to
above	behind	for	off	toward
across	below	from	on	under
after	beneath	in	onto	until
against	beside	inside	out	up
along	between	into	outside	upon
among	by	like	over	with
around	down	near	past	within
at	during	next to	through	without

EXERCISE

24.8

Supply the correct present tense verb in the following sentences.

1. The young woman with the expensive leather planner and briefcase
   _____ late every day.
   (to arrive)

2. Another of my friends _____ a new car.
   (to have)

3. Those students, after their teacher's warning, _____ absent
   (to be)
   again.

4. The puppies inside the garage _____ loudly each night.
   (to bark)

5. The noise of the airplanes _____ area residents much
   (to cause)
   concern.

Inverted Sentence Order

Sentences in which the subject does *not* come before the verb also present special problems with subject-verb agreement.

▶ **Examples:**   Where are the vegetables you cooked? (vegetables *are*)

Where is the new shirt you bought? (shirt *is*)

In the door flies a bright yellow canary. (canary *flies*)

In the door fly several small birds. (birds *fly*)

There are three reasons I can't go. (reasons *are*)

There is a good reason for his not coming. (reason *is*)

Note: (*Hint:* You may reverse the order of a sentence to check for agreement problems. Example: *The vegetables you cooked are where?*).

EXERCISE

24.9

In each of the following sentences, locate the subject and underline it. Then choose the correct present tense form of the verb indicated.

1. There _____ several reasons why the plan failed.
   (to be)

2. Under the bed _____ an enormous cat.
   (to sleep)

3. _____ the computers been installed?
   (To have)

4. _____ the captain always obey his orders?
        (To do)

5. Here _____ the bus.
            (to come)

EXERCISE

24.10   The following paragraph contains ten errors in subject-verb agreement. Edit the paragraph by underlining the incorrect verb forms and then replacing them with the correct verb forms.

[1]Science fiction shows on television provides a look into the future. [2]These programs take a writer's dreams about the future and makes them seem real to the television viewers. [3]The remarkable thing about these shows is that what the television audience considered science fiction twenty or thirty years ago is science reality today. [4]In the fifties and sixties, for example, robots and computers began to appear on television. [5]Now everyone consider these marvels of technology rather commonplace. [6]Industry, as well as our homes, are increasingly dependent on computers. [7]And even robots are fairly commonplace in our complex society. [8]They may not look like the ones on the early science fiction shows, but they can do basically the same things. [9]Early television also showed man in space years before he actually accomplished this remarkable feat. [10]Neither television nor its viewers was aware that within a few years our astronauts would actually be able to orbit the earth in space ships. [11]Today movies on television often portrays man moving across the galaxies, visiting various planets. [12]There is several reasons to expect that this fantasy too will come true in the near future. [13]It will not be long before our technology, together with our talented scientists, have us to the point that we are ready to undertake these types of space voyages. [14]Not all the science fiction shows on television becomes a reality, but many of them seem to be a reliable prediction of what the future hold.

CHAPTER REVIEW

- Subjects and verbs must agree in number: Singular subjects take singular verbs; plural subjects take plural verbs.
- The singular form of third-person present tense verbs ends in an *s*.
- Special problems in subject–verb agreement occur with indefinite pronoun subjects, compound subjects, intervening prepositional phrases, and inverted sentence order.

  1. Most indefinite pronouns are singular, but several indefinite pronouns, including *few, many, both, some,* and *several,* take plural verbs. (See charts on pp. 329–330.)
  2. Subjects joined by *and* are usually plural. Subjects joined by *or* or *nor* are usually singular, but if one subject is plural, the verb takes the number of the nearer subject.
  3. When a prepositional phrase occurs between a subject and a verb, the verb always agrees with the subject rather than the object of the preposition.
  4. The subject comes after the verb in some sentences, but reversing the sentence order makes agreement clearer.

WRITING ASSIGNMENT

Write a paragraph in the present tense in which you describe what a friend of yours is doing today. Be sure all of your subjects and verbs agree.

PARTICIPATING IN THE ACADEMIC COMMUNITY

Meet with a group of your classmates to edit your paragraphs. Read each paragraph orally, checking to be sure the subjects and verbs agree.

CHAPTER

25

Pronoun Usage

When you are editing your writing, you need to pay special attention to three areas of pronoun usage: **reference, agreement,** and **case.** In addition, you should make sure your point of view is consistent and that you have avoided using pronouns in a sexist manner.

PRONOUN REFERENCE AND AGREEMENT

A pronoun is a noun substitute; it stands for a noun or another pronoun. The noun or pronoun to which a pronoun refers is called the **antecedent.** Thus, in the following sentence, *it* and *its* refer to *cat,* so *cat* is the antecedent:

▶ **Example:**   The **cat** arched **its** back, and then **it** hissed loudly.

For reference to be clear, each pronoun must have a clear antecedent:

UNCLEAR: While she was driving to work, **it** ran out of gas.

CLEAR: While she was driving to work, **her car** ran out of gas.

UNCLEAR: The professor gave the student **her** book.

CLEAR: The **professor** gave **her** book to the student.

A pronoun should also agree with its antecedent in number, gender, and person. The most frequently used pronouns are **personal pronouns,** which have various forms to indicate number, gender, and person.

	Singular	*Plural*
First person	I (me, my)	we (us, our)
Second person	you (your)	you (your)
Third person	he, she, it	they (them)
	(him, his, her, its)	

Agreement in number means that if the antecedent is plural, the pronoun that refers to it must also be plural. And, if the antecedent is singular, the pronoun should be singular.

▶ **Examples:**   The **computer** was down again, so I called the service department to have **it** repaired. (singular)

The **computers** were down again, so I called the service department to have **them** repaired. (plural)

For a pronoun to agree in gender with its antecedent, the pronoun should be masculine if the antecedent is masculine and feminine if the antecedent is feminine.

▶ **Examples:**   The **ballerina** posed gracefully on **her** toes. (feminine)

Mr. Chiang delivered **his** lecture and left before we could speak with **him.** (masculine)

For a pronoun to agree in person with its antecedent, it should be first person (*I, me, my, mine, we, us, our, ours*) if the antecedent is first person, second person (*you, your, yours*) if the antecedent is second person, and third person (*he, him, his, she, her, hers, it, its, they, them, their, theirs*) if the antecedent is third person.

▶ **Examples:**   **We** lost **our** way in the dense fog. (first person)

You lost **your** way in the dense fog. (second person)

They lost **their** way in the dense fog. (third person)

You usually follow most of these agreement rules without really thinking about them. But occasionally these rules are more difficult to understand and apply. The following sections on indefinite, relative, and demonstrative pronouns explain how to avoid agreement errors with these types of pronouns.

Indefinite Pronouns

Indefinite pronouns are always third person and have only one form, but problems sometimes arise in using these pronouns if the writer does not know which are singular and which are plural.

The following chart lists most singular and plural indefinite pronouns:

Indefinite Pronouns			
Singular			
anybody	each	everybody	somebody
anyone	either, neither	everything	someone
anything	nobody, nothing, none	one	something

(Continued on next page)

Plural			
all	few	most	several
any	many	none	
both	more	some	

If an indefinite pronoun functions as the antecedent of another pronoun, that pronoun must agree with it in number.

▶ Examples   **Everyone** left **his** or **her** shoes outside the door. (singular pronouns)

All of them left **their** shoes outside the door. (plural pronouns)

EXERCISE

25.1   Correct the pronoun reference and agreement errors in these sentences.

1. Does anybody have their reports ready to submit?

_____

_____

2. At the library they told Sonya she had an overdue book.

_____

_____

3. Ms. Brown gave their annual donation to United Way.

_____

_____

4. The teacher wants everyone to furnish their own paper for the examination.

_____

_____

5. Each of the students has their own opinion about the course.

_____

_____

Relative and Demonstrative Pronouns

A frequent problem in using **demonstrative pronouns** (*this, that, these,* and *those*) and **relative pronouns** (*who, whom, which, what,* and *that*) is that sometimes the antecedents are not clear (see also page 328).

▶ **Example:**   I had to wait two hours, **which** made me angry.

Two hours is not the antecedent of the pronoun *which;* rather, the *waiting* made the writer angry. But because the pronoun does not have a clear antecedent, the sentence is unclear and awkward. The revised sentence below eliminates the pronoun reference problem.

▶ **Example:**   Because I had to wait two hours, I was angry.

(*Note:* In using relative pronouns, it is also important to remember that *who* refers only to people and *which* refers only to animals and inanimate objects, whereas *that* can refer to people, animals, or objects.)

EXERCISE

25.2   Correct the pronoun reference errors in the following sentences.

1. We found the gun in his car which suggests he is guilty.

   _____

   _____

2. The person which called failed to give his name.

   _____

   _____

3. Jim told Tom a lie. This caused a lot of trouble.

   _____

   _____

4. I frequently called home long distance, which annoyed my father.

   _____

   _____

5. My friend often works in her garden, which is obvious.

   _____

   _____

EXERCISE

25.3   Edit the following paragraph for errors in pronoun reference and agreement.

   [1] Three of my early teachers are special to me because they took the time to show an interest in me and to challenge me to

work harder. ²This made me a better student. ³I remember my English teacher Mrs. Johnson, which always encouraged me with my writing. ⁴They were always hard to write, but with their encouragement I made them even better. ⁵In my history class, Mr. Krelinski pushed me to be a better student by giving me challenging questions and making me rethink and support them. ⁶In my math class, Dr. Kline gave me the extra time I needed by explaining difficult problems to me. ⁷I never would have come to college if she hadn't encouraged me and if he hadn't taught me how to think. ⁸A hard-working teacher like this can really make a difference in a student's life. ⁹He certainly did in mine.

PRONOUN CASE

The correct pronoun form, or **case**, of a personal pronoun is determined by its use in a sentence. As illustrated in the following chart, pronouns occur in subjective, objective, and possessive cases:

Number	Subjective	Objective	Possessive
Singular			
First person	I	me	my, mine
Second person	you	you	your, yours
Third person	he, she, it	him, her, it	his, her, hers
	who, whoever	whom, whomever	its, whose
Plural			
First person	we	us	our, ours
Second person	you	you	your, yours
Third person	they, who	them, whom	their, theirs, whose
	whoever	whomever	

1. *Subjective case:* Pronouns that function as a subject or a subject complement that renames the subject takes the **subjective case:**

   ▶ **Examples:**   The children and **I** went on a picnic in the park. (subject)

   The winner of the race is **she.** (subject complement)

2. *Objective case:* Pronouns that function as direct objects, indirect objects, and objects of a preposition take the **objective case:**

▶ **Examples:**   The car nearly hit **us** before it stopped on the median. (direct object)

Professor Gonzalez gave **him** a B⁺ on his midterm exam. (indirect object)

Please give this message to **them** before you leave. (object of preposition)

3. *Possessive case:* Pronouns that show ownership are in the **possessive case:**

▶ **Examples:**   **His** baseball went through **their** window on **its** way out of the ballpark.

Is this book **yours, mine,** or **ours**?

The simple possessives *my, your, his, its, our,* and *their* are followed by nouns; the possessives *mine, yours, hers, ours, yours,* and *theirs* refer to (or modify) nouns or pronouns that have occurred earlier. See also page 332. Possessive pronouns function as modifiers.

Who (Whoever) and Whom (Whomever)

The pronouns *who* and *whoever* are subject forms; the pronouns *whom* and *whomever* are object forms. In general, these pronouns function much like other subjective and objective pronouns. As shown here, the two primary uses of these words are to introduce questions and relative clauses:

Questions

Who knows the answer? (subject)

Whom did you call? (object)

Relative Clauses

The politician **who spends the most** often wins the election. (subject of relative clause: *who spends the most*)

The judge will give the prize to **whomever she chooses.** (direct object of relative clause: *she chooses whomever*)

The manager should hire **whoever will do the best job.** (subject of relative clause: *whoever will do the best job*)

As shown in these examples, the correct pronoun form is determined by how the pronoun is used in the relative clause, not by how the clause is used in the complex sentence.

Because questions use inverted word order and complex sentences have more than one subject and verb, the use of *who* (*whoever*) and *whom* (*whomever*) can sometimes be tricky. To help you choose the right form of these words, rephrase questions as statements and substitute more common pronoun forms, such as *he* and *him*, for *who* or *whom* in relative clauses.

▶ **Examples**

Whom did you call? = You did call **whom**?

Who spends the most = **He** spends the most.

Whomever she chooses = She chooses **him**.

Compound Elements

A pronoun is often used as one of the elements in a compound subject, a compound direct or indirect object of a verb, or a compound object of a preposition:

SUBJECT:	**Jonikka** and **I** studied until midnight.
DIRECT OBJECT:	The dog followed **Wayne** and **her** all the way home.
INDIRECT OBJECT:	Please give **Deanna** and **him** the book.
OBJECT OF PREPOSITION:	The surprise is just for **Jason** and **me**.

To help you choose the correct pronoun case in a compound element, restate the sentence with only the pronoun. For example, if you are tempted to write *The surprise is just for **Jason** and **I*** in the last example, omit the first item in the compound element (*Jason*) and compare the resulting sentences. Clearly, *The secret is just for **me*** is preferable to *The secret is just for **I**.*

Comparisons

Pronouns are often used in implied comparisons such as those in the following sentences:

SUBJECT FORM:	Her father was more upset than **she**. (Her father was more upset than *she was upset*.)
OBJECT FORM:	The scholarship would mean more to Waylon than **me**. (The scholarship would mean more to Waylon than *it would mean to **me**.*)

EXERCISE

25.4   In each of the following sentences, select the correct form of the pronoun.

1. David and _____ go hiking in the Colorado mountains every
   (she, her)

   summer.

2. It's not fair that, as members of the head table, you got _____
   (your, yours)

   dinner an hour before we got _____.
   (our, ours)

3. To _____ did you give the money from the concession
   (who, whom)

   stand?

4. My younger sister is two inches taller than _____.
   (I, me)

5. _____ boss gave _____ a 10 percent raise.
   (She, her)   (she, her)

6. The district championship will be decided in the final game between

   _____ and _____
   (they, them)   (we, us)

7. The first-place spelling medal should go to _____
   (whoever, whoever)

   earns it.

8. We watched _____ as _____ waved goodbye to
   (they, them)   (they, them)

   _____ daughter.
   (their, theirs)

9. Jandy said that the loss of the championship hurt the assistant coach

   more than _____.
   (she, her)

10. _____, personally, would like to learn as much as I can in
    (I, Me)

    college.

EXERCISE

25.5   Find and correct the eight errors in pronoun case in the following paragraph.

¹ On the long flight to Italy, I sat next to a young mother and her five-year-old son whom were flying home to Jordan. ² Early in the flight, the attendant distributed peanuts and soft drinks to they and I. ³ The child, whom was named Abdul, quickly gobbled up his peanuts and looked hungrily at mine. ⁴ Of course, I gave he not only my peanuts but also my soft drink. ⁵ In fact, in a few hours, after I had shared part of a complete meal with him, Abdul and me were good friends. ⁶ I was certainly tired and hungry when I arrived in Rome. ⁷ However, I realized that they were more exhausted than me, and I felt sorry for whomever sat next to Abdul on the rest of the flight.

USING PRONOUNS WITH *-SELF* AND *-SELVES*

Pronouns with *-self* or *-selves* (*myself, yourself, yourselves, himself, herself, itself, themselves*) can be used as intensives or reflexives. An intensive pronoun is a personal pronoun plus *-self* or *-selves* that emphasizes the noun or pronoun to which it refers:

> **INTENSIVE PRONOUN:**   She **herself** won the essay contest.
>
> She won the essay contest **herself**.

A **reflexive pronoun** has the same form as an intensive pronoun but indicates that the subject of the sentence receives the action of the verb.

> **REFLEXIVE PRONOUN:**   The child hurt **herself**.

An intensive pronoun functions as a modifier; a reflexive pronoun functions as an object. Remember that a pronoun with *-self* or *-selves* can never be used as the subject of a sentence. Remember also that *hisself* and *theirselves* are not standard English words.

EXERCISE

25.6   Write the correct intensive or reflexive pronoun form in the blanks in each of the following sentences.

1. The children wanted to plan their party _____.
     (theirselves, themselves)

2. When the little girl fell, she hurt _____ .
   (her, herself)

3. Although his employees were on time, he _____ was late.
   (himself. no other pronoun)

4. The elderly woman changed the tire _____ .
   (herself, her own self)

5. The rock singer gave _____ a new car for his birthday.
   (himself, hisself)

USING A CONSISTENT POINT OF VIEW

First-person pronouns (*I* and *we*) always refer to the person who is speaking or writing. The second person (*you*), which is the same in the singular and plural, refers to the person spoken to or addressed (the audience). The third-person pronouns (*he, she, it,* and *they*) refer to a person or thing spoken or written about.

▶ **Examples**

I need to exercise each day because I feel better when I am active. (first-person point of view)

You need to exercise each day because you feel better when you are active. (second-person point of view)

People need to exercise each day because they feel better when they are active. (third-person point of view)

When you are writing, it is important to be consistent in your point of view. If you choose to write from the first-person point of view (*I* or *we*), you should use this point of view throughout your paper. Avoid shifting casually from one point of view to another unless there is a good reason for doing so. In formal writing, it is usually best to avoid the second-person unless you are giving directions or explaining a process.

EXERCISE

25.7   Revise the following sentences to eliminate unnecessary shifts in point of view.

1. I like math because it is easy for me, and you can grasp it on your own.

_____

_____

2. When we had received our sheets and blankets, we were shown how to make one's bed according to army regulations.

_____

_____

3. I need to improve my writing skills. To be able to express yourself in writing is of great importance.

_____

_____

4. To me, graduation marks the beginning of a new life, a demanding life, from which a person can expect to receive only as much as you give.

_____

_____

5. I want to learn all the rules you need to know in order to stay out of trouble with the authorities.

_____

_____

USING NONSEXIST PRONOUNS

Because pronouns frequently indicate gender, a writer is often faced with a decision about which gender to choose if the sex of the antecedent is not apparent. Traditionally, masculine pronouns were used when the sex of the antecedent was not stated.

▶ Example: A **teacher** should motivate **his** students.

However, this solution is increasingly considered unacceptable. A fairer practice is to alternate masculine and feminine pronouns.

▶Example: A **teacher** should motivate **her** students.

Or you can use both the masculine and feminine pronouns.

▶ Example: A **teacher** should motivate **his** or **her** students.

Using both pronouns is perhaps fairer, but the result is somewhat awkward and wordy. Another way to solve this problem is to use the plural form of the noun and thus avoid the dilemma completely.

▶ Example: **Teachers** should motivate **their** students.

25.8
Revise the following sentences to eliminate sexist pronouns.

1. A judge usually delivers his decision at the end of a trial.

   _____

   _____

2. Anyone who arrives late must take his place in line.

   _____

   _____

3. A pediatrician often dictates his notes into a recorder.

   _____

   _____

4. The politician asked everyone to give his best for the campaign.

   _____

   _____

5. A great writer, like a great actor, must practice his craft.

   _____

   _____

25.9
Edit the following paragraphs, correcting the errors in pronoun usage (reference, agreement, case, *-self* words, point of view, and sexist pronouns). Use the third person consistently.

[1] All teachers need a broad liberal arts education as well as training in a special area of study. [2] This is very important to prepare teachers to face a variety of challenges in a classroom for which a narrow, specialized education is inadequate. [3] For example, a social studies teacher needs to develop his knowledge of literature, art, and music. [4] In my teaching profession, I will use my courses from the university's general studies program as much as the courses in our major fields.

[5] Many colleges require students whom are preparing to teach to work in the field as practice teachers for a year before he

graduates. ⁶This is probably more helpful to young, inexperienced teachers than to those whom have already worked as substitute teachers. ⁷However, being in the classroom theirselves is no doubt helpful to all whom are preparing to teach.

⁸Teachers cannot be too well prepared because in the classroom students will ask you a variety of questions and expect you to know about the world in general as well as about how to teach your subject. ⁹Teachers should realize that the students who they teach will depend on they and the administrators to provide a quality education.

CHAPTER REVIEW

- A pronoun should have a clear antecedent—a noun or other pronoun to which the pronoun refers.
- A pronoun and its antecedent must agree in number, gender, and person.
- Problems in pronoun reference and agreement often occur with indefinite, relative, and demonstrative pronouns.
- Personal pronouns take the subjective, objective, or possessive case depending on whether they are used as subjects, objects, or modifiers.
- Special problems with pronoun case sometimes occur with *who* and *whom*, compound elements, and comparisons.
- Pronouns with *-self* and *-selves* can be intensive or reflexive, but *hisself* and *theirselves* are not standard words and should never be used.
- The point of view of personal pronouns should be consistent.
- Writers should be careful to use nonsexist pronouns.

WRITING ASSIGNMENT

Write a paragraph in which you tell about something that one of your friends or family members has done recently. Be sure to use pronouns clearly, correctly, and consistently in your paragraph.

PARTICIPATING IN THE ACADEMIC COMMUNITY

Meet with a group of your classmates to edit your paragraphs. Check each paragraph carefully for correct pronoun usage. (You may want to refer to the Chapter Review as you edit your paragraphs.)

Verb Tenses and Forms

A good writer needs a clear understanding of verb tenses and forms. **Verb tense** shows the time at which the stated action or being takes place. Each verb has many tenses (see Chapter 19, pages 241–243), but the tenses that you will probably use most often—and that you will study in this chapter—are listed here:

Present:	I **study** every night.
Past:	I **studied** last night.
Future:	I **will study** tomorrow night.
Present perfect:	I **have studied** all day.
Past perfect:	I **had studied** before I took the test.
Future perfect:	I **will have studied** by the time I take the test.
Present progressive:	I **am studying** right now.
Past progressive:	I **was studying** when you called.
Future progressive:	I **will be studying** tomorrow night.

English verbs are of two general types: regular and irregular. Regular verbs form their past and past participle tenses by adding *-d* or *-ed* to the present tense (*work, worked, worked*); irregular verbs form their past and past participle by changing their internal spellings (*give, gave, given*).

REGULAR VERBS

The following chart lists the forms of a few of the most common **regular verbs.** Notice that each past tense and past participle form ends in *-d* or *-ed.*

Present Tense *First- and Second-* Person Singular	*Third-Person* Singular	*Present Participle (Use with* form of *to be)*	*Past Tense*	*Past Participle (Use with* have, has, *or* had*)*
ask	asks	asking	asked	asked
look	looks	looking	looked	looked
talk	talks	talking	talked	talked
use	uses	using	used	used
wait	waits	waiting	waited	waited

(*Note:* Because writers don't easily hear the *-d* or *-ed* ending in some regular past tense verbs, they sometimes omit this ending. Remember that the past tense forms of *use* and *suppose* are *used* and *supposed.*)

EXERCISE
26.1

Fill in the appropriate past tense forms of the regular verbs in parentheses.

1. My great-grandfather _____ two miles to school.
   (walk)

2. Mark _____ for an hour while Dr. Lieberman _____
   (wait)   (examine)
   the new patient.

3. My roomate _____ me if I was _____ to be at
   (ask)   (suppose)
   work by 8:00 A.M.

4. Anita _____ the house while Rita _____
   (paint)   (mow)
   the lawn.

5. My mother _____ so hard that she _____
   (work)   (pass)
   her teacher's examination in one attempt.

EXERCISE

26.2

Edit the following paragraph, changing the present tense verbs to past tense. All of the verbs in the paragraph are regular verbs.

¹Every summer, I visit my cousin in the small, sleepy town of Miller's Cove. ²In good weather we skateboard down the sidewalk of my cousin's street. ³In rainy weather, we play Nintendo and computer games. ⁴And at night, we watch videos of old horror movies. ⁵Year after year, we manage to amuse ourselves so well that I always hate to leave.

IRREGULAR VERBS

Irregular verbs change their forms in both the past and past participle. The following list of common irregular verbs will help you choose the correct verb forms as you write and edit your papers. Notice that each of these irregular verbs changes its internal spelling to form its past and past participle forms.

Present Tense First- and Second-Person Singular	Third-Person Singular	Present Participle (Use with form of to be)	Past Tense	Past Participle (Use with have, has, or had)
arise	arises	arising	arose	arisen
awake	awakes	awaking	awoke (awaked)	awoken (awaked)
bear	bears	bearing	bore	borne
beat	beats	beating	beat	beaten
become	becomes	becoming	became	become
begin	begins	beginning	began	begun
bend	bends	bending	bent	bent
bite	bites	biting	bit	bitten
bleed	bleeds	bleeding	bled	bled
blow	blows	blowing	blew	blown
break	breaks	breaking	broke	broken
build	builds	building	built	built
burst	bursts	bursting	burst	burst
buy	buys	buying	bought	bought

(Continued on next page)

Present Tense First- and Second- Person Singular	Third-Person Singular	Present Participle (Use with form of to be)	Past Tense	Past Participle (Use with have, has, or had)
catch	catches	catching	caught	caught
choose	chooses	choosing	chose	chosen
cling	clings	clinging	clung	clung
come	comes	coming	came	come
creep	creeps	creeping	crept	crept
deal	deals	dealing	dealt	dealt
dig	digs	digging	dug	dug
dive	dives	diving	dove (dived)	dived
do	does	doing	did	done
draw	draws	drawing	drew	drawn
drink	drinks	drinking	drank	drunk
drive	drives	driving	drove	driven
dwell	dwells	dwelling	dwelt (dwelled)	dwelt (dwelled)
eat	eats	eating	ate	eaten
fall	falls	falling	fell	fallen
feed	feeds	feeding	fed	fed
feel	feels	feeling	felt	felt
fight	fights	fighting	fought	fought
find	finds	finding	found	found
fling	flings	flinging	flung	flung
fly	flies	flying	flew	flown
forget	forgets	forgetting	forgot	forgotten (got)
forgive	forgives	forgiving	forgave	forgiven
freeze	freezes	freezing	froze	frozen
get	gets	getting	got	gotten
give	gives	giving	gave	given
go	goes	going	went	gone
grow	grows	growing	grew	grown
hang	hangs	hanging	hung (hanged)	hung (hanged)
have	has	having	had	had
hear	hears	hearing	heard	heard
hide	hides	hiding	hid	hidden
hit	hits	hitting	hit	hit
hold	holds	holding	held	held
hurt	hurts	hurting	hurt	hurt
keep	keeps	keeping	kept	kept
know	knows	knowing	knew	known
lay	lays	laying	laid	laid

Present Tense First- and Second-Person Singular	Third-Person Singular	Present Participle (Use with form of to be)	Past Tense	Past Participle (Use with have, has, or had)
lead	leads	leading	led	led
leave	leaves	leaving	left	left
lend	lends	lending	lent	lent
let	lets	letting	let	let
lie	lies	lying	lay	lain
light	lights	lighting	lit (lighted)	lit (lighted)
lose	loses	losing	lost	lost
make	makes	making	made	made
mean	means	meaning	meant	meant
meet	meets	meeting	met	met
pay	pays	paying	paid	paid
quit	quits	quitting	quit	quit
read	reads	reading	read	read
ride	rides	riding	rode	ridden
rise	rises	rising	rose	risen
run	runs	running	ran	run
see	sees	seeing	saw	seen
sell	sells	selling	sold	sold
send	sends	sending	sent	sent
set	sets	setting	set	set
shake	shakes	shaking	shook	shaken
shine	shines	shining	shone (shined)	shone (shined)
shrink	shrinks	shrinking	shrank (shrunk)	shrunk (shrunken)
sing	sings	singing	sang	sung
sink	sinks	sinking	sank	sunk
sit	sits	sitting	sat	sat
sleep	sleeps	sleeping	slept	slept
slide	slides	sliding	slid	slid
sling	slings	slinging	slung	slung
speak	speaks	speaking	spoke	spoken
spend	spends	spending	spent	spent
spit	spits	spitting	spat (spit)	spat (spit)
split	splits	splitting	split	split
spoil	spoils	spoiling	spoilt (spoiled)	spoilt (spoiled)
spread	spreads	spreading	spread	spread
spring	springs	springing	sprang	sprung
stand	stands	standing	stood	stood

(Continued on next page)

Present Tense First- and Second- Person Singular	Third-Person Singular	Present Participle (Use with form of to be)	Past Tense	Past Participle (Use with have, has, or had)
steal	steals	stealing	stole	stolen
stick	sticks	sticking	stuck	stuck
sting	stings	stinging	stung	stung
stink	stinks	stinking	stank (stunk)	stunk
string	strings	stringing	strung	strung
swear	swears	swearing	swore	sworn
swell	swells	swelling	swelled	swelled (swollen)
swim	swims	swimming	swam	swum
swing	swings	swinging	swung	swung
take	takes	taking	took	taken
teach	teaches	teaching	taught	taught
tear	tears	tearing	tore	torn
tell	tells	telling	told	told
think	thinks	thinking	thought	thought
throw	throws	throwing	threw	thrown
wake	wakes	waking	woke (waked)	woken (waked)
wear	wears	wearing	wore	worn
weep	weeps	weeping	wept	wept
win	wins	winning	won	won
wring	wrings	wringing	wrung	wrung
write	writes	writing	wrote	written

EXERCISE

26.3   Fill in the correct past tense forms of the irregular verbs in parentheses.

1. I _____ to write my history paper last night, so I
   (forget)

   _____ it early this morning.
   (write)

2. Dora _____ the bus home for spring break last week.
   (ride)

3. The two mallards _____ gracefully from one side of
   (swim)

   the lake to the other.

4. The ice in the lake _____ two inches thick overnight.
   (freeze)

5. We _____ the new campus production of *The Crucible*
   (see)

   last week.

6. At the campus store yesterday I _____ my books from
   (sell)

   last semester and _____ my books for next semester.
   (buy)

7. My parents recently _____ a new house two streets
   (build)

   away from their old house.

8. The man from the moving company _____ all night
   (drive)

   to get the furniture delivered.

9. The elderly widow _____ most of her money out of the
   (draw)

   bank and _____ it to the homeless in her city.
   (give)

10. I _____ I _____ the answers to the test.
    (think)   (know)

PROBLEM VERBS: *SIT/SET, LIE/LAY, RISE/RAISE*

Three pairs of verbs often give writers special problems. The definitions, forms, and uses of these verbs are given here:

Verb	Present	Past	Past Participle	Present Participle
to sit	sit	sat	sat	sitting

   Definition: to assume a seated position
   Example: Please *sit* in the chair.

| *to set* | set | set | set | setting |

   Definition: to place something
   Example: Please *set* the vase on the table.

| *to lie* | lie | lay | lain | lying |

   Definition: to recline
   Example: The book *lies* unopened on the table as he *lies* on the couch.

(Continued on next page)

to lay	lay	laid	laid	laying

Definition: to place

Example: Please *lay* the book on the table.

to rise	rise	rose	risen	rising

Definition: to ascend; to move upward

Example: As she *rises* in the morning, the sun *rises* in the east.

to raise	raise	raised	raised	raising

Definition: to lift or cause something to move upward

Example: Jennifer *raised* the window to let in some air.

Set, lay, and *raise* refer to actions performed on things and thus have objects; *sit, lie,* and *rise* refer to states of being and do not have objects.

EXERCISE

26.4

In the spaces provided, fill in the correct forms and tenses of the six problem verbs.

1. The physical trainer _____ the weights high above
   (rise, raise)

   her head.

2. I like to _____ near the front of my history class, but
   (sit, set)

   my friend Haleigh _____ in the back yesterday.
   (sit, set)

3. Did you _____ the alarm for early in the morning?
   (sit, set)

4. Professor Kim _____ his violin carefully in its case while
   (lie, lay)

   he _____ and talked with his students.
   (sit, set)

5. Because he felt ill when he _____ this morning, Aaron
   (rise, raise)

   has _____ in bed all morning.
   (lie, lay)

SPECIAL USES OF THE VERBS
TO BE AND *TO HAVE*

The verbs *to be* and *to have* are probably the most frequently used verbs in the English language. Each is irregular and thus has multiple forms. Each of these two verbs may be used alone or as helping verbs to form the special types of verbs discussed in the following sections. The forms of these two verbs are given for you here:

Person	Present Tense		Past Tense	
	Singular	Plural	Singular	Plural
To Be				
First person	I am	we are	I was	we were
Second person	you are	you are	you were	you were
Third person	he, she, it is	they are	he, she, it was	they were
To Have				
First person	I have	we have	I had	we had
Second person	you have	you have	you had	you had
Third person	he, she, it has	they have	he, she, it had	they had

Irregular Verbs *To Be* and *To Have*

EXERCISE

26.5   In the spaces provided, fill in the correct forms of the verbs *to be* and *to have*.

1. So far this year, our home team _____ won all
   (to have)

   its games.

2. The quarterback _____ a good candidate for "Most
   (to be)

   Valuable Player in the District."

3. Yes, I heard that he _____ in the running for a
   (to be)

   scholarship at the state university.

4. The local newspaper reported that the team _____ an
   (to have)

   excellent chance of winning state this year.

5. _____ you and your brother seen them play this season?
      (to have)

6. No, he and I _____ going to the game last night but we
             (to be)

we were delayed by an accident on the freeway.

7. The assistant coach _____ a minor accident last night
             (to have)

and _____ late for the game.
    (to be)

8. Perhaps that _____ the accident we saw.
         (to be)

9. Well, we _____ tickets for last night, but we
        (to have)

_____ not planning to go tonight.
   (to be)

10. I _____ certainly happy to have such an excellent team
     (to be)

this year.

Simple Past and Past Participle Forms

The **past participle** is always used with a helping verb, such as a form of the verb *to have:*

SIMPLE PAST:

I **walked** this morning. (regular verb)

I **gave** a presentation today. (irregular verb)

PAST PARTICIPLE:

I **have walked** for 30 minutes. (regular verb)

I **have given** my best effort. (irregular verb)

As shown in the next section, the past participle and the helping verb *have* are used to form the perfect tenses.

Present and Past Perfect Tenses

The **perfect tenses** describe action or events already completed or to be completed before a specific point in time. Forms of the verb *to have* and the past participle are used to form the perfect tenses. The most frequently used perfect tenses are the **present perfect** and **past perfect.** To form the present perfect, use *has* or *have* plus the past participle; to form the past perfect, use *had* plus the past participle.

PRESENT PERFECT: Action has taken place and is still taking place

I **have cooked** all day. (regular verb)

I **have beaten** the eggs for several minutes. (irregular verb)

PAST PERFECT: Action in past perfect occurs before another action in the past

I **had cooked** the cake before I made the icing. (regular verb)

I **had beaten** the eggs before I added the sugar. (irregular verb)

EXERCISE

26.6

Change the verbs in the following sentences from the simple past to the past perfect, altering the sentence as necessary to show the change in time.

1. The United States imported many luxury automobiles recently.

   _____

2. Unethical accounting practices damaged several corporations.

   _____

3. The child's mother overlooked his misbehavior for several years.

   _____

4. The conductor gave the orchestra the signal to begin playing.

   _____

5. The visiting lecturer began his lecture.

   _____

EXERCISE

26.7

Use each of the following verbs to write one sentence in the present perfect tense and another sentence in the past perfect tense:

1. to work

   Present perfect: _____

   Past perfect: _____

2. to choose

   Present perfect: _____

   Past perfect: _____

3. to drive

   Present perfect: _____

   Past perfect: _____

    4. to grow

    Present perfect: _____

    Past perfect: _____

    5. to talk

    Present perfect: _____

    Past perfect: _____

Progressive Tenses

The **progressive tenses** of a verb show continuing or ongoing action. The progressive tenses use a form of the verb *to be* with the present participle (*-ing*) form of the verb.

PRESENT PROGRESSIVE:	I **am beating** the eggs now.
PAST PROGRESSIVE:	I **was cooking** the filling earlier.
FUTURE PROGRESSIVE:	I **will be icing** the cake later.
PRESENT PERFECT PROGRESSIVE:	I **have been beating** the eggs for ten minutes.
PAST PERFECT PROGRESSIVE:	I **had been cooking** all morning.
FUTURE PERFECT PROGRESSIVE:	By dinnertime, I **will have been working** in the kitchen all day.

EXERCISE

26.8

Fill in the correct forms of the progressive tenses in the following sentences. In each sentence, you will need to provide a form of the main verb and a form of *to be* or *to have*. (*Note:* You may need to refer to the chart on pages 343–346 for irregular verbs.)

1. _____ you _____ well in your chemistry class
             (to do/present progressive)

2. No, I _____ _____ _____ to drop
              (to plan/present perfect progressive)

  the course all semester.

3. I _____ _____ about dropping, but my last
        (to think/past progressive)

  exam was much better.

4. Last night, some of the students _____ _____

(talk/past progressive)

about forming a study group.

5. Well, at least we _____ _____ most of our

(pass/present progressive)

English compositions!

6. I hope that tomorrow I _____ _____

(celebrate/future progressive)

_____ a good grade on my chemistry test.

Passive Voice

The verb *to be* and the past participle of the verb are used to form the passive voice. In **active voice,** the subject performs the action; in **passive voice,** the subject receives the action.

ACTIVE VOICE: The pitcher **throws** the ball. (present tense)

The batter **hit** the ball. (past tense)

PASSIVE VOICE: The ball **is thrown** by the pitcher. (present tense)

The ball **was hit** by the batter. (past tense)

Passive voice is useful when you want to emphasize the receiver of the action rather than the one who performs the action, but active voice is always more vivid and concise.

EXERCISE

26.9   Change the following sentences from active to passive voice, using a prepositional phrase that begins with *by* to indicate who performs the action of the verb.

1. The senate confirmed the judge's appointment.

_____

2. The terrorists abducted the journalist.

_____

3. The publisher shipped the books to the campus book store.

_____

Change the following sentences from passive voice to active voice.

1. The robber was caught by the police officer.

_____

2. The rock concert was enjoyed by the crowd.

_____

3. The woman on the sidewalk was hit by a drunk driver.

_____

EXERCISE

26.10   Fill in each blank in the following paragraphs with the appropriate form of the verb in parentheses.

Paragraph A

Yesterday, the weather forecaster _____ a night temperature of 20
                                    (1/predict)

degrees, but my roommate and I _____ the warning. My mother had
                                 (2/ignore)

_____ me an electric heater to use in our apartment, but I _____
  (3/give)   (4/forgot)

to turn it on. When we _____ to bed, the temperature was about 50
                        (5/go)

degrees, but when we _____ up this morning, it was 18 degrees. In
                      (6/wake)

the night, a water pipe had _____and _____. When the water
                             (7/freeze)   (8/burst)

_____ about noon, it _____ all over our new carpet. The water
  (9/thaw)   (10/run)

also _____ our new VCR that was _____ on the floor. Next time
      (11/ruin)   (12/sit)

the weather forecast _____ the temperature will _____ below
                      (13/say)   (14/drop)

freezing, my roommate and I will _____ and prepare.
                                  (15/listen)

Paragraph B

Last year's vacation in Florida _____ delightful. I had
                                  (1/is)

_____ forward to the trip all year, and I was not _____. I
  (2/look)   (3/disappoint)

have never _____ the water as blue or the sky as clear as it
            (4/see)

_____ last year. We _____ from the pier, _____ fresh
    (5/is)   (6/fish)   (7/eat)

shrimp every day, _____ every afternoon, and then _____
                  (8/swim)   (9/lie)

on the beach under the stars at night. I _____ another trip to the
                                             (10/plan)

coast this year. In fact, I _____ for a reservation just this morning.
                          (11/write)

CONSISTENCY IN TENSE

Good writers avoid unnecessary shifts in tense. If you start a paragraph or essay in the present tense, you should keep it in the present; if you start it in the past tense, you should keep it in the past. Awkward shifts in tense, such as the one in the following example, can confuse your reader:

INCONSISTENT: The plumber **installs** the new faucets and **connected** the disposal.

This sentence is confusing because the writer shifts needlessly from the present tense (*installs*) to the past tense (*connected*). Because the following actions occurred at approximately the same time, the tense of both verbs is the same:

CONSISTENT: The plumber **installs** the new faucets and **connects** the disposal. (present tense)

                The plumber **installed** the new faucets and **connected** the disposal. (past tense)

Changing tenses is permissible, however, if the context indicates that the events or actions occurred at different times.

EXAMPLE: The plumber **installed** the new faucets yesterday, **is repairing** the drain today, and **will connect** the disposal tomorrow. (past, present, and future tenses)

As a rule, do not confuse your readers by changing tenses unless a shift is clearly justified.

EXERCISE

26.11   Underline needless shifts in tense you find in the following sentences. Then rewrite the sentences correctly.

    1. The war was horrible, and anyone who goes through it had to endure great hardships.

    _____

    _____

2. The plane passes over the highway but barely missed the tower.

_____

_____

3. The concert started at eight o'clock, will last two hours, and ends at ten o'clock.

_____

_____

4. Out of the jungle creeps a large spotted leopard, which turned suddenly when he sees the hunters on the other side of the river.

_____

_____

5. The train engineer rounded the curve, sees a car on the track, and will pull the emergency brake.

_____

_____

EXERCISE

26.12   Underline the eighteen present tense verbs in the following paragraph. Then edit the paragraph by changing the tense from present to past. (One verb will be in past perfect tense, and the two will be in passive voice.)

¹The game begins promptly at eight o'clock as the teams run out and line up at opposite ends of the field. ²The crowd of cheering fans grows quiet, the official gives the signal, and the two lines of uniformed players begin to run toward each other. ³The ball is kicked by one player so that it arches high above the field before dropping with a decisive thud into the hands of the player who has been waiting for it. ⁴At this point, the receiver begins to fight his way down the field. ⁵As he runs, he is the target of every player on the opposing team. ⁶At the same time, his own teammates attempt to protect him. ⁷After a long run, he is tackled by a large player, and there is a pile-up as players from both teams tangle in a mass of colorfully uniformed arms and legs. ⁸The crowd lets out screams of delight and anguish as another football game gets underway.

CHAPTER REVIEW

- Regular verbs form the past tense and past participle by adding -*d* or -*ed*.
- Irregular verbs form the past tense and past participle by internal spelling changes.
- Three pairs of verbs with special usage problems are *sit/set, lie/lay,* and *rise/raise.*
- The most frequently used irregular verbs are *to be* and *to have*.
- The past participle is always used with a form of the verb *to have* or *to be* as a helping verb.
- The present, past, and future perfect tenses include a form of the verb *to have* as a helping verb.
- The present, past, and future progressive tenses consist of a form of the verb *to be* and a present participle (*-ing*) form of the verb.
- The passive voice, in which the subject receives the action of the verb, consists of the appropriate from of the verb *to be* and the past participle.
- Good writers avoid unnecessary shifts in tense.

WRITING ASSIGNMENT

Write a paragraph describing one of the most important events in your childhood. Be sure to use various past tenses correctly in your paragraph.

PARTICIPATING IN THE ACADEMIC COMMUNITY

Meet with a group of your classmates to edit your paragraphs. Check each paragraph to be sure the writer uses the past, past perfect, and past progressive tenses correctly and consistently.

Modifiers

Modifiers give information about other words in a sentence. A modifier may function as either an adjective or an adverb, and it may be either a single word or a group of words (a phrase or a clause).

ADJECTIVES AND ADVERBS

Adjectives modify nouns or pronouns and explain what kind, which one, or how many.

▶ **Examples:** The old storekeeper is an **unhappy** person. (adjective modifying noun *person*)

As the newest teacher, she was **nervous**. (adjective as subject complement modifying noun *teacher*)

Adverbs modify verbs or other modifiers—adjectives or adverbs—and tell how, when, in what manner, and to what extent.

▶ **Examples:** The patient is breathing **norimally** again. (adverb modifying verb *breathing*)

The new hotel is **extremely** expensive. (adverb modifying adjective *expensive*)

We went to the park **yesterday**. (adverb modifying verb *went*)

The mail came **very** late this morning. (adverb modifying adverb *late*)

In the last example, *very* is an adverb **intensifier**. Intensifiers (such as *very, too, really, much*, etc.) add emphasis to the words they modify.

Sometimes writers have trouble knowing whether to use an adjective or an adverb. Remember that the linking verb *to be* may be followed by an adjective but is never followed by an adverb.

▶ **Example:**   The figure skater is **graceful**. (adjective)

This same rule applies when the verb is a sense verb (such as *feel, taste, smell, hear,* and *look*) that is followed by a modifier describing the subject.

▶ **Example:**   The skater looks **graceful** on the ice. (adjective)

On the other hand, use an adverb rather than an adjective with a verb other than a linking verb:

▶ **Example:**   The contestant skates **gracefully**. (adverb)

You should also remember that *good* is an adjective and *well* is an adverb.

▶ **Example:**   Jim barbecues **well**, and his hamburgers always taste **good**.

For additional explanation of different types of adjectives and how to use them, see Chapter 20, pp. 252–255.

EXERCISE

27.1   Underline the correct adjective or adverb in each of the following sentences.

1. The steak was burned _____ and tasted _____.
   (bad, badly)   (awful, awfully)

2. I slept _____ _____ last night.
   (real, really)   (good, well)

3. She walked _____ into the room and spoke _____
   (confident, confidently)   (easy, easily)

   to the audience.

4. Her skating routine was _____; indeed, it was
   (graceful, gracefully)

   _____ performed.
   (perfect, perfectly)

5. Are you _____ that she is _____
           (sure, surely)   (real, really)

_____?
  (angry, angrily)

COMPARATIVES AND SUPERLATIVES

Adjectives and adverbs have three basic forms: simple, comparative, and superlative. The **comparative** form is used to compare two things; the **superlative** form is used to compare three or more things. To form the comparative of an adjective or adverb, add *-er* or *more* to the simple form; to form the superlative, add *-est* or *most* to the simple form. The following chart illustrates these forms and the patterns for creating them:

	Simple	*Comparative*	*Superlative*
One syllable:	cold	colder	coldest
Ending in y:	easy	easier	easiest
Multisyllable:	famous	more famous	most famous
	gratefully	more gratefully	most gratefully
Irregular:	good, well	better	best
	bad, badly	worse	worst

EXERCISE

27.2   Write the correct form (comparative or superlative) of the adjectives and adverbs in parentheses:

1. One of the _____ stars in the sky is the North Star.
               (bright)

2. Are Wal-Mart stores_____ than K-Mart stores?
                        (busy)

3. What is your _____ career goal?
                 (important)

4. I watch my diet _____ than I did as a child.
                    (carefully)

5. The temperature was _____ today than yesterday.
                        (hot)

6. Tracie made a _____ grade on her last essay than on her
   (high)

previous one, but her grade on her last history quiz is the

_____ she has made all semester.
(bad)

Correct the errors in adjective/adverb usage in the following paragraph.

> [1]The campaign started quick. [2]One day there were no candidates; the next day six people were compaigning for the nomination. [3]All of the candidates wanted to win real bad, so they each tried to convince the voters that he or she was more better than the others. [4]Some didn't do good initially but became more popular as the campaign progressed. [5]As the campaign became more intense, the candidates became famouser. [6]Voters became weary of the television ads and inevitable polls as the candidates struggled more hard to become well known. Most of the voters only wanted to live normal again. [7]In the end, everyone was definite relieved that it was all over for another four years. [8]It was hard to tell which group was most grateful—the voters or the candidates.

MISPLACED AND DANGLING MODIFIERS

Although a writer has options in placing some modifiers, sometimes a misplaced or dangling modifier can confuse a reader (see also pages 252–255).

Misplaced Modifiers

Avoid **misplaced modifiers** by placing each modifier as near as possible to the word it modifies. Otherwise, the meaning may not be clear.

▶ **Example:**   The clown entertained the children **wearing baggy pants and an old top hat**.

In this example, it is not clear who is wearing the baggy pants and old top hat. If it is the clown who is dressed in this way, then that phrase should be placed immediately before or after the word *clown*.

▶ Examples: **Wearing baggy pants and an old top hat**, the clown entertained the children.

The clown, **wearing baggy pants and an old top hat**, entertained the children.

Note that commas separate nonrestrictive modifiers from the rest of the sentence.

EXERCISE

27.4   Rewrite the following sentences by moving each modifier (bolded) next to the word it modifies.

1. The men watched the hockey match **eating sandwiches**.

_____

_____

_____

2. As his playmates continued to tease him, the child was ready to **almost** cry.

_____

_____

_____

3. She found a scorpion **on the floor doing exercises.**

_____

_____

_____

4. **Hanging on a hook in the bedroom closet**, my sister found her lost umbrella.

_____

_____

_____

5. I cautioned the movers **carefully** to carry the dishes.

_____

_____

_____

Dangling Modifers

Sometimes a modifier occurs in a sentence in which there is no antecedent (or word for it to modify). Such modifiers are called **dangling modifiers.**

▶ **Example:** **Sweeping the porch with a straw broom,** the dust filled the air.

In this example, the modifying phrase *sweeping the porch with a straw broom* is dangling because there is no word in the sentence for it to modify. We need to know *who* is doing the sweeping.

▶ **Example:** **Sweeping the porch with a straw broom,** the old woman filled the air with dust.

In this corrected example, the modifying phrase describes the old woman.

Participles

Most dangling modifiers are participial phrases that occur at the beginnings of sentences. Because participles are modifiers that derive from verbs (*sweeping* is the present participle of the verb *to sweep*), they must modify words that can perform the actions stated by the participles. Usually the subject of the sentence is the word modified by the participial phrase. The subject must, therefore, be the person or thing that is performing the action implied by the participle or participial phrase.

EXERCISE

27.5   Rewrite the following sentences, correcting the dangling modifier in each one.

1. Rowing frantically, the boat began to sink.

_____

_____

_____

2. Using brainwashing techniques, the captives began to weaken in their resolve.

_____

_____

_____

3. Arriving by ship, Los Angeles looked like an enormous city.

_____

_____

_____

4. By reading late that night, the examination was passed.

_____

_____

_____

5. Driving too fast on a sharp curve, the car had a serious accident.

_____

_____

_____

EXERCISE

27.6   The following paragraph contains eight misplaced or dangling modifiers. Rewrite the paragraph, correcting these errors.

¹She remembered the stream from her childhood. ²Then it was a small, clear stream that wound its way in and out of the trees in the wooded area behind her home. ³Looking at the stream now, it had changed drastically. ⁴Her parents had taught her always never to throw anything into the stream. ⁵Now it was littered with all kinds of debris obviously. ⁶Her parents had cautioned her about contaminating the water repeatedly. ⁷Now it was contaminated clearly because dead fish floated on its surface. ⁸Flowing sluggishly among the trees, she looked at the stream with tears in her eyes, ready to almost cry. ⁹The stream no longer burbled and murmured as it once had. ¹⁰It was silent,

sluggish, and stinking. [11]Other people had not been taught to respect and preserve nature evidently as she had. [12]The stream was now dead.

CHAPTER REVIEW

- Adjectives modify nouns; adverbs modify verbs and other modifiers.
- The comparative form of adjectives and adverbs is used to compare two things; the superlative form is used to compare three or more things.
- The comparative form of an adjective or adverb is formed by adding -er or *more* to the simple form.
- The superlative form of an adjective or adverb is formed by adding -est or *most* to the simple form.
- To avoid creating a misplaced modifier, a writer should place a modifier as near as possible to the word it modifies.
- To avoid creating a dangling modifier, a writer should always include a clear antecedent for each modifier.

WRITING ASSIGNMENT

Write a paragraph comparing and contrasting two people or places. Be sure to use adjectives and adverbs correctly in your paragraph—including comparative and superlative forms.

PARTICIPATING IN THE ACADEMIC COMMUNITY

Meet with a group of your classmates and edit your paragraphs for correct usage of adjectives and adverbs.

Sentence Style

Good writing goes beyond mere correctness. To grow as a writer, you also need to develop a clear, concise, vivid, and original **style** of writing. This chapter provides you with suggestions for improving your writing style by helping you avoid wordiness, triteness, and awkwardness and by helping you achieve effective sentence variety, comparisons, and parallelism.

AVOIDING WORDINESS

An age-old maxim says "Never use two words when one will do." Like most old sayings, this one is not completely true. You know from experience that you often need to develop your writing by adding details and examples. However, this old saying does suggest the important principle that writers should not use empty, meaningless words. Every word in a sentence or paragraph or essay should be necessary to express the writer's meaning. No words should be wasted.

The writing problem that results from using unnecessary and meaningless words is called **wordiness**. Following are some suggestions to help you avoid wordiness:

1. *Avoid using several words when one will do.* For example, avoid meaningless phrases such as *have a tendency to, because of the fact that, due to the fact that, at this point in time,* and *in my opinion.*

    WORDY: I have a tendency to be bashful around people.

    REVISED: I am shy.

2. *Use words that are clear, direct, and to the point.* Although you should use complex words when you need them to make a particular point, avoid using big words for the sake of using such words.

   WORDY: As for my own self, I have always had a preference for people of diminutive stature.

   REVISED: I like short people.

3. *Avoid the passive voice.* Active voice is much more direct and less wordy than passive voice. (See Chapter 26, page 353, for additional explanation of the passive voice.)

   WORDY: The assignment was finally completed by Bill.

   REVISED: Bill finally completed the assignment.

4. *Avoid overusing the verb* to be. Try to use more specific verbs.

   WORDY: My sister **is** a parent who demands good behavior from her children.

   REVISED: My sister **demands** good behavior from her children.

5. *Avoid clauses with postponed subjects.* Sentences with postponed subjects are often introduced by *it* or *there.*

   WORDY: It was a miracle that the groom found his cuff links.

   REVISED: Miraculously, the groom found his cuff links.

6. *Change adjective clauses to participles whenever possible.*

   WORDY: The men who were fighting the fire were exhausted.

   REVISED: The men fighting the fire were exhausted.

EXERCISE

28.1   Rewrite the following sentences to make them less wordy.

1. What are the basic underlying causes that motivate students to affiliate with a fraternity or sorority?

   _____

   _____

2. At this point in time, I have been overcome by a strong desire to sleep.

_____

_____

3. The reason he went was that he wanted to meet Rosemary.

_____

_____

4. It can truly be said that this is a great university.

_____

_____

5. The horse that won was ridden by the new jockey.

_____

_____

ACHIEVING SENTENCE VARIETY

Another hallmark of an effective writing style is **sentence variety.** You can achieve this goal by applying the following strategies to your own writing.

1. *Alternate longer sentences with shorter ones.* Achieving variety and avoiding wordiness often go hand in hand. Because student writers are concerned about punctuating long sentences correctly, they often write a series of short, choppy sentences. As shown in the following example, this practice usually results in both unnecessary repetition of information, or wordiness, and a lack of sentence variety:

Weak

One time I remember was on Christmas Eve. An angry man knocked on our door. He was the chief of police. He told us that someone had reported seeing a man on our roof. Supposedly, this man wore a red and white suit.

Revised

One Christmas Eve an angry chief of police knocked on our door. Someone had reported a man in a red and white suit on our roof.

As shown in this example, you can often achieve sentence variety and avoid unnecessary wordiness by combining short, choppy sentences into longer ones.

However, not all short sentences are bad. Indeed, sometimes a very short sentence can be quite effective in emphasizing a point or varying the rhythm of a passage. For example, one of the most effective sentences in the Bible is the two-word sentence *Jesus wept,* which appears among much longer sentences.

2. *Combine the ideas expressed in simple sentences into longer sentences.* As shown below, two or more simple sentences can be combined in a number of ways.

    a. Combine sentences into a compound sentence:

ORIGINAL:	Both girls studied all night. Haleigh made an A on her exam.
COMBINED:	**Both girls studied all night, and Haleigh made an A on her exam.**

    b. Combine sentences with identical subjects or verbs into one sentence with a compound subject or a compound verb.

ORIGINAL:	Haleigh studied all night. Lynn studied all night too.
COMBINED:	**Haleigh** and **Lynn** studied all night. (compound subject)
ORIGINAL:	Haleigh studied all night. Haleigh passed her exam.
COMBINED:	Haleigh **studied** all night and **passed** her exam. (compound verb)

    c. Change one sentence into a dependent clause.

ORIGINAL:	Haleigh was exhausted from studying all night. Haleigh still made an A on her exam.
COMBINED:	**Although she was exhausted from studying all night**, Haleigh still made an A on her exam. (adverb clause)
ORIGINAL:	Haleigh is one of the best students in her class. Haleigh made an A on her exam.
COMBINED:	Haleigh, **who is one of the best students in her class**, made an A on her exam. (adjective clause)

    d. Change one sentence into a participial phrase.

ORIGINAL:	Haleigh prepared for her exam. She studied all night.
COMBINED:	**Preparing for her exam**, Haleigh studied all night. (present participial phrase)
ORIGINAL:	Haleigh was exhausted from studying all night. Haleigh still made an A on her exam.
COMBINED:	**Exhausted from studying all night**, Haleigh still made an A on her exam. (past participial phrase)

e. Change one sentence into an appositive phrase.

ORIGINAL: Haleigh is one of the best students in the class.
              Haleigh made an A on her exam.

COMBINED: **One of the best students in her class,** Haleigh made
              an A on her exam.

f. Change one sentence into an infinitive phrase.

ORIGINAL: Haleigh studied all night. She made an A on her exam.

COMBINED: **To make an A on her exam,** Haleigh studied all night.

By using these strategies in your writing, you can achieve a variety of complex, compound, and simple sentences. Moreover, your simple sentences will themselves include various types of phrases. (See Chapters 20, 21, and 22 for more detailed explanations of ways to combine short sentences and for more sentence-combining practice.)

3. *Vary sentence beginnings.* In addition to varying the types of sentences you use, you may also vary the way you begin your sentences. The most common way to write a sentence is to begin with the subject and then add the verb and various modifiers.

ORIGINAL: **The band** performed skillfully during the game.

However, you may add variety and emphasis to your writing if you begin with one of the following types of modifiers (note punctuation):

PREPOSITIONAL PHRASE: **During the game,** the band performed
                          skillfully.

PARTICIPIAL PHRASE: **Performing skillfully,** the band played
                          during the game.

ADVERB: **Skillfully,** the band performed during
                          the game.

EXERCISE

28.2   The following paragraphs are composed of short, choppy sentences. Using several of the preceding suggestions, rewrite these paragraphs for greater sentence variety.

[1] My grandfather was a real cowboy. [2] His life made him hard. [3] It also made him set in his ways. [4] He taught me honesty. [5] He also taught me respect. [6] My grandfather was a big influence on my life. [7] He was not tall. [8] He was only 5 feet and 9 inches.

⁹But he was built like a bulldog. ¹⁰He was strong willed. ¹¹He demanded respect. ¹²I sometimes thought he was hard. ¹³I thought he was mean. ¹⁴I realize now that I was seeing him as a child would see him. ¹⁵Now I respect him for his role in my life.

¹⁶My grandfather told stories of his youth. ¹⁷He told about riding fences for days under the hot sun. ¹⁸He was checking the cows. ¹⁹He often spent the nights under the stars. ²⁰He slept with his pistol beside him. ²¹His stories reminded me of western movies. ²²He never got to ride off into the sunset. ²³He never rode with the pretty lady. ²⁴My grandfather remains a strong, positive memory for me.

WRITING EFFECTIVE COMPARISONS

We all use figurative comparisons without realizing it. Have you ever heard of *the eye of a hurricane* or gossip that spreads *like wildfire?* Statements that use the words *like, as,* or *than* to make a comparison are called **similes;** statements that make a comparison without using *like, as,* or *than* are called **metaphors.**

> SIMILE: The policeman butted through the crowd **like a bull.**
>
> METAPHOR: The policeman was a real **bull charging through the crowd.**

Simply saying that your friend is a stubborn person or that the floor is slippery is not as expressive as saying that your friend is *as stubborn as a cork in a bottle* or that *the floor is as slippery as egg white.* As these examples show, the keys to effective comparisons are vividness and originality.

Avoiding Triteness

Original comparisons can make your writing more effective, but you should avoid using comparisons or other statements that have become **trite,** or overused. For example, expressions such as *cold as ice* were once effective but are now so worn out by overuse that they are no longer interesting. Unoriginal and overused expressions such as *stubborn as a mule* or *green with envy* are called **clichés,** from an old French word meaning "stereotype." Be sure your comparisons and descriptions are fresh and original.

Also, be sure a comparison is consistent in tone and nature with the thing being compared. For example, the sentence *The athlete went as fast as a paycheck in the supermarket* may be original, but it is not as effective as the sentence *The athlete raced down the field like a comet through space.* Although both "go fast," the image of the comet suggests the actual movement of the athlete more than the image of the paycheck does. (*Note*: If you cannot think of an original comparison, you should still avoid the cliché. For example, "She is extremely intelligent" is more effective than "She is as smart as a whip.")

EXERCISE

28.3

Rewrite each of the following trite comparisons into a fresh new one. Use each new comparison in a sentence.

▶ **Example:**   as light as a feather

New Comparison: <u>as light as an empty eggshell</u>

Sentence: <u>Old Buck nonchalantly picked up</u>
<u>the 300-pound crate as if it were an</u>
<u>empty eggshell.</u>

1. as quiet as a mouse

    New Comparison: _____

    Sentence: _____

    _____

2. as old as the hills

    New Comparison: _____

    Sentence: _____

    _____

3. as big as a house

    New Comparison: _____

    Sentence: _____

    _____

4. as free as a bird

    New Comparison: _____

    Sentence: _____

5. as pretty as a picture

New Comparison: _____

Sentence: _____

_____

USING PARALLELISM

You can achieve effective rhythms and avoid awkwardness in your writing by using parallel structures. Parallel structures express similar ideas so their similarity is emphasized. **Parallelism** is achieved by balancing words with similar words—nouns with nouns, adjectives with adjectives, adverbs with adverbs, and so forth. Parallelism also balances groups of words with similar groups of words—prepositional phrases with prepositional phrases, participial phrases with participial phrases, infinitives with infinitives, main clauses with main clauses, subordinate clauses with subordinate clauses, and sentences with sentences. In simple terms, parallelism is the balancing of one grammatical structure with another of the same kind.

Some specific types of parallelism are illustrated for you in the following examples (see also Chapter 8, pages 90–93):

Parallel Word Forms

Jennifer's favorite hobbies are **reading, painting**, and **swimming**. (parallel -*ing* words)

Note: Parallel words should have the same grammatical form.

Parallel Phrases

Winter visitors to Reno, Nevada, like **to shop, to gamble**, and **to ski**. (parallel infinitive phrases)

Parallel Clauses

Kari prayed **that the war would end soon** and **that her father would return safely**. (parallel noun clauses)

Parallel Sentences

Good students are involved. **They ask questions. They do their homework**. And **they apply their knowledge**. (parallel sentences)

Note: When a writer uses similar ideas in structures that are not parallel, the result is usually awkward, as shown in this example:

AWKWARD: I like **bowling** better than **to swim**.

PARALLEL: I like **bowling** better than **swimming**.

EXERCISE

28.4   Identify the awkward and unparallel structures in the following sentences. Then revise the sentences to make these structures parallel.

1. She enjoys tennis more than playing volleyball.

   _____

   _____

2. I hear the seagulls that sing above me, the fish splashing as they swim, and the toads burp on the shore.

   _____

   _____

3. I resolved my problems involving family, with my friend, and my conscience.

   _____

   _____

4. Make your choices with the future in mind, keeping the present in control, and because you have the past to guide you.

   _____

   _____

5. At the lake, I have a chance to enjoy the silence and for gathering my thoughts.

   _____

   _____

EXERCISE

28.5   The following two paragraphs have serious weaknesses in sentence style. Read these paragraphs carefully and then rewrite them. In your revision, try to achieve sentence variety and parallelism and to avoid wordiness and triteness.

Paragraph A

¹Needless to say, most people agree that in today's world a great influence can be exerted by a good teacher. ²It is unfortunate that there are not many good teachers available. ³In

fact, one is lucky to have five or six top-notch instructors in an entire academic career. ⁴One of the best teachers I have ever had the privilege of studying under was Dr. Glenn Foster, who was a biology professor who taught at the tried and true state university. ⁵It can be said without any exaggeration that he was as sharp as a tack. ⁶At the same time he was one of those rare geniuses who could also communicate with undergraduate college students at their own level. ⁷On a few occasions in his biology class, his students were left behind by his powerful intellect. ⁸However, when the class was perceived to be having trouble following the lesson, Professor Foster stopped in the middle of his sentence, would throw up his hands, cross his eyes, and made unintelligible jabbering sounds until everyone cracked up. ⁹It was in this amusing manner that he offered his apologies to the class for going too fast. ¹⁰He also apologized for being too obscure in his explanations. ¹¹Then he would retrace his steps. ¹²He would find out at what point in time he had lost us in the course of the day's lesson. ¹³Being popular was not something that he ever worried about. ¹⁴Popularity was something that came naturally as a result of his concern for students. ¹⁵Popularity also resulted from his ability to explain difficult concepts in an entertaining and memorable way.

Paragraph B

¹In today's modern society many married women must go above and beyond the call of duty because they are trapped between a rock and a hard place. ²This trap is between the old-fashioned notion that the responsibilities of keeping the house and rearing the children are primarily woman's work and the financial reality that requires women in the United States to work outside the home in order to supplement their husband's income in order to make ends meet. ³Too many husbands expect their

wives to live up to the ideals of the past as well as meeting the challenges of the present. ⁴These husbands aren't willing to accept their fair share of the household chores or helping with child-care duties. ⁵Any modern American husband worth his salt should recognize the inequities of the present system. ⁶The husband should be willing to meet his wife half way or even go the extra mile in order to relieve his spouse of the extra burden of holding down a job outside the home. ⁷The wife also has the burden of keeping the home fires burning. ⁸At this point in time, the high divorce rate in this country today is a scourge upon our land, and one of the major contributing factors is the unrealistically high expectations that are placed on women at the sacred altar of marriage.

CHAPTER REVIEW

- Strategies for avoiding wordiness include the following:
  1. Omit unnecessary words and meaningless phrases.
  2. Use clear and direct language.
  3. Avoid the passive voice, the verb *to be*, and postponed subjects.
  4. Change *which, that,* and *who* clauses to participles.

- Strategies for achieving sentence variety include the following:
  1. Alternate longer sentences with shorter ones.
  2. Vary ways of combining ideas expressed in simple sentences.
  3. Vary sentence beginnings.

- A good writer uses effective figurative comparisons (similes and metaphors) and avoids trite language and clichés.
- A good writer uses parallel structure.

WRITING ASSIGNMENT

Pick one of the following topics and write a short descriptive paragraph using fresh comparisons (similes and metaphors) to describe it.
   1. Rain
   2. Fire

3. Thunder

4. A child

5. Freshly baked bread (apple pie, chocolate chip cookies, etc.)

PARTICIPATING IN THE ACADEMIC COMMUNITY

Make copies of your descriptive paragraph and work with a small group of your classmates to revise your paragraphs for effective sentence style. Edit carefully to avoid wordiness and triteness and to achieve sentence variety and parallel structure.

Punctuation and Capitalization

Conventions are standards, or rules, that speakers and writers of a language agree to use to communicate effectively. In order to proofread your writing effectively, you need to be familiar with the conventions of **punctuation** and **capitalization**. This chapter explains rules for using the most common marks of punctuation and the conventions for capitalization.

PUNCTUATION

The common marks of punctuation are the apostrophe, comma, colon, dash, period, question mark, quotation marks, and semicolon. The primary uses of each of these marks of punctuation are explained in the following sections.

Apostrophe

1. Use an apostrophe to indicate the possessive form of a noun.

   The giraffe's neck is too long.

2. Use an apostrophe for a contraction (examples: *it's, can't, doesn't, wasn't, couldn't*).

(See Chapter 30, pages 407–408, for rules about forming the possessives of nouns.)

Comma

1. Use a comma to *separate* the following elements:
   a. Two independent clauses connected by a coordinating conjunction

      I took my giraffe for a walk, but my cousin stayed at home with his elephant.

b. Items in a series

I would like to adopt an aardvark, a walrus, and a crocodile.

c. Coordinate adjectives that precede a noun

A neat, courteous rhinoceros would not be a bad pet either.

d. An introductory modifier from the main clause, especially if it is long or loosely connected to the rest of the sentence

Wandering through the zoo, I saw several interesting animals.

e. Nouns of direct address

Scott, will you please feed the animals?

f. An introductory adverbial clause from the main clause

Until we move to a larger house, I guess I'll have to be satisfied with my giraffe and kangaroo.

g. Items in dates and addresses

Until then, we'll continue to live at 4321 Animal Crackers Avenue, Beastville, Iowa.

But by January 1, 2005, I hope to move to New York, New York, and rent a large penthouse to hold several new animals.

2. Use commas to *enclose,* or *set off,* the following:

a. A nonessential adjective clause

My cousin, who also owns a buffalo, lives in a smaller house.

b. An appositive

The buffalo, a large male with an impressive hump on its back, stays in the back yard.

c. A parenthetical expression or interrupter

My cousin, of course, is not married.

d. A noun used in direct address

"Don't worry, Cousin George. Someday you will find a woman who loves animals."

e. Expressions designating the speaker in direct quotations

"I'm not worried," he said, "just lonely."

Note: Do *not* use a comma to separate a subject from its verb or to separate compound elements:

The chimpanzee and the orangutan jumped and played.

Colon

1. Use a colon at the end of a sentence to direct attention to a list, summary, or appositive.

   George and I would like to own a park that has the following animals: a walrus, a rhinoceros, a sea lion, and a laughing hyena.

2. Use a colon after the salutation of a business letter or formal e-mail correspondence.

   Dear Ms. Wolf:

3. Use a colon between a title and subtitle, between figures indicating the chapter and verse of a biblical reference, and between the hour and minute of a time reference.

   Adopting Animals: Theory and Practice

   Luke 2:13

   Monday at 4:30 P.M.

Dash

1. Use a dash to mark a sudden break in thought or tone.

   Most animals—notice that I said *most*, not *all*—are friendly and gentle.

2. Use a dash to set off a brief summary or an appositive that is loosely related to the sentence in which it appears.

   My giraffe—the animal I have had the longest—is named Alfred.

3. Use a dash to set off a parenthetical element or appositive that has commas within it.

   I have never met an ugly animal—an animal that I couldn't love, admire, and enjoy.

Period

1. Use a period after a sentence that is not a question.

   A zebra cannot change its stripes.

2. Use a period after an abbreviation (examples: *Mr., Ms., U.S., approx., P.M., A.M.*).

Question Mark

Use a question mark after a direct question.

Does this elephant belong to you?

Quotation Marks

1. Use quotation marks to enclose a direct quotation.

   My cousin asked, "Can my elephant get through the door?"

2. Use quotation marks to enclose the title of a short work (story, essay, song, or poem) to which you are referring.

   I like the song "Giraffes Are a Man's Best Friend."

   (*Note:* Italicize, or underline, the titles of longer works such as books, plays, and movies.)

   Dances with Wolves is my favorite movie.

Semicolon

1. Use a semicolon to join two independent clauses.

   The elephant belongs to my cousin; the giraffe is mine.

2. Use a semicolon with a conjunctive adverb to join two independent clauses.

   The elephant is too wide; however, the giraffe is too tall.

3. Use a semicolon to separate items in a series if the items include internal commas.

   The awards were presented to Big Foot, the elephant; Crooked Tusk, the walrus; and Long Neck, the giraffe.

EXERCISE

29.1   Correct the following sentences, providing appropriate punctuation where it is needed.

1. My offer and its my final bid is $200.

2. Please mail the order form to Discount Records 4206 Beverly Street Albany New York 60639.

3. Mr B. W Swanson who was defeated for governor last year will speak at the Boy Scout Annual Banquet

4. Even though Mr Brinkley the most successful salesman insisted on a raise in salary the boss replied Its out of the question.

5. John what is the subject of your paper

6. Ms Cheevers purchased a water hose garden shears and plant food.

7. Before setting a time for the trial Judge Thompsons clerk checked the judges calendar for a day when his case load was light.

8. Most of the old books were worthless but a first edition of *The Scarlet Letter* turned out to be quite valuable.

9. Mr. Johnson the chief of Fire Station 109 will hold a press conference on Wednesday June 9 at 2 00 P M.

10. The defense lawyer argued a brilliant convincing case but the jury found his client guilty anyway.

EXERCISE
29.2

Correct the following sentences, providing appropriate punctuation where it is needed.

1. On July 20 1987 the First National Bank of Orion Tennessee will have been in business for fifty years.

2. After answering the phone Professor Reynolds secretary stated that the report was due today.

3. Dr L M Weber who won the Lions Club Award last year will give the major address.

4. Please address your response to Liz Keller 2208 Peachtree Street Atlanta Georgia 30309

5. The labor organizations usually support the Democratic nominees for national state and local offices

6. When Ms. Russell the new personnel manager asked about the afternoon mail Hal responded Its already here.

7. We lost the Miller account however we gained two new accounts Morton Department Store and the Security National Bank.

8. We have branch offices in the following cities San Francisco California Denver Colorado and Houston Texas.

9. Jason wrote his paper on Stephen Cranes short story The Open Boat.

10. Sharon what score did you make on your last examination

CAPITALIZATION

Like punctuation, capitalization follows certain standardized convertions. The major rules of capitalization apply to (1) sentences and direct quotations; (2) names of specific people, places, organizations, things, and times; and (3) titles and specific elements of letters.

Sentences and Direct Quotations

1. Capitalize the first word of every sentence.

   The repairman took the television set with him.

2. Capitalize the first word of a direct quotation.

   I said, "We'll leave for the game from my house."

   "Be sure," John said, "to leave on time."

Names of Specific People, Places, Organizations, Things, and Times

1. Capitalize **proper nouns** (names of specific persons, places, or things).

   During the 1940s, Ernest Hemingway lived in a village near Havana, Cuba, and often fished from his boat, the *Pilar*.

   The Mississippi River is the longest river in the United States.

2. Capitalize adjectives and nouns that are derived from proper nouns.

The former Soviet Union was dominated by Stalinism during the 1940s.
She was an expert in Marxist philosophy.

3. Capitalize titles of persons when they precede proper names.

Senator Smith and Admiral Lacy came to the party for Professor Andrews.
Ms. Murray called Dr. Brinkman for an appointment.

4. Capitalize names of family members only when used in place of proper names.

Today Mother called to tell me about my father's trip.

My mother gave Dad a new fishing rod for his birthday.

5. Capitalize names referring to the people or language of a nation, religion, or race.

Most of the French and the Spanish who settled Louisiana were Catholic.

Mary took German and Russian courses to satisfy her foreign language requirements.

6. Capitalize cities, states, and countries and adjectives derived from them.

On vacation we flew to Paris, France, and then to London, England.

The bus broke down in Denver, Colorado, on its way to Amarillo, Texas.

We hope to take an Alaskan cruise next summer.

7. Capitalize organizations such as clubs, churches, corporations, governmental bodies and departments, and political parties.

The members of the Senate passed a resolution praising the American Cancer Society.

The J. P. Stone Insurance Company made large contributions to both major parties, the Democrats and the Republicans.

8. Capitalize geographical areas. Do not capitalize directions.

Mark Twain writes about his boyhood adventures in the South.

Go north when you get to Lee Street.

9. Capitalize brand and commercial names.

I bought a can of Right Guard deodorant spray at Wal-Mart.

The local store received new shipments of aspirin, including Bayer and St. Joseph's.

10. Capitalize days of the week and names of months.

    My birthday, June 9, will fall on a Tuesday this year.

    The annual company Christmas party will be held on Friday, December 23.

    Notice that the names of seasons are *not* capitalized.

    The first Monday in January was the coldest day of winter.

    Last Thursday marked the end of summer and the beginning of autumn.

11. Capitalize abbreviations when the words they stand for would be capitalized.

    My brother transferred to UCLA (University of California, Los Angeles).

    The USMC (United States Marine Corps) has a long, proud tradition.

12. Capitalize only the official title of a particular course unless the course refers to a nationality or language.

    My history class for next semester will be History 122.

    I hate math and science, but I enjoy my French class.

13. Capitalize the pronoun *I*.

    I passed my examination.

    Although I worked until two o'clock in the morning, I didn't finish my paper.

Titles and Letters

1. Capitalize the first word, last word, and all nouns, verbs, adjectives, and adverbs in the titles of books, plays, articles, movies, songs, and other literary or artistic works. Do not capitalize articles (*a, an,* and *the*), conjunctions, and prepositions.

   To Kill a Mockingbird is a famous novel by Harper Lee.

   The professor wrote an article entitled "Too Far from the Shore" about Hemingway's *The Old Man and the Sea.*

2. Capitalize the first word in the greeting and complimentary close of a letter. Also capitalize names and titles in the greeting.

   Dear Madam, Dear Mr. President, Dear Sir

   Sincerely yours, Yours very truly

EXERCISE

29.3   Correct the following sentences, adding capital letters wherever needed.

1. The international students organization is planning a pancake sale to raise funds for the victims of the turkish earthquake.

2. The cities of new york, london, and madrid are all popular vacation sites.

3. Some people prefer pepsi or coca-cola, but my favorite soft drink is dr. pepper.

4. Mother cried out, "shut that door, and be quick about it!"

5. If you begin in san diego, go north to los angeles, head east to st. louis, and then go down to baton rouge, you will be in the south.

6. When I finally got my children to bed, I settled down to read larry mcmurtry's book *lonesome dove*.

7. I live in berry hall, but I spend most of my time in the hall of languages, which is where the english, spanish, and french classes are held.

8. The battle of gettysburg was an important battle for both the north and the south.

9. As we studied in my history 121 class, the mexican war was very important to american history, but it is one of the least studied events in history today.

10. My interest in going to college at the university of oklahoma is to major in business and computer science.

EXERCISE

29.4   Correct the following sentences, adding capital letters wherever needed.

1. The university of wisconsin played a football game against the nebraska cornhuskers last fall on saturday, october 27, at memorial stadium in lincoln, nebraska.

2. Bill doesn't like his french class or his history class, but he enjoys sociology 111.

3. Members of the U.S. house of representatives will fly south on a fact-finding mission to brasília, brazil, and then east to volgograd, russia.

4. When my grandfather was a young man, he and grandma traveled throughout the west selling bottles of a homemade medicine called "fountain of youth serum and colic chaser."

5. Roberta wasn't sure if she should begin her letter to the white house in washington with "dear sir" or "dear mr. president."

6. My mother's article about her vacation, which she entitled "Around the world in eight days," was printed in *reader's digest*.

7. "The picnic will be held tomorrow," said ms. wilson, "unless it rains."

8. "Come over and watch the game," Sam said. "the dallas cowboys are playing football."

9. The winter p.t.a. meeting will be held at jefferson high school on wednesday, january 5, at eight o'clock.

10. My father made A's in english and in math as a freshman in college, and mom got A's in chemistry and european history 251.

EXERCISE

29.5

Correct the following paragraph by adding capitals wherever necessary. (You will need to capitalize twenty-four letters.)

¹People in the southern part of texas can visit mexico and stay as long as they wish, but citizens of mexico often find it difficult to visit texas. ²Because many mexican citizens like to come to south texas not only to visit but also to work, the united states border patrol checks visiting permits very carefully— particularly in the summer months of june, july, and august. ³why do you suppose this is so? ⁴One reason is that during these months many mexican citizens try to stay in texas illegally in order to work for the farmers during this busy season. ⁵in the past the government has discouraged such illegal labor because many american citizens believe that these migrant workers deprive them of jobs. ⁶also, although many farmers treat all workers fairly, migrant workers are often the objects of discrimination and cruelty. ⁷Such cruelty is described by john steinbeck in his novel *the grapes of wrath*.

CHAPTER REVIEW

- Effective writers know and use the basic conventions of punctuation and capitalization.
- The common marks of punctuation are the apostrophe, the comma, the colon, the dash, the period, the question mark, quotation marks, and the semicolon.
- Basic rules of capitalization apply to the following:
    1. Sentences and direct quotations
    2. Names of specific people, places, organizations, things, and times
    3. Titles and certain elements of letters

▦ WRITING ASSIGNMENT

Review the rules for punctuation and capitalization in this chapter. Then edit one of your previous essays, focusing on your punctuation and capitalization. You may also want to write a journal entry identifying the areas of punctuation and capitalization on which you need to concentrate as a writer.

▦ PARTICIPATING IN THE ACADEMIC COMMUNITY

After you have revised your essay, work with a group of your classmates to edit and proofread one another's essays. Focus especially on punctuation and capitalization. If you wrote a journal about problems you have with punctuation and capitalization, discuss these problems with your instructor, a tutor, or a small group of your classmates.

CHAPTER

30

Spelling

Many talented writers struggle with poor spelling skills, but they work to improve their spelling because they know misspelled words are distracting to readers. Because misspelled words may even give the impression the writer is careless or irresponsible, more experienced writers develop ways to improve their spelling and to compensate for their problems. If you have difficulty with spelling, you need to learn how to minimize spelling errors so your reader is not unduly distracted by them.

The following strategies can help you become a better speller:

- *Use your dictionary.* You should accept the fact that you will always need to check on the spellings of some words and learn to rely on your dictionary. Remember that you can use a **dictionary** to check a word's definition as well as its spelling so that you can be sure you have both used the word appropriately and spelled it correctly. Keep your dictionary handy and use it during the editing and proofreading stages of your writing process.

- *Use your spell checker.* The **spell checker** that is a feature on most word processors is a fast and convenient way to check the spelling in your document. If you use a computer to write your papers, you should *always* use the spell checker as a part of your final proofreading. Be careful, however, about relying too heavily on this feature. Most spell checkers simply identify words not listed in the computer's database of correct words and then give you options for editing these words. You are still responsible, however, for selecting the correct options. Remember, too, that spell checkers cannot determine when you have used a word with an inappropriate meaning for the context (e.g., *there* for *their*).

- *Improve your vocabulary.* Your spell checker cannot identify misspellings of words that look or sound alike (*quiet, quite*) or other misuses of **vocabulary.** Hence, being aware of the meanings of words as you read and write is also important to developing your spelling skills. Each time you learn a new word, be sure you master its spelling as well as its meaning. You can often determine the meaning of a word from its context, but remember that you can also consult your dictionary when you are unsure of the definition of a word you encounter in your reading or want to use in your writing.

Using your dictionary, using your spell checker, and developing your vocabulary should all help you to improve your spelling. The following techniques can also help you improve your spelling:

- Concentrating on your personal spelling problems
- Learning how to spell the most commonly misspelled words
- Learning basic spelling rules and patterns

The remainder of this chapter concentrates on these three strategies.

PERSONAL SPELLING PROBLEMS

Students often misspell the same words over and over again. One of the most helpful strategies for improving your spelling is to concentrate on your personal spelling problems. To do this, follow these steps:

1. Keep a list in which you record each misspelling you discover in your own writing as you edit and proofread your work and as you review your instructor's comments. (If you misspell the same word more than once, record it each time you misspell it.)

2. After you have recorded twenty or more words, review your list.

3. Circle any words you have misspelled more than once and study these words regularly until you master them.

4. Study each word and its misspelling to determine why you misspelled it and write a note to help you remember how to spell it correctly. Can you think of a memory device to help you remember the correct spelling? (For example, the adverb of place *there* includes the word *here.*) Does it fit into one of the categories of words listed in the chart on page 393? If so, record the word under the appropriate category.

5. Review your list each week to identify words that you misspell frequently and to analyze the reasons you misspell them.

EXERCISE
30.1

The following exercise sheet will help you begin your list, but you will need to continue it in a section of your notebook or journal.

PERSONAL RECORD OF MISSPELLED WORDS

CORRECT SPELLING	YOUR MISSPELLING	NOTES

▶ **Example:**

there	their	adverb there includes here

1.
2.
3.
4.
5.
6.
7.
8.
9.
10.
11.
12.
13.
14.
15.
16.
17.
18.
19.
20.

EXERCISE

30.2   Each time you record your misspelled words, analyze the type of error you made. If the error corresponds to one of the categories on this chart, write the word in the appropriate block. You should soon begin to see a pattern of the types of spelling errors you are making. Study especially those parts of this chapter that apply to the types of errors you make consistently. (*Note:* You may not be able to complete your initial analysis of your spelling errors until you have studied the later sections of this chapter.)

SPELLING ERROR PROFILE

LOOK ALIKE/ SOUND ALIKE WORDS	PROBLEM WORDS	COMPOUND WORDS
PLURALS	**POSSESSIVES**	**FINAL *e* WORDS**
FINAL *y* WORDS	***ei/ie* WORDS**	**DOUBLING FINAL CONSONANT**
OTHER WORDS		

COMMONLY MISSPELLED WORDS

Almost everyone misspells words occasionally, especially difficult words. However, educated people do not misspell common, frequently used words. You can improve your spelling ability by studying the following alphabetized list of words that look and sound alike. In addition, you can improve your spelling by memorizing the lists of commonly misspelled problem words and compound words provided on pages 401–404.

Words That Look and Sound Alike

Some commonly misspelled words are especially difficult because they look or sound like other words with which they can easily be confused. Misuse of some of these words occurs because writers do not know the meanings of the words they are using and therefore use the wrong one, as in using *affect* (verb, meaning "to influence") for *effect* (noun, meaning "result"). Misuse of other look alike and sound alike words occurs because writers confuse possessive pronouns, such as *its*, with contractions, such as *it's* (*it is*).

Word	Correct Meaning/Use
a	article used before a consonant sound (*a* book, *a* lamp, *a* unicorn)
an	article used before a vowel sound (*an* orange, *an* hour)
accept	to receive (I *accept* your apology.)
except	not included (Everyone *except* the teacher laughed.)
advice (noun)	an opinion as to what should or should not be done (Your *advice* was helpful.)
advise (verb)	to recommend or suggest; to inform or notify (Please *advise* your employer that you have been *advised* to resign.)
affect (verb)	to have an influence on (The illness *affected* his mind.)
effect (noun)	a result or consequence (What *effect* will the new law have?)
a lot	a large amount, many (two words; not *alot*)
already	previously or by this time; one word (Summer is *already* here.)

Word	Correct Meaning/Use
all ready	completely prepared; two words (I am *all ready* to go.)
are	present tense form of *to be;* used with *you, we,* and *they* and plural nouns (You and they *are* free to go, but we *are* required to stay.)
our	possessive pronoun (We lost *our* way.)
or	coordinating conjunction (Joe *or* I will stay with you.)
capital (noun)	a city; a sum of money (Legislators in Austin, the *capital* of Texas, control the flow of *capital* in the state.)
capital (adjective)	chief or excellent (What a *capital* suggestion!)
capitol	a building where legislative sessions are held (The state *capitol* has a large dome.)
conscience	knowledge of right and wrong (Your *conscience* should hurt you.)
conscious	aware or alert (Was he *conscious* after the accident?)
complement	to make complete (Her blond hair *complemented* her tan.)
compliment (verb)	to praise (He *complimented* her tan.)
compliment (noun)	an expression of praise (She gave him a *compliment*.)
council	an assembly of persons called together for consultation or deliberation (The student *council* met with the faculty.)
counsel	advice or guidance, especially from a knowledgeable person (She sought the *counsel* of her minister and school counselor.)
coarse	low or common, of inferior quality or lacking in refinement; not fine in texture (That cake has a *coarse* texture.)
course	route or path taken; regular development or orderly succession; a prescribed unit of study (In the *course* of a year, twelve new buildings were built.)
of course	naturally, without doubt (*Of course*, I will.)

Word	Correct Meaning/Use
dessert	what is eaten at the end of a meal (I like ice cream for *dessert*.)
desert (verb)	to leave; to abandon (The father *deserted* his son.)
desert (noun)	land area characterized by sand and lack of water (The camel is used for transportation in the *desert*.)
fill	to make full (Please *fill* the dog's water dish.)
feel	to experience; to touch (I didn't *feel* very happy.)
fourth	number 4 in sequence (We are *fourth* in line.)
forth	onward; in view; forward in place or time (Please step *forth*.)
idea (noun)	a thought, mental image, or conception (My *idea* would be helpful.)
ideal (adjective)	perfect; without flaw (The gulf is an *ideal* place to fish.)
ideal (noun)	a standard or model of perfection (Her teacher was her *ideal*.)
imply	to suggest; to express indirectly (The candidate *implied* the opponent had lied.)
infer	to conclude, as on the basis of suggestion or implication (A reader *infers* from what has been written.)
its	possessive pronoun meaning "belonging to it" (Virtue is *its* own reward.)
it's	contraction meaning "it is" or "it has" (*It's* a shame you are sick.)
knew	past tense of *to know* (He *knew* the name of the song.)
new	not old (She was *new* in town.)
know	to be mentally aware of (Do you *know* the answer?)
no	opposite of *yes;* not any (That is *no* way to treat a lady.)
lie	to recline (The book *lies* unopened on the table.)

Word	Correct Meaning/Use
lay	to place (Please *lay* the book on the table.) *Note:* The past tense of *lie is lay;* the past tense of *lay is laid*.
loose (adjective)	not tight; unfastened (The car has a *loose* wheel.)
lose (verb)	to allow to get away; to misplace (Did you *lose* your umbrella?)
mine (pronoun)	possessive pronoun meaning "belonging to me" (That book is *mine*.)
mind (noun)	mental capacity (Your *mind* can play tricks on you.)
mind (verb)	to obey (You should *mind* your mother.)
passed (verb)	past tense of *to pass* (The train *passed* through the town.)
past (noun)	former times or belonging to former times (It is easy to forget the *past*.)
past (preposition)	beyond in time or position (The burglar slipped *past* the guard.)
peace	opposite of war; tranquillity (The U.N. was determined to keep the *peace*.)
piece	a part of something (May I have a *piece* of cake?)
personal (adjective)	of or pertaining to a particular person; private (Is this a *personal* call?)
personnel (noun, adjective)	those employed by an organization or business (Mr. May oversees personnel and personnel files.)
principal (noun)	a governing officer of a school (The *principal* of our high school is Mr. Drake.)
	a sum of money on which interest is calculated (I was able to pay the interest on my loan but not the *principal*.)
principal (adjective)	first in importance (The *principal* actor in the play was ill.)
principle (noun)	a fundamental truth, law, or doctrine; a rule of conduct (Mr. Adams is a man of *principle*.)
quiet (adjective)	not noisy (The library was unusually *quiet*.)

Word	Correct Meaning/Use
quite (adverb)	somewhat or rather (The girl was *quite* shocked by the remark.)
rise	to ascend; to move upward (The sun *rises* in the east.)
raise	to lift or cause something to move upward (He wants to *raise* his grades in French class.)
sight	a spectacle; view; scene (The *sight* of the mountains awed him.)
site	a location (They chose a new *site* for the building.)
cite	to quote or use as evidence (He *cited* me as an authority.)
sit	to assume a seated position (Please *sit* in that chair.)
set	to place something (Please *set* the chair by the window.)
than	used in a comparison (Ray is faster *than* George.)
then	at that time (Can you leave *then?*)
there	an adverb of place (*There* is our room.)
their	possessive pronoun meaning "belonging to them" (Where is *their* living room?)
they're	contraction of *they are* (*They're* in that room.)
threw	past tense of *to throw* (They *threw* the frisbee across the room.)
through	in one side and out the other; by way of (It went *through* the rear window.)
though	despite; commonly used with *as* or *even* (He looked as *though* he were exhausted.)
to	used as a preposition (*to* the stars) or with a verb as an infinitive (*to* go)
too	also; to an excessive degree (The car was *too* crowded for him to go *too*.)
two	the number 2 (The child was *two* years old.)
weather	the state of the atmosphere (The *weather* is expected to turn cold.)

Word	Correct Meaning/Use
whether	if it is the case that; in case (I'm not sure *whether* he is going.)
who's	a contraction meaning "who is" or "who has" (*Who's there?*)
whose	a possessive pronoun meaning "belonging to whom" (*Whose* car are we taking?)
your	possessive pronoun meaning "belonging to you" (I like *your* idea.)
you're	contraction meaning "you are" (*You're* wrong about that!)

EXERCISE

30.3   Choose the correct word in parentheses to complete each of the following sentences.

1. Your (conscious, conscience) should hurt you for defending the robber.

   The motorists were still (conscious, conscience) after the accident.

2. There's (a, an) antelope in my yard. I was expecting (a, an) moose.

   The antelope has eaten (alot, a lot) of grass.

3. The letter (implied, inferred) that he had not paid his phone bill.

   I (implied, inferred) from that remark that he wouldn't be able to balance the budget.

4. My pet elephant (rises, raises) slowly in the mornings.

   She has (risen, raised) two baby elephants.

5. A rabbit is (lose, loose) in my garden.

   I would hate to (lose, loose) all that lettuce.

6. Afraid he would be lost in the (dessert, desert), the soldier (desserted, deserted) his platoon.

   My favorite (dessert, desert) is strawberry shortcake.

7. If (your, you're) not careful, she'll make you a member of her committee.

   Why didn't you answer (your, you're) phone when he called?

8. (Who's, Whose) books are these?

   (Who's, Whose) going to clean up the kitchen?

9. (Its, It's) difficult to make up for lost time.

   The monkey caught (its, it's) tail in the cage.

10. I will eat any vegetable (accept, except) okra.

    Will you (accept, except) a collect call from your son?

EXERCISE

30.4   Choose the correct word in parentheses to complete each of the following sentences.

1. I (advice, advise) you to eat more vegetables.

   Why don't you take my good (advice, advise)?

2. That (knew, new) song is simply horrible.

   The student (knew, new) all the answers.

3. Be sure to (site, sight, cite) the source of your quotation.

   The sunset was a beautiful (site, sight, cite).

   The architect will meet us at the building (site, sight, cite).

4. Even (through, threw, though) the boy (through, threw, though) the ball with force, it did not go (through, threw, though) the window.

5. The actress gave (quiet, quite) a performance.

   The audience was (quiet, quite) throughout the play.

6. The zoo had more monkeys (than, then) it knew what to do with.

   First he took out his harmonica; (than, then) he began to play.

7. (There, They're, Their) fun-loving people.

   The fishermen mended (there, they're, their) nets every night.

   (There, They're, Their) is the spot where I had my wreck.

8. I went (too, two, to) the store (too, two, to) buy some candy for Uncle Monroe.

   Uncle Monroe eats (too, two, to) much candy; Aunt Sophie does (too, two, to).

   The (too, two, to) of them really love candy.

9. I will (lie, lay) my books on the sofa.

Then I will (lie, lay) down and rest for a while.

10. My pet monkey was (sitting, setting) in my favorite chair.

He was watching me (sit, set) the table for dinner.

EXERCISE

30.5

Choose the correct spelling of each word in parentheses to complete the following letter:

Dear Mr. Jones:

We regretfully (accept, except) (you're, your) resignation, which you plan to submit to our (personal, personnel) office next month. (You're, Your) leaving will (effect, affect) our entire organization. I hope that your (advice, advise) and (council, counsel) will continue to be available to us after your retirement.

I realize that (personal, personnel) reasons force you (to, two, too) take this step, but I certainly do hate to (loose, lose) such an (idea, ideal) employee. Your (principal, principle) contribution has been your patience and (conscience, conscious) effort to be a good employee. Of (coarse, course), I will miss your (personnel, personal) friendship also.

Many years have (past, passed) since you first came to work at Smith & Smith, Inc. (Your, You're) going to miss our organization, and we are certainly going to miss you.

(Its, It's) with sincere regret that I see you leave.

Sincerely yours,

J. R. Smith

J. R. Smith

President

Additional Problem Words

Although, as a rule, spelling lists are practically useless in improving spelling skills, a few words are so consistently misspelled by students that it is worth your time to master them. Notice, as you look at this list of problem spelling words, that many are misspelled because they are often not pronounced correctly. The words are divided into syllables, with the accented syllables marked so you can check your pronunciation. Say the words aloud as you study them. If you are saying the words incorrectly, try to correct your pronunciation. Pay particular attention to the boldfaced letters because that is the part of the word that usually causes the spelling error.

athlete (ath′ lete)—two syllables, not three, not athelete

different (dif′ fer ent)—three syllables, not two

environment (en vi′ ron ment)—notice the *n*

February (Feb′ ru ar y)—notice the *r*

finally (fi′ nal ly)—three syllables, not two

government (gov′ ern ment)—notice the *n*

grammar (gram′ mar)—ends in *ar*, not *er*

interest (in′ ter est)—three syllables, not two

library (li′ brar y)—notice the *r*

listening (lis′ ten ing)—three syllables, not two

probably (prob′ a bly)—three syllables, not two

quiet (qui′ et)—two syllables, not one; do not confuse with *quite*

recognize (rec′ og nize)—notice the *g*

separate (sep′ a rate)—middle vowel is *a* not *e*

similar (sim′ i lar)—last syllable is *lar* not *ler* or *liar*

sophomore (soph′ o more)—three syllables, not two; notice the *o*

supposed (sup posed′)—don't forget the *d* if you are using past tense (*He was supposed to call.*)

used (used)—don't forget the *d* if you are using past tense (*I used to sing.*)

EXERCISE

30.6

Underline each of the fifteen misspelled words and write the correct spelling above it.

1. Mrs. Rodriguez is suppose to speak at the city council meeting.

2. The coaches at our college are establishing a program to promote scholarship among our atheletes.

3. I use to detest grammer, didn't you?

4. Are you going to the libary to study tonight?

5. Yes, I probly will study for my history test in the study room where it is quite.

6. I will be a sophmore next semester if I pass all of my final exams.

7. The speaker at the symposium in Febuary will talk about enviromental problems.

8. We will be listning to an intresting lecture.

9. Wasn't last year's symposium theme similiar to this year's?

10. Yes, but this year we are focusing on what the goverment and seperate individuals can do to solve these problems.

Compound Words

Many words are formed in English by a process known as *compounding*. That is, a new word is made by combining two familiar words. *Truck stop*, for example, is a relatively new compound that is still written as two words.

The tendency, however, is for compound words to be written (eventually) as one word, as in *hangover, handbook, babysitter,* and *typewriter.* Historically, a compound word is initially written as two words, then as a hyphenated word, and finally as one word. For example, *week end* became *week-end* and then *weekend*. Recently, the trend has been for compound words to change from two words to one without going through the hyphenated stage.

Most compound words are easy to spell because they are made up of two familiar words. However, it is sometimes difficult to remember whether the compound is written as one word or two. Occasionally, also, the spelling of the compound word is altered slightly when it becomes one word. Thus, the word *although* is spelled with one *l* in *all* rather than two.

The following categories of compound words will help you remember whether the compounds in them should be written as one word or two. However, you should consult your dictionary if you are in doubt.

1. Compound words spelled as two words

    a lot, all right (These two words are frequently misspelled as one word rather than two.)

2. Hyphenated compound words

    a. *mother-in-law, son-in-law,* etc.

b. *self-concept, self-image, self-hypnosis* (all compounds beginning with *self*)

c. *ex-husband, ex-wife, ex-president,* etc.

d. *pro-Communist, pro-abortion,* etc.

3. Compound words spelled as one word

a. *everybody, somebody, anything, everyone, someone, something, anybody, sometime, anyplace, someplace,* etc.

b. *whenever, wherever, whatever, whichever,* etc.

c. *although, altogether, always, already, almost* (Note that each of these compound words has only one *l.*)

d. *moreover, therefore, however, nonetheless*

EXERCISE

30.7   Ten compound words are misspelled in the following sentences. Underline these words and correct them in the spaces provided.

1. Do you remember the old song "Every Body Loves Some Body Some Time"?

_____

2. Yes, my exhusband Robert used to sing it to me when ever we had a quarrel.

_____

3. You all ways had alot of trouble with that marriage, didn't you?

_____

4. Yes, I hated his singing, and he hated his mother in law.

_____

5. Well, your self concept certainly has improved all right since your divorce!

_____

EXERCISE

30.8   Proofread the following paragraph for problems with commonly misspelled words. Underline each misspelled word and write the correct spelling above it. (You will find twenty-two misspelled words in the passage. Two words are each misspelled twice, for a total of twenty-four mispellings.)

[1] The school and city goverment officials that are choosing the cite for the new football stadium are involved in a serious

controversy. [2] The principle, the coaches, the atheletes, and alot of parents want to put the stadium on the edge of the city where it's enviroment will be pieceful and quite. [3] However, every body on the city counsel, including the exmayor, would like to put the field beside the high school and save the residential area for a new public libary. [4] The city counsel members argue that increased traffic will have a negative affect on the residential area, but the school officials argue that the new cite will have more room for a seperate parking lot that will be better in bad whether conditions. [5] Before a decision is reached, both groups are suppose to ask the advise of the city zoning officer. [6] At that point, the too groups will have to meet and determine what is in the best intrest of the city as a whole. [7] Their calling a meeting for tomorrow night in the Civic Center to announce there decision.

SPELLING RULES AND PATTERNS

Although some spelling rules are so complicated or have so many exceptions that they are not worth learning, a few spelling rules and patterns actually do work most of the time and can therefore be quite helpful. Included in this section are the rules for forming the plurals of nouns, the rules for forming the possessives of nouns and pronouns, and four of the most useful spelling patterns.

Forming the Plurals of Nouns

By far the most common way to change a singular noun to a plural noun is to add s (*car, cars; feeling, feelings; note, notes*). Several other rules for the formation of plurals, however, can be helpful.

1. To form the plurals of words that end with an s sound (*s, x, z, ch, sh*), add *es* (*boss, bosses; fox, foxes; buzz, buzzes; ditch, ditches; dish, dishes*).
2. To form the plurals of words that end in y preceded by a single vowel, add just an s (*tray, trays; key, keys; toy, toys; guy, guys*). But to form the plurals of words that end in y preceded by a consonant, change the y to i and add *es* (*baby, babies; enemy, enemies*).
3. To form the plurals of words that end in *is*, change the *is* to *es* (*basis, bases; analysis, analyses; synopsis, synopses*).

4. To form the plurals of some words that end in *f* or *fe*, change the *f* to *v* and add *es* (*leaf, leaves; knife, knives; wife, wives; loaf, loaves; self, selves*).

5. To form the plurals of words that end in *o*, add *s* or *es*. The plurals of many of these words can be formed either way; with some, however, there is no choice. The following clues are helpful in determining which ending some words require:

   a. To form the plurals of words that end in a vowel plus *o* (*ao, eo, io, oo, uo*), add just an *s* (*stereo, stereos; duo, duos; studio, studios*).

   b. To form the plurals of musical terms that end in *o*, add just an *s* (*piano, pianos; solo, solos; combo, combos; cello, cellos*).

   c. To form the plurals of *tomato* and *potato*, add *es* (*tomato, tomatoes; potato, potatoes*).

   To determine whether other words that end in *o* require an *s* or *es*, check your dictionary.

6. Some words form the plural irregularly by changing internally rather than by adding *s* or *es* (*man, men; woman, women; child, children; mouse, mice; foot, feet*).

7. Some words have the same form in both the singular and the plural (*fish, moose, sheep, deer*).

EXERCISE

30.9   Change the following singular nouns to plural nouns. (Check your dictionary if in doubt.)

1. radio _____   6. foot _____
2. teacher _____   7. thesis _____
3. match _____   8. fox _____
4. beauty _____   9. alley _____
5. leaf _____   10. sheep _____

EXERCISE

30.10   Change the following singular nouns to plural nouns.

1. friend _____   4. ally _____
2. joy _____   5. wife _____
3. tomato _____   6. chair _____

7. thief _____   9. dress _____

8. crisis _____   10. industry _____

Forming Possessives

Both nouns and pronouns have possessive forms, but the rules for forming possessive nouns and pronouns differ.

Possessive Nouns

Failure to indicate correctly that a noun is possessive causes many needless spelling errors. The rules for forming the possessive are regular and easy to apply.

1. To form the possessive of a singular noun, add an apostrophe and an s ('s) to the noun.

   George's car was in the garage.

   My **boss's** hat is ridiculous.

   Today's mail needs to be sorted.

   Notice that it does not matter what letter the noun ends in; all singular nouns form the possessive by the addition of an apostrophe and an s to the noun.

   Note: The rule for forming the singular possessive is presently in some dispute. If the singular noun ends in an s, some writers add just an apostrophe after the s. Others believe that only if the singular noun is a proper noun of one syllable may you omit the s and add just the apostrophe. To avoid confusion and controversy, it is better to apply the simple rule of adding 's to all singular nouns, regardless of their final letter or whether they are common or proper.

2. To form the possessive of a plural noun that does not end in an s, also add an apostrophe and an s ('s) to the noun.

   The **children's** coats were unbuttoned.

   He looked into the **deer's** eyes.

   The **women's** club is meeting in the auditorium.

3. However, to form the possessive of a plural noun that ends in s, add just an apostrophe after the s (s').

   The **cats'** tails have all been cut off.

   Dust covered the **books'** covers.

   The **boys'** teachers were invited to the meeting.

Now review the steps in forming the possessive of a noun:

1. Determine if the noun is possessive.
2. Determine if the noun is singular or plural.
3. Apply the appropriate rule.

Possessive Pronouns

The possessive pronouns are *my, mine, your, yours, our, ours, his, her, hers, their, theirs, its,* and *whose.*

> **My** dress is torn.
>
> That book is **hers.**
>
> The tree has shed **its** leaves.
>
> Do they want **their** papers returned?

Notice that possessive pronouns *do not* require apostrophes. Rather than adding an apostrophe and *s* or just an apostrophe, as you do in forming the possessive of nouns, you form the possessive of pronouns by changing the word itself. Thus the pronoun *I* changes to *my* or *mine; we* becomes *our* or *ours: you* becomes *your* or *yours,* and so on.

Note: Four possessive pronouns (*its, your, their,* and *whose*) are pronounced exactly the same as four contractions (*it's, you're, they're,* and *who's*) that do require apostrophes. *It's* is a contraction of *it is; you're* is a contraction of *you are; they're* is a contraction of *they are;* and *who's* is a contraction of *who is.* Be careful in your writing not to confuse the contraction with the possessive form. (See also pages 333 and 396–399.)

EXERCISE

30.11   Some nouns in the following sentences should be possessive. Rewrite correctly any noun that requires the possessive form. Write *C* if no nouns in the sentence need to be changed to the possessive form.

1. My sisters have all married.

   _____

2. My brothers wife was in a terrible accident yesterday.

   _____

3. My brothers wives are both in school.

   _____

4. The realities of the situation must be faced.

   _____

5. My fathers attitudes about education differ from mine.

_____

6. All politicians promises are worthless.

_____

7. The waiters served the food skillfully.

_____

8. Several students papers had been plagiarized.

_____

9. Is this car yours or your best friends?

_____

10. Dr. Johnsons secretary took the message.

_____

EXERCISE

30.12   Use each of the following nouns in three sentences. In the first sentence, use the noun as a singular possessive; in the second sentence, use the same noun as a plural possessive; in the third sentence, make the noun plural but not possessive.

1. uncle

a. *singular possessive* _____

_____

b. *plural possessive* _____

_____

c. *plural* _____

_____

2. nation

a. *singular possessive* _____

_____

b. *plural possessive* _____

_____

c. *plural* _____

_____

3. child

    a. *singular possessive* _____

    _____

    b. *plural possessive* _____

    _____

    c. *plural* _____

    _____

4. waitress

    a. *singular possessive* _____

    _____

    b. *plural possessive* _____

    _____

    c. *plural* _____

    _____

5. soldier

    a. *singular possessive* _____

    _____

    b. *plural possessive* _____

    _____

    c. *plural* _____

    _____

EXERCISE

30.13   Choose the correct word in parentheses to complete each of the following sentences.

    1. (Its, It's) (their, they're) car that was in the accident.

    2. (Its, It's) body was in need of repair.

    3. Where are (your, you're) books?

    4. (Their, They're) sitting on the table.

    5. (They're, Their) not very happy about being here.

6. This is (they're, their) last visit; you can be sure of that.

7. (Your, You're) going to have to stay up late tonight to finish (your, you're) paper.

8. (Their, They're) teacher is Mr. Jones.

9. (Their, They're) in big trouble about taking (their, they're) father's car without permission.

10. (Its, It's) an important meeting for the entire university.

EXERCISE
30.14

Add apostrophes where needed in the following sentences. Write *C* if no apostrophes are needed.

1. The boys hat was on the chair.

2. Its not her fault.

3. Two weeks vacation is provided by our company.

4. The Continental Mens Shop is having a sale on sport coats.

5. The childrens section of the library is always crowded.

6. Viewing the Pacific Ocean with Balboas crew would have been exciting.

7. Grandmothers new house was designed by a famous architect.

8. Was the colonists desire for equal representation the cause of the American Revolution?

9. The expansion of Napoleons army over Europe posed a threat to England in the nineteenth century.

10. His novels are widely read by the general reading public.

11. A students study time is often reduced by the pressure of social activities.

12. The reward is ours.

13. Theyre late again.

14. The snake has shed its skin.

15. The Filipinos government is based on that of the United States.

30.15   Proofread the following paragraph for problems with the spellings of plurals and possessives. Underline each misspelled word and write the correct
spelling above it. You will find fifteen misspelled words.

> [1]Local police officers' announced on the 10:00 P.M. news
> last night that a series of attempted robberys and arsones had
> taken place in our cities high school. [2]The superintendents
> statement will be printed in tomorrow mornings' newspapers, but
> he wants to reassure parents that all student's books and other
> belongings' will be safe. [3]Thus far, the thiefs have only broken
> into the hall of the building, so they haven't been able to get inside
> the teachers classrooms. [4]A few matchez were found beside one
> group of lockers' but the night guard scared the vandal's away
> into the back alleys before any harm was done. [5]Several theorys
> are being considered to determine the cause of the problem, but
> until the situation is resolved, students should take they're
> valuables home each afternoon.

Useful Spelling Patterns

There are no simple rules that will eliminate all spelling problems, but knowing the following spelling patterns will help you improve your spelling.

Dropping or Keeping Final e

1. To add a suffix beginning with a vowel to a word ending in a final *e*,
   drop the silent *e* (*usage, safest, caring*).

   EXCEPTIONS

   Words that have a *c* or *g* before the final *e* keep the *e* before the suffixes
   -able and *-ous* (*noticeable, courageous, changeable, advantageous,
   peaceable*).

2. To add a suffix beginning with a consonant to a word ending in a final
   e, keep the silent *e* (*lovely, useless, safely*).

   EXCEPTIONS

   a. Words ending in *ue* drop the final *e* before a suffix beginning with
      a consonant (*argument, duly, truly*).

   b. awe + ful = awful

   c. whole + ly = wholly

EXERCISE

30.16

Apply the spelling pattern for dropping or keeping final *e* to the following words. Some of the words are exceptions to the pattern.

1. change + able _____
2. come + ing _____
3. outrage + ous _____
4. shine + ing _____
5. fame + ous _____
6. scarce + ly _____
7. write + ing _____
8. awe + ful _____

9. mere + ly _____
10. resource + ful _____
11. argue + ment _____
12. care + less _____
13. complete + ly _____
14. love + ly _____
15. guide + ance _____

Final *y*

1. To add a suffix not beginning with an *i* to a word that ends in *y* preceded by a consonant, change the *y* to *i* (*happiness, copier, cried*).

2. To add a suffix to a word that ends in *y* preceded by a vowel (*a, e, i, o, u*), do not change the *y* to *i* (*employer, keys, enjoyment*).

3. To add a suffix beginning with an *i* to a word that ends in *y*, do not change the *y* to *i* (*copying, fortyish, playing*).

EXCEPTIONS: *daily, gaily, paid, said, laid, shyly, shyness, slyly, slyness, dryly, dryer* (the machine), all proper nouns (Kennedy + s = Kennedys; Harry + s = Harrys)

EXERCISE

30.17

Apply the spelling pattern for final *y* to the following words. Watch for exceptions.

1. survey + ed _____
2. pity + ed _____
3. chimney + s _____
4. happy + ness _____
5. accompany + es _____
6. shy + ly _____
7. enjoy + able _____
8. study + ing _____

9. hurry + ed _____
10. defy + ance _____
11. Grady + s _____
12. day + ly _____
13. beauty + ful _____
14. wealthy + er _____
15. twenty + ish _____

ei/ie Words

1. The *i* comes before the *e* if a *c* does not immediately precede it (*believe, niece, yield*).

2. The *e* comes before the *i* if these letters are immediately preceded by a *c* (*receive, deceit, ceiling*).

3. If the sound of *ei/ie* is a long *a*, the *e* comes before the *i* (*vein, weight, neighbor*).

This pattern is most often stated in the form of this familiar rhyme:

Write *i* before *e*

Except after *c*

Or when sounded as *a*

As in *neighbor* and *weigh*.

Exceptions: There are a number of exceptions to this rule. Concentrate on remembering the five most common: *either, neither, seize, weird,* and *leisure*.

EXERCISE

30.18
Apply the spelling pattern for *ei/ie* words to the following sentences. Again, watch for exceptions.

1. I cannot be_____ve that she is so conc_____ted.

2. The fr_____ght train was long and slow.

3. The president is also commander in ch_____f of our armed forces.

4. Will the parents y_____ld to the kidnappers' demands?

5. They will s_____ze him when he returns.

6. How much do these apples w_____gh?

7. His reputation as a th_____f followed him everywhere.

8. She gave a p_____ce of candy to her little brother.

9. The class was rel_____ved that the exam was postponed.

10. The blood in his v_____ns ran cold at the sight.

11. The r_____gn of the queen was br_____f.

12. They ach_____ved more than _____ther had expected.

13. My mother rec_____ved a c_____ling fan for her birthday.

14. Our n_____ghbors came for dinner.

15. I have no l_____sure time this semester.

Doubling the Final Consonant

Double the final consonant when adding a suffix beginning with a vowel if the word ends in a single consonant preceded by a single vowel and meets either of the following additional criteria:

1. It consists of only one syllable (examples: *bigger, dimmer*).
2. It is accented on the last syllable (examples: *referred, occurred*).

Note: Some exceptions exist for this pattern (*beginning*), and some words have two acceptable spellings (*benefited, benefitted*).

EXERCISE

30.19   Apply the rule for doubling the final consonant to the following words.

1. forgot + ten	_____	9. equip + ment	_____
2. counsel + ing	_____	10. compel + ed	_____
3. drop + ed	_____	11. hit + ing	_____
4. commit + ment	_____	12. refer + ence	_____
5. begin + ing	_____	13. honor + able	_____
6. hope + ing	_____	14. refer + ed	_____
7. occur + ence	_____	15. hinder + ed	_____
8. plan + ing	_____		

EXERCISE

30.19   Underline each misspelled word in the following paragraph and write the correct spelling above it. If you are unsure whether a word is spelled correctly, review the four useful spelling patterns on pages 412–415. You will find twenty misspelled words in the passage.

[1]Last summer when I visited Walden Pond in Concord, Massachusetts, I was shocked at what has happened to the place. [2]In writting his book *Walden*, Henry David Thoreau had produced a classic arguement for living simply. [3]As I was driveing to Concord, I beleived I would find a beautyful, clear, and peaceful lake. [4]I expected this body of water to be several miles from the closest nieghbor or other intruder, just as Thoreau had described it in his book. [5]As I hurryed to veiw this literary shrine, I remembered Thoreau's description of the battle and seige of the ants, the playfullness of the loon on the pond, and the beauty of the ice cakes as they were loaded onto horse-drawn sledes. [6]I also remembered the lovly arrangment of the viens of the leafs caught in the ice. [7]I was totaly shocked to find the pond filled with bathers and swimers who didn't even know who Thoreau was. [8]I left Walden Pond angryer than I had been in a long time.

CHAPTER REVIEW

- Misspelled words are distracting to readers and may give a negative impression of the writer.
- Strategies for improving your spelling include the following:
  1. Use your dictionary.
  2. Use your spell checker.
  3. Improve your vocabulary.
  4. Concentrate on your own personal spelling problems by keeping a list of the words you misspell and analyzing this list to determine the kinds of spelling problems you have.
  5. Learn to spell the most commonly misspelled words, including words that look and sound alike, special problem words, and compound words.
  6. Use the spelling rules for forming plurals and possessives of nouns.
  7. Apply the spelling patterns for final silent *e*, for final *y*, for *ei/ie* words, and for doubling the final consonant.

WRITING ASSIGNMENT

Edit one or more of your essays for spelling problems. Then review the spelling problems you and your instructor discovered in your work. Record your misspelled words on the sheets provided for you in this chapter and then analyze your spelling habits, strengths, and weaknesses in a journal entry. What spelling problems occur regularly in your own writing? Before reading this chapter, how did you handle these problems? In your opinion, which of the suggestions in this chapter will be most helpful to you? Which will be the least helpful?

PARTICIPATING IN THE ACADEMIC COMMUNITY

Meet with a small group of your classmates to analyze and discuss your spelling problems and compare your ideas about which strategies will be most helpful to you in improving your spelling. You might even compare your personal spelling list with those of your classmates. What spelling problems do you have in common? What spelling problems are most troubling to each of you?

PART 4

Critical Reading and Writing Strategies

You use critical reading and writing skills in almost every college course. Reading critically means being an active reader who engages in a dialogue with the text. It means being aware of the writer who produced the text, identifying main ideas, distinguishing between fact and opinion, evaluating sources and evidence, and reaching your own conclusions about what you read.

In order to be an effective critical reader, you must be able to comprehend what you read. You can improve your reading comprehension by using the following strategies:

- Preview the selection to be read, focusing on the introduction, topic sentences, headings, and conclusion. This preview will not only provide you with an overview of the selection but also enable you to form a general idea of its important points.
- Read the selection carefully, marking the text freely as you read.
- Review the selection to reinforce your comprehension and to be sure you have identified the writer's main points.
- Respond to the selection in some way—ideally, in writing.

In this unit, you will not only learn how to become a critical reader but also how to become a critical writer. The unit focuses on critical reading skills, outlining and summarizing, reviewing books and films, and taking essay exams.

Reading Critically

Being a good reader involves more than comprehending and retaining what you read. In addition, you need to be able to *evaluate* what you read—in other words, to read critically. Reading critically means reading not only the words on the page but also between the lines and even beyond the page.

DEVELOPING CRITICAL READING SKILLS

Reading critically is primarily a habit of mind acquired through years of practice. To read critically, you must become a skeptic, evaluating the accuracy, value, and relevance of what you read and questioning the intentions and credibility of the author. Although no simple rules exist for becoming an effective critical reader, the following strategies will help you learn to read more critically and develop the skills essential to critical reading:

1. *Understand the writer's purpose.* It has been said that "learning to read is learning that you have been written to."* In other words, readers become *critical* readers when they realize the writer behind the text is as important as the text itself. Of course, you may not always know much about the writers of the texts you read. Your textbooks, for example, are probably written by people you have never heard of. How can you know a writer who is just a name to you?

All writers reveal themselves in certain ways in their texts. It is up to you to discover the clues that will tell you what you need to know about the author of the text you are reading. First, you need to identify the

*(Deborah Brandt, *Literacy as Involvement: The Acts of Writers, Readers, and Texts* [Carbondale, IL: Southern Illinois UP, 1990], p. 5).

writer's purpose—why he or she is writing this particular text. People obviously write for many reasons, but some of the more common purposes for writing include the following:

- To express oneself
- To remember information
- To learn
- To amuse
- To reconstruct past experiences
- To communicate
- To inform
- To instruct
- To record information
- To evaluate
- To persuade

Knowing *why* someone wrote something—what he or she hoped to accomplish by writing a particular text—will help you evaluate it. For example, if a writer's purpose is to instruct, you should not complain if the text is not entertaining. On the other hand, if a writer's purpose is to amuse or entertain, you should not expect the text to be informative or useful. Determining the writer's purpose is a good first step when you are doing a critical reading of a text. (See Chapter 1 for more information on the writer's purpose).

Although people write for a variety of purposes, in one sense all writing is persuasive. Some writing is clearly and openly persuasive (editorials, propaganda, recommendation reports). Other writing—narratives, instructions, textbooks—is less obviously persuasive but still includes arguments. It is up to you as a reader to recognize the persuasive nature of a text whether or not the writer states this purpose overtly.

2. *Understand the writer's main idea.* Inexperienced readers often confuse a writer's purpose with his or her thesis, but the two are not the same. A writer's *purpose* is the reason the text was written; a writer's *thesis* is the controlling argument of the text. For example, a writer's purpose may be to persuade, but his or her thesis may be something like *Technology has robbed us of our privacy.*

Although not all writers place the thesis statement in the introduction, most writers—especially writers of textbooks, newspapers, magazines, and reports—include in their introduction a thesis statement that explains clearly the point they wish to make. It is a good idea, therefore, to read the introduction carefully, looking for the thesis statement.

Because everything else in the essay relates to the thesis, you must identify it before you can understand the essay as a whole.

Occasionally, a writer will not include a thesis statement. Just as a paragraph may have an implied rather than a stated topic sentence, an essay may have an implied rather than a stated thesis. Nevertheless, every essay has a controlling idea. If there is no stated thesis, you should formulate in your own words what you think the writer's thesis is.

For example, read the following paragraph carefully and try to determine its main idea.

> Once upon a time, college students needed little more than a pen or pencil and some paper to be prepared for class. Now, students need to own or at least have access to a computer. In addition, they must purchase computer disks, plastic envelopes or boxes for the disks, various types of folders and notebooks, and miscellaneous tools such as hole punchers and staplers. In the past, students bought only a few relatively inexpensive textbooks. Now, it is not unusual for each course to require three or more texts, each of which may cost $50 to $100. And these expenses are just considered the necessities. Many college students also expect to be provided with cell phones, televisions, refrigerators, and, of course, cars of their own. It's difficult to imagine how much it will cost to send the next generation of students to college!

Although this paragraph does not have a stated main idea or topic sentence, each sentence is an important detail that suggests or implies that the cost of a college education has increased significantly in recent years.

When you encounter a text that has an implied rather than a stated thesis, you must use the supporting details to help you determine—or *infer*—the thesis. The thesis you formulate from these details is an **inference.** The process of inferring the thesis of a text from the supporting details is similar to the process of inferring the main idea of a paragraph that does not include a topic sentence. In both situations, you use the information given to help you infer what the writer implies.

EXERCISE
31.1

The following paragraphs are taken from college textbooks. Read each paragraph carefully. The main idea is stated in some of these paragraphs; in others it is implied. In each paragraph, underline the main idea statement or the words that give clues to the main idea. Then, in the space provided, write the main idea in your own words.

Paragraph A

Some of the resources you have read about—air, water, soil, plants—have been important to people for thousands of years. Some mineral resources have also been important for a long time. For example, early hunters used a certain kind of rock (flint) to make their spearpoints and arrowheads. And people have long valued gold for its beauty. But many other minerals were not resources for early people. They did not know how to use coal or oil. They did not know how to process iron to make tools from it. Therefore none of these minerals were resources for them. Many of the minerals people use today have only become important resources in the past century or two.

—Arthur Getis and Judith M. Getis, *Geography*

Main idea: _____

_____

_____

Is the main idea stated or implied? _____

Paragraph B

As we read a work of literature, at some point we develop a sense of its quality. In the case of fiction, we may decide that the story it tells is "great," "good," or just "so-so," and thus we begin to evaluate. Often our initial response is subjective, based largely on personal tastes and prejudices. Such a reaction is natural; after all, we must start somewhere. No doubt many professional critics first come to an assessment of an author's work by way of preference and bias. But sheer curiosity might get the better of us and make us ask: Why? Why is this story so enjoyable or moving, and that one not quite satisfying? To find out, we need to probe the elements of fiction and study its techniques. We need to examine the parts so that we might gain a fuller understanding and appreciation of the whole.

—Anthony Dubé et al., *Structure and Meaning: An Introduction to Literature*

Main idea: _____

_____

_____

Is the main idea stated or implied? _____

Paragraph C

Obviously, beyond the very necessities for life itself, the distinction between needs and wants is not clear, at least not for society as a whole. . . . If you live in the suburbs or in a rural area where there is no public transportation, you may believe that you need a car. Others might need only a bicycle and occasional taxi fares. You may also believe that you need a college education in order "to succeed." Again, others may well reject this idea. Likewise, some families need a washer and dryer, some don't. Most profess the need for a refrigerator and a stove; others need only a cafeteria meal ticket or a hot plate and a cold cellar. The point is that most things an individual or family considers to be needs are not really vital to life but are simply higher-order wants.

—Daniel McGowan, *Contemporary Personal Finance*

Main idea: _____

_____

_____

Is the main idea stated or implied? _____

Paragraph D

The Court is neither free to rule on all controversies in American society nor capable of correcting all injustices. Not only do institutional obstacles prevent the Court from considering certain major questions, but even when it has the authority, the Court exercises considerable self-restraint. Judicial restraint can be based on philosophical as well as practical considerations. Many justices believe certain types of questions should not be considered by the Court. Furthermore, the Court often evades those issues on which it can expect little political or public support. John P. Roche states that the Court's power "has been maintained by a wise refusal to employ it in unequal combat."

—Robert S. Ross, *American National Government*

Main idea: _____

_____

_____

Is the main idea stated or implied? _____

Paragraph E

[During the Middle Ages] London's narrow streets were lined with houses and shops, most of them built of wood. Fire was an ever-present danger. The streets were mostly unpaved and during the day were crowded with people, dogs, horses, and pigs. . . . But from the perspective of the twelfth century, London was a great, progressive metropolis. The old wooden bridge across the River Thames was being replaced by a new London Bridge made entirely of stone. Sanitation workers were employed by the city to clear the streets of garbage. There was a sewer system—the only one in England—consisting of open drains down the centers of streets. There was even a public lavatory.

—C. Warren Hollister, *Medieval Europe: A Short History*

Main idea: _____

_____

_____

Is the main idea stated or implied? _____

3. *Distinguish between fact and opinion.* As a reader, you must be careful to distinguish between fact and opinion. A **fact** may be defined as a statement that can be proved or disproved by concrete evidence. An **opinion** is a subjective statement that cannot be proved or disproved.

> ► **Example**
>
> FACT: The *New York Times* has the largest circulation of any newspaper in the country.
>
> OPINION: The *New York Times* is the best newspaper in the country.

A fact is an objective statement about a person, place, act, or thing. Some factual statements are erroneous, but they are still factual if they can be disproved. An opinion is a subjective belief, feeling, or judgment about a person, place, act, or thing. Opinions may be based on facts, but they can never be proved because they are personal and subjective.

Both facts and opinions have valid purposes, and most experienced writers use both. If a writer makes a statement that appears factual, you as a reader should be able to verify it. If a writer states an opinion, you should expect arguments to support that opinion.

EXERCISE

31.2

Study the following statements carefully and indicate which are statements of fact and which are statements of opinion by marking an *F* or *O* beside each.

_____   1. Students of today are smarter than those of ten years ago.

_____   2. More high school students attend college today than attended ten years ago.

_____   3. Franklin D. Roosevelt founded the March of Dimes.

_____   4. Franklin D. Roosevelt was a great president.

_____   5. It is better to save than to spend.

_____   6. As a rule, women are poor drivers.

_____   7. Alaska is the largest state in the union.

_____   8. The Washington Monument is taller than the Statue of Liberty.

_____   9. Christmas Day was on Tuesday in 2001.

_____   10. Schools spend too much money on athletic programs.

4. *Evaluate the writer's evidence.* Another way to determine the validity of a text is by evaluating the writer's evidence—the material he or she uses to support arguments. One writer may use a personal example to support an argument while another may cite a large statistical study. Both of these types of evidence are valid, but the personal example is clearly less impressive than the large statistical study. Statistical evidence can be seriously flawed, however, if not downright inaccurate. For this reason, you should examine statistics as critically as you do other types of evidence.

As a critical reader, you should always determine what kind of evidence a writer is using and then evaluate it as best you can. If the writer has done his or her job well, you will have enough information to judge the evidence that is included. For example, statistical studies should always be identified precisely in terms of who or what the study involved (subjects), when it was conducted, and what the conclusions were. This type of information can then be used by readers to evaluate the quality of the evidence.

Beware of writers who cite unidentified examples to support their assertions or who use studies and statistics that are not really pertinent. Some unscrupulous writers have been known to make up examples or cases that conveniently support their arguments. Responsible writers include only evidence that is clearly identified and relevant to their arguments.

It is also important to distinguish between *logical* and *emotional* arguments. Read the following paragraphs, both of which support the idea that technology is robbing us of our privacy, and decide which uses logical arguments and which uses emotional arguments:

Paragraph A

Phones ringing, beepers beeping, cursors blinking—all of these intrusions into our privacy are the result of modern technology, which is out of control. Our lives are no longer our own; our homes are no longer places of refuge. Technology has invaded every aspect of our lives, leaving us at the mercy of anyone who can learn our telephone or Social Security numbers.

Paragraph B

More people own cellular phones, computers, and pagers than ever before. And in the near future, even more people will be purchasing these types of communication devices. As a result, our peace and privacy are becoming increasingly compromised, and more of us are becoming aware of the price we pay for these conveniences.

It is not difficult to see that the first example is more emotional than the second. Although some emotional arguments are perfectly valid and can be extremely effective, as a critical reader you should know when a writer is appealing to you emotionally. Reasonable, logical arguments are not always better or even more ethical, but you certainly want to recognize emotional appeals for what they are and to evaluate them on the basis of their fairness and appropriateness. In general, you should suspect the motives of a writer who uses only emotional arguments or who uses arguments that appeal to negative emotions such as fear, prejudice, greed, and hate. (For more on evaluating evidence, see Chapter 18, Persuasion.)

5. *Evaluate the writer's sources.* To read critically, you must also evaluate a writer's sources—the people a writer cites to support his or her arguments. All sources are not equal. Someone who once received welfare may be a good source for a writer who is arguing in favor of the traditional welfare system, but someone who has written an article or book on the subject is usually considered a more knowledgeable, unbiased source. Writers should identify their sources clearly and should indicate their experience or credentials. In addition, a writer should not rely exclusively on sources that are obviously biased. A writer arguing against gun control, for example, should not depend entirely on sources published by the National Rifle Association. And a writer who is arguing that national forests should be preserved should include sources other than those produced by the environmentally friendly Sierra Club.

In general, a writer's sources should be

- clearly identified and acknowledged
- qualified by experience or credentials
- unbiased
- relatively current

6. *Arrive at your own conclusions.* Although it is important for you to focus on the writer when you read critically, you must also be able to separate yourself from the writer and reach your own conclusions. You should not accept without question the conclusions of the writer.

While a writer's conclusions may be stated in the introduction or conclusion of the text, they may also be implied rather than stated. In this case, you must infer from the text the conclusions the writer wants you to reach and also determine your own thinking on the subject. In effect, you must figure out what the writer is saying, evaluate his or her arguments, and arrive at your own conclusion.

EXERCISE

31.3   In the following two paragraphs, the main ideas are not stated. Read each one, studying the information that is given to draw an appropriate conclusion.

Paragraph A

Hands stained and brow dripping perspiration, the young man struggled to complete the task before him. He had been working for hours, and his body ached with exhaustion. His back hurt from hours of bending over his task; his head hurt from the intense concentration and mental effort he had expended; and his hand hurt from gripping the tool with which he was working. Furthermore, his mind had never felt so fatigued—so utterly depleted. Moaning to himself, he picked up his leaking pen and bent once more over his smudged paper. He must go on. The essay was due in the morning.

Conclusion: _____

_____

Paragraph B

Henry VIII became king of England in 1509. His first wife was Catherine of Aragon, who was unable to give him a male child. Dissatisfied with Catherine, Henry became interested in Anne Boleyn, for whom he challenged the Church and divorced Catherine. Ann, too, failed to bear him a male child, so she was charged with adultery and beheaded. Next, Henry married Jane Seymour, who gave him a male heir, Prince Edward, and then conveniently died. Later, Henry married Anne of Cleves on the strength of her portrait. Being disappointed in the real Anne, however, he bought her off and sent her away to a remote castle. He then married Catherine Howard, a pretty young woman who was unfaithful to him and who, not surprisingly, was beheaded for her infidelity. Finally, Henry married Catherine Parr, a young widow to whom he remained happily married until his death.

Conclusion: _____

_____

EXERCISE

31.4   In the following reading selection, the main idea is not stated in a thesis statement. However, the writer provides the information needed to draw a conclusion about the main idea.

> ¹They didn't say anything about this in the books, I thought, as the snow blew in through the gaping doorway and settled on my naked back.
>
> ²I lay face down on the cobbled floor in a pool of nameless muck, my arm deep inside the straining cow, my feet scrabbling for a toe hold between the stones. I was stripped to the waist and the snow mingled with the dirt and the dried blood on my body. I could see nothing outside the circle of flickering light thrown by the smoky oil lamp which the farmer held over me.
>
> ³No, there wasn't a word in the books about searching for your ropes and instruments in the shadows; about trying to keep clean in a half bucket of tepid water; about the cobbles digging into your chest. Nor about the slow numbing of the arms, the creeping paralysis of the muscles as the fingers tried to work against the cow's powerful expulsive efforts.
>
> ⁴There was no mention anywhere of the gradual exhaustion, the feeling of futility and the little far-off voice of panic.
>
> ⁵My mind went back to that picture in the obstetrics book. A cow standing in the middle of a gleaming floor while a sleek veterinary surgeon in a spotless parturition overall inserted his arm to a polite distance. He was relaxed and smiling, the farmer and his helpers were smiling, even the cow was smiling. There was no dirt or blood or sweat anywhere.
>
> ⁶That man in the picture had just finished an excellent lunch and had moved next door to do a bit of calving just for the sheer pleasure of it, as a kind of dessert. He hadn't crawled shivering from his bed at two o'clock in the morning and bumped over twelve miles of frozen snow, staring sleepily ahead till the lonely farm showed in the headlights. He hadn't climbed half a mile of white fell-side to the doorless barn where his patient lay.
>
> —James Herriot, *All Creatures Great and Small*

Using the facts and details given in this reading selection, draw a conclusion about the author's main point.

_____

_____

_____

_____

GUIDELINES FOR CRITICAL READING

Reading critically means engaging in a dialogue with the writer, questioning, evaluating, and responding to the ideas and arguments he or she presents. Although critical reading cannot be reduced to a formula, the following guidelines will help you evaluate what you read:

1. Read the introduction carefully to identify the writer's thesis and purpose, and preview the entire selection before beginning to read.

2. As you read, identify the writer's primary arguments, evaluating the evidence and sources used to support the arguments and distinguishing between facts and opinions.

3. After you read, review the selection, deciding your own position on the issues addressed by the writer. On what points do you agree and disagree? If you disagree, what are your counterarguments?

4. Finally, arrive at your own conclusions on the subject.

These guidelines should be useful to you in any assignment that requires critical reading and writing. However, the skill of reading and writing critically is one that is developed slowly as you gain experience. There is no formula or set of rules that can automatically give you these complex skills. Most of all, critical reading and writing require *thinking*—a skill that cannot be acquired instantly. The more you think seriously about what you read and write, the more accomplished you will become as a critical reader and writer.

The following essay has been annotated to show you how a critical reader might respond to a text:

¹Baltimore Maryland. I was waiting for breakfast in a coffee shop the other morning and reading the paper. The <u>paper</u> had sixty-six pages. The waitress brought a <u>paper place mat</u> and a <u>paper napkin</u> and took my order, and I paged through the paper.

What does this term mean?

²The headline said, "House Panel Studies a Bill <u>Allowing</u> <u>(Clear-Cutting)</u> in U.S. Forests."

³I put the paper napkin in my lap, spread the paper out on the paper place mat, and read on: "<u>The House Agriculture</u>

Fact

Committee," it said, "is looking over legislation that would once again open national forests to the clear-cutting of trees by private companies under government permits."

Evidence?

4The waitress brought the coffee. I opened a paper sugar envelope and tore open a little paper cup of cream and went on reading the paper: "The Senate voted without dissent yesterday to allow clear-cutting," the paper said. "Critics have said clear-cutting in the national forests can lead to erosion and destruction of wildlife habitats. Forest Service and industry spokesmen said a flat ban on clear-cutting would bring paralysis to the lumber industry." And to the paper industry, I thought. Clear-cutting a forest is one way to get a lot of paper, and we sure seem to need a lot of paper.

Is this fact or opinion?

More evidence

5The waitress brought the toast. I looked for the butter. It came on a little paper tray with a covering of paper. I opened a paper package of marmalade and read on: "Senator Jennings Randolph, Democrat of West Virginia, urged his colleagues to take a more restrictive view and permit clear-cutting only under specific guidelines for certain types of forest. But neither he nor anyone else voted against the bill, which was sent to the House on a 90 to 0 vote."

Fact

6The eggs came, with little paper packages of salt and pepper. I finished breakfast, put the paper under my arm, and left the table with its used and useless paper napkin, paper place mat, paper salt and pepper packages, paper butter and marmalade wrappings, paper sugar envelope, and paper cream holder, and I walked out into the morning wondering how our national forests can ever survive our breakfasts.

Writer's conclusion

—Charles Kuralt, "Down with the Forests," *Dateline America*

The first paragraph of the following response summarizes Kuralt's essay, identifying his thesis and his two major points. The second paragraph evaluates the essay, giving the reader's reasons for agreeing with Kuralt's stand but pointing out an omission, or weakness, in the essay.

Main idea

Summary

1 In his essay "Down with the Forests," Charles Kuralt points out that **our widespread use of paper products is a serious threat to our national forests.** He argues that Americans use huge, and probably unnecessary, quantities of paper products; he also implies that this dependence on paper is one reason the government is reluctant to pass laws that prohibit the destruction of entire forests. Kuralt not only implicitly argues against legislation that allows "clear-cutting" in U.S. forests but also indirectly blames American consumers for their thoughtless overuse of paper.

Agreement

Reasons for agreement

Overall strength/ weakness

2 I agree with Kuralt's basic argument that our forests are in danger and with his implied argument that Americans use too many paper products. By describing in detail how much paper we use in a typical breakfast served in a restaurant, Kuralt dramatically illustrates how we waste paper. Because my own experience confirms that of Kuralt, I too realize that we use a lot of paper products—probably more than we need. Moreover, because paper is made from trees, it is obvious that our extravagant use of paper is directly related to the destruction of forests and perhaps specifically to the loss of our national forests. However, although Kuralt's essay does identify a potentially serious problem, it does not suggest possible solutions.

EXERCISE

31.5   Read the following selection from *Future Shock*, by Alvin Toffler. Annotate the selection as you read, identifying the author's purpose and thesis and evaluating his arguments, evidence, sources, and conclusions.

1 Our attitudes toward things reflect basic value judgments. Nothing could be more dramatic than the difference between the new

breed of little girls who cheerfully turn in their Barbies for the new and improved model and those who, like their mothers and grandmothers before them, clutch lingeringly and lovingly to the same doll until it disintegrates from sheer age. In this difference lies the contrast between past and future, between societies based on performance, and the new, fast-forming society based on transience.

2That man-thing relationships are growing more and more temporary may be illustrated by examining the culture surrounding the little girl who trades in her doll. This child soon learns that Barbie dolls are by no means the only physical objects that pass into and out of her young life at a rapid clip. Diapers, bibs, paper napkins, Kleenex, towels, non-returnable soda bottles—all are used up quickly in her home and ruthlessly eliminated. Corn muffins come in baking tins that are thrown away after one use. Spinach is encased in plastic sacks that can be dropped into a pan of boiling water for heating, and then thrown away. TV dinners are cooked and often served on throw-away trays. Her home is a large processing machine through which objects flow, entering and leaving, at a faster and faster rate of speed. From birth on, she is inextricably embedded in a throw-away culture.

3The idea of using a product once or for a brief period and then replacing it runs counter to the grain of societies or individuals steeped in a heritage of poverty. Not long ago Uriel Rone, a market researcher for the French advertising agency Publicis, told me: "The French housewife is not used to disposable products. She likes to keep things, even old things, rather than throw them away. We represented one company that wanted to introduce a kind of plastic throw-away curtain. We did a marketing study for them and found the resistance too strong." This resistance, however, is dying all over the developed world.

4Thus a writer, Edward Maze, has pointed out that many Americans visiting Sweden in the early 1950's were astounded by its cleanliness. "We were almost awed by the fact that there were no beer and soft drink bottles by the roadsides, as, much to our shame, there were in America. But by the 1960's, lo and behold, bottles were suddenly blooming along Swedish highways. . . . What happened? Sweden had become a buy, use and throw-away society, following the American pattern." In Japan today throw-away tissues are so universal that cloth handkerchiefs are regarded as old fashioned, not to say unsanitary. In England for sixpence one may buy a "Dentamatic throw-away toothbrush" which comes already coated with toothpaste for its one-time use. And even in France, disposable cigarette lighters are commonplace. From cardboard milk containers to the rockets that power space vehicles, products created for short-term or one-time use are becoming more numerous and crucial to our way of life.

5We develop a throw-away mentality to match our throw-away products. This mentality produces, among other things, a set of radically altered values with respect to property. But the spread of disposability through the society also implies decreased durations in man-thing relationships. Instead of being linked with a single object over a relatively long span of time, we are linked for brief periods with the succession of objects that supplant it.

—From Alvin Toffler, *Future Shock*

CHAPTER REVIEW

- Critical reading includes the following steps:
    1. Understand the writer's purpose
    2. Understand the writer's thesis
    3. Distinguish between fact and opinion
    4. Evaluate the writer's evidence
    5. Evaluate the writer's sources
    6. Arrive at your own conclusions
- Reading critically means engaging in a dialogue with the writer.

WRITING ASSIGNMENT

Using the guidelines on page 430, reread the selection from *Future Shock*, by Alvin Toffler, and write a response in which you evaluate Toffler's ideas. The annotations you wrote in Exercise 31.5 may be helpful.

PARTICIPATING IN THE ACADEMIC COMMUNITY

Discuss with your classmates your response to the selection by Alvin Toffler, comparing your evaluation with theirs.

Outlining and Summarizing

Two of the most important strategies for improving your textbook reading skills are outlining and summarizing. You may know how to outline and summarize in general, but in this chapter you will learn specifically how these two strategies can reinforce reading.

OUTLINING TO STUDY

Outlining can be an important aid to reading when your purpose is to learn the material being read. If you outline what you read, you force yourself to focus on your reading task and to analyze the content and structure of what you are reading. Because it involves writing, outlining also reinforces learning and retention. Furthermore, an outline provides a written record of the most important ideas from your reading—a record that can be invaluable when the time comes for a written assignment or a test.

Study outlines are informal outlines that help you understand and remember what you read. Study outlines, like planning outlines, do not have to conform to any one format or any specific restriction. They can be as informal and individual as you want to make them. (See the examples of informal planning outlines on pages 26–30 in Chapter 3.)

A useful study outline is one that is still comprehensible to you weeks or even months after you have written it, so your outline needs to be clear and complete. A useful study outline is also comprehensive and accurate; it includes all of the important ideas and does not distort their meaning.

Guidelines for Outlining

If you have not previously constructed study outlines, you will find the following general guidelines helpful:

1. Read the *entire* passage carefully.
2. Determine the author's main idea and state it in your own words.

3. Decide on the major subdivisions. (Be sure all of the major support-ing points are of equal importance.)

4. Under each major division, list the more specific supporting points. (Do not include too many minor details.)

EXERCISE

32.1

Use the preceding guidelines to outline the following paragraph:

1. Read the entire passage carefully.

[1]Comedy is usually defined as the opposite of tragedy. [2]One reason definitions of comedy are rarely given is that there are two distinct types of comedy, and these two types are very different. [3]The first type, low comedy, is loud, uninhibited, occasionally physical, and often vulgar. [4]For example, slapstick comedy is considered low comedy. [5]The second type, high comedy, is sophisticated, subtle, and usually romantic. [6]The situation comedies so popular with television viewers are an example of high comedy. [7]Because these two types of comedy are so different, it is difficult to define comedy.

2. Determine the author's main idea and state it in your own words.

_____

3. Decide on the major subdivisions. (Be sure these major points are of equal importance.)

First major point: _____

_____

Second major point: _____

_____

4. Now list the more specific supporting points. (Do not include minor details or, as a rule, examples.)

Specific supporting points under first major point: _____

_____

_____

Specific supporting points under second major point: _____

_____

_____

You probably did not include information from either the first or last sentence of the paragraph. Because the first sentence is not the topic sentence but merely an introduction to the main idea (which is stated in the second sentence), it has no information that must be included. The last sentence serves as a conclusion and restates the main idea, so it, too, contains no new information. You may have also omitted the examples of the two types of comedy. However, if these examples helped you understand the difference between the two types, you may have included them as minor supporting points.

Now you are ready to construct your outline. Use any format or arrangement with which you are comfortable, but be sure you (1) indicate accurately the order in which the points occur and (2) show the appropriate relationships among major and minor supporting points.

When you have completed your outline, you may want to compare it with those of your classmates. Notice that the same basic outline can assume many forms. (For more information on the forms outlines may take, see Chapter 3.)

EXERCISE

32.2   Read the following paragraphs from a chemistry textbook. The main idea of this selection could be stated as follows: *The origins of modern chemistry can be traced back to ancient civilizations.* As you read, annotate by identifying the major supporting points.

1 The earliest attempts to explain natural phenomena led to fanciful inventions—to myths and fantasies—but not to understanding. Around 600 BC, a group of Greek philosophers became dissatisfied with these myths, which explained little. Stimulated by social and cultural change as well as curiosity, they began to ask questions about the world around them. They answered these questions by constructing lists of logical possibilities. Thus, Greek philosophy was an attempt to discover the basic truths of nature by thinking things through, rather than by running laboratory experiments. The Greek philosophers did this so thoroughly and so brilliantly that the years between 600 and 400 BC are called the "golden age of philosophy."

2 During this period, the Greek philosophers laid the foundation for one of our main ideas about the universe. Leucippus (about 440 BC) and Democritus (about 420 BC) were trying to determine whether there was such a thing as a smallest particle of matter. In doing so, they established the idea of the atom, a particle so tiny that it could not be seen. At that time there was no way to test whether atoms really

existed, and more than 2,000 years passed before scientists proved that they do exist.

[3]While the Greeks were studying philosophy and mathematics, the Egyptians were practicing the art of chemistry. They were mining and purifying the metals gold, silver, and copper and were making embalming fluids and dyes. They called this art *khemia*, and it flourished until the seventh century AD, when it was taken over by the Arabs. The Egyptian word *khemia* became the Arabic word *alkhemia* and then the English word *alchemy*. A major goal of the alchemists was to transmute (convert) "base metals" into gold. That is, they wanted to transform less desirable elements such as lead and iron into the element gold. The ancient Arabic emperors employed many alchemists for this purpose, which, of course, was never accomplished. The alchemists also tried to find the "philosopher's stone" (a supposed cure for all diseases) and the "elixir of life" (which would prolong life indefinitely). Unfortunately they failed in both attempts; but they did have some lucky accidents. In the course of their work, they discovered acetic acid, nitric acid, and ethyl alcohol, as well as many other substances used by chemists today.

[4]The modern age of chemistry dawned in 1661 with the publication of the book *The Sceptical Chymist*, written by Robert Boyle, an English chemist, physicist, and theologian. Boyle was "skeptical" because he was not willing to take the word of the ancient Greeks and alchemists as truth, especially about the elements that make up the world. Instead, Boyle believed that scientists must start from basic principles, and he realized that every theory had to be proved by experiment. His new and innovative scientific approach was to change the whole course of chemistry.

—From Alan Sherman, Sharon Sherman, and Leonard Russikoff,
Basic Concepts of Chemistry

EXERCISE

32.3   Using the guidelines on pages 435–436, outline the selection from the chemistry textbook that you have just read and annotated.

SUMMARIZING

Many of the skills you use in outlining are also used in writing a summary—a concise restatement of a reading selection. To summarize, you

must have a good understanding of what you have read and be able to identify clearly the main idea and the major supporting points. Then you must
restate these ideas in your own words. Thus, **summarizing,** like outlining, requires both reading and writing skills.

Guidelines for Summarizing

Summarizing requires two important reading skills: (1) finding the main
idea and (2) determining major supporting points. Neither of these skills
is new to you. You simply need to see how they apply to summarizing.
Following are some suggestions for how to read a selection you plan to
summarize:

1. *Read through the entire selection before you start to summarize.* If you
   try to summarize as you read, you will very likely fail to recognize the
   major ideas, and your summary will be too long and inclusive.

2. *Identify the author's main idea.* If the main idea is expressed in a topic
   sentence or thesis statement, underline this sentence.

3. *Determine the major supporting points and their relationship to the
   main idea.* Again, underlining may be helpful.

After you have read the selection carefully and have gone back over
it to determine the main idea and major supporting details, you are ready
to begin writing your summary. The length of a summary depends on the
length of the original selection. For example, a summary of a thirty-page
textbook chapter might be several pages long. In summarizing a paragraph, however, you would probably write only two or three sentences.

Writing a summary requires all of the writing skills you have studied
so far. In addition, here are several specific suggestions that may prove
helpful:

1. *Include the title and author of the selection you are summarizing in
   your summary.* You may combine this information and the main idea
   statement in one sentence. (See page 440, the summary of the selection
   by Langacker.)

2. *Include only the author's main ideas and the important supporting
   details.* Do not insert your own ideas or unimportant details.

3. *Write in your own words.* Use the author's ideas but not the author's
   words unless you include a direct quotation.

4. *Be brief and to the point.* The idea of summarizing is to condense the
   main ideas of the original work into as few words as possible.

To get a clearer idea of summaries, read the following paragraph and the summary of it that follows:

Children display an amazing ability to become fluent speakers of any language consistently spoken around them. Every normal human child who is not reared in virtual isolation from language use soon comes to speak one or more languages natively. The child's learning of his native language is not dependent on special tutoring. Parents may spend many hours "reinforcing" every recognizable bit of their child's verbal activity with a smile or some other reward, or trying by means of "baby talk" to bridge the gap between their mature language competence and the child's immature one. But there is no particular reason to believe that such activity has any bearing on the child's ultimate success in becoming a native speaker of his parents' language. Children can pick up a language by playing with other children who happen to speak it just as well as they can through the concentrated efforts of doting parents. All they seem to need is sufficient exposure to the language in question.

—From Ronald W. Langacker, *Language and Its Structure*

One possible summary of this passage:

In *Language and Its Structure*, Ronald W. Langacker points out that children learn to speak any language that is spoken around them. No special instruction is required.

EXERCISE

32.3

Read the following paragraphs and write a summary of each:

Paragraph A

Good written instructions are easy to read, easy to follow, and easy to remember. Unfortunately, they are also rare. Everyone has had the frustrating experience of trying to follow badly written instructions that are open to different interpretations, leave out important information, assume too much knowledge on the part of the reader, or do not explain what needs to be done in a straightforward manner. When you read instructions, your primary purpose is usually to accomplish something— to improve your vocabulary, dress more stylishly, save money, find a job, lose or gain weight, and so on. Thus reading instructions is usually a means to an end, a way of accomplishing some goal. Few other types of reading are so focused and specific in purpose.

—Adapted from Jeanette Harris and Donald Cunningham, *The Simon & Schuster Guide to Writing*, 2nd ed.

Summary: _____

_____

_____

_____

_____

Paragraph B

Let me put this in another way. It is true that there are bad teachers—teachers who do not prepare for class, who are arbitrary, who subject their students to sarcasm, who won't tolerate (let alone encourage) questions and criticism, or who have thought little about education. But there are also bad students. By "bad students" I do not mean students who get low grades. Instead, I mean students who do not participate sufficiently in their own education and who do not actively demand enough from their teachers. They do not ask questions in class or after class. They do not discuss the purposes of assignments with their teachers. They do not make the teacher explain the importance and significance of the subject being studied. They do not go to office hours. They do not make the teacher explain comments on papers handed back to the student. They do not take notes on the readings. They just sit in class, letting the teacher do all the work. Education can only be a cooperative effort between student and teacher. By actively participating in these and other ways, you play your proper and necessary part in this cooperative process.

—Jack W. Meiland, *College Thinking: How to Get the Best Out of College*

Summary: _____

_____

_____

_____

_____

Paragraph C

The best means of benefiting the community is to place within its reach the ladders upon which the aspiring can rise—free libraries, parks, and means of recreation, by which men are helped in body and mind; works of art, certain to give pleasure and improve the public taste; and public institutions of various kinds, which will improve the general condition of the people; in this manner returning their surplus wealth to the mass of their fellows in the forms best calculated to do them lasting good.

—Andrew Carnegie, "The Gospel of Wealth"

Summary: _____

_____

_____

_____

_____

Summarizing Essays

Writing a summary of a longer composition, such as an essay or a text-book chapter, is similar to writing a summary of a paragraph. Whether you are summarizing a paragraph or a longer passage, you must read through the entire selection and identify both the author's main idea and major supporting details. In summarizing a paragraph, you look for a stated or implied *topic sentence*. In summarizing an essay or chapter, you look for a stated or implied *thesis statement*. In writing a summary of a paragraph, you determine the major supporting details; in writing a summary of an essay, you determine the main ideas of each paragraph or each section.

In the following passage, the thesis is identified and the main supporting points are bolded:

Limitations of Word Processing

THESIS: Word-processing programs are useful writing tools, but they have several limitations.

[1] Word-processing programs are tools that facilitate writing much as the fountain pen and the typewriter have in the past: They make writing easier and faster. Numerous word-processing programs are available, and more are being developed all the time. Each program differs in execution and function, but most programs offer essentially the same assistance: They enable a writer to make changes in a text—

insertions, deletions, substitutions, and rearrangements—without having to retype the manuscript repeatedly. In addition, most word-processing programs are supplemented by programs that check spelling and help writers edit and proofread their texts. As marvelous as such assistance is to a writer, these programs have limitations.

[2]**First, word-processing programs do not improve a person's writing**. Writing with the aid of word processing does encourage writers to revise what they have written, but writers must still know how to revise. Revision, which involves reseeing and rethinking, involves substantive modifications in a text. Inexperienced writers will frequently produce several drafts when they use a word processor, but the modifications they make are often minor changes in word choice or punctuation rather than substantive changes in content and organization.

[3]**A second limitation is that the editing programs** that frequently accompany word-processing programs usually **focus on problems with spelling or punctuation and thus reinforce the idea that revising involves making small changes rather than substantive modifications in content and organization**. Furthermore, these text-editing programs **give inexperienced writers a false sense of security**. For example, writers who use spell-check programs usually feel confident that they have eliminated all spelling errors. However, if a writer has written *their* instead of *there* or *effect* instead of *affect*, the spell-check program will not identify the error. Existing programs simply cannot determine if the writer has used the correct word. All they can do is alert the writer if he or she writes a word that is not in its dictionary.

[4]Word processing does offer writers some real advantages, but writers should not assume that their writing will magically be more coherent or convincing or even more correct simply as a result of their using word processing.

—Frances Gregory

EXERCISE
32.4

In your own words, write a one-paragraph summary of the passage you have just read. If you include specific phrases from the passage, be sure to enclose them in quotation marks. Begin your summary by identifying the author and title.

_____

_____

_____

_____

_____

_____

_____

_____

_____

_____

_____

_____

_____

_____

_____

_____

_____

_____

_____

CHAPTER REVIEW

- Outlining and summarizing include the following steps:
    1. Read the *entire* selection.
    2. Determine the writer's main idea.
    3. State it in your own words.
    4. Identify major supporting points.
- Outlines may take various forms but should always indicate the relationship between main ideas and major supporting points.

WRITING ASSIGNMENT

Write an informal study outline of a textbook reading selection that is required reading for you. Use that outline to write a brief summary of the same reading selection.

PARTICIPATING IN THE ACADEMIC COMMUNITY

Discuss outlining and summarizing with your classmates and instructor, focusing on their usefulness and/or limitations as reading strategies.

CHAPTER 33

Reviewing Books and Films

Instructors often ask you to review a book or a film. For example, a history teacher may ask you to read and review a biography of a president, or an English teacher may ask you to review a movie based on a well-known novel. This type of assignment involves several critical reading and writing skills. First, you must read the book or view the film with a critical eye, not only comprehending its basic meaning but also evaluating it. Second, you must construct a review that not only summarizes the book or film but also argues for your evaluation or interpretation of the work.

READING/VIEWING THE WORK TO BE REVIEWED

Whether you are reviewing a book or a film, you always begin with the work itself. If you are reviewing a book, you will, of course, begin by reading it carefully. As you read, you will need to annotate the book, marking passages you may want to reread or refer to later, underlining important names or events, defining words you don't know, and making general comments in reaction to what you read. If you do not own the book and thus cannot write in it, you will want to do the same sort of thing by taking notes (perhaps on note cards that can also serve as page markers, or on the computer, if you prefer to keep notes in a computer file). Writing as you read not only improves your comprehension but also provides you with a record of your thoughts—thoughts that can later become the basis of your review.

If you are reviewing a film, you may want to take notes as you watch the film. If not, you should write a summary of the film, your reaction to it, and any ideas you want to remember as soon as possible after you have viewed it. You may need to view the film twice rather than just once. A second viewing nearly always provides the viewer with new insights, more details, and a generally better understanding of the film. In addition to viewing the film several times, be sure you know not only the leading and supporting actors and the roles they play but also the director and perhaps the cinematographer, scriptwriter, music director, or costume designer (depending on the focus of your review). This information is available in the credits displayed at the beginning and/or end of the film. This type of information sometimes appears on the cover of the box if you rent the movie as a video or DVD.

WRITING THE REVIEW

Reviews vary widely. Two people who read the same book or view the same movie will not produce the same review. However, a book or film review usually consists of the following elements:

- Introduction
- Summary
- Analysis/discussion
- Evaluation

In addition, a review may include background information about the work, comparisons to similar works, and discussions of major themes, motifs, or arguments.

Introduction

The introduction sets the stage for your review. Thus, you may choose to give your reader background information about the work or its topic, discuss the author or director, or simply tell something about your reading experience. Most writers also include pertinent information about the work and the person or people who produced it. You may also include a discussion of the writer's or director's purpose and intended audience. If you omit this information in your introduction, be sure to include it elsewhere in the review. You cannot fairly critique a book or film without establishing its purpose and audience. Finally, you may want to end your introduction with a statement of your own thesis or argument—or, at least, an indication of the focus of your review.

Summary

Your summary should provide your reader with an overview of the work you are reviewing but should not go into great detail. It should constitute only one-fourth to one-third of your total review. Inexperienced writers often make the mistake of trying to summarize the work in too much detail; thus, the entire review is merely a summary. Remember that your summary is only a part of the total review and not necessarily the main part.

Because books and movies continue to exist after they are published or produced, the present tense is customarily used in summarizing them. For example, you would write "The protagonist never **realizes** that she has been deceived" or "The setting of the movie **is** a small town in New Hampshire."

Analysis/Discussion

After providing your readers with a summary of the work, you are ready to begin your own analysis and/or discussion of it. If you have not previously indicated the focus of your review, you will want to include in this section a thesis statement or a clear indication of your main point. Some reviews are persuasive in that the writer is making a particular argument. For example, you might argue that a movie is well written and directed but that one actor's performance is disastrous, or that a book is suspenseful and dramatic but poorly written. You may choose to emphasize some other element of the work—the setting of a novel, the bias of a historical or scientific work, or the emotionally manipulative ending of a movie, for example. But it is important to have a focus. You cannot do justice to every element of a work, so you must decide what element or elements you consider most significant to the work's success or failure.

In effect, as a writer of a report or review, you are making an argument for your evaluation or interpretation. To do this, you may need to analyze some element of the work. To analyze means to take something apart, examine its individual parts, and determine how they function in relation to the whole work. For example, you might analyze a writer's skillful use of irony, a director's pacing of the action, a cinematographer's camera angles, or a music director's use of music to heighten mood or suspense.

It may help you to think of this part of your review as your opportunity to discuss the work's strengths and weaknesses. To be convincing, however, you must do more than mention what you liked and did not like about the work. By analyzing certain elements of a work—pointing out not only **what** happens but also **how** and **why**—you will be more informative and, ultimately, more persuasive.

Experienced reviewers also use specific examples from the work itself to prove their arguments. In effect, the examples you use constitute your evidence and support your arguments. A good review is not just a summary of the work with an opinion tacked on but rather a discussion of the work that includes a well-supported argument. For example, if you claim that the author of a book is biased, you must point out instances of bias. If you argue that the dialogue in a movie is unconvincing, you must cite specific lines of dialogue and point out why they are inappropriate.

Evaluation

Your final evaluation of a work usually constitutes the conclusion of your review. It need not be either totally positive or negative. Most reviewers identify both the strengths and weaknesses of a work—although, on occasion, you may want to focus strictly on one or the other. One word of caution, however: It is difficult to write an effective review if you are completely positive about everything. You can be completely negative and still write an interesting review, but if you are completely positive, your review will be bland at best.

ANNOTATED BOOK REVIEW

In the following book review from the March 31, 2002, issue of *The New York Times Review of Books*, we indicate the introduction, summary, analysis/discussion, and evaluation.

OUT OF AFRICA

W. Jeffrey Bolster

The Diligent: A Voyage Through the Worlds of the Slave Trade,
by Robert Harms.

■ **Introduction (includes background information)**

The largest forced migration in human history, the Atlantic slave trade, endured for centuries. It transformed Africa and the Americas by setting in motion millions of people, and by giving the concept of race enduring power. The sheer scale and brutality of this business beggars the imagination, even among those who admit that economic development has a human cost.

Contemporary Americans know the fundamentals: unwilling people crammed into the holds of stinking little ships, destined for death or a short lifetime of slavery. Collective white guilt and black nationalist assertions, however, reduce this epic to a simple, if horrifying, morality tale. There is much more to it.

Robert Harms's quietly passionate account of a single voyage of the Diligent, a French slave ship, shifts attention away from the idea of a monolithic Atlantic slave trade, expertly uncovering the local events, decisions and endeavors that made up this enduring commerce in human beings. An excellent section on slavery and serfdom in early modern France is part of the story, as is another addressing war and political squabbling on the African coast. The structures of racism are examined repeatedly, notably in a section on the Cape Verde islands, which, according to Harms, were "a kind of cultural 'halfway house' between the society" the sailors "had left behind in France and the ones they would encounter in Africa." Smuggling, fraud and seamanship on a grand scale play out here, as does the voyeurism of slave traders, who, "looking for symptoms of syphilis, gonorrhea or yaws . . . carefully examined the private parts of both men and women."

▪ **Summary**

"The Diligent" can be read as a good detective story in which Harms has pursued lead after lead to reconstruct the slave trade. More than 40 period illustrations, including paintings, line art and maps, add to the book's somber appeal.

At its heart lies the remarkable journal of Robert Durand, a 26-year-old French ship's officer with a gift for watercolors, who in 1731 departed from Vannes, a French Atlantic port, for his first voyage to West Africa. Historians know of at least 27,000 slaving voyages across the Atlantic, and considerable information about many of them exists. But very few detailed accounts, much less illustrated detailed accounts, exist for individual voyages. Harms, a professor of African history at Yale, has transformed Lieutenant Durand's banal and businesslike journal of the Diligent's voyage into an informative book that challenges readers to think historically. "Although shocking to 21st-century bourgeois culture," Harms writes, the inhumanity of the slave trade "was distressingly ordinary in its own time and place."

The story is laced with ironies. As was often the case, the death rate of the Diligent's French crewmen exceeded that of their African captives. And when those captives finally arrived at Martinique, in the French Caribbean, they confronted slaves producing cotton that would be woven into cloth in France and then traded for more slaves in Africa.

▪ **Analysis/ discussion**

Works of nonfiction are driven (and restricted) by their sources, and Harms had to transcend the limitations of a seaman's journal. Much of his book's success originates in a larger-than-life cast of characters. Harms has chosen to portray the 18th-century slave trade through stories of the participants, some of them well removed from the Diligent itself. Pauline Villeneuve, a West Indian slave girl who achieved freedom in France by becoming a nun in the Benedictine Sisters of Calvary, is introduced to explore racial attitudes in France. The insatiable King Huffon, whose magnificent furniture, imported delicacies and fine wines in the Guinea coast port of Whydah rivaled those of any palace in Europe, exemplifies the African elites who profited from slaving. Then there are individuals double-crossed in this business of few scruples: Bulfinche Lambe, an English slave trader who became a slave himself to King Agaja in Dahomey, and "Captain Tom," a Dahomean who was variously a slave, a slave trader and a cosmopolitan traveler. Manuel do Rosário Pinto, the black archdeacon of the

Portuguese diocese of São Tomé, appears as a successful 18th-century man of color who was neither a slave nor a slave trader. Such engaging vignettes convey a "feel" for the worlds of the slave trade. As a comprehensive and multilayered appreciation of that trade, "The Diligent" has no peer.

▪ **Evaluation (includes both weaknesses and strengths)**

Harms's sympathies clearly lie with the Africans below decks on the Diligent, but he knows virtually nothing about them: neither their names nor ethnicities, their origins or ultimate fates. Sources from their perspective do not exist. Given the narrative nature of the book, however, and its orientation to personalities, some readers may yearn for that missing connection.

Call this the "predicament of the protagonist" in a history related as story. Harms has drawn extensively on Lieutenant Durand's journal, corroborating and elaborating on it. But Harms's humanist values do not allow him to develop any affinity for Durand, an ambitious seaman who sought to elevate himself in the status-conscious French society of the mid-18th century, and who took risks, endured sacrifice and inflicted suffering on others to achieve his goals. Durand is certainly more knowable than the African captives, but even so, his journal reveals little of the inner man. In short, the would-be heroes, the slaves, remain veiled, and the man around whom the story revolves, the French lieutenant, never entirely steps to the fore. Readers are left in the wake of the Diligent, picaresquely following various venues and villains.

Harms has brought to this undertaking decades of training, deep knowledge of his subject and a historian's fascination with the strangeness of the past. He has produced an original book that will endure. Yet his determination to reconstruct the numerous worlds of the slave trade has impeded his ability to tell one story. The African slave trade was—and still is—so overwhelming that no single narrative can do it justice. This book's strengths, and its shortcomings, must be seen in that light.

EXERCISE

33.1   After you have read the annotated review, answer the following questions:

1. Although the reviewer does not include a clear thesis statement, can you determine his focus, or main point? Write it in your own words.

2. Identify and underline several specific examples from the book the reviewer includes to support his own arguments.

3. Identify and circle at least one positive comment the reviewer makes about this book.

4. Identify and draw a square around at least one negative comment the reviewer makes about this book.

▦ CHAPTER REVIEW

- Reviewing a book or film begins with a careful reading or viewing of the work.
- A review includes the following:
  1. Introduction
  2. Summary
  3. Analysis/discussion
  4. Evaluation

▦ WRITING ASSIGNMENT

Read a book or view a film and write a review that includes the elements identified in this chapter.

▦ PARTICIPATING IN THE ACADEMIC COMMUNITY

Exchange reviews with one of your classmates. Read your classmate's review to determine whether or not it includes introduction, summary, analysis/discussion, and evaluation. Also answer the following questions about the review:

1. Does the review have a clear focus?
2. Does the writer give an adequate summary of the work?
3. Does the writer analyze and discuss at least one specific element of the work?
4. Does the writer include specific details and examples from the work itself to support his or her own arguments?
5. Does the writer clearly evaluate the work?

Taking Essay Exams

Many of the courses you take in college will require you to take **essay exams**. Although students often dread this type of exam, you should view it as an opportunity to demonstrate for your instructor what you have learned. Because an essay exam requires both reading and writing skills, the previous chapters in this book have prepared you for this type of examination. The chapters on writing effective paragraphs and essays have taught you how to structure an essay exam (which is, in effect, simply an essay). The chapters on methods of development have provided you with terminology and patterns commonly used in essay exams. And the chapters on reading have taught you to read more critically and to outline and summarize—skills that will be extremely useful to you when you take an essay exam. For example, essay exam questions often ask you to outline the steps in a process or summarize something you have read.

Most instructors assume that your response to an essay question will be based on a critical reading of a text. So your preparation for taking an essay exam should, of course, include a careful, critical reading of the material on which the test will be based. This reading should include extensive annotation of the text; careful notes on lectures and what you have read; possibly an outline and/or summary; a thoughtful evaluation of the writer's arguments, evidence, and sources; and your own conclusions.

UNDERSTANDING ESSAY EXAM TERMINOLOGY

The following list defines common types of instructions you may encounter when taking an essay exam:

> *Analyze.* Identify and discuss the various elements of an issue or an event, as in analyzing causes or effects.

Compare. Examine specific events, beliefs, individuals, qualities, or problems to show similarities. (Differences may also be mentioned.)

Contrast. Examine specific events, beliefs, individuals, qualities, or problems to show differences.

Discuss. Examine and analyze in detail a specific issue or problem, considering all sides.

Enumerate. Although you may answer this type of question in paragraph form, you should answer concisely, listing items instead of discussing them thoroughly. Some instructors prefer items listed and numbered in columns.

Explain. Clarify and interpret fully, showing how and why a certain event occurred or a certain belief developed. Often this requires a discussion of causes and effects, as in the question *Explain the causes. . . .*

Illustrate. Present a clear, complete example to clarify your answer.

Relate. Show connections and relationships among ideas, individuals, or events.

Summarize. Present the main ideas in concise summary form.

Trace (Narrate). Describe the progress, sequence, or development of events or ideas, usually in chronological order.

GUIDELINES FOR TAKING ESSAY EXAMS

Understanding the terms in the preceding list will help you understand the questions and directions on an essay exam. The following guidelines will also help you perform more successfully on essay examinations:

1. *Read through the entire examination.* Pay close attention to the directions and note whether you are to answer all questions or only a specified number. Reading through the entire test gives you an overview of the information to be covered and may prevent unnecessary and time-consuming overlapping in your answers. As you read each question, you may want to jot down ideas and examples in the margin so you will not forget them later.

2. *Budget your time.* After reading through all of the questions, determine the total time for the test, the total number of questions to be answered, and the point value for each question. Then quickly plan how you will use your time, allowing a short planning period and a review period but saving the bulk of your time for actually answering the questions. Consider the point value of each question and divide your total time into blocks. The following illustration shows how you might budget your time for a one-hour examination with four test questions of different point values:

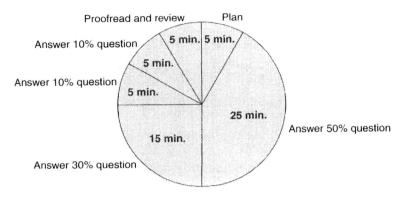

3. *Analyze the question carefully.* Circle or underline key words such as *compare, explain,* and *summarize,* and think carefully about what each key word requires of you. Also be sure to notice whether the question contains more than one part.

4. *Follow directions.* Be sure you understand the directions and then follow them closely. If you have been asked to list, don't discuss; if you have been asked to discuss, don't list.

5. *Plan your answer to each question.* Use scratch paper or the inside cover of your test booklet to make a rough outline of the ideas you intend to include in your answer.

6. *Answer each question clearly and completely.* Give your thesis or main idea in the first sentence. If there are two or more subpoints to your answer, you may indicate this in your thesis. (Example: *The Native Americans of North and South America differed in their civilizations, their governments, their religions, and their property concepts.*) As you develop your thesis, include specific and thorough support, but don't ramble. In a short essay question, your thesis can probably be developed in a paragraph; a longer essay question may require three or more paragraphs. In either case, pay close attention to transitions and include a concluding statement.

7. *If you don't remember the answer to a question, leave a blank space for it.* Return to it after you have finished the other questions. You might remember the answer before you finish the exam. (Sometimes there are clues in other questions.) It is also a good idea to leave wide margins and blocks of blank space after each answer so you can add information you remember later.

8. *Proofread your answers.* Rereading your answers will give you a chance to catch careless mistakes in spelling and punctuation. Reviewing your answers may also jog your memory and help you think of points that did not occur to you earlier. If so, you will be glad you left extra time and space to add to your answers.

EXERCISE
34.1

Read and annotate the following passage from a history textbook, identifying the thesis and major supporting points.

The European Background

What drove Europeans to leave their native lands and explore unknown parts of the globe? Why did some of them stay in the New World? This surge of activity was part of a complex process of change which had been building in Europe for centuries. These changes— economic, political, and religious—were to shape the destiny of the New World. They deserve a closer look.

The Commercial Revolution

Before Columbus's voyages, there was little interest in colonizing far-off territories. The excitement which began in 1492 can be explained in part by economic changes in Europe between the eleventh and fifteenth centuries.

In AD 1000, when Leif Ericson was exploring the northern coastal areas of Canada, Europe was divided into countless small duchies, principalities, and estates. The chief economic unit was the manor, a virtually self-supporting landed estate ruled by a hereditary nobility. All food and labor required to sustain the community were supplied by its serfs, servants who were in permanent bondage to the soil and who were never permitted to leave the manor. In return for a guarantee of personal safety, the serfs devoted much of their time to serving the lord of the manor. This meant plowing and tilling the fields, repairing the castle, and fighting as foot soldiers in the periodic battles with neighboring lords.

The dominant role of the manor in European life began to change slowly during the Crusades. Between 1095 and 1291 the Christian church of western Europe attempted to recover Palestine from the Moslems and to liberate Middle Eastern Christians from Islamic authority. These efforts were ultimately unsuccessful, but most modern historians believe that the Crusades helped transform the European way of life by increasing commercial activity.

During and after the Crusades long-distance trade became safer and cheaper. Money in the form of gold and silver coins also came into widespread use, providing the means for more people to buy goods without relying on the barter system.

As a result, the small amount of trade between the towns of southern Italy and the eastern Mediterranean was enlarged to include Venice, Genoa, and other port cities in the western Mediterranean. Since the exchange of goods took place mainly in towns, these trading centers grew larger and more influential as commercial activity increased.

In addition, to raise funds for the long voyage to the Holy Land, feudal knights often sold towns the right to incorporate. Townsfolk were able to buy from their ruling baron or bishop a charter granting them the right to levy taxes, enroll a militia, and name their own officials. The growth of cities in turn encouraged the expansion of commerce. Nobles, eager to buy new products, raised money by selling freedom to their serfs. More and more of these freed serfs moved into the towns, increasing their populations and swelling the number of people engaged in producing goods for trade. This further heightened the demand for manufactured goods and for luxury items from the eastern Mediterranean.

Merchants

As trade between towns, countries, and even continents increased, the merchant became an increasingly important figure. Emphasis slowly shifted from making goods for local consumption to producing for distant markets. This trend was accelerated during the fifteenth century, when the new sea routes to the Orient and the Americas brought a great upsurge in trade, especially in such bulk commodities as lumber, rice, tea, and sugar. Heavy industries such as ship-building and cannon manufacture were also stimulated. This intercontinental trade, as well as trade within Europe, enlarged the role of the middleman. The merchants of this period often functioned as bankers and manufacturers, too. If they did not make the goods they were selling, they frequently financed their production.

These successful European merchants directly affected the development of America in at least two ways. First, the merchants had made international trade such a vital part of the European economy that the New World provided necessary new raw materials as well as a potentially large new market. Second, the rise of the merchant class enabled some European countries to colonize the New World, for it was the merchants, not the government, who financed the first English colonies.

Laborers

As merchants steadily improved their position in European society, the gap between the wealthy middle class and the impoverished laborers widened year by year. One reason was the great inflation of the sixteenth and seventeenth centuries, caused in part by the importation of vast amounts of precious metal from the Spanish colonies in America. Inflation caused prices to rise while wages lagged far behind. In 1560 workers in Spain, France, Germany, and England had 50 percent less purchasing power than their great grandparents had had a hundred years earlier.

At the same time, the guild system—and thus the opportunity to improve one's station in life—was declining. In the twelfth and thirteenth centuries any worker could rise from apprenticeship to journeyman status and eventually become a master craftsman. But by the sixteenth century master craftsmen tended to hand their positions down to their sons, so that journeymen had little hope of ever improving their status. Thus for many laborers the only way to share in the New World's wealth was to actually go there.

—Rebecca Brooks Gruver, *An American History*, Brief ed., Vol. I

EXERCISE
34.2

The following essay exam question is based on the passage from the history textbook in Exercise 34.1. Analyze the question below, thinking about what the instructor is asking and how you plan to answer the question.

QUESTION: Trace the major economic and social changes that took place in Europe between the eleventh and fifteenth centuries. Explain how these changes affected trade and the economy.

Now read the following analysis of the question to see if you have considered all aspects of it:

ANALYSIS OF QUESTION: This question consists of two parts. In the first part, you are asked to trace the major economic and social changes that occurred in Europe between the eleventh and fifteenth centuries. To *trace* is to narrate the progress of an event, historical sequence, or development. Thus the first part of your answer will be largely narrative in organization (see Chapter 11, Narration).

In the second part of the question, you are asked to explain or show how and why these events affected American colonization. Explanation often requires discussion of causes and effects. Thus, the second part of your answer will follow the pattern for cause and effect (see Chapter 16, Cause and Effect).

Now read the following answer to this question. As you read, try to determine whether the essay follows the instructions given in the question and whether it effectively answers the question. Then read the analysis of the answer that follows and compare it to your own analysis.

ANSWER: [1]Between the eleventh and fifteenth centuries, the economic and social situation in Europe evolved from a feudal system to a middle-class, or merchant's, system. [2]In AD 1000 the major economic unit was the feudal manor, which was ruled by a hereditary noble and peopled with serfs bound to the soil. [3]These serfs were given a guarantee of personal safety in return for working the soil and serving in the lord's army. [4]The Crusades of the twelfth and thirteenth centuries, however, began to change this system. [5]Money was in more frequent use, and nobles released some of their feudal power by selling towns the right to incorporate and by selling freedom to many of the serfs, who then moved to the new towns. [6]As these towns and cities grew, so did trade and the economy.

[1]As trade grew, the merchants became more and more important and began to look for new products and new markets. [2]The New World provided both a source of raw materials for products and, through the practice of colonization, sources for investment and new markets. [3]As the middle class rose, however, the position of the laborer declined. [4]His buying power decreased in the sixteenth and seventeenth centuries when Spanish gold created inflation, and his hope of improving his social and economic status was reduced when the guild system declined. [5]Thus, the New World became a source of investment for merchants and a last source of hope for the laborers who moved there.

ANALYSIS OF ANSWER: This answer is developed by narration and by cause and effect relationships. The thesis, which is stated in the first sentence of the first paragraph, is that between the eleventh and fifteenth centuries the economic and social situation in Europe changed from a feudal system to a middle-class system. Sentences 2 and 3 describe the feudal system, and sentences 4 and 5 show how the Crusades began to alter this system so that the manors were superseded in power by the growing towns. Sentence 6 concludes this paragraph and looks forward to the next paragraph. (This question could have been answered in one paragraph, but a logical break occurs here between the end of the feudal system and the growth of the middle class.)

Sentence 1 in paragraph 2 introduces the idea of the importance of the merchants, and sentence 2 explains how the New World helped this new merchant class. Sentences 3 and 4 explain the position of the laborers in Europe, and sentence 5 sums up the effects of the New World on both merchants and laborers. Thus, the entire answer is well organized, including a stated thesis, clear transitions between ideas, and a concluding sentence.

EXERCISE

34.3   Read the following passage on memory from a psychology textbook. As you read, annotate the text by identifying the main idea and major supporting points.

Basic Memory Processes

Most people have a favorite story about forgetfulness. For example, one of the authors sometimes drives to work and sometimes walks. On one occasion he drove, forgot that he had driven, and walked home. When he failed to find his car in its normal spot the next morning, he called the police to report the car stolen. After about twenty-four hours, the police called to let him know that they had found the car parked next to the psychology building on campus and that it had been towed to a storage area. When he went to retrieve the car, it was embarrassing enough for the author to explain that he had made a mistake, but particularly so when he realized that he was once again stranded because he had forgotten to bring his car keys. What went wrong? There are several possibilities, because remembering the contents of episodic, semantic, or procedural memory requires the flawless operation of three fundamental processes—encoding, storage, and retrieval. . . . A breakdown of any one of these processess will produce some degree of forgetting (Melton, 1963).

First, information must be put into memory, a step that requires *encoding*. Just as incoming sensory information must be coded so that it can be communicated to the brain, information to be remembered must be put in a form that the memory system can accept and use. In the memory system, sensory information is put into various memory codes, or mental representations of physical stimuli. As discussed in Chapter 9, on thought, mental representations can take many forms. For example, people sometimes put information into *acoustic codes*, which represent information as sequences of sounds. *Visual codes* represent stimuli as pictures. *Semantic codes* represent an experience by its general meaning. Thus, if you see a billboard that reads "Huey's Going Out of Business Sale—50% Off Everything in Stock," you might encode the sound of the words as if they had been spoken (acoustic coding), the image of the letters as they were arranged on the sign (visual coding), or the fact that you saw an ad for Huey's (semantic coding). The way stimuli are coded can influence what is remembered. For example, semantic coding might allow you to clearly remember seeing a car parked in your neighbors' driveway just before their house was robbed, but because there was little or no other coding, you might not be able to remember the make, model, or color (Bahrick & Boucher, 1968).

The second basic memory process is *storage*, which simply means maintaining information in the system over time. Episodic, semantic, and procedural memories can be stored for a very long time. When you find it possible to use a pogo stick or perform some other "rusty" skill or to recall facts and events from many years ago, you are depending on your memory's storage capacity.

Retrieval is the process of finding information stored in memory and bringing it into consciousness. Retrieving stored information like your address or telephone number is usually so fast and effortless as to seem automatic. Only when you try to retrieve other kinds of information—such as the answer to a quiz question that you know but cannot quite recall—do you become aware of the searching process.

Encoding, storage, and retrieval are all vital links in the memory chain. The author's forgetfulness might thus be traced to information about his car's location being (a) never properly encoded, (b) encoded but never stored, or (c) stored but never retrieved.

—Douglas A. Bernstein et al., *Psychology*

▨ CHAPTER REVIEW

- Essay exams require both reading and writing skills.
- Understanding the terms commonly used in essay exams is essential.
- Following these suggestions will improve your performance on essay exams:
    1. Read through the entire examination.
    2. Budget your time.
    3. Analyze each question carefully.
    4. Follow directions.
    5. Plan your answer to each question.
    6. Answer each question clearly, directly, and completely.
    7. If you don't remember the answer to a question, leave a blank space and return to it later.
    8. Proofread your answers.

▓ WRITING ASSIGNMENT

Following the guidelines for taking essay exams given in this chapter, answer the following question about the psychology passage in Exercise 34.3:

Identify and explain each step of the mental process that allows a person to encode, store, and retrieve information.

▓ PARTICIPATING IN THE ACADEMIC COMMUNITY

Compare your answer with those of your classmates, discussing the strengths and weaknesses of each. As a group, come to a conclusion about what information is essential to a "correct" answer.

A Mini-Reader on American Culture

The reading selections in Part Five, which focus on American culture, provide you with an opportunity to practice the writing and reading skills you learned in Parts One through Four of this book. As you read each selection, try to apply what you have learned about both reading and writing. For example, **preview** each selection before you read it, **annotate** the text as you read, and **review** the selection after you have finished reading it. In addition, you should analyze each selection to determine the writer's main idea and purpose. The questions at the end of each selection will guide your understanding and evaluation of it.

The selections are grouped into four units, each of which addresses a different theme related to American culture. The first unit focuses on identity—a person's sense of who he or she is and how that identity is formed. The second explores several issues related to college life, and the third focuses on lifestyles. Finally, the fourth unit addresses the issue of diversity in our society.

UNIT 1: IDENTITY

This unit explores the concept of identity—how we define ourselves and some of the issues we face as individuals within the American culture. To begin your exploration of this theme, freewrite about your image of yourself and the process by which you became who you are.

MOTHER AND FREEDOM

Maya Angelou

- **Reading Preview**

In this essay, Maya Angelou tells about her decision to leave home just after graduating from high school, giving you insight into not only her feelings but also those of her mother. Angelou, a well-known African American writer, is perhaps best known for her autobiography, I Know Why the Caged Bird Sings, *and for her poem "On the Pulse of the Morning," which she read at President Bill Clinton's first inauguration. This selection is taken from a collection of stories entitled* Even the Stars Look Lonesome.

- **Journal Assignment**

Recollect the first time you left home for an extended time. What did you enjoy about this experience? What was difficult for you? Did you learn anything about yourself as a result of this experience?

Write a journal entry about what it is like to leave home for the first time.

- **Reading Strategy**

This essay is easy to read because it is short and is essentially a narrative. However, like most stories, Angelou's has a thesis, which is not stated but is clearly implied. As you read, try to formulate in your own words the main point she is making.

She stood before me, a dolled-up, pretty yellow woman, seven inches shorter than my six-foot bony frame. Her eyes were soft and her voice was brittle. "You're determined to leave? Your mind's made up?" 1

I was seventeen and burning with passionate rebelliousness. I was also her daughter, so whatever independent spirit I had inherited had been nurtured by living with her and observing her for the past four years. 2

"You're leaving my house?"   3

I collected myself inside myself and answered, "Yes. Yes, I've found a   4
room."

"And you're taking the baby?"   5

"Yes."   6

She gave me a smile, half proud and half pitying.   7

"All right, you're a woman. You don't have a husband, but you've got   8
a three-month-old baby. I just want you to remember one thing. From the
moment you leave this house, don't let anybody raise you. Every time you
get into a relationship you will have to make concessions, compromises,
and there's nothing wrong with that. But keep in mind Grandmother Hen-
derson in Arkansas and I have given you every law you need to live by. Follow what's right. You've been raised."

More than forty years have passed since Vivian Baxter liberated me   9
and handed me over to life. During those years I have loved and lost, I have
raised my son, set up a few households and walked away from many. I have
taken life as my mother gave it to me on that strange graduation day all
those decades ago.

In the intervening time when I have extended myself beyond my reach   10
and come toppling Humpty-Dumpty-down on my face in full view of a
scornful world, I have returned to my mother to be liberated by her one
more time. To be reminded by her that although I had to compromise with
life, even life had no right to beat me to the ground, to batter my teeth down
my throat, to make me knuckle down and call it Uncle. My mother raised
me, and then freed me.

And now, after so many eventful years of trials, successes and fail-   11
ures, my attention is drawn to a bedroom adjoining mine where my once
feisty mother lies hooked by pale blue wires to an oxygen tank, fighting
cancer for her life.

I think of Vivian Baxter, and I remember Frederick Douglass's mother,   12
enslaved on a plantation eleven miles from her infant son, yet who, after toil-
ing a full day, would walk the distance to look at her child hoping that he would
sense a mother's love, then return to the plantation in time to begin another
day of labor. She believed that a mother's love brought freedom. Many African
Americans know that the most moving song created during the centuries of
slavery was and remains "Sometimes I Feel Like a Motherless Child."

As a mother and a daughter myself, I have chosen certain songs and   13
poems to take to my mother's room, and there we will laugh and cry together.

I pray I shall have the courage to liberate my mother when the time   14
comes. She would expect that from me.

■ **Summarizing**
What You
Have Read

Write a brief summary of this essay, focusing on not only the events in
the story but also the point that Angelou is making.

■ **Responding to What You Have Read**

Respond to this essay by describing how you felt when you left home and/or started to college.

■ **Discussing What You Have Read**

Discuss this essay with your classmates and instructor, focusing on the following questions:

1. How would you characterize the relationship between Angelou and her mother? (You might be interested to know that Angelou lived with her grandmother as well as her mother when she was a young child.)

2. How can a mother both raise and free a child? Why are both necessary?

3. Explain what Angelou means when she writes at the end of the essay that she hopes she will "have the courage to liberate [her] mother when the time comes."

4. At the end of the story, how have Angelou's and her mother's roles become reversed?

5. What is Angelou suggesting in this essay about how a person establishes a sense of identity?

■ **Writing Activity**

Write an essay based on a single experience you have had that helped you establish your sense of who you are. Be sure you make a point as well as tell a story. You need not state your thesis explicitly, but be sure that your readers understand the point you are making.

※ ※ ※ ※ ※ ※ ※ ※ ※ ※ ※ ※ ※ ※

LIVING IN TWO WORLDS

Marcus Mabry

■ **Reading Preview**

The author of this selection came from a poor family in New Jersey but was a student at Stanford when he wrote this essay. In the essay, he describes what it was like to "travel between the universes of poverty and affluence." His essay was initially published in Newsweek *as part of the "Newsweek on Campus" series.*

■ **Journal Assignment**

Think about the ways in which your life has changed since you started college. Then write a journal entry in which you compare your life now with your life before you were a college student.

■ **Reading**
Strategy As you read this essay, focus on the contrast between Mabry's experiences at home and his experiences at college. Think about how this contrast affected his sense of who he was.

A round, green cardboard sign hangs from a string proclaiming, "We built 1 a proud new feeling," the slogan of a local supermarket. It is a souvenir from one of my brother's last jobs. In addition to being a bagger, he's worked at a fast-food restaurant, a gas station, a garage and a textile factory. Now, in the icy clutches of the Northeastern winter, he is unemployed. He will soon be a father. He is 19 years old.

In mid-December I was at Stanford, among the palm trees and weighty 2 chore of academe. And all I wanted to do was get out. I joined the rest of the undergrads in a chorus of excitement, singing the praises of Christmas break. No classes, no midterms, no finals . . . and no freshmen! (I'm a resident assistant.) Awesome! I was looking forward to escaping. I never gave a thought to what I was escaping to.

Once I got home to New Jersey, reality returned. My dreaded freshmen 3 had been replaced by unemployed relatives; badgering professors had been replaced by hard-working single mothers, and cold classrooms by dilapidated bedrooms and kitchens. The room in which the "proud new feeling" sign hung contained the belongings of myself, my mom and my brother. But for these two weeks it was mine. They slept downstairs on couches.

Most students who travel between the universes of poverty and afflu- 4 ence during breaks experience similar conditions, as well as the guilt, the helplessness and, sometimes, the embarrassment associated with them. Our friends are willing to listen, but most of them are unable to imagine the pain of the impoverished lives that we see every six months. Each time I return home I feel further away from the realities of poverty in America and more ashamed that they are allowed to persist. What frightens me most is not that the American socioeconomic system permits poverty to continue, but that by participating in that system I share some of the blame.

Last year I lived in an on-campus apartment, with a (relatively) mod- 5 ern bathroom, kitchen and two bedrooms. Using summer earnings, I added some expensive prints, a potted palm and some other plants, making the place look like the more-than-humble abode of a New York City Yuppie. I gave dinner parties, even a *soirée française*.

For my roommate, a doctor's son, this kind of life was nothing extraor- 6 dinary. But my mom was struggling to provide a life for herself and my brother. In addition to working 24-hour-a-day cases as a practical nurse, she was trying to ensure that my brother would graduate from high school and have a decent life. She knew that she had to compete for his attention with drugs and other potentially dangerous things that can look attractive to a young man when he sees no better future.

Living in my grandmother's house this Christmas break restored all the forgotten, and the never acknowledged, guilt. I had gone to boarding school on a full scholarship since the ninth grade, so being away from poverty was not new. But my own growing affluence has increased my distance. My friends say that I should not feel guilty: what could I do substantially for my family at this age, they ask. Even though I know that education is the right thing to do, I can't help but feel, sometimes, that I have it too good. There is no reason that I deserve security and warmth, while my brother has to cope with potential unemployment and prejudice. I, too, encounter prejudice, but it is softened by my status as a student in an affluent and intellectual community.

7

More than my sense of guilt, my sense of helplessness increases each time I return home. As my success leads me further away for longer periods of time, poverty becomes harder to conceptualize and feels that much more oppressive when I visit with it. The first night of break, I lay in our bedroom, on a couch that let out into a bed that took up the whole room, except for a space heater. It was a little hard to sleep because the springs from the couch stuck through at inconvenient spots. But it would have been impossible to sleep anyway because of the groans coming from my grandmother's room next door. Only in her early 60s, she suffers from many chronic diseases and couldn't help but moan, then pray aloud, then moan, then pray aloud.

8

This wrenching of my heart was interrupted by the 3 A.M. entry of a relative who had been allowed to stay at the house despite rowdy behavior and threats toward the family in the past. As he came into the house, he slammed the door, and his heavy steps shook the second floor as he stomped into my grandmother's room to take his place, at the foot of her bed. There he slept, without blankets on a bare mattress. This was the first night. Later in the vacation, a Christmas turkey and a Christmas ham were stolen from my aunt's refrigerator on Christmas Eve. We think the thief was a relative. My mom and I decided not to exchange gifts that year because it just didn't seem festive.

9

A few days after New Year's I returned to California. The Northeast was soon hit by a blizzard. They were there, and I was here. That was the way it had to be, for now. I haven't forgotten; the ache of knowing their suffering is always there. It has to be kept deep down, or I can't find the logic in studying and partying while people, my people, are being killed by poverty. Ironically, success drives me away from those I most want to help by getting an education.

10

Somewhere in the midst of all that misery, my family has built within me, "a proud feeling." As I travel between the two worlds it becomes harder

11

to remember just how proud I should be—not just because of where I have come from and where I am going, but because of where they are. The fact that they survive in the world in which they live is something to be very proud of, indeed. It inspires within me a sense of tenacity and accomplishment that I hope every college graduate will someday possess.

■ **Summarizing What You Have Read**

Write a brief summary of this essay, focusing on the differences between Mabry's two lives and how the contrast between them affects him. Remember that in a summary you do not include examples and details.

■ **Responding to What You Have Read**

Respond to this essay by describing in detail one major difference between your life at home and your life at school.

■ **Discussing What You Have Read**

Discuss this essay with your classmates and instructor, focusing on these questions:

1. How have Mabry's two worlds shaped his identity—how he feels about and defines himself? Which of Mabry's two worlds has had the greater impact on his identity?

2. Explain what you think Mabry means by the following statement: "Ironically, success drives me away from those I most want to help by getting an education."

3. Why is Mabry's description of his younger brother in his first paragraph an effective introduction for this essay?

4. What other different worlds may an individual live in simultaneously?

■ **Writing Activity**

In an essay, contrast two different worlds in which you live.

■ ■ ■ ■ ■ ■ ■ ■ ■ ■ ■ ■ ■ ■ ■ ■

TOSSING IDENTITY AND A BOUQUET
Ellen Goodman

■ **Reading Preview**

Ellen Goodman, a well-known syndicated columnist, writes in this essay about the issue of whether women should keep their own names when they marry or remarry. Although, according to Goodman, more than 90 percent of young women "give up their names" when they marry, this issue is increasingly one that young women face as they struggle with their identities.

■ Journal
Assignment

In the past, in America a woman who married took her husband's last name. However, some American women now choose to keep their own last name. Write a journal entry in which you argue for or against women keeping their own names when they marry.

■ Reading
Strategy

Goodman's purpose in this essay is primarily persuasive, but her arguments are subtle and indirect. As you read, focus on what her main argument is and how she supports it.

Over the years, I have come to think of this as the Plumber Problem. I pick up the phone and the plumber asks, "Mrs. Levey?"   1

At that point, two possible responses run through my brain.   2

I can say, "No, I'm Ms. Goodman although I am married to Mr. Levey and no longer married to Mr. Goodman, but by the time I was divorced and remarried, it was too late to go back to my birth name, which was, by the way, Holtz, because Goodman was my byline."   3

Or, I can say, "yes."   4

To be frank, my answer on any given day depends on exactly how high the water is in the basement. But I offer up this brief history of plumbing, marriage and nomenclature to make it clear that I understand the complications that can arise when one couple carries two names.   5

Nevertheless, I always assumed that after all these years, a younger generation of brides would leave the altar with their birth names intact. I thought that keeping your name was a leading indicator, as the economists say, of an egalitarian era.   6

But as I read the bumper crop of summer wedding announcements, it has become clear that one of the last things to change is name-changing. The majority of college students are female, half of the new doctors and lawyers are women, but more than 90 percent of the brides still give up their names. We have more paychecks and rights but toss out our credit cards and identities like so much rice.   7

In short, married women are making a name for themselves. But the name is still his. Married men are changing a lot, even diapers, but not surnames.   8

Wives do not take their husband's name, I am told, because men demand they do. Grooms don't have to. Penn State's Laurie Scheuble, who has been studying the name phenomenon with David Johnson, her hus-   9 band of 18 years, says, "Bright boys know that if they say, 'you do whatever you want, dear,' the women are far more likely to change their name."

Women make this decision because, they have told her, "it's what's done." It's still seen as a part of marriage. Not the part that treats wives as property—the old reason women changed names—but the part that subtly and strongly makes women regard trading in their name as proof of commitment. **10**

One glance at the wedding pages of *The New York Times*, the paper of romantic record, is a pretty good indication of the ongoing power of tradition. Wives are no longer totally "disappeared" under their husband's names as Mr. and Mrs. John Jones. But even now a woman who is "keeping her name" is treated as if she were breaking news. Or breaking norms. **11**

Last month, for example, a Ms. Robischon, "who is keeping her name," got married. So too Ms. Olson; who is also "keeping her name." No such editorial tagline, need I say, accompanied Mrs. Galland? No editor said Mrs. Kirsch was giving away her birth name. **12**

There is the social subtext to all of these public announcements: Ms. Smith, *whose marriage will never make it*, is keeping her name. Ms. Brown, *a careerist who doesn't really believe in family*, will keep her name. **13**

Of course, Scheuble can tell you from her research that "names can never hurt" your marriage, that there is no difference in the satisfaction or duration of a marriage with one name or two. (Something else to tell the plumber?) But there is still the enormous weight of tradition coming down at precisely the moment in life when even the neurosurgeon is mystically drawn to chantilly lace. **14**

Yes, I know the thoroughly modern arguments for changing a name. I've heard them, done them. Why is it less patriarchal to keep a father's name than take a husband's? Shouldn't children all have the same name? One family, one name? Why confuse the teacher, let alone the plumber? But none of these explain why newlyweds don't pick a new name or why men almost never change their own. You may be certain that no editor announced to the reading public that Mr. Kirsch is "keeping his name." **15**

The truth is not only that the pull of tradition is strong, but that it pulls more on women. The burden of changing traditional assumptions and relationships from the wedding bells on still rests with wives. The name is just the first thing they "give" or "keep." **16**

This spring, a survey showed how the young are looking for soulmates. It seems to me that the trick of marriage is not merger but negotiation, managing two "I"s and a "we." **17**

Maybe the real symbol is when we bring something old—ourselves—to something new—our marriages. Two first names. Two last names. One marriage. **18**

The plumber will figure it out. **19**

- **Summarizing What You Have Read**

Write a brief summary of this essay, focusing on Goodman's argument rather than her examples and experiences.

- **Responding to What You Have Read**

Respond to this essay by explaining why or why not you found Goodman's argument convincing.

- **Discussing What You Have Read**

Discuss this essay with your classmates and instructor, focusing on these questions:

1. Did you find Goodman's use of humor an effective way to support her argument? Why or why not?
2. Did you find the statistics and studies she cited convincing evidence for her point of view? Why or why not?
3. Do you think that when women give up their names it affects their sense of who they are? Why or why not?
4. Do you think it is unfair for women to give up their names while men get to keep theirs? Why or why not?
5. What are some other ways to resolve this issue?

- **Writing Activity**

Write an essay in which you argue that women should or should not give up their own names when they marry.

CUMULATIVE ASSIGNMENTS FOR UNIT ONE

DISCUSSION QUESTIONS

1. Why is a strong sense of identity essential to a healthy personality?
2. What elements and forces other than those suggested by these three reading selections affect a person's sense of identity?
3. Why is conflict often instrumental in forging a clear sense of identity?

WRITING ASSIGNMENT

Drawing on the three essays you have just read and your own experiences, write an essay describing the forces you think shaped your own sense of identity.

This unit focuses on issues related to college life in America and the role education plays in shaping who we are. Before you begin the readings in this unit, make a list of current issues related to American education that you consider important. Then discuss with your classmates some of the ways in which being a college student in America differs from being a college student in other cultures.

IN PRAISE OF THE F WORD

Mary Sherry

■ **Reading Preview**

In this guest editorial for Newsweek, *Mary Sherry, who is both a mother and a teacher, argues that our educational system would be more effective if teachers and administrators were not reluctant to fail students. In defending the practice of flunking students, she cites her own son's experience to support her argument.*

■ **Journal Assignment**

Most parents are eager for their children to make good grades, but this author, who is both a teacher and a parent, argues that "flunking as a regular policy has just as much merit today as it did two generations ago." In a journal entry, predict the reason why Sherry might be in favor of schools' flunking students.

■ **Reading Strategy**

As you read, identify and number the arguments Sherry includes to support her thesis.

Tens of thousands of 18-year-olds will graduate this year and be handed 1 meaningless diplomas. These diplomas won't look any different from those awarded their luckier classmates. Their validity will be questioned only when their employers discover that these graduates are semiliterate.

Eventually a fortunate few will find their way into educational-repair 2 shops—adult-literacy programs, such as the one where I teach basic grammar and writing. There, high school graduates and high school dropouts pursuing graduate-equivalency certificates will learn the skills they should have learned in school. They will also discover they have been cheated by our educational system.

As I teach, I learn a lot about our schools. Early in each session I ask 3 my students to write about an unpleasant experience they had in school. No writers' block here! "I wish someone would have made me stop doing drugs and made me study." "I liked to party and no one seemed to care." "I was a good kid and didn't cause any trouble, so they just passed me along even though I didn't read well and couldn't write." And so on.

I am your basic do-gooder, and prior to teaching this class I blamed the 4 poor academic skills our kids have today on drugs, divorce, and other impediments to concentration necessary for doing well in school. But, as I rediscover each time I walk into the classroom, before a teacher can expect students to concentrate, he has to get their attention, no matter what distractions may be at hand. There are many ways to do this, and they have much to do with teaching style. However, if style alone won't do it, there is another way to show who holds the winning hand in the classroom. That is to reveal the trump card of failure.

I will never forget a teacher who played that card to get the attention 5 of one of my children. Our youngest, a world-class charmer, did little to develop his intellectual talents but always got by. Until Mrs. Stifter.

Our son was a high school senior when he had her for English. "He 6 sits in the back of the room talking to his friends," she told me. "Why don't you move him to the front row?" I urged, believing the embarrassment would get him to settle down. Mrs. Stifter looked at me steely-eyed over her glasses. "I don't move seniors," she said. "I flunk them." I was flustered. Our son's academic life flashed before my eyes. No teacher had ever threatened him with that before. I regained my composure and managed to say that I thought she was right. By the time I got home, I was feeling pretty good about this. It was a radical approach for these times, but, well, why not? "She's going to flunk you," I told my son. I did not discuss it any further. Suddenly English became a priority in his life. He finished out the semester with an A.

I know one example doesn't make a case, but at night I see a parade of 7 students who are angry and resentful for having been passed along until they could no longer even pretend to keep up. Of average intelligence or better, they eventually quit school, concluding they were too dumb to finish. "I should have been held back," is a comment I hear frequently. Even sadder are those students who are high school graduates who say to me after a few weeks of class, "I don't know how I ever got a high school diploma."

Passing students who have not mastered the work cheats them and the 8 employers who expect graduates to have basic skills. We excuse this dishonest behavior by saying kids can't learn if they come from terrible environments. No one seems to stop to think that—no matter what environments they come from—most kids don't put school first on their list unless they perceive something is at stake. They'd rather be sailing.

Many students I see at night could give expert testimony on unemployment, chemical dependency, abusive relationships. In spite of these difficulties, they have decided to make education a priority. They are motivated by the desire for a better job or the need to hang on to the one they've got. They have a healthy fear of failure.   9

People of all ages can rise above their problems, but they need to have a reason to do so. Young people generally don't have the maturity to value education in the same way my adult students value it. But fear of failure, whether economic or academic, can motivate both.   10

Flunking as a regular policy has just as much merit today as it did two generations ago. We must review the threat of flunking and see it as it really is—a positive teaching tool. It is an expression of confidence by both teachers and parents that the students have the ability to learn the material presented to them. However, making it work again would take a dedicated, caring conspiracy between teachers and parents. It would mean facing the tough reality that passing kids who haven't learned the material—while it might save them grief for the short term—dooms them to long-term illiteracy. It would mean that teachers would have to follow through on their threats, and parents would have to stand behind them, knowing their children's best interests are indeed at stake. This means no more doing Scott's assignments for him because he might fail. No more passing Jodi because she's such a nice kid.   11

This is a policy that worked in the past and can work today. A wise teacher, with the support of his parents, gave our son the opportunity to succeed—or fail. It's time we return this choice to all students.   12

■ **Summarizing What You Have Read**   Summarize this essay, focusing on the arguments you identified and numbered as you read.

■ **Responding to What You Have Read**   Write about whether you are or are not motivated by the fear of failing a particular assignment or course.

■ **Discussing What You Have Read**   Discuss this essay with your instructor and classmates, focusing on these questions:

1. How did Sherry's experiences as a mother and teacher shape her conviction that flunking is a useful policy? Do you think she would have

felt the same had her son actually flunked the English class rather than making an A?

2. Do you think her son's fear of flunking was the only factor in his success? What other factors might have been involved?

3. Do you agree or disagree with Sherry that our schools would be more effective if students knew they would fail if they did not meet the school's academic standards? Why or why not?

4. What are the positive and negative effects of flunking students?

▪ **Writing Activity**   Write an editorial arguing for or against the policy of flunking students who do not meet certain standards.

▪ ▪ ▪ ▪ ▪ ▪ ▪ ▪ ▪ ▪ ▪ ▪ ▪ ▪ ▪ ▪

FRESHMAN YEAR 101
Tim Madigan

▪ **Reading Preview**   *In this essay, Tim Madigan describes problems faced by first-year college students and argues that one of the main reasons students drop out during their first year in college is that they are lonely. He also offers suggestions for beginning students that will help them solve problems with which they have to deal.*

▪ **Journal Assignment**   Can you remember some of the emotions you experienced when you first entered college? What problems did you encounter? What were your expectations? Write a journal entry in which you describe how you felt when you first began college.

▪ **Reading Strategy**   As you read, number the problems encountered by students that Madigan identifies.

As a college freshman a quarter-century ago, my first-semester hous-   1
ing assignment was a dorm room in the basement, next to a janitor's closet, and away from almost everyone else. I didn't care for my roommate. On long treks across campus, to and from my classes, I passed thousands of anonymous fellow students, all of whom seemed to have legions of friends.

In late afternoons of my first term, I began to dread mealtime and the prospect of eating alone once again in a crowded dormitory cafeteria.

Needless to say, the first semester of my freshman year was among the loneliest, most miserable times of my life, misery compounded by the fact that I was certain I was the only loser at the University of North Dakota who spent his Friday nights alone in his room.

All these years later, I find that this might not have been the case after all. If statistics from recent years hold, nearly one in three freshmen enrolling this fall at American colleges and universities will not return for their sophomore year. And a leading cause of that attrition, experts say, is that same loneliness, that same sense of isolation I felt in my first year.

"This issue of isolation, or lack of involvement with their peers, with faculty, with staff, is a significant predictor of dropout," says Vincent Tinto of Syracuse University, author of *Leaving College: Rethinking the Causes and Cures of Student Attrition* (University of Chicago, 1993). "That is why, when talking about the issue, so many people talk about building communities of engagement or communities of involvement."

Wes Habley, of ACT, the Iowa-based education-information clearinghouse, puts it another way. By joining study groups, the marching band, student government or the chess club, etc., college freshmen can "reduce the psychological size of the campus, establish a community within a community," Habley says. Students who fail to find that niche, more so than those who are too social (i.e., party too much), are more likely to disappear from school during their freshman year, or not return as sophomores, he says.

Not that this phenomenon is particularly new. Statistics on this point have held fairly steady for decades. Traditionally, only 40 percent of the students entering higher education in any given year go on to earn degrees, and most of the dropouts occur during or soon after the freshman year.

In the most recent ACT statistics, for the year 2000, 32.9 percent of students at two- and four-year colleges and universities did not re-enroll as sophomores, though the numbers vary greatly depending on the type of institution. The dropout rate at two-year, community-based colleges is nearly half, for example, while freshman attrition at the most prestigious private schools is 16 percent. (Ivy League schools lose fewer than 10 percent of their students every year.)

Despite those perennially high attrition rates, student retention strategies have only recently become hot topics on college campuses, Habley says. In the mid-1980s, hanging onto students became a concern when the number of college-age Americans dropped by 400,000. More recently, state and federal governments have grumbled about tax dollars wasted when students don't come back.

Not that there are simple solutions to what has proved to be a com- 9
plex problem. "Everybody has an opinion. Let's put it that way," Habley
says. "It's almost impossible to say with any assurance what causes the
failure to complete college."

But anyone who has been a college freshman and had to confront the 10
daunting cocktail of transition that is the first year has a good idea. Tom
Kading, a class of 2000 graduate from Arlington High School, expected a
college lark until he walked into his freshman psychology class at the
University of Texas. Five hundred other students had joined him in the
classroom.

"In high school, I never had to put in much effort to get good grades," 11
says Kading, who did not re-enroll at UT this fall, though he plans to
attend college again in 2002. "I had a 4.0 in high school and didn't have
to do anything. At college, you have to be reading all the time, studying
all the time, and the commitment level was a lot higher. It was overwhelming at times. I wasn't ready."

The average student also faces homesickness, potential for alcohol 12
abuse, problems with money management—to name just a few of the
first year's challenges. Millions of new college students, isolated as I was
in the 1970s, try to contend with these problems alone, suffering in their
dorm rooms. Too often, truncated college experiences are the result,
experts say.

The solution for college freshmen seems simple. Join something. But 13
that can be asking too much of many college freshmen, for whom creating a study group or signing up for intramural football can be highly daunting tasks, experts say.

"If you come from a small town in Texas, and you're going to the Uni- 14
versity of Texas, your skills for reaching out and interacting are probably
dwarfed," Habley says.

Which puts the onus for reaching out on the colleges and universities, 15
Habley and other experts insist. The word they often use when describing the programs needed to help college freshman is "intrusive." New students need to get involved with their peers, with the faculty, with an
adviser, whether they feel comfortable doing so or not.

"It's too important to leave to chance," says Lana Low, a consultant who 16
helps universities develop student-retention programs. "With these programs, what we're saying to the new students is that we're serious about
your success. We're going to put some structure to this, and give you less
and less an opportunity to fail."

Among the most popular programs are "learning communities" in 17
which college freshmen co-register with several others with similar academic interests and attend multiple classes with the same students. They
are also required to interact with one another both in and out of the class-

room. Kading says one of the best parts of his University of Texas experience was meeting the 13 students with whom he attended all of his classes during his first semester.

"I found out about that program during freshman orientation, and I'm 18 glad I signed up for it," Kading says. "I wish you could do it every year not just in your first semester as a freshman. We met once a week to talk about classes and stuff. There was always someone to talk to, and we became good friends."

Increasing numbers of colleges and universities arrange dormitories by 19 academic area, another attempt to promote community. Some schools, such as Syracuse, train residence hall staffers to intervene if they see a student is isolated. Universities also increasingly urge faculty and staff members to cultivate mentoring relationships with students. Research shows that a student with at least one such relationship is at a reduced risk of dropping out.

I don't believe that faculty know how important they are to students," 20 says Low, the student-retention consultant. "A student's relationship with faculty via instruction and advising is one of the most important things that happen to them on campus."

I can attest to that, too. It was a creative writing teacher who took 21 me under his wing. I also joined the staff of the student newspaper. I made the baseball team. By the second semester of my freshman year, I had greatly reduced the "psychological size" of the University of North Dakota. By then the challenge was squeezing classes and study into a social life. Trust me. Compared with the anguish of my first semester, that was no challenge at all.

And somewhere, in a dusty corner of my attic, a college diploma sits 22 as evidence.

■ **Summarizing What You Have Read**

Referring to the problems you identified and numbered in this reading selection, write a brief summary of Madigan's essay.

■ **Responding to What You Have Read**

Write a response to this essay in which you argue for or against Madigan's view of college life.

■ **Discussing What You Have Read**

Discuss this selection with your instructor and classmates, focusing on the following questions:

1. What do you consider the most serious problem first-year students encounter? What is your solution for this problem?

2. Madigan not only identifies the problems faced by first-year students but also suggests solutions to these problems. Do you think the solutions he suggests are effective? Why or why not?

3. Are the stories about personal experiences of college students that Madigan includes in his essay convincing evidence? Why or why not?

4. Madigan also quotes several experts and cites statistics that support his arguments. Do you find these kinds of support more or less convincing than the stories he includes? Why is it usually a good idea to include different types of evidence?

■ **Writing Activity**   Write an essay in which you focus on a problem you have experienced or observed as a beginning college student and suggest a solution that would be helpful to other students.

COLLEGE VALUED LESS FOR LEARNING THAN FOR EARNING

Ethan Bronner

■ **Reading Preview**   *Ethan Bronner, a writer for the* New York Times, *reports in this article on a nationwide poll by researchers at the University of California at Los Angeles. The results of the poll suggest that most students now view getting an education as a way to gain financial security rather than as an opportunity to develop "a meaningful philosophy of life." The article also reveals several interesting trends among college freshmen nationwide.*

■ **Journal Assignment**   Write a journal entry in which you discuss whether you value college primarily for what you are learning or for what a college education will enable you to earn.

■ **Reading Strategy**   Skim the information about "Freshman Opinions" included with this article before you read the article itself. Then, after you have read the article, reread—this time more carefully—these "Freshman Opinions" (p. 482) and mark any that surprise you.

A survey of college freshmen confirms what professors and administra- 1
tors said they have been sensing: that students are increasingly disengaged
and view higher education less as an opportunity to expand their minds
and more as a means to increase their incomes.

The annual nationwide poll by researchers at the University of Cali- 2
fornia at Los Angeles shows that two suggested goals of education—"to
be very well off financially" and "to develop a meaningful philosophy of
life"—have switched places in the past three decades.

In the survey taken at the start of the fall semester, 74.9 percent of 3
freshmen chose being well off as an essential goal and 40.8 percent chose
developing a philosophy. In 1968, the numbers were reversed, with 40.8
percent selecting financial security and 82.5 percent citing the importance
of developing a philosophy.

It is a matter of using education more as a means to an end, rather 4
than valuing what you are learning, said Linda Sax, director of the survey at the Higher Education Research Institute at UCLA. The survey was
first taken 32 years ago.

The trend has long been in the making, with students' strong interest 5
in high incomes rising to a plateau in the mid-1980s. But the desire edged
down a bit through the 1990s, rising again slightly with this latest survey.

Sax said the trend took on more significance when added to the fact 6
that incoming students showed unprecedented levels of academic and political disengagement.

The percentage of students who said that during their last year in high 7
school they had been frequently "bored in class" hit a record high of 36 percent, compared with 26.4 percent in 1985, the second year the question
was asked.

At the same time, a record 34.5 percent said they had "overslept and 8
missed class," compared with a low of 18.8 percent in 1968.

Despite that, a record high of 39.4 percent said they aspire to obtain 9
a master's degree and 49.7 percent said they expect to earn a B average.

Some professors expressed little surprise at the seemingly contradic- 10
tory mix of boredom and ambition.

"Schooling has become more about training and less about transfor- 11
mation," said Mark Edmundson, a professor of English at the University
of Virginia who wrote of the growing consumerist view of education by students in the September issue of *Harper's* magazine.

"You go there to prepare yourself for the future," Edmundson said, 12
"to learn a skill, a capacity that you can convert into dollars later on.
And being trained is boring. Being educated is not, but that is going on
less and less."

The disengagement was also reflected in attitudes toward politics.   13

A record low 26.7 percent of freshmen thought that "keeping up to date   14
with political affairs" is a very important or essential life goal, compared
with 29.4 percent in 1996 and a high of 57.8 percent in 1966.

Similarly, an all-time low 13.7 percent said they frequently discuss pol-   15
itics, compared with 16.2 percent last year and a high of 29.9 percent in 1968.

Freshman Opinions

Some highlights of the UCLA annual survey of college freshmen nationwide. The fall 1997 survey analyzed data from 252,082 students at 464 institutions. The first survey was taken in 1966.

POLITICS

- A record low 27 percent believe that "keeping up to date with political affairs is an important life goal compared with the record high of 58 percent in 1966.

- 14 percent said they frequently discuss politics down from 30 percent in 1968.

- Some 55 percent consider themselves as "middle of the road," compared with 53 percent last year and a high of 60 percent in 1983.

ACADEMICS

- A record-high 36 percent reported being frequently bored in class during their last year of high school, compared with the all-time low of 26 percent in 1985.

- A record high 39 percent plan to obtain master's degrees and a record 15 percent plan to obtain doctorates.

SOCIAL ATTITUDES

- Support for legal abortion declined for the fifth straight year to 54 percent, compared with a high of 65 percent in 1990. This is the lowest level of support for legal abortion since 1979.

- The percentage of those who believe "it is important to have laws prohibiting homosexual relationships" increased to 34 percent, the second increase in a row. Fifty percent, however, said that "same sex couples should have the right to legal marital status."

ALCOHOL, DRUGS, TOBACCO

- Percentage of freshman smokers is at its highest level in 30 years, with 16 percent saying they smoke frequently. That compares with 9 percent a decade earlier.

- Support for legalizing marijuana again rose, with 35 percent agreeing that marijuana should be legalized. That compares with a low of 17 percent in 1989.

- Fifty-three percent acknowledged frequent or occasional beer drinking, compared with a high of 75 percent in 1981.

Source: The Associated Press.

■ **Summarizing What You Have Read**

Briefly summarize the article you have just read, focusing on the survey and its results rather than the quotations that are included.

■ **Responding to What You Have Read**

Identify one finding of the survey that does not reflect your opinions or attitude toward education. Then write a brief response in which you make the point that statistical surveys do not accurately represent everyone.

■ **Discussing What You Have Read**

Discuss the results of this survey with your instructor and classmates, focusing on these questions:

1. Which of the results do you find most surprising, and why?

2. Do an informal survey of your class to determine if you and your classmates agree with the students who participated in the poll about the purpose of an education. Discuss why the results of a survey may vary depending on who is surveyed.

3. Notice the quotes by Linda Sax, director of the survey, and Mark Edmundson, a professor who has written an article on the same topic for *Harper's* magazine. What effect do these quotations have on you as a reader?

4. Do you agree or disagree with Edmundson's statement that "Schooling has become more about training and less about transformation"?

5. The author of this article, Ethan Bronner, does not give his opinion of the survey and its results, but he suggests his opinion by what he chooses to report and the people he quotes. In addition, the inclusion of the other highlights from the survey ("Freshman Opinions") indicates something about the conclusion that the author has drawn. Can you infer Bronner's opinion from the clues that are provided? Do you agree or disagree with his opinion?

■ **Writing Activity**

Write an essay in which you explain what you think the purpose of a college education should be.

CUMULATIVE ASSIGNMENTS FOR UNIT TWO

DISCUSSION QUESTIONS

1. What do you think motivates students to learn?

2. Should colleges admit anyone who wants to attend or only those who have good high school records and excellent test scores? What

obligation do colleges have to help underprepared students if they choose to admit them?

3. What causes students to drop out of college? What can colleges do to keep students in school? What can students do?

4. How do you measure the quality of an education? What factors are involved?

WRITING ASSIGNMENT

Choose one of the issues addressed in these three reading selections. Survey the students in one of your classes about this issue. Next, interview one of your professors, focusing the interview on the same issue (see Chapter 7 for instruction on interviewing). Then, write an essay in which you report on the results of your survey and interview, and conclude with your own opinion on this issue.

This unit focuses on the American lifestyle—the elements and characteristics of our society that are distinctly and significantly American. To begin your study of this theme, write the word *America* in the center of a blank sheet of paper; then create a word map by branching out from that word with lifestyle features you think are distinctly American.

CHINESE SPACE, AMERICAN SPACE
Yi-Fu Tuan

■ **Reading Preview**

Yi-Fu Tuan was born in China but later moved to the United States, where he taught and studied geography, focusing on the ways in which people of different cultures view their environments. In this article, initially published in Harper's, *Tuan compares the way people in China and the United States view their environments.*

■ **Journal Assignment**

Think about the way you view your environment. Is your environment important to you? Do you need a lot of space, or do you prefer a small, intimate environment? Write a journal entry in which you describe in detail a particular environment that for you is special in some way.

■ **Reading Strategy**

As you read this brief selection, number the differences Tuan identifies between the way Chinese and Americans view space.

Americans have a sense of space, not of place. Go to an American home in exurbia, and almost the first thing you do is drift toward the picture window. How curious that the first compliment you pay your host inside his house is to say how lovely it is outside his house! He is pleased that you should admire his vistas. The distant horizon is not merely a line separating earth from sky, it is a symbol of the future. The American is not rooted in his place, however lovely: his eyes are drawn by the expanding space to a point on the horizon, which is his future. 1

By contrast, consider the traditional Chinese home. Blank walls enclose it. Step behind the spirit wall and you are in a courtyard with 2 perhaps a miniature garden around a corner. Once inside his private compound you are wrapped in an ambiance of calm beauty, an ordered world of buildings, pavement, rock, and decorative vegetation. But you have no distant view: nowhere does space open out before you. Raw nature in such a home is experienced only as weather, and the only open space is the sky above. The Chinese is rooted in his place. When he has to leave, it is not for the promised land on the terrestrial horizon, but for another world altogether along the vertical, religious axis of his imagination.

The Chinese tie to place is deeply felt. Wanderlust is an alien sentiment. The Taoist classic *Tao Te Ching* captures the ideal of rootedness in place with these words: "Though there may be another country in the neighborhood so close that they are within sight of each other and the crowing of cocks and barking of dogs in one place can be heard in the other, yet there is no traffic between them; and throughout their lives the two peoples have nothing to do with each other." In theory if not in practice, farmers have ranked high in Chinese society. The reason is not only that they are engaged in a "root" industry of producing food but that, unlike pecuniary merchants, they are tied to the land and do not abandon their country when it is in danger.

Nostalgia is a recurrent theme in Chinese poetry. An American reader of translated Chinese poems may well be taken aback—even put off—by the frequency, as well as the sentimentality, of the lament for home. To understand the strength of this sentiment, we need to know that the Chinese desire for stability and rootedness in place is prompted by the constant threat of war, exile, and the natural disasters of flood and drought. Forcible removal makes the Chinese keenly aware of their loss. By contrast, Americans move, for the most part, voluntarily. Their nostalgia for home town is really longing for a childhood to which they cannot return: in the meantime the future beckons and the future is "out there," in open space. When we criticize American rootlessness, we tend to forget that it is a result of ideals we admire, namely, social mobility and optimism about the future. When we admire Chinese rootedness, we forget that the word "place" means both a location in space and position in society: to be tied to place is also to be bound to one's station in life, with little hope of betterment. Space symbolizes hope; place, achievement and stability.

■ **Summarizing What You Have Read**

Briefly summarize this essay, focusing on the different ways that Chinese and Americans view space.

■ **Responding to What You Have Read**

Explain what you think Tuan means when he states that "Americans have a sense of space, not of place."

■ **Discussing
What You
Have Read**

Discuss this essay with your instructor and classmates, focusing on these questions:

1. Do you agree that Americans have a keener sense of space than of place? Why or why not?

2. Why do you think Americans are attracted by a sense of space, or spaciousness? Historically, how has space (in several senses of that word) been important to Americans?

3. How does the Chinese view of their environment differ from that of Americans? What does their preference for place, rather than space, reflect about their history and situation?

4. Tuan repeatedly uses the word *rooted* to describe the Chinese. What is he suggesting about the Chinese sense of place when he describes them as "rooted"? Would you also describe some Americans as "rooted" or tied to a certain place?

5. Do you agree with Tuan's assertion that Americans' rootlessness reflects their "social mobility and optimism about the future"? Why or why not?

6. Tuan makes rather large generalizations about both Chinese and American society in this essay. Ultimately, do you think his generalizations are accurate? Are they fair?

■ **Writing
Activity**

Write an essay in which you compare some attribute or attitude of American society to that of another society. For example, you might compare American eating habits with those of the French, the status of American women with the status of women in a Middle Eastern country, or American music to British or Latin music. If possible, go beyond a simple comparison to make a reasonable generalization about what the differences mean in terms of the values of the two cultures or societies you are comparing.

■ ■ ■ ■ ■ ■ ■ ■ ■ ■ ■ ■ ■ ■ ■ ■

WHAT YOU DO IS WHAT YOU ARE

Nickie McWhirter

■ **Reading
Preview**

In our society, it is common for someone to ask another person "What do you do?" The question refers, of course, to what the person does for a living—the job one holds or the career one pursues. The author of this article argues that defining a person on the basis of what he or she does is especially characteristic of Americans.

■ **Journal**
Assignment
Think about the relationship between what you do and what you are. Have you ever held a job that caused you to feel low self-esteem or one that made you feel good about yourself? In a journal entry, explore the relationship between work, or career, and identity.

■ **Reading**
Strategy
As you read this essay, focus on the evidence the author gives to support her assertion that Americans tend to define people by what they do rather than by who they are.

Americans, unlike people almost everywhere else in the world, tend to   1
define and judge everybody in terms of the work they do, especially work performed for pay. Charlie is a doctor; Sam is a carpenter; Mary Ellen is a copywriter at a small ad agency. It is as if by defining how a person earns his or her rent money, we validate or reject that person's existence. Through the work and job title, we evaluate the worth of the life attached. Larry is a laid-off auto worker; Tony is a retired teacher; Sally is a former show-girl and blackjack dealer from Vegas. It is as if by learning that a person currently earns no money at a job—and maybe hasn't earned any money at a job for years—we assign that person to limbo, at least for the present. We define such non-employed persons in terms of their past job history.

This seems peculiar to me. People aren't cast in bronze because of the   2
jobs they hold or once held. A retired teacher, for example, may spend a lot of volunteer time working with handicapped children or raising money for the Loyal Order of Hibernating Hibiscus. That apparently doesn't count. Who's Tony? A retired teacher. A laid-off auto worker may pump gas at his cousin's gas station or sell encyclopedias on weekends. But who's Larry? Until and unless he begins to work steadily again, he's a laid-off auto worker. This is the same as saying he's nothing now, but he used to be something: an auto worker.

There is a whole category of other people who are "just" something.   3
To be "just" anything is the worst. It is not to be recognized by society as having much value at all, not now and probably not in the past either. To be "just" anything is to be totally discounted, at least for the present. There are lots of people who are "just" something. "Just" a housewife immediately and painfully comes to mind. We still hear it all the time. Sometimes women who have kept a house and reared six children refer to themselves as "just" a housewife." "Just" a bum, "just" a kid, "just" a drunk, bag lady, old man, student, punk are some others. You can probably add to the list. The "just" category contains present non-earners, people who have no past job history highly valued by society and people whose

present jobs are on the low-end of pay and prestige scales. A person can be "just" a cab driver, for example, or "just" a janitor. No one is ever "just" a vice-president, however.

We're supposed to be a classless society, but we are not. We don't rec- 4
ognize a titled nobility. We refuse to acknowledge dynastic privilege. But we certainly separate the valued from the valueless, and it has a lot to do with jobs and the importance or prestige we attach to them.

It is no use arguing whether any of this is correct or proper. Rationally 5
it is silly. That's our system, however, and we should not only keep it in mind but we should teach our children how it works. It is perfectly swell to want to grow up to be a cowboy or a nurse. Kids should know, how-ever, that quite apart from earnings potential, the cattle breeder is much more respected than the hired hand. The doctor gets a lot more respect and privilege than the nurse.

I think some anthropologist ought to study our uncataloged system 6
of awarding respect and deference to each other based on jobs we hold. Where does a vice-president–product planning fit in? Is that better than vice-president–sales in the public consciousness, or unconsciousness? Writers earn diddly dot, but I suspect they are held in higher esteem than wealthy rock musicians—that is, if everybody older than 40 gets to vote.

How do we decide which jobs have great value and, therefore, the job- 7
holders are wonderful people? Why is someone who builds shopping cen-ters called an entrepreneur while someone who builds freeways is called a contractor? I have no answers to any of this, but we might think about the phenomenon the next time we are tempted to fawn over some stranger because we find out he happens to be a judge, or the next time we catch ourselves discounting the personal worth of the garbage collector.

■ **Summarizing What You Have Read**

Briefly summarize this essay, focusing on the author's arguments.

■ **Responding to What You Have Read**

In what way is your choice of career affected by your awareness that in our society "what you do is what you are"?

■ **Discussing What You Have Read**

Discuss this selection with your classmates and instructor, focusing on these questions:

1. In the first sentence of this essay, the author says we "tend to define and judge everybody in terms of the work they do." What is the differ-ence between defining and judging? Do you agree that Americans both define and judge people on the basis of what they do?

2. Americans are known for their work ethic—their attitude that work is important and even virtuous. Do you think this attitude is one reason why Americans tend to define and judge people on the basis of the work they do? Why or why not?

3. The author argues that "We're supposed to be a classless society, but we are not." Do you agree that our emphasis on the work people do has created a way of distinguishing among people? Is this way of judging and defining people better or worse than a class system based on wealth or family?

4. The author argues that defining people on the basis of what they do is typically American. Do you agree with this assertion? Why or why not?

▪ **Writing Activity**   Write an essay in which you agree or disagree with one or more of McWhirter's assertions. Support your thesis with examples from your own experience and observations.

※ ※ ※ ※ ※ ※ ※ ※ ※ ※ ※ ※ ※ ※

MADE IN AMERICA

Bill Bryson

▪ **Reading Preview**   *Hamburgers in general and McDonald's in particular are powerful symbols of American culture. In this selection, Bill Bryson traces the history of McDonald's and shows how this fast-food chain came to dominate this industry and to revolutionize the way in which food is marketed in the United States. He also analyzes McDonald's success and suggests how that success has shaped American lifestyle and culture.*

▪ **Journal Assignment**   What is your reaction when you visit a McDonald's franchise? Do you find it a familiar, comfortable place, or are you turned off by the way the food is prepared and served? Write a journal entry in which you describe your reaction to McDonald's in general or to a particular experience you have had at a McDonald's.

▪ **Reading Strategy**   As you read, focus on the reasons for the success of McDonald's.

Though the hamburger had been part of the American diet for half a   1
century, it underwent a kind of apotheosis in the 1950s. As late as 1950,
pork was, by a considerable margin, still the most widely eaten meat in

America, but two decades later Americans were eating twice as much beef as pork, nearly a hundred pounds of it a year, and half of that in the form of hamburgers. One company more than any other was responsible for this massive change in dietary habits: McDonald's.

The story as conveyed by the company is well known. A salesman of 2
Multimixers named Ray Kroc became curious as to why a small hamburger stand on the edge of the desert in San Bernardino, California, would need eight Multimixers—enough to make forty milkshakes at a time, more than any other restaurant in America could possibly want to make—and decided to fly out to have a look. The restaurant he found, run by the brothers Maurice and Richard McDonald, was small, only six hundred square feet, but the burgers were tasty, the fries crisp, and the shakes unusually thick, and it was unquestionably popular with the locals. Kroc was fifty-two years old, an age when most men would be thinking of slowing down, but he saw an opportunity here. He bought the McDonald's name and began building an empire. The implication has always been that the original McDonald's was an obscure, rinky-dink operation in the middle of nowhere, and that it was only the towering genius of Ray Kroc that made it into the streamlined, efficient, golden-arched institution we know and love today. It wasn't entirely like that.

By 1954, when Kroc came along, the McDonald brothers were already 3
legendary, at least in the trade. *American Restaurant* magazine had done a cover story on them in 1952, and they were constantly being visited by people who wanted to see how they generated so much turnover from so little space. With sales of over $350,000 a year (all of it going through one busy cash register) and profits above $100,000, McDonald's was one of the most successful restaurants in America. In his autobiography, Kroc makes it sound as if the McDonald brothers had never thought of franchising until he came along. In fact, by the time he visited them they had a dozen franchised operations going.

Almost everything later associated with the McDonald's chain was 4
invented or perfected by the brothers, from the method of making French fries to the practice of trumpeting the number of hamburgers sold. As early as 1950, they had a sign out front announcing "Over 1 Million Sold." They even came up with the design of a sloping roof, red-and-white-tiled walls, and integral golden arches—not for the San Bernardino outlet but for their first franchise operation, which opened in Phoenix in 1952, two years before Kroc came along.

The McDonalds were, in short, the true heroes of the fast-food 5
revolution, and by any measure they were remarkable men. They had moved to California from New Hampshire during the depression years, and opened their first drive-in restaurant in 1937 near Pasadena. It didn't sell hamburgers. But in 1940, they opened a new establishment at 14th and E Streets, at the end of Route 66, in San Bernardino in a snug

octagonal structure. It was a conventional hamburger stand, and it did reasonably well.

But in 1948 the brothers were seized with a strange vision. They closed 6 the business for three months, fired the twenty carhops, got rid of all the china and silverware, and reopened with a new, entirely novel idea: that the customer would have to come to a window to collect the food rather than have it brought to the car. They cut the menu to just seven items—hamburgers, cheeseburgers, pie, potato chips, coffee, milk, and pop. Customers no longer specified what they wanted on their hamburgers but received them with ketchup, mustard, onions, and pickle. The hamburgers were made smaller—just ten to a pound—but the price was halved to 15 cents each.

The change was a flop. Business fell by 80 percent. The teenagers on 7 whom they had relied went elsewhere. But gradually a new type of clientele developed, the family, particularly after they added French fries and milk shakes to the menu, and even more particularly when customers realized that the food was great and that you could feed a whole family for a couple of bucks. Before long, McDonald's had almost more business than it could handle.

As volume grew, the brothers constantly refined the process to make 8 the production of food more streamlined and efficient. With a local machine shop owner named Ed Toman they invented almost everything connected with the production of fast food, from dispensers that pump out a precise dollop of ketchup or mustard to the lazy susans on which twenty-four hamburger buns can be speedily dressed. Toman even improved on Kroc's Multimixers, modifying the spindles so that shakes could be made in their paper cups rather than in tin canister and then transferred. Above all, the McDonalds introduced the idea of specialization—one person who did nothing but cook hamburgers, another who made shakes, another to dress the buns, and so on—and developed the now universal practice of having the food prepared and waiting so that customers could place an order and immediately collect it.

The parallels between the McDonald brothers and Wright brothers are 9 striking. Like the Wrights, the McDonald brothers never married and lived together in the same house. Like the Wrights, they had no special interest in wealth and fame. (The McDonalds' one indulgence was to buy a pair of new Cadillacs every year on the day that the new models came out.) Both sets of brothers were single-mindedly devoted to achieving perfection in their chosen sphere, and both sets created something from which others would derive greater credit and fame. The McDonald brothers had just one distinction that set them apart from the Wrights. They dreaded flying, which presented a problem in keeping tabs on their expanding empire. So when Ray Kroc came along and offered to form a partnership in which he would look after the franchising side of the operation, they jumped at his offer.

Kroc was, it must be said, a consummate seller of franchises. By 1961, 10 the year he bought the brothers out for $2.7 million, there were two hundred McDonald's restaurants, and the company was on its way to becoming a national institution. Kroc achieved this success in large part by making sure that the formula of the original San Bernardino McDonald's was followed everywhere with the most exacting fidelity. His obsession with detail became legendary. He dictated that McDonald's burgers must be exactly 3.875 inches across, weigh 1.6 ounces, and contain precisely 19 percent fat. Big Mac buns should have an average of 178 sesame seeds. He even specified, after much experimentation, how much wax should be on the wax paper that separated one hamburger patty from another.

Such obsessiveness made McDonald's a success, but it also led to the creation of a culture that was dazzlingly unsympathetic to innovation. As he recounted in his autobiography, when a team of his most trusted executives suggested the idea of miniature outlets called MiniMacs, Kroc was "so damned mad I was ready to turn my office into a batting cage and let those three guys have it with my cane." Their failing, he explained, was to think small. One could be excused for concluding that their failure was to think at all.

- **Summarizing What You Have Read**

Briefly summarize this selection, focusing not only on major developments in the history of McDonald's but also on the main reasons for its success.

- **Responding to What You Have Read**

Do you view the amazing success of McDonald's and its influence on other fast-food restaurants as a positive or negative development in our culture? Why or why not?

- **Discussing What You Have Read**

With your classmates and instructor, discuss the selection you have just read, focusing on these questions:

1. According to Bryson, who were the "true heroes of the fast-food revolution"? What evidence does he provide to support this assertion?

2. What significant changes did the McDonald brothers make to their restaurants in 1948? As a result of these changes, who became the main customers of the McDonald's restaurants after 1948?

3. Which features of the McDonald's system do you think account for its success?

4. George Ritzer, who has written extensively about the McDonald phenomenon, coined the word *McDonaldization* and has widely criticized what he calls the "McDonaldization of society." Ritzer believes that

McDonaldization is the cause of the hyperefficiency and homoge- nization that increasingly pervade all aspects of American culture. Do you agree or disagree with this view?

5. McDonald's restaurants have now spread throughout the world. Do you think they are good representatives of American culture? Do they reflect American culture accurately? Why or why not?

■ **Writing Activity**

Write an essay based on an observation of a McDonald's restaurant (see Chapter 7). Spend 30 minutes to an hour observing what goes on at the restaurant and take extensive notes on what you see. You may also want to order food and take notes on its quality. Then write an essay in which you come to some conclusion about McDonald's that you support with your observations and experience.

◾ ◾ ◾ ◾ ◾ ◾ ◾ ◾ ◾ ◾ ◾ ◾ ◾ ◾

COULD YOU LIVE WITH LESS?

Stephanie Mills

■ **Reading Preview**

Stephanie Mills is a writer and an environmentalist. She is the author of Whatever Happened to Ecology? *(1989) and* In Service of the Wild: Restoring and Reinhabiting Damaged Land *(1995). In this essay, which appeared in* Glamour *magazine, Mills argues for a simple lifestyle uncomplicated by gadgets and technology.*

■ **Journal Assignment**

Think about the affluence of American society. How many of the things you own do you really need? Write in your journal an answer to the question posed by Mills's title: "Could You Live with Less?"

■ **Reading Strategy**

Identify Mills's main idea in her first paragraph and then number the exam- ples she gives to support this main idea.

Compared to the lifestyle of the average person on Earth, my days are lush with comfort and convenience: I have a warm home, enough to eat, my own car. But compared to most of my urban American contemporaries, I live a monastically simple life.

Since 1984 I've made my home outside a small city in lower Michi- gan, where the winters are snowy but not severely cold. My snug

1

2

720-square-foot house is solar- and wood-heated. No thermostat, just a cast-iron stove. There's electric lighting, indoor plumbing, a tankless water heater, a secondhand refrigerator and range—but no microwave oven, no dishwasher, no blow-dryer, no cordless phone. My gas-sipping compact station wagon has 140,000 miles on it and spreading patches of rust. I've never owned a television set. My home entertainment center consists of a thousand books, a stereo system, a picture window and two cats.

3 Part of the reason I live the way I do is that as a freelance writer, my income is unpredictable and at best fairly unspectacular. Thus it behooves me to keep in mind the difference between wants and needs. Like all human beings, I have some needs that are absolute: about 2,000 calories a day, a half a gallon of water to drink, a sanitary means of disposing of my bodily wastes, water to bathe in, something muscular to do for part of the day and a warm, dry place to sleep. To stay sane I need contact with people and with nature, meaningful work and the opportunity to love and be loved.

4 I don't need, nor do I want, to complicate my life with gadgets. I want to keep technology at the periphery rather than at the center of my life, to treat it like meat in Chinese cuisine—as a condiment rather than as a staple food. Technology should abet my life, not dominate or redefine it. A really good tool—like a sharp kitchen knife, a wheelbarrow or a baby carrier, all of which have been with us in some form for thousands of years— makes a useful difference but doesn't displace human intelligence, character or contact the way higher technologies sometimes do. Working people need the tools of their trade, and as a writer, I do have a fax, but I've resisted the pressure to buy a personal computer. A manual typewriter has worked well for me so far. Noticing that the most computer-savvy people I know are always pining for more megabytes and better software, I've decided not to climb on the purchasing treadmill of planned obsolescence.

5 Doing with less is easier when I remember that emotional needs often get expressed as material wants, but can never, finally, be satisfied that way. If I feel disconnected from others, a cellular phone won't cure that. If I feel like I'm getting a little dowdy, hours on a tanning bed can't eradicate self-doubt.

6 Why live in a snowy region when I don't use central heat? I moved here for love several years ago, and while that love was brief, my affection for this place has grown and grown. I like the roots I've put down; living like Goldilocks, moving from chair to chair, seems like not much of a life to me.

7 Being willfully backward about technology suits my taste—I like living this way. Wood heat feels good, better than the other kinds. (Central heating would make my home feel like it was just anywhere.) Fetching firewood gets me outdoors and breathing (sometimes gasping) fresh air in the wintertime when it's easy to go stale. It's hard, achy work to split and

stack the 8 or 12 cords of stove wood I burn annually. I've been known to seek help to get it done. But the more of it I do myself, the more I can brag to my city friends.

My strongest motivation for living the way I do is my knowledge, deep 8 and abiding, that technology comes at a serious cost to the planet and most of its people. Burning fossil fuels has changed the Earth's climate. Plastics and pesticides have left endocrine-disrupting chemicals everywhere—in us and in wildlife, affecting reproductive systems. According to Northwest Environment Watch in Seattle, the "clean" computer industry typically generates 139 pounds of waste, 49 of them toxic, in the manufacture of each 55-pound computer.

I refuse to live as if that weren't so. In this, I'm not unique. There are 9 many thousands of Americans living simply, questioning technology, fighting to preserve what remains of nature. We're bucking the tide, acting consciously and succeeding only a little. Yet living this way helps me feel decent within myself—and that, I find, is one luxury worth having.

■ **Summarizing What You Have Read**

Summarize this essay (in one sentence if possible).

■ **Responding to What You Have Read**

Compare the lifestyle advocated by Mills to your own.

■ **Discussing What You Have Read**

Discuss this essay with your instructor and classmates, focusing on these questions:

1. What is Mills's motivation for living as she does? Why does she avoid technology?
2. Do you agree with Mills that "There are many thousands of Americans living simply, questioning technology, fighting to preserve what remains of nature"? Why or why not?
3. Do you think Americans are more reliant on technology and modern conveniences than are people in other countries? Why or why not?
4. Whether it is practical or not, do you find the lifestyle Mills describes attractive? Why or why not?
5. Would the lifestyle Mills advocates be a solution to some of the American lifestyle problems identified in the other essays in this unit? Explain your answer.

■ **Writing Activity**

Write an essay in which you argue for or against the simple lifestyle Mills advocates.

CUMULATIVE ASSIGNMENTS FOR UNIT THREE

DISCUSSION QUESTIONS

1. Each of the four reading selections in this unit suggests a rather critical attitude toward the American lifestyle. Review the selections and discuss what generalization each author seems to be making about Americans or American culture. Do you think these generalizations are realistic and fair? Why or why not?

2. What are some positive aspects of American lifestyle also pointed out by these four authors?

3. Which of the selections in this unit do you think is most accurate in its depiction of American lifestyle? Support your answer.

4. How do you think American culture is typically viewed by the rest of the world? What aspects of American lifestyle are most envied and imitated? Which are most criticized?

WRITING ASSIGNMENT

Using the four essays in this unit and your own observations and experiences, write an essay in which you argue for a particular view of America's image or a particular element of American lifestyle. Alternatively, write an essay based on an interview with someone from another country (see Chapter 7 for instruction on interviewing). Your interview and essay should focus on a particular aspect of American lifestyle.

This last unit encourages you to examine America's cultural diversity and how it shapes this society. To begin thinking about this issue, make two lists—one of the problems that can result from cultural diversity and the other of the benefits that derive from cultural diversity.

CHILD OF THE AMERICAS
Aurora Levins Morales

■ **Reading Preview**

Aurora Levins Morales, the writer of this poem, calls herself a "Child of the Americas" because her background is Jewish and Puerto Rican, but she was raised in the United States. Thus, she is a "crossroads" for several cultures. The poem is from a collection entitled Getting Home Alive *by Morales and her mother, and it celebrates the diversity not only embodied in the poet but also of America.*

■ **Journal Assignment**

Write a journal entry in which you describe the ethnic and cultural influences in your family background. What effect have these influences—or the lack of them—had on you?

■ **Reading Strategy**

Underline the words that are unfamiliar to you; be prepared to contribute these words to a class discussion of the vocabulary of this poem.

I am a child of the Americas,
a light-skinned mestiza of the Caribbean,
a child of many diaspora, born into this continent at a crossroads.

1

I am a U.S. Puerto Rican Jew,
a product of the ghettos of New York I have never known.
An immigrant and the daughter and granddaughter of immigrants.
I speak English with passion: it's the tongue of my consciousness,
a flashing knife blade of crystal, my tool, my craft.

5

I am Caribeña, island grown. Spanish is in my flesh,
ripples from my tongue, lodges in my hips:

the language of garlic and mangoes,
the singing in my poetry, the flying gestures of my hands.
I am Latinoamerica, rooted in the history of my continent:
I speak from that body.

I am not african. Africa is in me, but I cannot return.
I am not taína. Taíno is in me, but there is no way back.
I am not european. Europe lives in me, but I have no home there.

I am new. History made me. My first language was spanglish.
I was born at the crossroads
and I am whole.

15

20

- **Summarizing What You Have Read**

Write a prose summary of this poem, focusing on your interpretation of its meaning.

- **Responding to What You Have Read**

Compare the "two Americas" (North America and Latin America) that produced the poet. What similarities and differences exist between the two?

- **Discussing What You Have Read**

Discuss this poem with your classmates and instructor, focusing on these questions:

1. Which images in the poem do you find most interesting and significant?

2. What does Morales value most from each of the cultures in her background?

3. In addition to the two Americas, what other cultures does she claim as part of her heritage?

4. Identify the words in the poem that are strange to you. What languages do these words come from? With your classmates, try to figure out the meaning of these words from their context and your knowledge of the languages from which they derive.

5. Notice that the word *crossroads* is used twice in the poem. Why do you think this is an important image for the poet?

- **Writing Activity**

Write an essay or a poem in which you explore your own heritage—its different elements and what they have contributed to who you are.

THE LEGACY OF GENERATION Ñ

Christy Haubegger

■ **Reading**
Preview

In this essay, which first appeared in Newsweek *magazine, Christy Haubegger predicts that the twenty-first century will be characterized by increasing growth in the Latino population of America. Already a significant minority, Latinos are increasing at a rate of "seven times that of the general population," according to Haubegger. Although Haubegger's tone is humorous, her arguments are serious and convincing.*

■ **Journal**
Assignment

Increasingly, Latin influences are shaping U.S. society. In a journal entry, describe some element of the Latino culture with which you are familiar (for example, music, food, dance, language).

■ **Reading**
Strategy

As you read, analyze Haubegger's tone, which ranges from light and humorous to bitingly ironic to deadly serious. Indicate in the margin those statements in which you think she is being most serious and straightforward.

About 20 years ago, some mainstream observers declared the 1980s the   1
"decade of the Hispanic." The Latino population was nearing 15 million! (It's since doubled.) However, our decade was postponed—a managerial oversight, no doubt—and eventually rescheduled for the '90s. What happens to a decade deferred? It earns compounded interest and becomes the next hundred years. The United States of the 21st century will be undeniably ours. Again.

It's Manifest *Destino.* After all, Latinos are true Americans, some of the   2
original residents of the *Américas.* Spanish was the first European language spoken on this continent. Which is why we live in places like *Los Angeles, Colorado* and *Florida* rather than The Angels, Colored and Flowered. Now my generation is about to put a Latin stamp on the rest of the culture—and that will ultimately be the Ñ legacy.

We are not only numerous, we are also growing at a rate seven times that   3
of the general population. Conservative political ads notwithstanding, this growth is driven by natural increase (births over deaths) rather than immigration. At 30, I may be the oldest childless Latina in the United States. More important, however, while our preceding generation felt pressure to assimilate, America has now generously agreed to meet us in the middle. Just as we become more American, America is simultaneously becoming more Latino.

This quiet *revolución* can perhaps be traced back to the bloodless coup   3
of 1992, when salsa outsold ketchup for the first time. Having toppled the

leadership in the condiment category, we set our sights even higher. Fairly soon, there was a congresswoman named Sanchez representing Orange County, a taco-shilling Chihuahua became a national icon and now everyone is *loca* for Ricky Martin.

We are just getting started. Our geographic concentration and repu- 5
tation for family values are making us every politician's dream constituency. How long can New Hampshire, with just four Electoral College votes—and probably an equal number of Hispanic residents—continue to get so much attention from presidential candidates? Advertisers will also soon be begging for our attention. With a median age of 26 (eight years younger than the general market), Latinos hardly exist outside their coveted 18–34 demographic. Remember, we may only be 11 percent of the country, but we buy 16 percent of the lipliner.

The media will change as well, especially television, where we now appear 6
to be rapidly approaching extinction. Of the 26 new comedies and dramas appearing this fall on the four major networks, not one has a Latino in a leading role. The Screen Actors Guild released employment statistics for 1998 showing that the percentage of roles going to Hispanic actors actually declined from the previous year. But, pretty soon, the cast of "Friends" will need to find some *amigos*. Seeing as they live in New York City, and there's almost 2 million of us in the metropolitan area, this shouldn't prove too difficult.

Face it: this is going to be a bilingual country. Back in 1849, the Califor- 7
nia Constitution was written in both Spanish and English, and we're headed that way again. If our children speak two languages instead of just one, how can that not be a benefit to us all? The re-Latinization of this country will pay off in other ways as well. I, for one, look forward to that pivotal moment in our history when all American men finally know how to dance. Latin music will no longer be found in record stores under foreign and romance will bloom again. Our children will ask us what it was like to dance without a partner.

"American food" will mean low-fat enchiladas and hamburgers served 8
with rice and beans. As a result, the American standard of beauty will necessarily expand to include a female size 12, and anorexia will be found only in medical-history books. Finally, just in time for the baby boomers' senescence, living with extended family will become hip again. "Simpsons" fans of the next decade will see Grandpa moving back home. We'll all go back to church together.

At the dawn of a new millennium, America knows Latinos as enter- 9
tainers and athletes. But, someday very soon, all American children can dream of growing up to be writers like Sandra Cisneros, astronauts like Ellen Ochoa, or judges like Jose Cabranes of the Second Circuit Court of Appeals. To put a Latin spin on a famous Anglo phrase: It is truly *mañana* in America. For those of you who don't know it (yet), that word doesn't just mean tomorrow; *mañana* also means morning.

■ **Summarizing What You Have Read**

Briefly summarize this essay, focusing on Haubegger's main predictions about how the increase in Latino population will change the United States.

■ **Responding to What You Have Read**

How do you respond to Haubegger's assertion that Latinos are "true Americans, some of the original residents of the *Américas.*"

■ **Discussing What You Have Read**

Discuss this essay with your classmates and instructor, focusing on these questions:

1. Why is Haubegger's use of the term *Generation Ñ* an effective allusion to terms such as *Generation X*? What marks the term as particularly Hispanic or Latino?

2. What are the major areas of our society that Haubegger predicts will be affected by the growing Latino population?

3. Do you agree that the United States will at some point in the future be a bilingual country? What would be the advantages of the country's being bilingual? What would be the disadvantages?

4. Would you characterize Haubegger's tone as primarily humorous, serious, disillusioned, or optimistic? Cite specific sentences from the essay to support your answer.

■ **Writing Activity**

Write an essay in which you explain some aspect of Latino culture you find interesting. You may need to research your subject by observing a particular location or event and/or interviewing someone who is knowledgeable about the Latino culture (see Chapter 7).

❋ ❋ ❋ ❋ ❋ ❋ ❋ ❋ ❋ ❋ ❋ ❋ ❋ ❋ ❋

TIME TO LOOK AND LISTEN
Magdoline Asfahani

■ **Reading Preview**

Although this essay was written before the September 11, 2001, terrorist attacks, it expresses the views of many Arab Americans today. The author, Magdoline Asfahani, describes what it is like to be feared and suspected by her fellow citizens. As she states in her introduction, "I learned at a young age that the country we loved so much did not feel the same way about us."

■ **Journal Assignment**

Since the September 11 attacks on the World Trade Center and the Pentagon, many Americans have realized they know very little about the Middle East. In a journal entry, write what you know about Middle Eastern culture and identify the primary sources of your knowledge.

■ **Reading Strategy**

As you read, try to imagine how the author must feel now, after the terrorist attacks carried out primarily by people from the Middle East.

I love my country as many who have been here for generations cannot. Perhaps that's because I'm the child of immigrants, raised with a conscious respect for America that many people take for granted. My parents chose this country because it offered them a new life, freedom and possibilities. But I learned at a young age that the country we loved so much did not feel the same way about us.   1

Discrimination is not unique to America. It occurs in any country that allows immigration. Anyone who is unlike the majority is looked at a little suspiciously, dealt with a little differently. The fact that I wasn't part of the majority never occurred to me. I knew that I was an Arab and a Muslim. This meant nothing to me. At school I stood up to say the Pledge of Allegiance every day. These things did not seem incompatible at all. Then everything changed for me, suddenly and permanently, in 1985. I was only in seventh grade, but that was the beginning of my political education.   2

That year a TWA plane originating in Athens was diverted to Beirut. Two years earlier the U.S. Marine barracks in Beirut had been bombed. That seemed to start a chain of events that would forever link Arabs with terrorism. After the hijacking, I faced classmates who taunted me with cruel names, attacking my heritage and my religion. I became an outcast and had to apologize for myself constantly.   3

After a while, I tried to forget my heritage. No matter what race, religion or ethnicity, a child who is attacked often retreats. I was the only Arab I knew of in my class, so I had no one in my peer group as an ally. No matter what my parents tried to tell me about my proud cultural history, I would ignore it. My classmates told me I came from an uncivilized, brutal place, that Arabs were by nature anti-American, and I believed them. They did not know the hours my parents spent studying, working, trying to preserve part of their old lives while embracing, willingly, the new.   4

I tried to forget the Arabic I knew, because if I didn't I'd be forever linked to murderers. I stopped inviting friends over for dinner, because I thought the food we ate was "weird." I lied about where my parents had come from. Their accents (although they spoke English perfectly) humiliated me. Though Islam is a major monotheistic religion with many similarities to   5

Judaism and Christianity, there were no holidays near Chanukah or Christmas, nothing to tie me to the "Judeo-Christian" tradition. I felt more excluded. I slowly began to turn into someone without a past.

Civil war was raging in Lebanon, and all that Americans saw of that country was destruction and violence. Every other movie seemed to feature Arab terrorists. The most common questions I was asked were if I had ever ridden a camel or if my family lived in tents. I felt burdened with responsibility. Why should an adolescent be asked questions like "Is it true you hate Jews and you want Israel destroyed?" I didn't hate anybody. My parents had never said anything even alluding to such sentiments. I was confused and hurt. 6

As I grew older and began to form my own opinions, my embarrassment lessened and my anger grew. The turning point came in high school. My grandmother had become very ill, and it was necessary for me to leave school a few days before Christmas vacation. My chemistry teacher was very sympathetic until I said I was going to the Middle East. "Don't come back in a body bag," he said cheerfully. The class laughed. Suddenly, those years of watching movies that mocked me and listening to others who knew nothing about Arabs and Muslims except what they saw on television seemed like a bad dream. I knew then that I would never be silent again. 7

I've tried to reclaim those lost years. I realize now that I come from a culture that has a rich history. The Arab world is a medley of people of different religions; not every Arab is a Muslim, and vice versa. The Arabs brought tremendous advances in the sciences and mathematics, as well as creating a literary tradition that has never been surpassed. The language itself is flexible and beautiful, with nuances and shades of meaning unparalleled in any language. Though many find it hard to believe, Islam has made progress in women's rights. There is a specific provision in the Koran that permits women to own property and ensures that their inheritance is protected—although recent events have shown that interpretation of these laws can vary. 8

My youngest brother, who is 12, is now at the crossroads I faced. When initial reports of the Oklahoma City bombing pointed to "Arab-looking individuals" as the culprits, he came home from school crying. "Mom, why do Muslims kill people? Why are the Arabs so bad?" She was angry and brokenhearted, but tried to handle the situation in the best way possible: through education. She went to his class, armed with Arabic music, pictures, traditional dress and cookies. She brought a chapter of the social-studies book to life, and the children asked intelligent, thoughtful questions, even after the class was over. Some even asked if she was coming back. When my brother came home, he was excited and proud instead of ashamed. 9

I only recently told my mother about my past experience. Maybe if I had told her then, I would have been better equipped to deal with the thoughtless teasing. But, fortunately, the world is changing. Although discrimination and stereotyping still exist, many people are trying to lessen and end it. Teachers, 10 schools and the media are showing greater sensitivity to cultural issues. How-ever, there is still much that needs to be done, not for the sake of any par-ticular ethnic or cultural group but for the sake of our country.

The America that I love is one that values freedom and the differences   11
of its people. Education is the key to understanding. As Americans we need
to take a little time to look and listen carefully to what is around us and not
rush to judgment without knowing all the facts. And we must never be
ashamed of our pasts. It is our collective differences that unite us and make
us unique as a nation. It's what determines our present and our future.

- **Summarizing What You Have Read**

Write a brief summary of this essay, focusing on the author's feelings rather than her life story.

- **Responding to What You Have Read**

If you could, how would you respond to Asfahani?

- **Discussing What You Have Read**

Discuss this essay with your classmates and instructor, focusing on these questions:

1. Asfahani begins her second paragraph with the following assertion: "Discrimination is not unique to America. It occurs in any country that allows immigration." Can you think of other countries, now or in the past, that have struggled with the problem of discrimination? Do you agree that discrimination is linked to immigration?

2. Examine the national disasters that Asfahani discusses, the bombing of the U.S. Marine barracks in Beirut in 1985 and the bombing of the federal building in Oklahoma City a few years later. How and why did these events affect Arab Americans?

3. What was Asfahani's initial reaction to these events? What was her later reaction?

4. Asfahani's essay ends on a relatively positive note. What does she believe is the key to the type of discrimination she has experienced?

5. How do you think the events of September 11, 2001, affected the author and her family? How may these events and their repercussions have changed her optimism?

- **Writing Activity**

Write an essay based on an interview with someone who has immigrated to the United States (see Chapter 7). In your interview, focus on the per-son's reaction to a recent event or to some aspect of American life.

■ ■ ■ ■ ▓ ▓ ▓ ▓ ▓ ▓ ▓ ▓ ▓ ■ ▓ ▓

I HAVE A DREAM
Martin Luther King, Jr.

■ **Reading Preview**

Martin Luther King, Jr. delivered this famous speech in 1963, five years before he was assassinated. Throughout his life, King worked with the Southern Christian Leadership Conference to gain for African-American citizens the freedom and justice promised all Americans in the Constitution. This speech, with its famous refrain, "I have a dream," played a major role in the civil rights movement of the 1960s and continues to be cited frequently.

■ **Journal Assignment**

In a journal entry, describe your dream for this country—the kind of nation you would like to see America become.

■ **Reading Strategy**

Because this selection is a speech, it will be more effective if you read it aloud. As you read, notice the rhetorical devices (such as direct address, repetition, parallel structure, and Biblical and historical references) that contribute to the powerful effect of this speech.

I am happy to join with you today in what will go down in history as the greatest demonstration for freedom in the history of our nation. 1

Five score years ago, a great American, in whose symbolic shadow we stand today, signed the Emancipation Proclamation. This momentous decree came as a great beacon light of hope to millions of Negro slaves who had been seared in the flames of withering injustice. It came as a joyous daybreak to end the long night of their captivity. 2

But one hundred years later, the Negro still is not free; one hundred years later, the life of the Negro is still sadly crippled by the manacles of segregation and the chains of discrimination; one hundred years later, the Negro lives on a lonely island of poverty in the midst of a vast ocean of material prosperity; one hundred years later, the Negro is still languished in the corners of American society and finds himself in exile in his own land. 3

So we've come here today to dramatize a shameful condition. In a sense we've come to our nation's capital to cash a check. When the architects of our republic wrote the magnificent words of the Constitution and the Declaration of Independence, they were signing a promissory note to which every American was to fall heir. This note was the promise that all men, yes, black men as well as white men, would be guaranteed the unalienable rights of life, liberty, and the pursuit of happiness. 4

It is obvious today that America has defaulted on this promissory note 5
in so far as her citizens of color are concerned. Instead of honoring this
sacred obligation, America has given the Negro people a bad check; a check
which has come back marked "insufficient funds." But we refuse to believe
that the bank of justice is bankrupt. We refuse to believe that there are
insufficient funds in the great vaults of opportunity of this nation. And
so we've come to cash this check, a check that will give us upon demand
the riches of freedom and the security of justice.

We have also come to this hallowed spot to remind America of the fierce 6
urgency of now. This is no time to engage in the luxury of cooling off or
to take the tranquilizing drug of gradualism. Now is the time to make
real the promises of democracy; now is the time to rise from the dark and
desolate valley of segregation to the sunlit path of racial justice; now is the
time to lift our nation from the quicksands of racial injustice to the solid
rock of brotherhood; now is the time to make justice a reality for all of God's
children. It would be fatal for the nation to overlook the urgency of the
moment. This sweltering summer of the Negro's legitimate discontent will
not pass until there is an invigorating autumn of freedom and equality.

Nineteen sixty-three is not an end, but a beginning. And those who 7
hope that the Negro needed to blow off steam and will now be content,
will have a rude awakening if the nation returns to business as usual.
There will be neither rest nor tranquility in America until the Negro is
granted his citizenship rights. The whirlwinds of revolt will continue to
shake the foundations of our nation until the bright day of justice emerges.

But there is something that I must say to my people, who stand on 8
the worn threshold which leads into the palace of justice. In the process
of gaining our rightful place, we must not be guilty of wrongful deeds. Let
us not seek to satisfy our thirst for freedom by drinking from the cup of bit-
terness and hatred. We must forever conduct our struggle on the high plain
of dignity and discipline. We must not allow our creative protests to degen-
erate into physical violence. Again and again we must rise to the majestic heights of meeting physical force with soul force. The marvelous new
militancy, which has engulfed the Negro community, must not lead us to
a distrust of all white people. For many of our white brothers, as evidenced
by their presence here today, have come to realize that their destiny is
tied up with our destiny. And they have come to realize that their freedom is inextricably bound to our freedom. We cannot walk alone. And as
we walk, we must make the pledge that we shall always march ahead.
We cannot turn back.

There are those who are asking the devotees of Civil Rights, "When will 9
you be satisfied?" We can never be satisfied as long as the Negro is the
victim of the unspeakable horrors of police brutality; we can never be satisfied as long as our bodies, heavy with the fatigue of travel, cannot gain

lodging in the motels of the highways and the hotels of the cities; we cannot be satisfied as long as the Negro's basic mobility is from a smaller ghetto to a larger one; we can never be satisfied as long as our children are stripped of their selfhood and robbed of their dignity by signs stating "For Whites Only"; we cannot be satisfied as long as the Negro in Mississippi cannot vote and a Negro in New York believes he has nothing for which to vote. No! No, we are not satisfied, and we will not be satisfied until "justice rolls down like waters and righteousness like a mighty stream."

I am not unmindful that some of you have come here out of great tri-   10
als and tribulations. Some of you have come fresh from narrow jail cells. Some of you have come from areas where your quest for freedom left you battered by the storms of persecution and staggered by the winds of police brutality. You have been the veterans of creative suffering. Continue to work with the faith that unearned suffering is redemptive. Go back to Mississippi. Go back to Alabama. Go back to South Carolina. Go back to Georgia. Go back to Louisiana. Go back to the slums and ghettos of our Northern cities, knowing that somehow this situation can and will be changed. Let us not wallow in the valley of despair.

I say to you today, my friends, so even though we face the difficulties   11
of today and tomorrow, I still have a dream. It is a dream deeply rooted in the American dream. I have a dream that one day this nation will rise up and live out the true meaning of its creed, "We hold these truths to be self-evident, that all men are created equal." I have a dream that one day on the red hills of Georgia, sons of former slaves and the sons of former slave owners will be able to sit down together at the table of brotherhood. I have a dream that one day even the state of Mississippi, a state sweltering with the heat of injustice, sweltering with the heat of oppression, will be transformed into an oasis of freedom and justice. I have a dream that my four little children will one day live in a nation where they will not be judged by the color of their skin, but by the content of their character.

I HAVE A DREAM TODAY!   12

I have a dream that one day down in Alabama—with its vicious racists,   13
with its Governor having his lips dripping with the words of interposition and nullification—one day right there in Alabama, little black boys and black girls will be able to join hands with little white boys and white girls as sisters and brothers.

I HAVE A DREAM TODAY!   14

I have a dream that one day every valley shall be exalted, every hill   15
and mountain shall be made low. The rough places will be plain and the crooked places will be made straight, "and the glory of the Lord shall be revealed, and all flesh shall see it together."

This is our hope. This is the faith that I go back to the South with. With   16
this faith we will be able to hew out of the mountain of despair, a stone

of hope. With this faith we will be able to transform the jangling discords of our nation into a beautiful symphony of brotherhood. With this faith we will be able to work together, to pray together, to struggle together, to go to jail together, to stand up for freedom together, knowing that we will be free one day. And this will be the day. This will be the day when all of God's children will be able to sing with new meaning, "My country 'tis of thee, sweet land of liberty, of thee I sing. Land where my father died, land of the pilgrim's pride, from every mountain side, let freedom ring." And if America is to be a great nation, this must become true.

So let freedom ring from the prodigious hilltops of New Hampshire; let freedom ring from the mighty mountains of New York; let freedom ring from the heightening Alleghenies of Pennsylvania; let freedom ring from the snow-capped Rockies of Colorado; let freedom ring from the curvaceous slopes of California. But not only that. Let freedom ring from Stone Mountain of Georgia; let freedom ring from Lookout Mountain of Tennessee; let freedom ring from every hill and mole hill of Mississippi. "From every mountainside, let freedom ring."   17

And when this happens, and when we allow freedom to ring, when we let it ring from every village and every hamlet, from every state and every city, we will be able to speed up that day when all of God's children, black men and white men, Jews and Gentiles, Protestants and Catholics, will be able to join hands and sing in the words of the old Negro spiritual: "Free at last. Free at last. Thank God Almighty, we are free at last."   18

■ **Summarizing What You Have Read**

Write a brief summary of this speech, focusing particularly on King's dream—what he hoped to see happen in the future.

■ **Responding to What You Have Read**

This speech is noted for its poetry and effectiveness as oral discourse, but it also includes skillful arguments. Respond to King's speech, focusing on his arguments and how convincing you found them.

■ **Discussing What You Have Read**

Discuss this speech with your classmates and instructor, focusing on these questions:

1. What was King's purpose in giving this speech? That is, what did he hope to accomplish? What effect do you think the speech had on his audience?

2. It has been forty years since King delivered this speech. Do you think his dream is closer to realization today than it was then? Support your answer.

3. Notice that King begins his second paragraph with the phrase "Five score years ago," echoing Abraham Lincoln's famous Gettysburg Address, which begins "Four score and seven years ago." What purpose does this reference to Lincoln serve?

4. What is your dream for the future of this country?

■ **Writing Activity**   Write a review of this speech, beginning with a brief summary and then pointing out its strongest and weakest features. (See Chapter 33 for instruction on writing a review.)

CUMULATIVE ASSIGNMENTS FOR UNIT FOUR

DISCUSSION ASSIGNMENT

1. What do you think King's reaction would be to Haubegger's and Asfahani's essays?

2. What progress have we made toward racial equality and harmony since King delivered his "I Have a Dream" speech in 1963?

3. What racial issues remain to be solved in our society?

4. How does language contribute to both racial problems and solutions? Support your answer with examples.

5. How has ethnic diversity both divided and enriched our society?

WRITING ASSIGNMENT

Using the poem and essays you have just read as well as your own experiences and observations, write an essay in which you argue that diversity either strengthens or weakens our society.

Documenting and Citing Sources

Documenting and citing sources properly are important for two reasons. One reason is that your readers may want to look up one of your sources, and the information you provide should enable them to do so. Another reason is that it is honest to give credit for ideas or words that you have borrowed from others. If you do not credit borrowed information, you are guilty of the serious offense of **plagiarism**.

Several documentation styles exist. Two of the most popular are Modern Language Association (MLA) style, as explained in the *MLA Handbook for Writers of Research Papers*, and APA style, as described in the *Publication of the American Psychological Association*. Because MLA style is the one most often used in first-year English courses, we focus our discussion on it. (Note that Appendix B provides a brief explanation of APA style.)

CITING BORROWED MATERIAL WITHIN YOUR TEXT

You are responsible for crediting not only quotations but also original information and ideas from your sources. In general, you should know how to document three kinds of borrowed material: (1) direct quotations of four lines or fewer; (2) direct quotations of more than four lines; and (3) ideas and information you have paraphrased (rewritten) or summarized (condensed). Each of these three ways of crediting information is illustrated here:

1. *Citing and crediting short quotations (four lines or fewer).* Quote (a) material that cannot be effectively paraphrased or summarized, (b) passages that are especially well written, and (c) the words of well-known people and reliable authorities.

   In recent years the Latino population of the United States has greatly increased. Christy Haubegger argues that this population will continue to increase and points out benefits of this change: "If our children speak two languages instead of one," she asks, "how can that not be a benefit to us all (61).

2. *Citing and crediting long quotations.* Long, or block, quotations of more than four lines are blocked (set off and indented ten spaces). Use long quotations sparingly, and be sure to introduce and comment on such quotations. Remember that, even though you are using sources, *you* are the primary writer.

Tim Madigan reports on a new strategy many colleges are using to try to reduce dropout rates among freshmen:

> Among the most popular programs are "learning communities" in which college freshmen co-register with several others with similar academic interests and attend multiple classes with the same students. They are also required to interact with one another both in and out of the classroom. (F1)

3. *Using and crediting summarized or paraphrased material.* Be sure to rewrite completely, using your own style and phrasing. Changing only a few words is not just poor paraphrasing; it is actually plagiarism.

> How a student feels about college helps to determine success or failure. Pointing out that loneliness is a major reason many students drop out of college, Madigan describes his own loneliness during his first semester at the University of North Dakota (F1). Another student, however, explains that his determination to succeed outweighs the effects of separation from his family (Mabry 53).

Note: The reference to Madigan in the second sentence shows where the borrowed information begins, so the parenthetical citation includes only the page number of the source (a newspaper). In the final citation, the last name of the author as well as the page number is needed to identify the source.

PREPARING YOUR WORKS CITED

Your Works Cited is just what its name suggests: a list (alphabetized) of the works, or sources, you cite (quote or otherwise use) in your paper. Although the *MLA Handbook* includes sample citations for many kinds of sources, we include here examples of only the few types of citations we believe you are most likely to use. (The first line of each Works Cited entry begins at the left margin of your paper, but additional lines are indented five spaces.)

1. *Book (one or two authors)*

   Angelou, Maya. *Even the Stars Look Lonesome.* New York: Random House, 1997.

   Collier, Peter, and David Horowitz. *The Fords: An American Epic.* New York: Summit, 1987.

2. *Essay or Article in an Edited Anthology (or Collection)*

   Mabry, Marcus. "Living in Two Worlds." *Interactions: A Thematic Reader,* 5th ed. Ed. Ann Moseley and Jeanette Harris. Boston: Houghton, 2003. 51–53.

3. *Essay or Article in a Magazine*

   Haubegger, Christy A. "The Legacy of Generation Ñ." *Newsweek* 12 July 1999: 61.

4. *Essay or Article in a Scholarly Journal*

   Harris, Jeanette. "Student Writers and Word Processing: A Preliminary Evaluation." *College Composition and Communication* 36 (1985): 323–30. [Article in a journal with continuous pagination.]

Moseley, Ann. "Classics of Children's Literature for Adult Summer Reading." *The Pride* 54.3 (2001): 6. [Article in a journal in which each issue is paginated separately.]

5. *Item or Article in a Reference Work (print source and online data base)*

"Behaviorism." *The American Heritage Dictionary of the English Language*. 3rd ed. 1994.

"Junior College." *Britannica Online*. 2002. Encyclopaedia Britannica. 26 May 2002 <http://www.eb.com/>.

6. *CD-ROM Materials*

"Henry Ford." *Webster's New Bibliographical Dictionary*. New York: Merriam-Webster, 1983. *Infopedia*. CD-ROM. Future Vision Multimedia. 1995.

7. *Internet (online materials)*

"Model A Story." *Model A Ford Club of America Website*. 1996. Model A Ford Club of America. 20 April 2001 <http://www.ford.com/archive/ModelA.html>.

8. *Interviews (email, personal, telephone)*

Jones, Andrew. Personal interview. 15 May 2003.

9. *Newspaper Article or Editorial (with and without author)*

Madigan, Tim. "Freshman Year 101." *Star Telegram* [Fort Worth] 15 Aug. 2001: F1⁺.

"Our Children." Editorial. *The Dallas Morning News*. 26 May 2002: 2J.

10. *Review (see also item 11)*

Bolster, W. Jeffrey. "Out of Africa." Rev. of *The Diligent*, by Robert W. Harms. *New York Times Book Review* 31 Mar. 2002: 16.

11. *Reprinted Source / Printed Source Accessed Online*

Mills, Stephanie. "Could You Live with Less?" *Glamour* May 1998: 238. Rpt. in *Strategies for College Writing*. Ed. Jeanette Harris and Ann Moseley. New York: Longman, 2003. 494–496.

Schwarzbaum, Lisa. Rev. of *A Beautiful Mind*, dir. Ron Howard. *Entertainment Weekly* 4 Jan. 2002: 46. 23 May 2002 <http://newfirstsearch.oclc.org/>.

12. *Television Program, Videocassette, or Film*

"Frederick Douglass." *Civil War Journal*. Narr. Danny Glover. Dir. Craig Haffner. Arts and Entertainment Network. 6 Apr. 1993.

It's a Wonderful Life. Dir. Frank Capra. Perf. James Stewart, Donna Reed, Lionel Barrymore, and Thomas Mitchell. 1946. Videocassette. Republic, 1996.

The Wonderful Wizard of Oz. Dir. Victor Fleming. Perf. Judy Garland, Frank Morgan, Ray Bolger, and Bert Lahr. Metro-Goldwyn-Mayer, 1939.

(Titles of books, magazines, films, etc., may be italicized or underlined.)

Glossary of Research Terms

APA: refers to the documentation style set forth in the publication manual of the American Psychological Association. It differs from MLA documentation style primarily in its emphasis on dates. In addition to the author's last name, the date of the publication is included in each citation.

Examples:

According to Brewer (2001), "The problem is not serious" (p. 6).

However, "The problem is not serious" (Brewer, 2001, p. 6).

APA style does not require a page number in a parenthetical citation if the material to which it refers is paraphrased or summarized rather than quoted.

Example:

Brewer (2001) believes that the focus should be on the solution rather than the problem.

APA uses the term *References* rather than *Works Cited* as the title of the list of citations on the last page.

bibliographical information: information that is essential to identify and locate source material (usually includes title, author, place and date of publication, and name of publisher if it is a book; title, author, journal or magazine in which it appears, date, and page(s) if it is an article; title, author if available, name and address of site, and date of access if it is an electronic source).

bibliography: alphabetized list of all sources consulted (not just those cited) with appropriate publication data (included much less frequently than works cited/reference pages).

block quotation: a long quotation displayed as an indented block. MLA style requires a quotation of more than four lines to be indented ten spaces from the left margin. APA style requires quotations of more than forty words to be indented five spaces.

card catalog: a collection of individual listings for all books and other materials in a library that is categorized under title, author, and subject. Until recently, these collections were actually card files kept in wooden cabinets in a library. Most libraries have now put this information into computerized catalog systems.

CD-ROM sources: print sources such as dictionaries, encyclopedias, bibliographies, and indexes that are available in an electronic (CD) form.

citation: a reference to a source or information that identifies a source (usually includes name of author or title of source material, page number, and, for APA, date of publication).

cite, citing: to use or refer to a source

common knowledge: general information/knowledge commonly known by educated people; does not need to be attributed to a source (e.g., the information that terrorists attacked the World Trade Center in New York on September 11, 2001, is now common knowledge).

direct quotation: the exact words used by someone else (spoken or written); quotation marks are used to indicate direct quotations.

> Example:

> The fire chief stated, "The cause of the fire has not yet been determined."

documentation: the essential information about a source that a writer must include to acknowledge source material appropriately.

documentation style: the type of documentation used; usually refers to MLA, APA, Chicago, or Turabian styles.

ellipis: three spaced periods indicating material has been omitted from a direct quotation.

field research: the act of gathering information from sources other than written sources; includes observations, interviews, questionnaires, surveys (see Chapter 7, Gathering Information).

footnote: a note placed at the bottom of the page that was formerly used as a way of identifying sources; now largely replaced by the use of parenthetical citations. (*Note*: some documentation styles, notably Chicago and Turabian, still employ footnotes.)

indirect quotation: a paraphrase or summary of a direct quotation; indirect quotations do not require quotation marks and are often introduced by the word *that* (see below).

> Example:

> The fire chief reported that the cause of the fire was unknown.

MLA: refers to the documentation style of the Modern Language Association; it is widely used in disciplines such as English and foreign languages.

paraphrase: to put source material into your own words.

online sources: general term for sources available online; includes both Internet sources and computerized databases.

parenthetical reference/citation: information needed to identify a source; enclosed in parentheses and inserted at the end of quoted, summarized, or paraphrased material. (*Note*: the period comes *after* the parenthetical citation unless the quotation is longer than four lines.)

> Example:
>
> > Nursing actually became a profession during the Civil War ("The History of Nursing").

plagiarism: the act of quoting, summarizing, or paraphrasing source material without appropriate documentation.

quotation: source material reproduced in the exact words of the speaker or writer.

quotation within a quotation: quoted source material that includes a quotation. *Note:* Quotations within quotations are indicated by the use of single quotation marks unless the secondary quotation appears within a block quote.

> Example:
>
> > "As John Turner reminds us, a great president focuses on more than 'winning the next election' or 'making a name for himself'" (Moore 6).

search engines: tools, such as Yahoo! and Google, that enable you to search the Internet quickly and efficiently.

summary: source material condensed and put into your own words (see Chapter 32).

Works Cited: the title used by MLA to indicate the list of sources (works) used (cited) in a research paper.

Works Cited entry: the information provided on a single source in the Works Cited.

> Example:
>
> > Angelou, Maya. *Even the Stars Look Lonesome.* New York: Random House, 1997.

Sample Student Paper (MLA Style)

Moseley 1

Davy Moseley

Professor McCarron

English 102

1 May 2002

The Model A

Beginning in 1896, Henry Ford created a number of "horseless
carriages" and automobile models, including the famous Model T ("Henry
Ford"). However, the best was yet to come. The new Model A, first
produced in 1927, provided service and style to many early automobile
owners, including my grandfather.

The Model A was both practical and popular. It was a family car with
the extras usually found on more expensive models. This car was designed
to "deliver speed, power and comfort" ("Model A Story"). It had a four-wheel
braking system plus an independent safety brake, wire spoke wheels, an
electric starting and generating system, two-sheet safety glass for the front
windshield, two-tone paint, and many body styles. The unveiling of this
new car was second in popularity only to Lindbergh's flight across the
Atlantic. In New York, an estimated ten million people saw the car in the
first thirty-six hours it was on display, and about fifty thousand deposits
were made on new Model A's (Collier and Horowitz 126).

People today probably find it difficult to imagine just why this
seemingly slow and boxy "poor man's" car made such a huge impression.
The car's large buxom fenders, thin bicycle tires, and forty-miles-per-hour
speed don't begin to suggest what the car really stood for to the American

people. The car portrayed the coming age of luxury, convenience, and efficiency. Everyone wanted to be able to get what everyone else already had, and the Model A made that possible. Its low price allowed nearly anyone, from Franklin Delano Roosevelt to the local grocery store owner, to own one. According to "Model A Story," nearly five million Model A's were made from late 1927 to 1931, when the Model A was again discontinued. The Model A, however, became a symbol for the success of the ordinary man.

Anyone could own a Model A—even poor young farmers. Thus, on December 23, 1928, my grandfather Fred Moseley purchased a very special Model A Roadster at the local Ford dealership in Sulphur Springs, Texas. Model A's were so much in demand at the time that the dealers could not keep them on the lot. At the time of sale, the purchaser would take his receipt to the closest Ford assembly line—which for my grandfather was at the East Grand Ford Plant in Dallas, Texas—and exchange the receipt for a bright, shiny new car. My grandfather rode the train to Dallas, gave the salesman his receipt for $595, and drove home in his new 1928 dark blue Model A Tudor Roadster (Moseley).

The Model A represents a time when life was simpler, safer, and brighter. Everywhere, the world was growing and changing and building and improving. The many Model A's preserved and on exhibit in car museums and private homes make the period of the late 1920s and early 1930s so vivid that one can almost reach into the history books and grab it.

Works Cited

Collier, Peter, and David Horowitz. <u>The Fords: An American Epic</u>. New York: Summit, 1987.

"Henry Ford." <u>Webster's New Biographical Dictionary</u>. New York: Merriam-Webster, 1983. <u>Infopedia.</u> CD-ROM. Future Vision Multimedia. 1995.

"Model A Story." <u>Model A Ford Club of America Website</u>. 1996. Model A Ford Club of America. 20 April 2002 <http://www.ford.com/ archive/ModelA.html>.

Moseley, Fred, Jr. Personal Interview. 24 April 2002.

CREDITS

Chapter 5

p. 45: From *This Stubborn Soil,* by William A. Owens. Published by N. Lyons Books. Copyright © 1986. Reprinted with permission of Jessie Ann Owens and David Owens.

Chapter 8

p. 87: From Paul Weisz and R. Keogh, *The Science of Biology,* 4th ed. Copyright © 1977 by The McGraw-Hill Companies. Reproduced with permission of the publisher. **p. 89:** Excerpt from *Silent Spring* by Rachel Carson. Copyright © 1962 by Rachel L. Carson, renewed 1990 by Roger Christie. **pp. 97–98:** From *The Essentials of American Government: Continuity and Change,* 3rd ed. (pages 203–204) by Karen O'Connor and Larry J. Sabato. © 1998 HarperCollins Pubishers. Reprinted by permission of Pearson Education, Inc.

Chapter 10

p. 116: From *Earth Science* 7/e by Edward J. Tarbuck and Frederick K. Lutgens. Copyright © 1994 by Prentice-Hall, Inc. Reprinted by permission of Pearson Education, Inc., Upper Saddle River, N.J. **p. 118:** Excerpt from *A Walker in the City*, copyright 1951 and renewed 1979 by Alfred Kazin, reprinted by permission of Harcourt, Inc. **p. 119:** From N. Scott Momaday, *The Way to Rainy Mountain.* Copyright © 1969. Reprinted by permission of the University of New Mexico Press. **p. 120:** Excerpt from "The Inheritance of Tools," copyright © 1986 by Scott Russell Sanders; first appeared in *The North American Review;* from *The Paradise of Boms*; reprinted by permission of the author and the author's agents, the Virginia Kidd Agency, Inc.

Chapter 11

pp. 130–131: From N. Scott Momaday, *The Way to Rainy Mountain.* Copyright © 1969. Reprinted by permission of the University of New Mexico Press. **p. 132:** Excerpt from *A Thousand Days* by Arthur M. Schlesinger, Jr. Copyright © 1965 by Arthur M. Schlesinger, Jr. Reprinted by permission of Houghton Mifflin Company. All rights reserved. **pp. 133–134:** Excerpt from *Holy the Firm* by Annie Dillard.

Chapter 12

Chapter 13

Chapter 14

Chapter 16

Copyright © 1994 by Prentice-Hall, Inc. Reprinted by permission of Pearson Education, Inc., Upper Saddle River, N.J.

Chapter 17

pp. 206–207: From *Earth Science* 7/e by Edward J. Tarbuck and Frederick K. Lutgens. Copyright © 1994 by Prentice-Hall, Inc. Reprinted by permission of Pearson Education, Inc., Upper Saddle River, N.J.

Chapter 18

pp. 217–218: From Alan Pistorius, "Species Lost," *Country Journal,* vol. 24 (July/August 1977), pp. 36–39. Reprinted with permission of the author. **pp. 219, 220, 221:** Three excerpts from "Letter from a Birmingham Jail," by Martin Luther King, Jr. Reprinted by arrangement with the Estate of Martin Luther King Jr., c/o Writers House as agent for the proprietor New York, NY. Copyright 1963 Dr. Martin Luther King Jr., copyright renewed 1991 Coretta Scott King. **p. 222:** Excerpted from "Why Gun-Control Laws Don't Work" by Barry Goldwater. Reprinted with permission from the *Reader's Digest*, December 1975. Copyright © 1975 by The Reader's Digest Association, Inc.

Chapter 19

pp. 240–241: From *The Book of Lights* by Chaim Potok, copyright. Copyright 1981 by Chaim Potok Individually and Adena Potok as Trustee for Rena N. Potok, Naana S. Potok and Akiva N. Potok. Used by permission of Alfred A. Knopf, a division of Random House, Inc. **pp. 243–244:** Except from *The Water is Wide* by Pat Conroy. Copyright © 1972 by Pat Conroy. Reprinted by permission of Houghton Mifflin Company. All rights reserved.

Chapter 20

pp. 257–258: From *Invisible Man,* by Ralph Ellison. Copyright © 1952 by Random House, Inc. Reprinted with permission of the publisher.

Chapter 31

p. 429: Copyright © 1972 by James Herriot. From *All Creatures Great and Small,* by James Herriot. Reprinted by permission of St. Martin's Press, LLC. **pp. 430–431:** "Down with the Forests" from *Dateline*

America by Charles Kuralt, copyright © 1979 by CBS, Inc., reprinted by permission of Harcourt, Inc. **pp. 432–434:** From *Future Shock* by Alvin Toffler, copyright © 1970 by Alvin Toffler. Used by permission of Random House, Inc.

Chapter 32

pp. 437–438: From Sherman, Alan, Sharon Sherman, Leonard Russikoff, *Basic Concepts of Chemistry,* Third Edition. Copyright © 1984 by Houghton Mifflin Company. Used with permission.

Chapter 33

pp. 448–450: "Out of Africa" by W. Jeffrey Bolster from *The New York Times Book Review.* Copyright © 2002 by the New York Times Co. Reprinted by permission.

Chapter 34

pp. 455–457: From Rebecca Brooks Gruver, *An American History,* Vol. 1, Brief Edition. Copyright © 1985 by The McGraw-Hill Companies. Reprinted with permission of the publisher. **pp. 459–460:** From Bernstein, Douglas A., Edward J. Roy, Thomas K. Srull, and Christopher D. Wickens, *Psychology,* First Edition. Copyright © 1988 by Houghton Mifflin Company. Used with permission.

Part Five

pp. 464–465: From *Even the Stars Look Lonesome* by Maya Angelou, copyright © 1997 by Maya Angelou. Used by permission of Random House, Inc. **pp. 467–469:** From *Newsweek,* April 1988. Copyright © 1988 Newsweek, Inc. All rights reserved. Reprinted by permission. "Living in Two Worlds," by Marcus Mabry. Reprinted by permission of the author. **pp. 470–471:** "Tossing Identity and a Bouquet" by Ellen Goodman from *Fort Worth Star-Telegram,* September 5, 2001. **Copyright © 2001 by The Washington Post Writers Group. Reprinted with permission. pp. 473–475:** "In Praise of the F Word," by Mary Sherry. Reprinted by permission of the author. **pp. 476–479:** "Freshman Year 101" by Tim Madigan from *Fort Worth Star-Telegram,* August 15, 2001. Reprinted by permission of Fort Worth Star-Telegram. **pp. 481–482:** "College Valued Less for Learning Than for Earning" by Ethan Bronner. Copyright © 1998 by the *New York Times* Co. Reprinted by permission. **pp. 485–486:** "Chinese Space,

INDEX